Public Management

How effective are public managers as they seek to influence how public organizations deliver policy results? How, and how much, is management related to the performance of public programs? What aspects of management can be distinguished? Can their separable contributions to performance be estimated?

The fate of public policies in today's world lies in the hands of public organizations, which in turn are often intertwined with others in latticed patterns of governance. Collectively, these organizations are expected to generate performance in terms of policy outputs and outcomes. In this book, two award-winning researchers investigate the effectiveness of management in the public sector. First, they develop a systematic theory on how effective public managers are in shaping policy results. The remainder of the book then tests this theory against a wide range of evidence, including a data set of 1,000 public organizations.

Laurence J. O'Toole, Jr., is the Margaret Hughes and Robert T. Golembiewski Professor of Public Administration and Distinguished Research Professor at the University of Georgia, Athens. He also holds an academic appointment as a professor in the Faculty of Management and Governance at Twente University in the Netherlands.

Kenneth J. Meier is the Charles H. Gregory Chair in Liberal Arts at Texas A&M University, College Station. He is also Professor of Public Management at Cardiff Business School.

Public Management

Organizations, Governance, and Performance

Laurence J. O'Toole, Jr.,

and

Kenneth J. Meier

CAMBRIDGE
UNIVERSITY PRESS

CAMBRIDGE UNIVERSITY PRESS

Cambridge, New York, Melbourne, Madrid, Cape Town, Singapore,
São Paulo, Delhi, Dubai, Tokyo, Mexico City

Cambridge University Press
The Edinburgh Building, Cambridge CB2 8RU, UK

Published in the United States of America by Cambridge University Press, New York

www.cambridge.org
Information on this title: www.cambridge.org/9781107004412

First published 2011

Printed in the United Kingdom at the University Press, Cambridge

A catalogue record for this publication is available from the British Library

Library of Congress Cataloging-in-Publication Data

O'Toole, Laurence J., 1948–
  Public management : organizations, governance, and performance / Laurence J. O'Toole,
Kenneth J. Meier.
    p. cm.
  ISBN 978-1-107-00441-2 (Hardback)
  1. Public management. 2. Administrative agencies–Management. I. Meier, Kenneth J., 1950–
II. Title.
  JF1351.L68 2011
  351–dc22
                                                                                    2010040919
ISBN 978-1-107-00441-2 Hardback

Contents

List of figures	*page* vi
List of tables	vii
Preface	xi

1 Public management and performance: an evidence-based perspective — 1

2 A model of public management and a source of evidence — 23

3 Public management in interdependent settings: networks, managerial networking, and performance — 55

4 Managerial quality and performance — 100

5 Internal management and performance: stability, human resources, and decision making — 131

6 Nonlinearities in public management: the roles of managerial capacity and organizational buffering — 182

7 Public management in intergovernmental networks: matching structural networks and managerial networking — 240

8 Public management and performance: what we know, and what we need to know — 267

Glossary — 287
References — 291
Index — 309

Figures

4.1 Linear and nonlinear relationship *page* 120
4.2 Controlling for quality 121
4.3 Differences by size of central staff 123
5.1 The interaction of management quality with networking and stability: quartile regression coefficients 146
5.2 The interaction of superintendent stability with teacher stability, management quality, and networking 146
5.3 The interaction of networking with management quality and stability 147
5.4 The interaction of teacher stability with superintendent stability, management quality, and networking 147
6.1 The marginal impact of missed school days contingent on managerial capacity 206
6.2 The marginal impact of Katrina students contingent on managerial capacity 206

Tables

3.1 Factor loadings for nodes involved in managerial
     networking, 2007   *page* 60
3.2 Levels of interaction are fairly constant over time   60
3.3 Managerial networking improves environmental support   62
3.4 Mean scores for interactions between different groups
     of officers in English local authorities   65
3.5 Factor loadings for managerial networking, 2000 survey data 71
3.6 Management and organizational performance: additive
     linear estimation   73
3.7 Management and organizational performance: nonlinear impacts 74
3.8 Management and organizational performance: autoregressive
     and nonlinear models   76
3.9 Managerial networking at different levels of educational performance 79
3.10 Managerial networking interactions with resources and constraints 80
3.11 The impact of network interaction on disadvantaged student
     indicators   88
3.12 The impact of network interaction on advantaged student indicators 88
3.13 The impact of network interaction on advantaged student indicators 90
3.14 The impact of individual network nodes on disadvantaged
     student indicators   90
4.1 Determinants of superintendent salaries   109
4.2 The impact of management on performance: standardized tests 112
4.3 Management quality and other measures of performance   113
4.4 Management quality in an autoregressive specification   114
4.5 The nonlinear relationship between networking and performance 119
4.6 Nonlinear effects of networking, controlling for quality   121
4.7 Nonlinear effects of networking on performance: impacts
     of the relative size of central administrative staff   122
5.1 The impact of management on performance: standardized tests II 141
5.2 Management, stability, and other measures of performance   143

5.3	Management, stability, and performance: autoregressive estimation	143
5.4	Measuring the quality of human capital: factor loadings	154
5.5	The reliability of the human capital measure	155
5.6	The impact of human capital on organizational performance	156
5.7	The impact of human capital on alternative indicators of performance	158
5.8	The autoregressive impact of human capital on alternative indicators of performance	158
5.9	The impact of a 10 percent or greater budget shock on organizational performance	165
5.10	The impact of budget shocks on other indicators of performance	166
5.11	Superintendent priorities: what is your primary goal for improving your district?	167
5.12	The nonbarking dog: the relationship between a budget shock and instructional expenditures	168
5.13	Redistributing funds to core functions: percentage point reductions in allocations	169
5.14	Reducing core costs: teachers' salaries and class size	170
5.15	Reducing core support tasks: instruction, aides, and support staff	171
5.16	Seeking less expensive core personnel	171
6.1	The impact of a 10 percent or greater budget shock on students' state examination performance	190
6.2	The impact of a 10 percent or greater budget shock on the performance of college-bound students	191
6.3	The impact of a 10 percent or greater budget shock on students' state examination performance	192
6.4	The impact of a 10 percent or greater budget shock on the performance of college-bound students	194
6.5	Organizational shocks: Hurricanes Katrina and Rita	200
6.6	Environmental shocks and student performance: the impact of students and missed class days	202
6.7	Administrative capacity can overcome the impact of environmental shocks	205
6.8	How the interaction of managerial networking and managerial capacity affects organizational performance	212
6.9	How the interaction of managerial networking and managerial capacity affects organizational performance: attendance	215
6.10	How the interaction of managerial networking and managerial capacity affects organizational performance: college readiness	216

6.11   The impact of buffering on organizational performance   228
6.12   The impact of buffering on alternative indicators of performance   228
6.13   Buffering: is the relationship linear or reciprocal?   230
6.14   Does the interaction with M_2 add explanation to a linear model?   230
6.15   Does buffering interact with resources in a reciprocal manner?   231
7.1   Management and dependence on state aid   253
7.2   Management and dependence on state aid II   253
7.3   Management and dependence on state aid: college aspirations
       indicators   254
7.4   Management and state aid: low-end indicators   254
7.5   Management and funding diversity   255
7.6   Management and funding diversity II   255
7.7   Management and funding diversity: college aspirations indicators   256
7.8   Management and funding diversity: low-end indicators   256
7.9   Summary of results: state aid   257
7.10   Summary of results: funding diversity   257
8.1   Intercorrelations of management measures   275
8.2   Practical lessons for managers   276

Preface

How effective are public managers as they seek to influence the efforts of public organizations to deliver policy outputs and outcomes? How, and how much, is management related to public program performance? What aspects of management can be distinguished, and can their separable contributions to performance be estimated? How do managers deal with internal operations, opportunities in the environment, and threats or shocks from outside the organization? Can the networking behavior of managers and the networked structures in which many public organizations sit shape policy results – for good or ill?

In this book we address these salient questions – and more. Whereas in an earlier volume (Meier and O'Toole 2006) we explored the relationship between democratic governance systems and public bureaucracy via the literatures of political science and public administration, and used empirical analyses to sort through the issues, in this new book we put the politics-and-administration theme to one side – mostly – to focus on management and performance. This approach does not mean that we reconstruct some sort of implicit politics/administration dichotomy. Indeed, the role that public managers occupy includes some highly political elements, and some of our work on management and performance demonstrates some explicitly political patterns. It turns out, for instance, that managerial interactions with external stakeholders shape the outcomes of their organizations in ways that reflect the distribution of power in their settings. It is also the case, furthermore, that maintaining personnel stability within the organizations we have been studying provides particularly strong benefits for the least advantaged clientele of the agencies. Public management certainly involves political themes and potentially controversial outcomes. What is distinctive about this volume, instead, is that our focus is directly on managers and how they shape results.

Examining the link between public management and performance might seem to be covering rather well-trodden ground. Until fairly recently, however, the contributions of management to performance were either contestable or very difficult to estimate. One major theoretical approach, for example, the population ecology view of organizations, has strongly argued that management does not matter, that organizations succeed or fail because they are lucky. By "lucky," population ecology theorists mean that some organizations have favorable environments with ample resources and are assigned tasks that are tractable. What might appear to be good management, therefore, is an artifact of an organization's niche. Other analysts, for instance some who employ public choice as a theoretical lens, might even see public managers as impediments ("rent seekers") – or, at best, inefficient contributors – to the delivery of goods and services to the public.

At what might seem like the other extreme, a major international movement, the new public management (NPM), holds that management is the key to effective public programs and that, if governments were to adopt NPM's set of favored reforms (mostly borrowed from the private sector), citizens would get better government at a lower cost. The overly strong versions of this argument can be considered "managerialism": public management as the potential magic cure that converts failure into success. Despite these contesting theoretical approaches, the body of systematic research on whether and how much management really matters has been relatively slim – particularly so if one restricts the search to investigations drawing evidence from large numbers of public organizations and employing archival rather than perceptual measures of performance.

In recent years, however, the number of studies systematically examining the links between management and performance has grown. We incorporate many of these recent findings in this book. In the main, though, this volume integrates much of our own systematic theoretical and empirical work on public management and performance conducted over an extended period. The approach we take allows for the development of relatively clear and evidence-based answers to the questions of how effective various facets of management can be – that is, how much difference they make. This book develops its perspective and findings on such issues in a cumulative and progressively nuanced fashion over the course of several chapters.

We have opted to distill our reading of the theoretical literature into a simple, parsimonious theory about how organizations are managed. Our theory is built around a set of five principles. First, public organizations are autoregressive (or inertial) systems; they seek to counter the natural tendency toward entropy in the environment. As a result, what organizations do today will be very similar to what they have done in the past. Second, public management can be divided into two broad parts: managing within the organization and managing the organization's relationships with the environment. Both can be expected to have performance implications. Third, external management can be divided, at least theoretically, into efforts to exploit opportunities in the environment and efforts to buffer the organization from threats that the environment might generate.

Fourth, managers use structures, systematic processes, and procedures to regularize organizational actions. Put succinctly, organizations and their managers organize. They set up stabilizing routines that embed knowledge and experience so that cases can be handled quickly and consistently. Finally, the relationships between variables – that is, management, stabilizing elements such as structure, and the environment – are nonlinear. In simple terms, this point means that management is not just another input to program performance but, rather, that it interacts with a variety of other factors and can produce large gains in effectiveness relative to the resources that management consumes.

Our approach is to formalize these principles via a mathematical model and then to test aspects of it systematically through most of the chapters of this volume. In particular, we focus on large panel data sets that permit the inclusion of a wide variety of control variables. In this fashion we can isolate the independent effects of public management as the key variable, instead of mistaking as management effects those that are actually due to some other factor that has been omitted from the analysis.

The most frequently used data set in the book, and perhaps in the field of public management, is the Texas school district data set, which we have built and refined for ten years. It has several significant advantages over other public management data bases, as we explain in this volume. Although Texas schools constitute the primary data set, we recognize that even a state as diverse as Texas cannot contain all the relevant organizational and environmental variables. In this book, therefore, we incorporate additional analyses we have undertaken with data on local police departments, local governments in the United Kingdom, and state unemployment insurance agencies. Further, we explain relevant findings garnered in others' research, as appropriate, at several points in the coverage. We make no claim that we have looked at the universe of organizations and organizational characteristics, but we have assembled research results from several thousand public organizations.

The work represented here stems from a decision made about a dozen years ago to pool our interests in order to develop a long-term research agenda centered around the management-and-performance theme. One of us, O'Toole, had developed theoretical ideas about management and performance, especially in complex institutional settings including networks, and had worked empirically in a number of fields of public policy. Meier had also undertaken numerous studies in multiple policy fields, including public education, and was especially experienced at tapping the advantages of large-N statistical approaches. This book reflects a merging of these interests and an effort to speak broadly to the field of public management.

We gratefully acknowledge assistance we have received from others. We owe a special debt to school district superintendents in Texas, since they have served multiple times as respondents to our surveys, which are designed to learn about the management of those public organizations. These busy public managers have tolerated our questions thus far through five separate survey efforts (plus one more specialized one) over a ten-year period, with more currently planned. Four reviewers for Cambridge University Press offered thoughtful assessments of this book and helpful suggestions for strengthening it. We also thank George Boyne, Alisa Hicklin, and Richard Walker for permitting our use of some data in this volume that had been gathered for joint research efforts with these colleagues. We are grateful to doctoral students and alumni of doctoral programs in the Department of Public Administration and Policy at the University of Georgia, and the Department of Political Science at Texas A&M University. We have refined our ideas and – we think – improved them on the basis of our teaching and research experiences with these colleagues. The same can be said for many scholars elsewhere, who have engaged with us regarding some of the specifics of this research agenda and its progress. Among this broad group, aside from those already mentioned, we would like to thank in particular Rhys Andrews, Stuart Bretschneider, Gene Brewer, Amy Kneedler Donahue, Sergio Fernández, H. George Frederickson, Carolyn Heinrich, J. Edward Kellough, H. Brinton Milward, David Peterson, David W. Pitts, Hal G. Rainey, Bob Stein, and Søren Winter. Finally, we pay tribute to the immeasurable benefit we have derived from the many forms of support provided by our families: Mary Gilroy O'Toole, Conor Gilroy O'Toole, Katie Easton O'Toole, and Diane Jones Meier. Needless to say, the weaknesses and errors that may remain can be lodged firmly at our own feet.

1 Public management and performance: an evidence-based perspective

Governments around the globe cope with critical issues and thorny policy challenges: encouraging economic growth, combating climate change, educating young people, protecting against disease, building and maintaining infrastructure, planning urban communities, providing social security, and a great deal more. Talented policy designers, and the contributions of policy analysts, can render many of these difficult tasks less daunting. Governments can also learn from each other's experiences, so that mistakes do not necessarily have to be repeated in many places before policy learning can occur (Rose 1993). To convert sensible policy ideas into reliable and effective streams of programmatic action, however, much more is needed.

Few policies are self-executing.[1] Typically, public programs require the concerted effort of many people, often coordinated via formal organization, to achieve their intended results. While some policy interventions can avoid the need for substantial coordination – monetary policies and other governmental efforts to shape market conditions, for instance, rely for much of their effectiveness on individuals'[2] uncoordinated responses to reconfigured incentives – the great bulk of policies are delivered into the hands of intended implementers, whose responsibility it is to make policy come alive in patterns of goal-oriented behavior. Indeed, the promise of democracy in advanced nations is fundamentally tied to the ability of representative institutions to deliver regularly on their policy commitments through such processes of converting public intention into action.

Governments typically face these implementation challenges with regard to numerous policy objectives and programmatic initiatives. In the United States, for example, the national government is committed to thousands of such policy efforts, and several hundred of these are intergovernmental: they encourage or require subnational governments to be a part of the action as well through grant-in-aid programs, intergovernmental mandates, and other such approaches. Subnational governments also develop their own policy initiatives. In addition to the fifty states, the United States is home to

89,476 local governments – municipalities, counties, special districts, townships, and school districts (US Census Bureau 2008). Virtually all these entities engage in efforts to deliver on policy results, and the same pattern is followed in country after country.

In addition to plenty of people and considerable resources, accomplishing public purposes also requires public management. At multiple levels in large organizations, managers coordinate people and resources toward the accomplishment of collective purpose; they also tap the interdependent organizational environment in support of such purpose and to protect the organization's efforts from potential disturbances. This is what is meant by *public management*. Some individuals, in other words, have to orchestrate the myriad individuals, routines, resources, and possibilities into a policy-responsive mosiac – to make, in Paul Appleby's (1949) memorable phrase, a "mesh of things." The concerted efforts of perhaps thousands of people to move toward complex public objectives does not spontaneously emerge; it must be organized and induced, and the task is necessarily ongoing. This book is devoted to a close examination of what public managers do as they take on such responsibilities, and we do so from a particular perspective: we are interested in the link between management, on the one hand, and public program performance, on the other.

Performance is a highly salient notion in recent years among those around the world who care about public management. It has acquired even more importance as government agencies and other organizations have struggled to deliver results under conditions of austerity. The economic winds that have buffeted programs in many countries have often resulted in budget cuts just as public service needs and demands have escalated. The term "performance" is often used imprecisely, thus sometimes generating confusion. We mean by the concept of "performance" the achievements of public programs and organizations in terms of the outputs and outcomes that they produce. Performance can be considered to have numerous dimensions, such as efficiency (the cost per unit of output or of service delivery), effectiveness (the extent to which policy objectives are being achieved), equity (how fairly outputs and outcomes are distributed among key targets or stakeholders), and public satisfaction (Boyne 2003). Accordingly, performance covers a broad territory – especially when one considers that improvements on a given criterion (efficiency, for instance) might result in declines on another (equity, say). In this book, we pay particular attention to performance in terms of effectiveness, while also taking into account the resources available, and in certain analyses we address the theme of equity as well.

The management task is even more challenging than would seem apparent at first glance. Public organizations – agencies, departments, bureaus, authorities, and the like – are at the core of the apparatus for policy implementation. Indeed, the US federal government's "bureaucracy"[3] is impressively large – hundreds of organizations, approximately 2.7 million civilian employees. Even though the national civil service has actually declined in size during the past half-century,[4] its scope and reach have not, because many policy initiatives involve contributions to policy action from entities outside the national bureaucracy. Indeed, Paul Light (1999) estimates that in 1996 a "shadow" federal workforce of approximately 12.7 million people beyond those in the civil service were involved in carrying out national policy – including government contractors and state and local employees.

Policy implementation is complicated by the fact that many important public policies and public programs call for the joint efforts of actors in two or more – sometimes many more – organizations, frequently in more than one government, and often in the for-profit and nonprofit sectors. The expression *governance* is now often used to denote these broadened patterns of collective action. "Governance," as the saying goes, often means more than just governments (Rhodes 1997; Peters and Savoie 2000; Kooiman 2003). The need for such multiorganizational action in networked patterns means that the task of public management requires attention to such interunit coordination along with a focus on internal organizational responsibilities.

The fate of public policies in today's world lies in the hands of public organizations, which in turn are often intertwined with others in latticed patterns of governance, which collectively are expected to generate performance: policy outputs and outcomes. Public management, therefore, means dealing with organizations, governance, and performance. This book examines the intersection of these three themes and how managers address them.

Even though our focus includes the performance of public programs, this volume is not another study of performance measurement or performance management (for instance, Radin 2006 or Moynihan 2008). That is to say, we do not explore in detail the issues and controversies involved in measuring performance, nor do we systematically investigate how managers use performance information to help influence what the people in their organizations do. Instead, in our empirical analyses we rely mostly on performance information that is regularly collected and typically treated as relevant and important by managers and others. Where appropriate, we also report on performance-related findings by other researchers who have been exploring the relationship between public management and performance. In other words, this volume explores what public managers do, whether and how their efforts translate into policy results that are treated as relevant by those interested in the policy field in question, and the extent to which the impacts of management on results are modest or sizable.

A perspective on public management and performance

In the chapters that follow, we conclude with confidence that public management makes a difference to performance, and the impact is far from trivial. At the same time, it is important to avoid the leap to what some have called "managerialism": the "seldom-tested assumption that better management will prove an effective solvent for a wide range of economic and social ills" (Pollitt 1990: 1). We steer an evidence-based middle course here (Meier and O'Toole 2009b). Much like the similar movements in medicine (Guyatt, Cairns, Churchill, *et al.* 1992) and in public policy (Heinrich 2007), our research, grounded in evidence-based public management, has as its objective to assess the conventional wisdoms – what earlier scholars might have called proverbs (Simon 1946) – so as to separate the wheat from the chaff and determine what actually works in practice. Specifically, we consider the theory and literature of public management, look for ways of tapping the relevant aspects of what managers do, and estimate the effects of public management on public program performance, while controlling for other relevant factors – in particular the difficulty of the policy-relevant tasks and the resources available for their successful achievement.

Evidence-based public management can proceed in a variety of ways, including the careful analysis of key case studies. We have opted, however, to employ the approaches and quantitative techniques of the social sciences. These include formal and precise theories that generate testable hypotheses and the statistical analysis of organizations over a period of time.

In this fashion, our theoretical and empirical perspectives avoid two approaches that are sometimes adopted. As mentioned in the preface, at one extreme are the population ecologists. This approach, best represented in the research literature on public management by Herbert Kaufman (1991), holds that public organizations survive and flourish because they are lucky, not because they or their managers make sound decisions. Organizations, in this view, are simply at the mercy of their environments.[5]

Some political scientists offer a modified version of this notion by suggesting that, particularly in the United States, the broader political system imposes so many constraints on public managers that they are hamstrung in their efforts and thus mostly consigned to a rather weak role (Wilson 1989).

At the other extreme are the managerialists, those who appear to attribute virtually all performance to the purportedly heroic efforts of public managers. Some themes of the so-called new public management[6] (NPM) seem to imply a similar notion, since the oft-mentioned refrain is to "let the managers manage." In a more tempered fashion, a literature on public sector leadership suggests that key managers can have dramatic impacts on performance (Doig and Hargrove 1987). Contrary to such assertions, a great deal of evidence in fields such as management clearly points to limitations on what can be accomplished by management, especially in the short run, although there are also good reasons to expect the actions of managers to be consequential for performance. For this reason, we are careful in this book to specify some additional likely influences on policy outputs and outcomes, including features of the environment in which organizations must try to accomplish their tasks.

Our analysis indicates that managerial influences on public program performance are multiple, substantively as well as statistically significant, and yet accompanied by other influences that need to be taken into consideration in any adequate accounting for results. Demonstrating such patterns and explaining how managers "do their thing" with such effects on results is the primary task of this book.

To begin exploring the difference that management makes, we start by reviewing some of the core themes in the research literature on public management. This earlier work provides valuable signals about how to approach the subject of management and public program performance.

Themes from the research literature

In one way or another, researchers have explored the subject of public management for more than a century. Methods and insights have gradually evolved and become more sophisticated over time, although certainly there remain plenty of unverified – and doubtlessly invalid – assertions and assumptions. In a general sense, we can observe that remarkable progress has been made in researchers' efforts to build solid empirical findings about the world of public management – in the United States, in Europe, and in many other parts of the world. If anything, the array of issues addressed in serious studies of public organizations and their management has expanded in recent years, with notable investigations of such topics as public service motivation; red tape, its causes and consequences; government contracting and privatization; the use of discretion by supervisors and front-line workers; the differences between public and private management; the challenges of involving stakeholders in public decision making; the adoption of new public management and other managerial reforms; the development of interorganizational collaboration and networks for the delivery of public programs; innovations in public organizations; institutional isomorphism (the consequence of mimesis, or organizations' copying or deriving their institutional forms from other such organizations) in the public sector; emergency or crisis management; and diversity management. This list, furthermore, is merely a partial one.

On the specific theme of public sector performance, moreover, considerable important work has been accomplished by researchers. Even leaving aside the frequently studied issue of whether so-called "pay for performance" systems produce useful results (many studies raise serious questions about the notion), public organizational performance has been approached from a number of angles. Some, for instance, have explored the meaning and determinants of the US national government's recent efforts to assess program performance by means of so-called "PART" (Program Assessment Rating Tool) scores (see, for example, Dull 2006, Gilmour and Lewis 2006, Moynihan 2006, 2008; more about PART scores shortly). Researchers have sought to understand whether setting performance targets helps to improve performance (Boyne and Chen 2007). Others have sought to estimate the influence of such diverse factors as organizational goal ambiguity, institutional design and reputation, and individual characteristics on performance (respectively, Chun and Rainey 2005, Krause and Douglas 2005, and Kim 2005). Researchers have tried to determine how features of network structure can shape performance (Provan and Milward 1995; Schalk, Torenvlied, and Allen 2010).

Some broad meta-analyses of hundreds of studies related to governance and performance have attempted to develop some generalizations and themes from the work of many others (Forbes and Lynn 2005; Hill and Lynn 2005). In addition, there have been efforts to compile the results of a number of different studies of performance from different empirical contexts (for example, see the full set of papers in the October 2005 issue of the *Journal of Public Administration Research and Theory*, as well as Boyne *et al.* 2006).

It is clear that, although a number of important issues remain to be sorted out – such as the kinds of samples and data sets that might be most appropriate for studying management and performance – the systematic exploration of the performance theme is well under way. (We examine the subject of performance data later in this chapter.)

Research designs and findings have proliferated, and there is by no means a consensus about how to understand what makes for effective management (an important criterion of performance) in contemporary systems of government. Still, the broad study of public management has provided a set of building blocks that we can use to begin a systematic analysis of the relationships between management and performance. Some of the key themes and findings are deserving of brief review, since they provide a grounding for any serious and sustained research program focused on public management and performance.

Several of the most notable compilations on and reviews of public management offer general agreement on certain broad points (for example, see Moore 1995, Ferlie, Lynn, and Pollitt 2005, and Lynn 2006; by far the best coverage of the empirical and theoretical literature is that by Rainey 2009). The core literature of the field assumes or, more often, argues for some distinctiveness to the management of public programs and public organizations.[7] While the generic management literature often assumes otherwise, and while some proponents of the new public management advocate designing public sector settings to more closely approximate market-like ones, in the main the scholars of public management see sufficient distinctiveness that it should be investigated in its own right. In this book we do not make systematic public–private comparisons (but see Meier and O'Toole forthcoming (b)), although we do treat public organizations and public management as sufficiently different – even unique – that they should be explored on their own, and largely on the basis of insights from the literature on that subject in particular.[8]

Second, the literature is in agreement that public management matters – and, in particular, that it makes a difference in public program performance. A fair amount of this literature consists of case studies. Indeed, numerous richly textured case studies and comparative case studies of public management all make persuasive arguments that management matters. Many focus on management in and of individual agencies (for instance, Doig and Hargrove 1987, Behn 1991, Ban 1995, Riccucci 1995, 2005, and Holzer and Callahan 1998),[9] while others emphasize management in more multiorganizational, networked settings (Gage and Mandell 1990; Provan and

Milward 1995; Klijn 1996). More recently, several studies have sought to cover numerous public organizations and/or governments in making and seeking to validate this claim (examples include Donahue *et al.* 2004, Boyne and Walker 2006, Brewer 2006, and Walker and Boyne 2006; see also some of the literature referenced earlier in this chapter); and some of these assert, but do not really test, the effects of management on results (for instance, the products of the Government Performance Project (GPP): see Ingraham, Joyce, and Donahue 2003, and Ingraham 2007). Given the broad agreement that public management matters (a conclusion that this book also validates), the important question guiding the analyses here is this: *how effective* is public management at generating performance?

Third, the case study literature, as well as the literature based upon larger-N studies of many organizations, is mostly in agreement that public management is not a simple function but, rather, encompasses multiple aspects. Different scholars offer different lists of functions. Ingraham, Joyce, and Donahue (2003) treat financial management, human resources management (HRM), information technology management, and capital management as the central elements of the managerial function,[10] while, in their early work together, Boyne and Walker (2006; Walker and Boyne 2006) concentrate on both managerial strategy process and strategy content. A number of case study authors and others focus in particular on "leadership" by managers (for example, Doig and Hargrove 1987, Behn 1991, and Terry 2002). Studies emphasizing the external/network-related aspects of public management highlight in particular the brokering, framing, exchange-related functions – above all, collaboration. For instance, Agranoff and McGuire (2003) identify a number of vertical and horizontal aspects of collaborative activity in which local government managers engage, including information seeking, adjustment seeking, policy making and strategy making, resource exchange, and project-based work. Rainey (2009) draws numerous structural and procedural dimensions into public managers' purview, while also noting the assumed importance of variables such as organizational environment, technology and tasks, goals, and culture. So, although there is no clear consensus on the preeminent or essential functions of public management – no agreed-upon "POSDCORB"[11] for the twenty-first century – a widespread consensus holds that public management is not a simple, unidimensional activity. An implication is that, given that management is multifunctional and involves varied behaviors, determining systematically just what differences all these functions make in the performance of public programs is an exceedingly difficult task. In this book we identify a number of distinct aspects and estimate their independent impacts, as well as a more complete, combined assessment. Even here, though, we have certainly been forced to omit some aspects of what public managers do that probably carry implications for the outputs and outcomes of policy initiatives.

Fourth, public management in and of networks has emerged as a central theme among many researchers in the field. Some caution that attention to managerial actions in and on the network should not lead scholars to ignore the important role that internal management plays in shaping performance (Hill and Lynn 2005; O'Toole and Meier 2009). Impressively large numbers of public management scholars, however, focus on the externally oriented, often collaborative, efforts of managers to coproduce multiorganizational action (a small sampling includes Provan and Milward 1995, Bardach 1998, McGuire 2006, Agranoff 2007, Bingham and O'Leary 2008, and Rethemeyer and Hatmaker 2008). This emerging literature, furthermore, suggests a more significant and extensive set of cross-organizational links than those implied in the earlier open systems perspective in organization theory. Clearly, any serious effort to incorporate a range of managerial influences on public program performance needs to address this growing line of work and, possibly, growing empirical reality.[12]

Fifth, a review of the extant research literature reveals a somewhat cloudy but nonetheless potentially important insight: particularly in case studies of what public managers do and how that seems to shape outputs and outcomes, there is often an argument or observation that managers catalyze action. To be a little more concrete, it is often claimed that such managers do not simply contribute directly to what happens; they also extract more positive effort from available resources, including human resources (HR), and they have the potential to reduce the impacts of disruptive forces. In other words, the relationship between management and performance is nonlinear with respect to certain other influences and should be considered in terms of *interactions*. If this idea is correct, any effort to model the influence of management on results must take into account potential interactive effects.

There are a number of points of convergence in the research literature on public management, therefore. Nonetheless, it is important to note that there is no consensus among researchers regarding precisely how to theorize about the links between management and performance. There are at least three reasons, and noting these can help to explain why we take the approach evident in this volume. One reason for the lack of theoretical consensus is that, as indicated earlier, management is a complicated, multifaceted subject;

and what managers do undoubtedly has multiple influences on results. The implication for this book is that we should explore the management–performance connection by tapping different aspects of management and estimating their impacts. Second, even for relatively discrete and carefully researched aspects of management, there is no shortage of different and competing theoretical formulations. As Hal Rainey (2009) points out, researchers cannot agree about how to assess organizational effectiveness, how decisions get made inside organizations, how structure influences various aspects of organizational behavior, how motivation is shaped in organizations and why that matters, and what leadership in organizations actually consists of and how it generates results. There is a plethora of theoretical ideas on these points; indeed, there is a huge surplus of them. As a consequence, our approach – as is evident in the next chapter – is to distill from and build upon the public management literature certain notions that have some support there, even if that literature is often some-what ambiguous and even though there is no consensus on precise theoretical formulations.

A third reason for the lack of consensus in the literature is related to the difficulties with assessing organizational or public program performance – the issue explored next.

Tapping performance

It is not sufficient to say, as US Supreme Court Justice Potter Stewart did about pornography, that we know performance when we see it. For reasons explained more carefully in the next chapter, we think the best route for making progress in exploring the management–performance link is through large-N, systematic quantitative studies of many public organizations. An initial challenge already alluded to is that the concept of performance entails multiple aspects. We have indicated where our conceptual focus lies. In addition, and importantly, tapping any aspect of performance requires valid and reliable measures of performance. Unfortunately, another reason why it has been difficult to build validated theory, and therefore consensus, is related to this issue – a matter of method, and, in particular, a point about measurement. To test for relationships between any aspects of management, on the one hand, and performance, on the other, requires at least one acceptable measure of performance.[13] Preferably, several performance measures would be used, since most public programs and virtually all public organizations operate with multiple objectives. Consider the challenges of doing so, however. Different public organizations are charged with highly varied responsibilities: managing housing, determining eligibility for and delivering welfare or social security payments, running national parks and forests, cleaning wastewater, overseeing prisons, launching spacecraft, fighting fires, defending the nation from attack. It goes without saying that no common measure(s) can directly tap outputs or outcomes across such diverse objectives.

Indirectly, it might seem to be possible to develop a measure at one remove, by finding a way to calculate something akin to "degree of goal attainment." This approach too would be exceedingly difficult to execute, however. The goals of many public organizations are often ambiguous, the degree of goal ambiguity varies between agencies, and this variation also has performance-related consequences (Chun and Rainey 2005, 2006). For federal agencies, one might be tempted to rely on some sort of common measure, if such could be found; and at first glance there would seem to be some candidates. Most of them, nonetheless, have significant limits. This point can be seen by a brief overview of some candidates for analysis. The processes initiated in the United States by the Government Performance and Results Act of 1993 require agencies to develop strategic plans, compile annual performance plans, and provide performance reports. The results are not regularly audited, however, there is a great deal of leeway in agencies' framing of their own objectives, and often – despite the efforts of scholars to employ these data – there is no reliable way of compiling an overall measure of performance, not to mention multiple comparable measures. Furthermore, as the US General Accounting Office (now the Government Accountability Office) has noted, the agencies typically under-report information on public programs that span two or more organizations (General Accounting Office 1999).

During the administration of President George W. Bush, in 2002, the White House published *The President's Management Agenda*, with performance as one of its themes. Following that signal, the US Office of Management and Budget (OMB) began to issue "agency scorecards" for some, but not all, major agencies. Each scorecard graded an agency via traffic light signals (green, yellow, red) on how the agency was seen (by OMB and the experts with whom it consulted) to be doing in achieving five fairly abstract government-wide initiatives identified in the *The President's Management Agenda* – for instance, improved financial performance, or budget and performance integration. As of 2008 these continued to be published quarterly for a couple of dozen federal organizations. The methods and measurement were suspect to many scholars (but, for more information, see www.whitehouse.gov/results/agenda/Standards_for_Success_8_11_2008.pdf (last accessed October 14, 2008)), the initiatives were not closely related to the organizations' programmatic outputs and outcomes, and the number of organizations involved was rather limited, not to mention overly aggregated (Department of Homeland Security, Department of Transportation, etc.).[14]

A further development along these lines during the Bush administration was the so-called Program Assessment Rating Tool, created by OMB in 2003 and expanded since that time. PART aims to tap program purpose and design, strategic planning, program management, program results (performance related to strategic goals), and an overall rating created from all the other indicators. An advantage would be that PART scores were eventually developed annually for hundreds of federal programs, not simply for agencies. Unfortunately, there is no publicly available information on just how the scores are determined by OMB budget examiners, nor is there any assurance that different examiners are applying the same standards and criteria to different programs. At best, only certain aspects of PART could be plausibly associated with outputs or outcomes, and there is some evidence that the scores reflect partisan concerns (Gilmour and Lewis 2006).

Efforts to measure performance have extended beyond those used by the US national government. States and localities have struggled with these issues. In addition, the Government Performance Project, a foundation-supported research project referenced earlier, sought to develop consistent performance-related information across federal agencies, across the fifty states, and across a set of major US local governments. The effort resulted in a great deal of valuable information regarding management and management systems, but no common or comparable information on performance itself was produced by the effort. The GPP, therefore, did not really test the management–shapes–performance relationship, nor did it generate performance measures that could be used for others' analysis. Some scholars have used the measures of management capacity that were generated by the project as partial explanation for other interesting dependent variables, such as state policy priorities (Coggburn and Schneider 2003), but not to explain performance itself.

Individual-level perceptual data on public organizational performance can be garnered from certain sources, most prominently data gathered by the US Merit Systems Protection Board in its Merit Principles Survey, which has been completed by thousands of federal employees in many national agencies. Other data sets also record similar perceptual data. Survey items ask for responses on some performance-related matters. Drawbacks, however, include the points that (1) it is not clear to what extent federal employees are knowledgeable and *impartial* with regard to their larger organization's overall performance, (2) several of the most relevant survey items are focused on the individuals' work units rather than their overall organization's outputs or outcomes,[15] and (3) models of performance estimated with independent as well as dependent variables drawn from the same respondents may be prone to common-source bias (Brewer 2006; for a test of common-source bias through a comparison of subjective and objective measures of performance, see Meier and O'Toole 2010).

One locus of interesting and useful data on the performance of a substantial number of general-purpose governments is the Comprehensive Performance Assessment (CPA) of the United Kingdom's Audit Commission, and especially the Core Service Performance (CSP) aspect.[16] The CPA and CSP have been applied to local authorities throughout the United Kingdom. The CSP is determined for each of seven service specialties and is based largely on archival performance indicators, supplemented by the results of the inspection and assessment of plans (Andrews *et al.* 2005). The archival performance indicators cover six aspects of organizational performance: quantity of outputs, quality of outputs, efficiency, formal effectiveness, equity, and consumer satisfaction. The inspection of services draws upon internal improvement plans, field visits, and other documentation. Statutory plans are assessed against the criteria of the service's relevant central government department. Evaluators external to the local authority conduct all assessments. Each service area is given a performance score by the Audit Commission from 1 (lowest) to 4 (highest). After calculating the CSP score for each service area, the Audit Commission derives a score for the whole organization by weighting services to reflect their relative importance by budget, then combining these weights with the performance score for each service area.

The CSP therefore offers a number of measurement advantages, but there are disadvantages as well. One is that using an overall measure of the performance of a local authority does not easily allow for exploration of individual service areas, and thus analysis is largely limited to relatively underspecified models. A second is that individual services are grouped into four rough performance categories (omitting much valuable information), and the adding of these weighted categories creates a false sense of precision that may not exist in practice. Also, of course, additional data on management must be gathered to try to model the management–performance link.

Some such studies have been completed (for instance, Andrews, Boyne, and Walker 2006 and Walker and Boyne 2006).[17] In any event, the British government has now modified its approach to assessing the performance of local authorities. The newer Comprehensive Area Assessment (CAA), created in 2009, was not comparable to the CSP approach, and explicitly placed significant discretion into the hands of the auditors. Furthermore, in May 2010 the newly elected Conservative/Liberal Democrat coalition government scrapped the CAA as well.

Perhaps the best way of making progress is to draw from many public organizations in one or other policy sector or service area, ideally in settings in which there is substantial consensus that certain performance measures are relevant, even highly salient. If such measures are collected systematically, in time series, and if additional data on control variables are likewise available, it may be possible to supplement this information with data on management to explore the difference that management makes. This is the approach we have taken here (see Chapter 2). Most of our empirical work draws from one field of public service: education. Results from education can be supplemented by similar studies in other policy fields, and valid general findings about public management and performance can be developed. In fact, a number of such studies have been conducted in other substantive fields of policy and management, both by us and by other investigators. The results of many such studies are included in later chapters of this book as appropriate, along with more detailed analyses of management and performance in public education. Although the other study areas have not produced a volume of research equal to that produced for public education, they have generated sufficient work to indicate that the theory and the approach can be generalized.

Our perspective: a parsimonious and formal approach

More than a decade ago we initiated a research program aimed at analyzing the influence of management on the performance of public organizations and public programs. We were convinced that, to be successful, such a program would need to be theoretically based and empirically grounded, and it would definitely need to consist of far more than a single study. After examining the literature on public management, performance, and organizational effectiveness, and after noting its many and tantalizingly interesting assertions and not fully validated conclusions, we decided to ground our own efforts on a parsimonious model of management and performance.[18] Doing so would mean leaving aside some of the subtleties in the research literature in favor of focusing on some especially critical aspects of management.

On the other hand, it would also require us, to make real progress, to be fairly specific about the theoretical ideas being explored. This approach contrasts with an alternative that would stipulate a broad notion of governance, as has been done by Lynn, Heinrich, and Hill (2001). They indicate that their "reduced-form model" can frame the logic of governance they explore:

$$O = f(E, C, T, S, M)$$

"where
O = outputs/outcomes (individual-level and/or organizational outputs/outcomes)
E = environmental factors
C = client characteristics
T = treatments (primary work/core processes/technology)
S = structures
M = managerial roles and actions" (2001: 81).

A limitation here, however, is that these researchers have not fully specified theoretical, causal linkages and therefore have not derived a set of precise, testable hypotheses.[19] Consequently, little progress has been made through this approach in validating or further specifying an appropriate model.

In other words, Lynn, Heinrich, and Hill explicitly "emphasize the distinction between a logic of governance and the specific theories that researchers use to investigate questions within this logic." Their aim is to suggest a more abstract logic that should be able to fit any number of theories. The approach "identifies an array of dependent and independent concepts that investigators encounter in empirical governance research, whether they analyze those concepts through lenses of political economy, network analysis, systems models or institutional approaches" (81).

Our approach, by contrast, aims at theoretical specification, hypothesis testing, and the validation of various forms of managerial influence – as appropriate. The perspective adopted in this book fits within a theoretical tradition developed by scholars such as James Thompson (1967), Charles Perrow (1986), and Herbert Simon (1997). The theoretical approach sketched in this book works at the organizational level. Another tradition, one not chosen here, operates or is driven primarily at and from the individual level (for instance, Argyris 1957, and subsequent publications; Golembiewski 1962, 1990, and subsequent publications; Katz and Kahn 1978). Both traditions have their strengths. We are interested in organizational and programmatic outputs and outcomes – and the effectiveness of management in shaping these – and judge that the former tradition offers a more direct and appropriate means for theory building and testing for this purpose.

In building from the tradition we have chosen, it is not imperative that we make a choice between socialized choice-based notions of individual decision making, on the one hand, and economic rationality, on the other (see the discussion in Lynn, Heinrich, and Hill 2001: 60–71). In tying our investigations of public management and performance to this earlier line of work in organization theory, furthermore, we are doing what Steven Kelman (2008) proposes for researchers in public management.

We also chose to generate such a model on the basis of our reading of the literature – in other words, inductively. Our approach has been to specify and formalize into mathematical expression what we understood to be some of the key theoretical assertions in the extant set of studies. Sometimes these earlier studies were not precise about the nature of the relationships in the theoretical arguments, so where we thought it necessary we added specificity. One reason why many apparent theoretical insights in the field remain neither validated nor refuted, we believe, is that they are sometimes not formulated with sufficient specificity to be tested and given a chance to be found wanting. Our approach, therefore, is the opposite: a formal, reductive model that is constructed inductively but that is in some respects more precise than the literature from which it springs. As we indicated at the time of the first publication of the model (O'Toole and Meier 1999), we would not be surprised to learn that some aspects of the model might need to be reconfigured on the basis of the evidence, but we would rather be precise so as to learn of the need for such modifications than persist in imprecision without progress.

We concluded that the model needed to offer a prominent role for what might be called internal management – the hands-on activities that managers undertake in seeking to organize and coordinate people and resources to get things done, as well as to reinforce and possibly enhance the routines and standard processes through which their organizations generate results. Equally importantly, we also concluded that the model would need to reflect the burgeoning emphasis on networks of organizational actors – the interdependent environment of the core organization that may be involved in supporting, opposing, and/or co-producing outputs and outcomes. A model reflective of much of the literature would, therefore, have to include some recognition of the structure or institutional arrangements through which policy-relevant action takes place, as well as the externally oriented actions of managers as they seek to deal with their context.

These and other aspects of the model are explained further in Chapter 2. Here we shift the focus briefly to some of the strengths of the approach we have taken, as well as some of the limitations or sacrifices inherent in such a research strategy.

The strengths have largely been alluded to above, and they are considerable. Working with a formal model allows for precision and the clear testing of hypotheses that are deductively drawn from the inductively built specification. Our particular approach, as will be evident in the several chapters of the book that lay out empirical evidence, is not to test the model all at once in its entirety; we consider that impossible. Rather, we have chosen to focus on certain relationships and conduct studies that explore those facets in particular. Much but not all of our empirical evidence has been drawn from a large-N data set that is still in the process of being built but that itself has considerable advantages – particularly given the difficulties, outlined earlier, of tapping common performance measures across many organizations. Chapter 2 explains the main data set and its advantages more thoroughly.

What is sacrificed by adopting such an approach? First, by using a parsimonious model we forgo the chance to explore many of the details and nuances in the case study literature on public management. We ignore, for instance, the personality traits of managers, as well as organizational culture, mission valence, the motivation of front-line workers,[20] and many other topics and variables that the literature discusses as being potentially important. We put the behavior and priorities of public managers front and center. Those who prize thick description will be disappointed with this aspect of our parsimonious approach, but they will also be rewarded nevertheless with findings and insights that would be impossible to glean from a smaller-N approach.[21]

Second, adopting a large-N approach means, furthermore, that aspects of the networks/public management theme in the research literature must largely be set aside at present. The fascinating and provocative research findings on networks have been generated from case studies and comparisons across small numbers of cases. This is so because detailing the many structural aspects of networks requires intensive investigation and the validation of many complex interactions (for instance, Provan and Milward 1995). Intensive analysis forecloses extensive larger-N comparisons. We explore some structural aspects of networks in this book, and we offer carefully developed findings on the networking behavior of top managers, but we do not explore the full details of networks. We view the tradeoff as worth it (for a detailed methodological argument to this effect, see Meier and O'Toole 2005), but the gains come at some cost as well. Over time, and with sustained attention by enough researchers, sufficient data may be able to be gathered for larger-N, more thoroughgoing network-focused studies to be possible.

Third, we focus on what can be measured, and thus ignore or overlook the intangibles that come into play. To be sure, we try to push the boundaries on what can be measured, such as with our measure of managerial quality (developed in Chapter 4). At the same time, we miss the unique behaviors and insights that make some managers stellar. We think the tradeoff – producing results that most organizations can attain versus identifying the absolute *best* practice – is worthwhile. We seek to sketch the broad parameters linking management to performance rather than undertake an exhaustive determination that requires excessively complex explanations.

Plan of the book

This volume is about public management and performance. It is not written from a naive perspective that would suggest that questions of management can be isolated from themes of politics, and, indeed, such themes are woven into several parts of our coverage. We focus first and foremost on management, however. Our efforts to address how some of the big questions of politics, and especially of democratic theory, intertwine with public management and bureaucratic structures resulted in an earlier book, which can be seen as a companion volume to this one (Meier and O'Toole 2006).

Our plan to unpack the difference that management makes begins in Chapter 2 with our theory of public management and its formalization in terms of mathematical modeling. The basic model is explained and distinguished from some other approaches that have appeared recently in the research literature. The chapter also attends to the subject of data. Most of our findings are drawn from a data set of about a thousand public organizations. The organizations and the nature of the data are explained in some detail, and we also demonstrate some of the major advantages of using such data in a research program such as this one.

Chapters 3 through 7 provide coverage of the management–shapes–performance evidence. Each chapter concentrates on an aspect of management, with the major managerial functions carved from the general model for focused attention. Systematic evidence is adduced in these chapters: detailed findings, especially from our work in public education, plus summary empirical evidence from other fields of policy and management and from numerous other venues.

Chapter 3 addresses the important themes of networks and managerial networking with other interdependent actors. Among the findings the chapter reports are: both network structure and networking behavior are appropriate foci of research for those interested in program performance; networking patterns of managers exhibit some similarities even when one compares data across national settings; networking by managers is not a product of pressure from outside the organization but, rather, reflects choices and actions by the managers themselves; the networking behavior of managers contributes positively to performance; managers' networking behavior interacts with some resources and constraints in the environment to boost the effects of networking in nonlinear ways; these positive outputs and outcomes are not equally distributed among interested parties, a pattern thus raising an issue of equity; and the direction(s) in which managers interact outward, and the nature of the interaction partner(s), help to explain who benefits from managerial networking.

Managers exhibit more than a mere degree of activity or "busyness" when performing their responsibilities. Some managers are highly skilled at what they do, while others frequently make mistakes. In Chapter 4 we develop a measure of managerial quality and estimate the separate impact of quality on public program outputs and outcomes. We also show that managerial quality can limit the onset of diminishing returns in the case of networking.

The management of people and operations within the core public organization charged with delivering results is a huge topic. Indeed, it is the primary focus of much of the literature on public management. Chapter 5 is devoted to analyses of some aspects of internal management. Among the results developed there are: personnel and managerial stability contribute positively to performance; and, more broadly, the management of an organization's human capital has a substantial positive influence that can be seen in organizations as diverse as those dealing with education and those charged with law enforcement. Chapter 5 also shows that good internal management can be used to deal with major events, such as budget cuts, that can harm the organization and its outputs.

Chapter 6 turns to two often neglected aspects of public management: the protective dimension and the nonlinearity of management's impact. Not only must managers be creative, help their organizations to exploit opportunities and resources in their setting, and jump-start new operations, they also can serve a crucial performance function by buffering public programs from perturbations and protecting them from negative shocks. Even when shocks enter the organizational system, management capacity plays a key role in allowing the organization to weather the disruption. In this chapter we demonstrate how important such functions can be in dealing with such sources of turbulence as budget cuts and natural disasters. We also explore the form of the managerial buffering function, and we show how this general process appears to benefit the organization's most disadvantaged clientele.

Chapter 7 presents an initial foray into the distinction between behavior and structural networks. This book focuses on behavioral networks, even though much of the literature deals with the structural dimension. Our measure of structural networks is the set of intergovernmental fiscal ties on which local governments depend, and we explore how variation in such funding sources between governments might shape results. We then show how behavioral networking, as well as other managerial aspects, affect performance within different types of structural networks.

In the final chapter we draw together the results of the research program to date, examine how all these managerial influences aggregate, sketch additional questions that remain to be explored, and summarize the difference that management makes.

NOTES

1. An exception is symbolic policies – those not intended to accomplish anything apart from signaling approval or disapproval of some person, event, or institution. Symbolic policies are obviously not intended to be implemented.
2. Here the individuals might be either people or organizations such as business firms. This point should not imply that such policies can operate without the benefit of public management to oversee the incentives and adjust them as priorities change or as the incentives generate unintended consequences.
3. As is often observed, the term "bureaucracy" typically appears as one of opprobrium in standard conversation – a shorthand for large, heavy-handed, intrusive, red-tape-encrusted,

inefficient government organization. Ever since Max Weber analyzed the concept nearly a century ago (Gerth and Mills 1958), however, social science has used the term to reference formal organization with certain distinctive features, including a hierarchy of superior–subordinate relations, the appointment of experts on the basis of merit criteria, fixed and limited jurisdictions, decision making on the basis of rules, and reliance on written records. Note that, by such a designation, bureaucracy as an organizational form applies to many for-profit and not-for-profit organizations as well as governmental ones.

4. The budget, on the other hand, has grown considerably.

5. A much less extreme version of such an argument holds that management matters, but what managers should do is largely driven by features of the organization's environment (see, for example, Woodward 1965). As becomes clear later in this book, we believe that this approach underestimates too much the potential effect of public management.

6. As many commentators have noted, NPM is less a coherent approach than a loosely linked cluster of ideas and reforms. Many of the specific NPM proposals have to do with bringing business management practices into public organizations and/or tapping market forces – for instance, by contracting functions out from public organizations. For varying versions of and emphases within NPM, see Hood (1991), Ferlie *et al.* (1996), Pollitt and Bouckaert (2000), and Barzelay (2001). NPM has shaped practices and ideas in many countries.

7. There is even a literature covering alternative ways that "publicness" might be defined and measured. We ignore such details in the coverage here, but revisit the subject briefly in the concluding chapter of the book.

8. It may be that private management has the same impact as public management; we do not know, and the literature has not demonstrated findings on this point, one way or another. We study public organizations because we are interested in public programs.

9. For an attempt to review the relevant literature and distill a set of testable propositions regarding the determinants of effective public organizations, see Rainey and Steinbauer 1999.

10. Overlying these four, three additional aspects are interwoven: leadership influence and emphasis, integration and alignment, and managing for results (see Ingraham, Joyce, and Donahue 2003: 16).

11. POSDCORB was Luther Gulick's (1937) way of summarizing the core managerial functions in the relatively early days of public administration as a self-aware field. The acronym stands for "planning, organizing, staffing, directing, co-ordinating, reporting, and budgeting."

12. On the one hand, many studies indicate that networks and collaboration are on the rise in today's world. The emerging theme of governance is reflective of this argument. On the other hand, diachronic studies of US legislation find little evidence of change across a nearly thirty-year period (Hall and O'Toole 2000, 2004). The actual trends over time, if any, await further empirical research.

13. Another requirement, of course, is measures of management. We address the set of issues related to this measurement challenge in various chapters of this book.

14. Many Cabinet departments have a wide variety of programs that are frequently not tied closely together. These aggregations reflect a wide variety of historical and political factors rather than any effort to group programs next to similar ones (see Seidman 1998).

15. Using work units might mean suboptimization at the work-unit level rather than optimal performance by the entire organization.
16. The CPA includes a subjective assessment of management style, which can bias the results if management is an independent variable in the analysis.
17. For management to play a major role, there must be discretion available to managers. In many UK service areas, such as education, the national government restricts the range of actions that local managers can take, thus limiting their impact.
18. More recently, one of us has suggested that the model might be used to explore performance-related relationships across a wide range of political institutions, not merely in bureaucratic organizations and networks of such implementing organizations (Meier 2007). This possibility is discussed in Chapter 8.
19. Lynn, Heinrich, and Hill do indicate that their reduced-form model implies an "essentially hierarchically" framed perspective on governance (e.g. legislative preferences driving the formal structures and process of public agencies, the latter then shaping the de facto organization and management of agencies and programs, this last set of forces influencing the "core technologies and primary work of public agencies," etc.; 2001: 32), although they also note that "there is likely to be endogeneity in these interactions, and one should not assume that the causal arrow always points downward" (39, note 14). The hierarchical formulation is based in part on the fact that many available empirical studies test for hierarchical effects. This finding, while undoubtedly partially valid, unfortunately does not take into account other under-researched causal paths – for instance, from front-line bureaucrats to managers to political leaders. Where such reverse or reciprocal causal paths have been hypothesized, evidence has validated such channels of influence; see Meier, O'Toole, and Nicholson-Crotty (2004).
20. The exception is when the motivation of front-line workers is reflected in lower turnover – a variable that we can measure directly.
21. Our approach is not divorced from the real work of practice. We have much experience interacting with managers in these organizations, as will be evident from our qualitative discussions in various places. All analysts of organizations and performance need to understand how organizations operate and how they generate the results that they do.

2 A model of public management and a source of evidence

How do organizations and governance systems shape performance, and how do managers influence what happens? In this chapter, we develop a model to answer these questions and guide our exploration of the real world of management. We model two distinct levels: the organizational and the network. While much of the empirical work developed later in this book focuses on how management makes a difference on the organizational level, many programs are implemented via complex networks that combine the efforts of multiple organizations. This structural variance means that it is important to discuss management in the context of the broader patterns of governance now evident in many public programs.

Since much of the rest of the book explores these theoretical ideas empirically, we also discuss data and data requirements. We start with an assessment of the type of data needed to test our theories. We then discuss the Texas schools data set, our primary data set, and its relative strengths and weaknesses. We then note other data sets used in various work in the public management–performance research agenda, including in some of our own studies. Several of these other data sets have enabled researchers to explore in other venues some of the important questions examined in this book, and we refer to a number of such studies in later chapters. Finally, we provide a specific discussion of performance measures for the Texas schools data set as well as the production function used in subsequent analyses.

Elements of a model

Our model of the relationship between public management and public program performance begins with a set of core concepts: hierarchy, stability, network, and management. We introduce a formal model at the organizational level and then move the modeling ideas to the network level. First, however, it is necessary to clarify some basic concepts that are both common in the literature and also central to our approach.

Public organizations are almost always structured as hierarchies. Indeed, bureaucracy as an organizational form is defined in part in terms of structures of superior–subordinate relations. In Chapter 1 we observed that frequently public organizations are also linked to other organizations of various sorts as they coproduce outputs and outcomes of public programs. So networks, as defined in the last chapter, often contain hierarchies embedded within them. At a more abstract level, we can think of hierarchy and network as structural forms at two ends of a continuum. That continuum would array structural forms – stable sets of relations – in terms of the degree to which each such structural form is governed by superiors who hold formal authority to compel action on the part of others.

Although we present hierarchies as a single type at one pole of the continuum, in practice they vary considerably in structure. They can be centralized or decentralized; they can vest extensive discretion in employees or seek to limit discretion with extensive rules; they can permit the lateral entry of employees or require that all promotions are from within the organization. These formal arrangements themselves tell only part of the story, since "informal organization," which develops in every functioning organization, is also important. For present purposes, however, we simplify by treating hierarchy as a stabilizing arrangement. In other words, at the extreme a "pure" hierarchy would be highly stable, even rigid, and would resist forces that might otherwise perturb or modify it.

Formal hierarchy is not the only stabilizing force in bureaucratic organizations. Among the other stabilizing aspects of formal organization, aside from structural stability, are mission stability (constancy over time in the stipulated goal(s) of the organization), procedural stability (constancy in the routines, rules, and standard operating procedures of the organization), production or technology stability (constancy in the tools used by the organization to get things done), and personnel stability (retention of the same individuals in the organization; see O'Toole and Meier 2003b). Indeed, some of these stabilizing forces are likely to reinforce each other; hierarchy, or structural stability, for example, can contribute to procedural stability.[1] These aspects of stability are discussed further in Chapter 5.

In short, we expect hierarchies to be relatively stable systems, and we also note that other forces also contribute to stable organizational systems. These features of public organizations will prove to be useful in our efforts to model management and performance, and some of them are also examined in the empirical parts of this book.

If "pure" hierarchy, or completely stable organization, is at one pole of the continuum mentioned earlier, pure networks can be considered to sit at the other end.[2] There is considerable evidence demonstrating that many public programs are not executed within or by a single hierarchical agency but are spread across parts of two or more organizations. These can be different organizations within a common government, but in many cases they are parts of multiple governments, and sometimes they also include businesses and/or nonprofit organizations. Such patterns are what we mean by networks. The nodes of networks can be occupied by individuals, organizations (including hierarchies), or parts of organizations.

As with hierarchies, networked structures can vary greatly in structural terms, from simple dyads to breathtakingly complex arrays of several dozen organizations, and with great variation as well on a number of structural dimensions that are typically used to characterize networked patterns: network centrality, multiplexity, and so forth (O'Toole 1997). Networked action is typical in the United States (see, for instance, Bardach 1998 and Bingham and O'Leary 2008) as well as in other settings, from the United Kingdom (Huxham 2000; Stoker 1999) to Sweden (Lundin 2007) and the Netherlands (Schalk, Torenvlied, and Allen 2010), and even Thailand (Krueathep, Riccucci, and Suwanmala 2010).

Despite the absence (or low level) of formal authority possessed by "leaders" in a network, such patterns may over time acquire some considerable degree of stability. In fact, some types of networks have become known for their relatively closed and impenetrable features – for example, the "iron triangles" of administrative agency, legislative committee, and interest groups sometimes seen operating for extended periods in certain US policy fields (Freeman 1965). Our particular interest is in networks of actors involved in implementing public programs and delivering public services. Networks for implementation can also acquire stability over time, but those that are not well established, but are in formation or flux due to the establishment of a new program or significant modification in an existing one, can be quite fluid. Indeed, in pluralist governance settings such as in the United States, we expect networks to be structurally more open and shifting than in implementation settings in more corporatist contexts where there is broad agreement on processes and procedures.

Networks are particularly interesting to public management scholars because public managers have the responsibility for trying to weave the interdependent parts of an implementation apparatus together into a functioning policy delivery system. Networks such as these, quite common for public programs, represent a considerable degree of structural fluidity and therefore contain considerable uncertainty regarding relations, commitments, understandings, power, and information (Frederickson 1999). Governments often tap networks to deliver policy results but face a common dilemma. The enhanced capacity of networks for action across multiple units increases the odds of generating outputs and outcomes, but, at the same time, adding actors in networked arrays introduces substantial challenges of coordination and associated uncertainty.

In short, structural variation – between rigid hierarchies at one extreme and fluid, emergent networks at the other – can be an important aspect of the institutional setting of public programs, and it can influence the challenges that managers face as they seek to contribute to program performance. Although most programs operate somewhere between the poles of this continuum, we want to include this range of variation in our approach to modeling to make sure that our theory is as general as possible.[3]

Public management involves the coordination of people and other resources toward the accomplishment of public purpose. The particular activities that are encompassed by the notion of management here constitute an exceedingly long list. Public managers undertake traditional POSDCORB-like functions, as well as creative and subtle efforts. They are involved in managing budgets, for instance, and also in devising creative ways of gaining access to resources. Their responsibilities involve planning, and also risk evaluation and mitigation. They manage people, while also trying to create and motivate teams that work together across the organization – and sometimes across different organizations. Public management, in other words, includes myriad specific challenges and activities.

It is impossible for us to specify and estimate the effect of all these detailed elements of public management. So, while we build our model inductively from the literature, we must perforce generalize and move to a somewhat more abstract level in sketching managerial functions. One way to do so is to distinguish managerial efforts to manage within the organization from other activities directed externally – that is, toward the environment of the organization. These two aspects of management are not neatly partitioned from each other, and we should avoid any implication that there is some sort of simple, zero-sum tradeoff between the two. For reasons that will become apparent shortly, nonetheless, it can be helpful when formalizing the role of management in shaping performance to distinguish and recognize both broad components of what managers do.

In this sense, then, our discussion of structure is related to our conceptualization of management. It is common to assume that "management" operates in and through a hierarchical structure, and it often does. Given the prominence of networks in the practical world, however, we do not want to assume that programs operate as hierarchies in advance of examining them. Accordingly, we encompass as part of "management" the efforts by actors to concert patterns of behavior across organizations and not just within them. A part of management might involve persuasion, signaling, and diplomacy with regard to others rather than simply issuing communications and directives along formal bureaucratic channels. This point, along with the observation that even the management of individual organizations operates in an open-system context, in which the core organization is inevitably and regularly interdependent with its environment, suggests that public management encompasses these distinguishable functions or lines of activity.

An additional point about public management, broadly construed, needs to be mentioned. Multiple individuals operating in the setting in which a public program is being executed may have responsibility for, or may take upon themselves part of the task of, management. The job is typically not consigned to a single position or individual, and perhaps not even to actors operating within a single organization. Managers populate multiple levels within large organizations, and, for networks of organizations, managers operate across the network as well. Nor is it a foregone conclusion that the managers are all operating in coordination with the other managers. Some managers may try to do so and fail, and other managers may also use their managerial effort and ability to move action in directions opposed by others – including other managers – in the setting. These possibilities make for exceedingly complex and possibly confusing patterns of behavior.

We address these complications in two ways. The reality that there may well be multiple managers and managerial influences, possibly pressing in different directions, is treated by us here via a simplification: theoretically, we model management as a vector sum of the full set of managerial efforts of various types. In other words, we include multiple managerial functions, but we treat different managerial vectors for each function only in terms of the vector sum for that function.[4] In most of the empirical work presented in later chapters, we draw our data from the top manager in each public organization. In terms of there being different managerial efforts at different levels of a complex institutional setting, we both simplify and complicate in our work. With regard to the former, we largely focus our empirical work on the efforts of top management in the core production organization and thus mostly leave aside the additional managerial forces at lower echelons of the organization. With regard to the latter, we undertake our modeling in two stages, each reflecting a different level in a governance system (organizations and networks). We thereby seek to capture the complexity of management in networks, even if we also simplify in other ways for the purposes of empirical analysis.

Modeling public management and performance

Our approach to modeling and exploring the relationship between public management and program performance is to draw some basic ideas from the extensive case study literature and to formalize some of it in terms of a mathematical model. In this section we proceed in this fashion, step by step, to build the model. We use the basic concepts covered in the preceding section of the chapter, as well as some of the points of scholarly consensus introduced in Chapter 1. Here we model management's relationship to performance from the perspective of a core production unit, and in the section following we continue by modeling at the network level. Our approach is to begin with some basic features of an organizational or program system and then gradually introduce additional elements. Once we have some of the basic features in place, we add aspects of management to the model.

Inertial systems and stability

Organizations and programs, as has often been noted, are inertial systems. What they do and what they produce today is typically very much like what they did and produced yesterday. The pattern holds for both empirical and normative reasons. Empirically, it is difficult to induce significant change overnight when the routines and operations of hundreds or thousands of individuals would need to be adjusted and coordinated anew, and perhaps in a different direction. Normatively, one of the major advantages of bureaucracy as an organizational form is consistency and relative stability (Gerth and Mills 1958); organizations, as a result, are designed to be inertial. An inertial system means that current outputs[5] can be expected to be strongly influenced by past outputs. If one defines outputs at time t as O_t, a very simple model of organizational or program output is

$$O_t = \beta_0 O_{t-1} + \varepsilon \tag{2.1}$$

where current performance is the result of past performance at time t–1, discounted by a rate of stability, β_0, and a set of shocks to the system, ε. In this general modeling effort, we ignore the nature of the relevant outputs, how they would be measured, and whether multiple dimensions should be considered.[6] In mathematical terms, such an inertial system is called an autoregressive system. An autoregressive system is not the equivalent of a static system. A static system does not change from one time period to the next; an autoregressive system can build in change over time either internally or in response to environmental change.[7] The rate of stability of this system is constrained to a value between zero and one. As β approaches one, the system becomes highly stable. As the value approaches zero, the system moves toward entropy.[8]

Shocks to the system, ε, can originate from a variety of forces in the environment. Some of them are intentionally generated by other actors – for instance, decisions from the courts that alter or constrain program activity, actions by legislatures or executives that change priorities or alter program funding, or antagonistic moves by those who oppose the program or the organization that operates it. Some shocks may emanate from other influences, such as changes in the economic or social environment. The examples mentioned thus far are exogenous, but some may have their source from within the system itself, such as planned organizational change, or organization development. As will become clear shortly, we distinguish some of the exogenous parts of ε and incorporate them into the modeling process.

In rigid hierarchies, as indicated earlier, we expect systems to be highly autoregressive, whereas with fluid and emerging networks there is much less inertia. If we consider both structure and other stabilizing features of such systems (standard operating procedures, civil service rules, and the like), we can introduce another term, S, as an expression for the set of stabilizing features. If we had a good measure of the set of stabilizing features, and if we normalize it to approach 1.0 at the highest level of stability and to approach 0 at the extremely fluid and flexible end of the continuum, we could say

$$\beta_0 = f(S) \tag{2.2}$$

or that the rate of stability, β_0, can be partitioned into the structural and other related stabilizing features, S, along with other inertial elements, now β_1. The general equation would be

$$O_t = \beta_1 SO_{t-1} + \varepsilon \tag{2.3}$$

which indicates that an increase in organizational structure and/or other stabilizing elements results in a more inertial system.

Shocks

A major difference between fluid networks and highly stable structures such as bureaucratic hierarchies lies in how they are affected by external shocks from the environment. Later in this book we consider in some detail how shocks affect organizational performance and what can be done to mitigate any potentially negative effects. For now, we consider the issue in general and abstract terms. Stable hierarchies generally tend to buffer or protect the organization fairly effectively. Shocks that do penetrate a system's protections, nonetheless, have different impacts on stable organizations from the impacts they have on fluid networks. Although shocks are less likely to pass through a hierarchy's buffering apparatus, when they do they can have a very significant impact. To see why, we return to the initial autoregressive relationship in Equation (2.1) from above for an approximation to the pattern in a highly stable hierarchical system (where $\beta_0 \rightarrow 1$):

$$O_t = \beta_0 O_{t-1} + \varepsilon \tag{2.4}$$

If we partition the ε into some shock X_t that penetrates the system's buffers with an initial impact of β_2 and a random component, ε_t, this yields

$$O_t = \beta_0 O_{t-1} + \beta_2 X_t + \varepsilon_t \tag{2.5}$$

Note that, in this case, a one-unit change in X_t produces a β_2 change in O_t, all other things being equal. This effect is the impact of X_t on O for time t only, however. Because X_t has increased the value of O_t, then in time t+1 this larger value of O_t will also influence the size of O_{t+1}. Because O_t is β_2 larger as the result of X_t, O_{t+1} will be $\beta_0\beta_2$ larger as the result of the impact of X_t in the preceding year. Such impacts continue to reverberate through the system in future years, gradually becoming smaller (forming what is known as a geometrically distributed lag; see Hamilton 1994) but still cumulating into a relatively large impact.

The overall impact, I, of a one-unit change in X can be determined by the following formula, where the terms are defined as above:

$$I = \beta_2/(1 - \beta_0) \tag{2.6}$$

A relatively small shock that gets through the system's buffering apparatus, consequently, can have a major, long-term influence on the system, depending on the size of the coefficient of stability. As an illustration, suppose the initial-year impact, β_2, had a value of 1. If the coefficient of stability is 0.99 (indicating a highly stable system), then the total impact is 100, or $100 = 1/(1 - 0.99)$.[9] If the coefficient of stability is only 0.7, the total impact of X in this case falls all the way to 3.33.[10] Two important points merit reemphasis. First, relatively small changes in a system can have major, long-run implications simply because the program structures are inertial systems. Second, shocks that penetrate to the organization have a much larger long-run impact in highly inertial systems than they do in less inertial systems, because the impact of the shock continues to influence outcomes well into the future.

Buffering

As noted above, organizations establish units or processes to buffer shocks from the environment. Several forms of buffering can be identified (O'Toole and Meier 2003a). Abstractly speaking, these include buffers structured as a barricade or "wall" of some height that stops all external shocks smaller than a given size from penetrating the organization and its operations. Alternatively, some buffers are designed more like filters: certain issues or stakeholders – ones more central to the organization's goals or survival – are screened in, while others are screened out. Another form that buffers might take is as a dampener: external perturbations have impact, but the magnitude is reduced by some amount (for empirical evidence on this last variant, see Meier and O'Toole 2008). We explore this variant more carefully in Chapter 6 of this book. Regardless of the type of buffer, in more fluid networks buffering is more difficult to accomplish simply because the nature of networks creates additional interdependences that cannot be isolated from the technical core of the system. Because organization A is interdependent with (read "linked to") organization B, any shocks that penetrate organization A's buffers are likely to influence organization B regardless of the strength of B's buffers.

Given the different functional forms that buffers may take, for modeling purposes we would need to take into account the form of the buffer to represent it mathematically. We do so here for one of the types mentioned above: that of buffer as dampener. We can conceive of the stabilizing features of a system (here subscripted with an "e" to indicate that the feature is designed to interface with the environment rather than generate internal stability – for instance, a legislative affairs or public affairs office), including the system (such as organizational) structure, as reducing the impact of shocks via a discounting term in the model, thus:

$$O_t = \beta_1 SO_{t-1} + \beta_2 X_t (1/S_e) + \varepsilon_t \tag{2.7}$$

In this way, an increase in stabilization, S_e, acts directly on the exogenous shock to limit its impact on the system. Any shock that penetrates the buffers of the system can still have a substantial, long-run impact on the organization, however, if the organization is highly inertial. For a fluid network, in contrast, buffering is relatively weak, so shocks easily reach the system. The impact of such shocks over time is far less, however – simply because the networks are more loosely coupled.

Equation (2.7) indicates how one might model a buffer that operates as a dampener, reducing all environmental impacts by a given amount. Other types of buffers would take different mathematical forms. A buffer that operated as a barricade or a levee, for example, would be operationalized as a more additive (subtractive in practice) process, as follows:

$$O_t = \beta_1 SO_{t-1} + \beta_2 (X_t - S_e) + \varepsilon_t \tag{2.8}$$

The important theoretical point about buffers is that they can be designed in very different ways; models of organizations need to reflect the different buffering processes with appropriate mathematical representations.

Introducing management into the picture

Hierarchies and networks are human systems for executing policy; as such, they are not merely inertial structures and buffers but managed entities as well. Obviously, therefore, we need to represent some of the core features of public management in our mathematical representation – but how, exactly? We know that all signs point to management often contributing positively to program performance. If this contribution were to take the form of another standard input in the production process, we could include management – "M" – as an additive term in the model. In this fashion, if we were to add management to Equation (2.5) from earlier, we would represent its contribution as follows:

$$O_t = \beta_0 O_{t-1} + \beta_2 X_t + \beta_3 M + \varepsilon_t \tag{2.9}$$

If X_t represents a vector of all other factors that affect the system (and therefore are viewed as shocks, whether positive or negative), such as resources, constraints, external demands, and so forth, then the test for whether management matters in a program structure would be whether the coefficient for management, β_3, is significantly greater than zero.

Such a simple linear impact for management is inconsistent with our reading of the literature, however. Much of the rich literature on public management and performance indicates that management interacts with other features of the system to shape results. Trying to represent this idea in the model means considering various nonlinear mathematical forms. Several options of this sort are possible (see O'Toole and Meier 1999 for some possibilities), but it is also important to consider the program structure, along with other stabilizing features of the system. Indeed, one crucial task of management is to maintain some of these stabilizing features: to frame the goals, set the incentives, buttress the structure, and negotiate the contributions from members and from those with whom the system interacts (Barnard 1938; Simon 1997). This system maintenance function of management, we think, can best be modeled as in the following representation, where management supplements the set of stabilizing elements in the system in the inertial portion of the model:

$$O_t = \beta_1 (S + M) O_{t-1} + \beta_2 X_t + \varepsilon_t \tag{2.10}$$

In this equation, as stability increases, the role of management becomes less necessary because the other stabilizing system features generate a relatively inertial system.[11] As stable structure and other such features decline, however, this system tends toward entropy unless management increases its impact on the maintenance of steady production.

Many of the standard accounts of public management emphasize this managerial function, and it would be possible to unpack many of the ways that management supports the coordination and maintenance of production efforts: managing human resources, planning and organizing and assessing risks, allocating financial resources among production tasks so as to support the generation of outputs and outcomes, and much more. Later in this book we devote some attention to specific managerial subfunctions such as these, as well as to internal management overall. For the moment, however, we simply note that one broad managerial function is to support and maintain performance.

Of course, maintenance is only one function of management.[12] We can call this first managerial function M_1. An equally important function of management is to guide how the system interacts with its environment – in modeling terms, how it deals with shocks to the system. We designate this latter aspect of management M_2. As indicated earlier in the chapter, the two are not fully partitioned from each other, and a given manager may allocate considerable time and effort to both (for an analysis of how shocks to the system can generate internal managerial adjustments, see O'Toole and Meier 2010). We use different subscripts nonetheless to allow for the possibility that these two functions can vary independently of each other yet still have something in common that we would consider management.

M_2 can be modeled, but only if the management strategy of the system is known relative to the interdependent environment. Management could adopt a strategy of buffering, or protecting, against environmental influences; or management could actively seek to exploit or tap the environment for the benefit of the program's performance. If management adopts a buffering approach, we can model this choice as follows, with management externally interacting with the set of stabilizing influences in the buffering process:

$$O_t = \beta_1(S + M_1)O_{t-1} + \beta_2 X_t(1/S_e M_2) + \varepsilon_t \tag{2.11}$$

In this equation, management dampens the impact of environmental shocks and works with stabilizing features such as structure in this process.[13]

Management that seeks to exploit the environment rather than buffer from it will attempt to tap or magnify some of these influences from outside – financial resources, supportive stakeholders, and suchlike – so that they have a performance-enhancing impact on the system. In this case, we model the impact of management as leveraging at least some of the "X" term, as in the following equation:

$$O_t = \beta_1(S + M_1)O_{t-1} + \beta_2 X_t(M_2/S_e) + \varepsilon_t \tag{2.12}$$

To put it simply, management moves from the denominator to the numerator of the second term of the equation, and in the process increases the impact of some environmental force rather than diminishing it.

Of course, a more nuanced and realistic notion would be that management does not simply adopt a buffering or an exploiting strategy, but, rather, seeks to do both: buffering some influences while tapping and using others.[14] To represent both exploiting and buffering in the same model, we combine Equations (2.11) and (2.12) and partition – and relabel – M_2 as managerial efforts to exploit, M_3, and managerial efforts to buffer, M_4, as follows:

$$O_t = \beta_1(S + M_1)O_{t-1} + \beta_2 X_t(M_3/S_e M_4) + \varepsilon_t \tag{2.13}$$

Rearranging the terms of this equation, we get

$$O_t = \beta_1(S + M_1)O_{t-1} + \beta_2 X_t/S_e(M_3/M_4) + \varepsilon_t \tag{2.14}$$

Equation (2.14) represents our general model of public management. The ratio of M_3 to M_4 in the second, or environmental, portion of the model is a characterization of how risk-seeking (or risk-averse) the management of the system is. As the effort devoted to tapping environmental forces increases, this ratio increases. As the management of the system devotes more effort to buffering, the system becomes more risk-averse and the size of this ratio decreases. In theory this risk ratio can be viewed as management-imposed risk versus the normal risks associated with an uncertain environment. The normal risks of environmental uncertainty can be tapped via an examination of how the "X" factor, the environment, affects the degree of variation in outcomes, O. This implies that greater risk will be associated with a larger standard deviation in O. Within this view, management's attempts to increase or decrease risk by manipulating the ratio of exploiting to buffering should also affect the standard deviation of O.

Finally, we note that we have distinguished stabilizing influences from managerial influences in this modeling effort. Though sensible and defensible, this approach omits an additional subtlety: that, over more extended periods, stabilizing forces influence (constrain) the actions of management, and the actions of managers can also shape the system's structure and other such stabilizing forces. Therefore,

$$S_t \rightarrow M_t \rightarrow S_{t+1}$$

The theory and the model, moreover, treat stabilization and some parts of management as substitutes for each other. The interrelationships between management and stabilization can be empirically examined with a variety of time-series techniques, such as vector autoregression or an instrumental variables approach within a normal time-series model. While we note these hypothesized relationships here, however, and while we explore M and some aspects of S in this book, we do not pursue further the interrelationship of

S and M over extended periods. This line of research must be left to future work, but it is a promising area in which to merge the study of public management with the study of organization theory (Kelman 2008).

We have developed a model that includes a number of managerial functions and a set of contingent relationships. Modeling management and performance at this level has incorporated some assumptions and simplifications, but a big advantage is that we have specified precisely a set of empirical relationships that might or might not hold in practice. Although we begin to test many of them later in this volume, at this point the model can be treated as a set of hypotheses. It is quite possible that this theoretical effort will eventually be shown to be in error on certain points (one such possibility is introduced later in the book; see Chapter 6), but we care less about being correct in the details than about catalyzing work along these lines. Progress can be expected only through precise and ultimately falsifiable predictions about managing public programs.

Our approach differs from others that have been taken in the research literature on public management. First and most obviously, this approach varies markedly from the most common approach in the field of public management. Although the model has been built by relying on the extensive case study literature, and although there is nothing about the model that could not be explored via additional case studies, we have formalized several of the assertions and intuitions of that earlier literature for the purposes of more precise, large-N statistical tests. We think the advantages of this approach in terms of reliability and external validity make the effort potentially valuable. It should also be clear that, given the complexity of the model and the number of hypothesized relationships, it is not a simple matter of generating one study that can see if all the theoretical ideas set forth here are valid or invalid. The model, in short, initiates and catalyzes a research program that needs to encompass multiple kinds of empirical investigations. As we mentioned at the conclusion of our initial articulation of the model, "[T]his perspective suggests the initiation of a research *agenda* rather than the sketch of a one-shot research design" (O'Toole and Meier 1999: 524, emphasis in original). Indeed, this book synthesizes a number of the investigations that have been part of that research agenda as it has developed over several years.

Second, the theoretical ideas sketched here are somewhat different from those offered by certain other researchers. Even among those analysts who frame public management in terms of multiple functions, there can be different ways of slicing such functions aside from the way we have done here. Mark Moore (1995), for example, carves managerial effort into three different portions: managing upward, downward, and outward. The model developed in this book largely does so in terms of internal management, external exploitation, and external buffering (sometimes we combine the latter two into a simpler measure of managing outward). We also differ from those who have argued that managing networks is fundamentally different from managing hierarchies (see, for instance, Provan and Milward 1995, Mandell 2001, and Agranoff and McGuire 2003). Our model can be adapted to the network level (see below); it also stresses managing in an organization's networked setting by its extensive focus on how managers deal with manifestations arising outside the organization.

Third, our approach is different from – and, we would argue, more specific than – other recent efforts to suggest the components of a model of governance. The most well-known such governance model is that offered by Lynn, Heinrich, and Hill (2001), which was discussed in Chapter 1. That conceptualization is an interesting and potentially useful way of thinking about governance, but it is not a theory of governance. The latter would make relatively precise predictions about variables and their relationships. The former can integrate extant research, identify over- and underexamined foci of investigation (see, for instance, Hill and Lynn 2005), and thereby provide a checklist for future work to consider. Other than clarifying a listing of relevant variables that should be considered in theory building, it does not generate specific research hypotheses and is largely agnostic in choosing between theoretical perspectives.

In short, we see a logic of governance as useful but insufficient; theory building is necessary. Our particular perspective in this regard explicitly incorporates management into the process, provides precise predictions about how the variables relate to each other, allows and specifies certain relationships to be nonlinear, frames a set of research questions so that conceptual and measurement issues can be identified and addressed, and mimics in the abstract how organizations and their managers operate in practice (contingent decision making that takes place in an autoregressive system open to environmental influences). These advantages, we would argue, are not inconsiderable; but the ultimate test is empirical.

We readily admit that we have a reductive model, one that emphasizes parsimony. Such parsimony is always open to the charge that we have omitted a key variable or concept. At the same time, parsimony is an advantage, because the limited number of concepts permits us to test some highly complex relationships (as illustrated by the nonlinear and interactive relationships). We think the gains from parsimony exceed the costs.

Much of the rest of this volume consists of empirical analyses, and considerable support for several parts of the model has accumulated. It is important to keep the overall emphasis on the model as a set of partially tested hypotheses, though, rather than as received wisdom or fully validated knowledge about public management in all places and for all times.

Before turning to empirical findings, however, two additional tasks ought to be addressed. First, we should expand the modeling effort to present some tentative ideas about managing in more complex settings – networked settings. We do this to illustrate our belief that, although managing a network is more difficult than managing a hierarchy, the general processes are similar and can be managed and modeled in similar terms. Second, we should place the ensuing empirical work in context by discussing the data requirements for empirical studies of this model, or other models of this sort.

Modeling management and performance in networks

Earlier in this chapter we explained that management's institutional setting is expected to be important; such settings range from rather stable structures such as hierarchies to highly fluid networks of organizations (which them-selves may contain hierarchies within them). Thus far, the model we have developed incorporates this structural variation as part of the stabilizing forces through the "S" term. If we try to be more precise and also complete, nonetheless, we have to think in terms of multi-level systems, with manage-ment operating at different levels, with different foci, and to different effects. Although the modeling ideas that result from grappling with this further feature of the real world generate enormous complexity, as will be seen shortly, and although the remainder of this volume works from the more simplified model developed in the preceding section, we think it useful here to suggest more fully how modeling might proceed in multi-level systems involving networks of actors. Doing so is helpful because it alerts us to some of the issues that can arise for managers operating in complex institutional settings, and taking this step now also suggests certain items yet to be dealt with by researchers in the field of public management.

Moving the theoretical ideas developed here up to the network level, with clusters of organizations and their management partially linked in pursuit of public objectives, involves increasing the model's complexity by an order of magnitude (for an early development of these ideas, see Meier and O'Toole

2004a). Although the core concepts and the basic ideas remain the same, the number of possible relationships and the demands that these place on data and models increase significantly. This section merely indicates the direction that such modeling and estimation may need to take; a full elaboration would take substantial additional space, and the data requirements for systematic testing of these ideas surpass significantly the kinds of data now available. For that reason, we restrict this presentation to the outlines of how such a modeling effort should develop.

We begin this sketch by reintroducing our basic model, but with a subscript, h, to indicate that the concepts are measured for a formal hierarchy – that is, at the organizational level. This modification in symbolization, but not conceptualization, yields the following:

$$O_{th} = \beta_{1h}(S_h + M_{1h})O_{(t-1)h} + \beta_{2h}(X_{th}/S_{eh})(M_{3h}/M_{4h}) + \varepsilon_{th} \qquad (2.15)$$

For the sake of simplicity, one can define the internal (that is, first-term) nonoutput portion as Y and the external (environmental) term as Z, yielding the following simple equation for a hierarchy:

$$O_{th} = \beta_{1h}(Y_h)O_{(t-1)h} + \beta_{2h}(Z_h) + \varepsilon_{th}, \qquad (2.16)$$

where $Y_h = S_h + M_{1h}$ and $Z_h = (X_{th}/S_{eh})(M_{3h}/M_{4h})$.

A network established or used to implement a program would also have similar internal and external terms. We theorize in terms of the same kind of functional form, now subscripted with an "n" to reference the network level:

$$O_{tn} = \beta_{1n}(Y_n)O_{(t-1)n} + \beta_{2n}(Z_n) + \varepsilon_{tn} \qquad (2.17)$$

Even networks should be expected to be somewhat inertial, though less so than individual formal organizations. The internal term of the model becomes much more complex, however, because it must now include both the internal management terms for the network $(S_n + M_{1n})$, and also the same terms for the hierarchies $(S_h + M_{1h})$ that compose the nodes of the network:

$$Y_n = [(S_n + M_{1n})\Omega\Phi(S_h + M_{1h})], \qquad (2.18)$$

with two new symbols (Ω, Φ) introduced, to be explained shortly. Similarly, the environmental term must now include both the environmental factors for the network $(X_{tn}/S_{en})(M_{3n}/M_{4n})$ and the environmental factors for the hierarchies $(X_{th}/S_{eh})(M_{3h}/M_{4h})$ that comprise the nodes of the network:

$$Z_n = [(X_{tn}/S_{en})(M_{3n}/M_{4n})]\Omega\Phi[(X_{th}/S_{eh})(M_{3h}/M_{4h})] \qquad (2.19)$$

When combined, the overall formal presentation of network management becomes

$$
\begin{aligned}
O_t = {} & \beta_{1n}[(S_n + M_{1n})\,\Omega\Phi\,(S_h + M_{1h})]O_{(t-1)n} \\
& + \beta_{2n}[(X_{tn}/S_{en})(M_{3n}/M_{4n})]\Omega\Phi[(X_{th}/S_{eh})(M_{3h}/M_{4h})] + \varepsilon_t
\end{aligned}
\tag{2.20}
$$

The two new symbols require explanation. The "Φ" term is used to indicate that the internal management terms of the individual organizations comprising a network are aggregated in some manner, as yet undefined; the external management terms of these units are also aggregated in some manner. The form of aggregation, we theorize, depends on the type of interdependence among the units comprising the network. Thompson (1967) has sketched a simple typology of such patterns for organizations, and his notions can be applied across units as well (see, for instance, O'Toole and Montjoy 1984). Whether networks of organizations are pooled, sequential, or reciprocal carries implications for how one models management.

Pooled environments around a core or focal organization and its management, whereby multiple external organizational actors contribute to impacts on the targets of public policy but do not deal directly with each other during their own efforts, are by definition less interdependent than other patterns; thus resources (or constraints) from them can likely be summed. Maintaining a supply of a particularly strategic resource from one part of a pooled environment does not require managing relations with the remainder of the organizational actors. Similarly, controlling the impact of constraints imposed from a particular direction does not necessarily entail orchestrating coalitions of actors across multiple units.

Sequentially structured environments – arrays in which an output of one unit serves as an input for the next, and so on – suggest certain other critical management issues: eliminating any blockages in the flows of production between units in the environment, and taking advantage of how resources may be aggregated. Sequential environments, or networks of organizations subject to sequential interdependence, should be aggregated in a multiplicative manner; a probability of failure (or success) in one relationship affects the probability of failure (or success) of all the subsequent units in the sequential chain.

Reciprocal environments, in which the outputs of some units serve as inputs for others, which in turn provide critical inputs for the first set, cannot be modeled in such simple ways. These require mathematical techniques that permit both positive and negative feedback in a pattern in which the resources are not wholly exogenous to the focal organization.

The implications of these various archetypes of environments, or networked patterns, for management (separate from their implications for modeling) should be obvious. In a pooled environment, the manager merely has to be concerned with factors that directly affect his or her own organization. Unless other organizations are linked into its environment, the actions that they take are of little concern to the focal organization except as competitors. In a simple pooled relationship, the aggregate operator is likely a simple vector summation (Σ). In a sequential setting, the managers have to be concerned with the operations of all the other organizations in the sequence. Each must either convince an errant organization to change or adapt his or her own organization to the change in inputs. In a pure sequential relationship, the aggregation parameter is likely a multiplicative one (Π). In networks bound by reciprocal ties, organizational management becomes similar to network management, with a web of relationships and concerns that have to be incorporated into any decisions. Reciprocal relationships may need to be translated into sequential relationships in two or more directions for mathematical estimation.

Of course, any organization's environment can contain resource (or constraint) linkages that fit all three types of interdependence. One can put the point in the language of networks: networks can differ from one another in the kinds and extensiveness of interdependent relationships between and among the various nodes.[15] Mixed relationships are likely to have some combination of different aggregation operators, perhaps including some we have not introduced here. Aggregation questions become rather important when one moves to the network level, because the question of aggregation and its form applies not only to the environment of a core organization of interest but to the network itself – for instance, regarding how the management function is aggregated across units. In short, the new arithmetic operator Φ introduced in Equation (2.20) signifies different operations, depending on the structure of interdependence within the network.

The second term (Ω) is included to show that the internal network management needs to be related to the aggregated internal management of the hierarchies, and that the environment of the network needs to be related to the aggregated environments of the hierarchies. Exactly how these elements are combined (addition, multiplication, and so forth) remains to be discovered.

The network-level model outlined sketchily here suggests why deciphering management in and of networks is more complex and demanding than the management of simple hierarchies. In a two-node network, the demands might not be insurmountable; as the number of nodes increases, however, the ability of either analysts or managers to consider all factors simultaneously soon exceeds the bounds of rational capacity. Managers, we think, use a variety of coping techniques to allow themselves to manage the network, and they may be able to make use of some heuristics from bodies of work such as game theory to sort through certain kinds of circumstances (see, for instance, O'Toole 1996). Coping techniques might include satisficing, rational shielding from nodes, ignoring some interdependences, decoupling or "negative coordination" (Scharpf 1993) from nodes, adding structure to the network environment, and so forth. The exact strategies can be determined only via empirical analysis of how managers operate in these networked situations.

For reasons that should be obvious at this point, data are not available that would allow us to fully specify and test the network-level model in enough cases to glean patterns of findings. Accordingly, the ideas in this section should be considered initial, untested steps toward a fully developed theory of public management and performance in networks. We also saw in Chapter 1 that challenges often make it difficult to test performance-related theoretical ideas of any sort across large numbers of cases. The next section describes the main data set that we employ to explore the relationship between management and performance in much of the remainder of this book.

The Texas school district data set

An important challenge to the development of evidence-based public management is the availability of adequate data sets for systematic investigation of these theoretical notions to see if they are actually valid. Public management in particular has been slow to develop general data sets that can be used to answer multiple questions important to the field (this coverage is drawn from Meier and O'Toole 2009b). There is no public management equivalent of the American National Election Study or the Panel Study of Income Dynamics, two widely used data sets important in other realms of social science. In our work we have tapped data on the management of various other public services, but the bulk of our empirical work has relied on another data set with some important advantages for this purpose. We have started the construction of a data set on the school districts in the state of Texas (we say "started" because the process is ongoing). Rather than beginning from scratch, we have opted to build on an existing data set that had a wide range of performance indicators for more than 1,000 public organizations over an established period of time – the Texas school district data set. To that data set we have added managerial measures with a series of surveys of top managers undertaken in 2000, 2002, 2005, 2007, and 2009,[16] plus an additional survey of top managers concerning how they responded to the devastating effects of Hurricanes Katrina and Rita, which unexpectedly ravaged that region in 2005.

The Texas context

Because we rely heavily on school districts in one state, some description of the Texas policy context is in order. In response to a nationwide study questioning the performance of public education (*A Nation at Risk*; see National Commission on Excellence in Education 1983), Governor Mark White launched a radical reform of Texas schools in the mid-1980s. Standards for both students and teachers were raised. Students were required to take more courses and more rigorous courses. State aid to local school districts was increased in order to address the problems generated by local variation in property values. The reforms were so fundamental that academics took precedence over the cultural lynchpin of Texas schools: football.[17]

Along with the reforms a state-level accountability system was established. Students were required to take a series of standardized tests, with the aggregate results published widely. The release of these test results is front-page news throughout the state. Many top managers have performance clauses related to these tests in their contracts. In addition to test scores, the Texas Education Agency (TEA) also collects a wide array of data on system finances and the characteristics of the student population. These additional data permit the estimation of statistical models with elaborate controls.

Education has remained on the statewide agenda continuously since the early reforms. Subsequent governors have also stressed issues of performance. Testing systems have been refined and some early problems in regard to validity were identified and addressed. The level of financial commitment has not necessarily corresponded with the rhetorical efforts, and there are continued concerns with equity issues.

The structure of Texas districts

Texas districts tend to be very similar on some structural dimensions but vary dramatically on others. All districts but one are independent school districts, which means that they are governed by a locally elected school board that has the power to levy taxes in support of education. The school boards hire a professional administrator, the superintendent, to be the chief operating officer of the schools. The superintendent has a great deal of discretion; he or she sets the agenda for school board meetings, proposes the district budget, establishes the schools' curriculum, and oversees all personnel processes. The superintendent has the formal authority to hire and fire managers (principals, assistant superintendents, etc.) and general authority to move personnel to different locations or positions. Teachers' unions are relatively weak in the state; and, even in the large districts, managers have substantial control over who teaches for them. These formal powers are limited somewhat by a significant teacher shortage in the state as well as informal norms and traditions.

These structural commonalities contrast dramatically with the vast other differences – differences that are to be expected in a highly diverse state that contains 8 percent of all US school districts. The districts range from wealthy to poor. Even with substantial state aid, per student instructional spending ranged from a low of $3,069 in 2007 to a high of $21,206. Correspondingly, the percentage of students who qualify for free or reduced school lunches (a poverty measure) ranged from 0.0 percent to 99.9 percent. Racially, the state is highly diverse; the student population is 14 percent African American, 47 percent Latino, 35 percent Anglo, 3.4 percent Asian, and 0.3 percent Native American. Individual districts vary greatly on these dimensions. To illustrate, the percentage of black students in a district ranges from 0.0 percent to 86.9 percent while the Latino percentage runs the full range from zero to 100.

In sum, these units of analysis are all school districts and share some characteristics, but they are exceptionally varied on many other dimensions and thus constitute a valuable source of information about public management. It is worth emphasizing that more public employees work in the field of education in the United States than in any other policy sector, and this Texas sample represents more than 1 percent of all governments of any type in the country.

We did not seek to become the foremost experts on the management of Texas school districts and to purposely irritate readers, reviewers, and editors with a narrowly focused set of studies. As the research has unfolded, however, each survey, each development of a new measure, has made this data set more and more valuable and more and more superior to alternative, available data sets – in five ways. First, the data set contains multiple measures of management and multiple measures of performance in addition to a wide variety of control variables. The control variables are chosen to fit with the rather well-developed production function research literature on public education. In this book we explain the details of the management measures and control measures, as well as the different ways of tapping performance. The multiple measures of performance allow investigation of the fact that public organizations have multiple goals and may need to emphasize one goal at the expense of another. The multiple measures of management and the extensive controls mean that we can rule out alternative explanations of our findings and thus provide evidence that the results are not spurious due to underspecification. The multiple measures of management also reflect the inherent complexity of the process by which public managers influence performance.

Second, by having data on the same organizations over time, we can address questions of causality (see O'Toole and Meier 2004b) and can replicate studies for different time periods to determine if findings remain valid (O'Toole and Meier 2004a, 2006). Both processes augment the existing general advantages of a large-N approach. Third, the large size of the data set – as many as 1,000 cases over a ten-year period – means that complex relationships that include multiple interactions can be tested without being limited by collinearity. Too frequently complex theories of management are based on only a small number of cases (for example, Miles and Snow 1978). Fourth, school districts have some valuable characteristics. They are the most common public organization in the United States, and similar organizations exist in virtually all countries. They are highly professionalized organizations that are generally decentralized and vest substantial discretion in street-level bureaucrats. To be sure, many public organizations have different characteristics and thus limit generalizations, but a large number of public organizations share these characteristics. Fifth, the data set is accessible; we provide the data to all scholars who request it, and we have invited other scholars to suggest additional items to include. These factors have made the returns to investment increasingly positive.[18]

We should also note, however, that the evidence-based research agenda has also used a wide variety of other data bases, including local law enforcement agencies (Nicholson-Crotty and O'Toole 2004), Columbian local governments (Avellañeda 2009b), UK local authorities (Walker, O'Toole, and Meier 2007), the federal government and its use of PART scores (Petrovsky 2006), institutions of higher education (Hicklin 2006), unemployment insurance agencies (Wenger, O'Toole, and Meier 2008), and the US presidency (Vaughn and Villalobos 2009). While we rely primarily on the Texas school district data set in the coverage that follows, we also tap some of our studies from other fields and data sets in our examination of public management and performance. Further, where appropriate we review findings from a number of others' empirical settings and relevant data sets, when these bear on our efforts to understand the effects of management on performance. Accordingly, several such analyses are summarized in relevant portions of the empirical chapters that constitute the bulk of this book.

Measures of performance

Although virtually all programs have multiple goals and are therefore subject to multiple performance indicators, some objectives are defined by the political environment as being more important than others (O'Toole and Meier 2004a). This study incorporates eleven different performance indicators in an effort to determine how public management affects a variety of organizational outcomes.

Although each performance indicator is salient to some portion of the educational environment, the most noticeable by far is the overall student pass rate on the statewide examination; called the Texas Assessment of Academic Skills (TAAS) until 2002, it was then replaced by the Texas Assessment of Knowledge and Skills (TAKS). The exams are standardized, criterion-based tests that all students in various grades have to take. Initially the exam was given in grades 3, 5, and 7, and as an exit exam. Currently grades 3 to 8 must take the exam as well as the exit exam, which at different times has been given in grades 10 or 11. The current system is also developing a series of end-of-course exams, such as 9th grade algebra, to assess the learning of specific course material. The exit exam is a high-stakes test, and students are required to pass it to receive a regular diploma from the state of Texas. TAAS/TAKS scores are used to rank districts, and the examination results are without question the most visible indicator of performance used to assess the quality of schools. Our measure is the percentage of students in a district who passed all (reading, writing, and mathematics) sections of the TAAS/TAKS.

The TAAS/TAKS exam has not been without controversy and challenges. Standardized tests clearly do not measure all the relevant aspects of an education system. There have also been unsuccessful court challenges arguing that the tests are discriminatory on the basis of race and ethnicity. Much concern has been expressed about cheating, given the high-stakes nature of the test. Cheating is made more difficult because Texas keeps control of the tests until administration and also is responsible for grading the tests. Elaborate statistical procedures scan the tests for evidence of cheating (erasures of wrong answers changed to right answers, etc.). In the few cases in which cheating has been found, teachers and administrators have been fired, and schools have had their state-assigned performance score reduced.

The institutionalized methods of cheating on the exams have been more interesting. Bohte and Meier (2000) provide an extensive study of efforts to manipulate exam scores by exempting students from the test, particularly exempting students as a result of limited English skills or because they are assigned to special education. They find not just sizable incentives to exempt students from the exam but also patterns that correlate with theoretical reasons to cheat (lack of resources, smaller districts, etc.). In 1997 the Texas state legislature attempted to restrict this process by requiring that all students be tested.

Despite the criticisms of the TAAS/TAKS, it has become generally accepted as a measure of performance for evaluating schools. Many districts use these scores to evaluate their superintendents, and many districts also use them to assess the performance of principals. The Houston Independent School District (HISD) and some of the other larger districts use the test scores to evaluate and reward teachers. Over time these evaluation tools have become far more sophisticated, moving from simply looking at raw test scores to the use of elaborate econometric models that seek to isolate the value added by the teacher or the school.

TAAS/TAKS scores have some useful statistical and practical advantages. The scores are normally distributed except when the scores become too high and a ceiling effect (districts cannot score above 100 percent) limits the upper end of the distribution. This occurs because districts improve over time, either because their education has improved or because students become more used to the test form. The Texas Education Agency, as a result, periodically adjusts the tests to make them more difficult (the transformation from TAAS to TAKS involved a significant increase in difficulty). These year-to-year movements and adjustments mean that all statistical models need to account for these annual fluctuations with a set of fixed-effects controls.

One of the contributions of the Texas school reform movement was a focus on racial and economic equity. The reforms required that data be gathered and reported on the basis of both race and income. The formal state accountability system, in fact, requires a given level of performance on all racial subgroups. Four other TAAS/TAKS measures are also useful as performance indicators: pass rates for Anglo, black, Latino, and low-income students.[19] Low-income students are defined as those eligible for free or reduced-price school lunches; this is an income criterion, established by the federal government, that is linked to the official poverty level.

Many parents and policy makers are also concerned with the performance of school districts regarding college-bound students. Four measures of college-bound student performance were used: the percentage of students who took either of the college board exams, the average ACT (American College Testing) score, the average SAT (Scholastic Aptitude Test) score, and the percentage of students who score above 1,110 on the SAT (or its ACT equivalent). Texas is one of the few states in which both the ACT and the SAT are taken by sufficient numbers to provide reliable indicators of both; as with samples drawn from other states, there is no correlation between these scores and the number of students taking them if the proportion of tested students is more than 30 percent of the total eligible to be tested (Smith 2003). Texas scores on the ACT and SAT are generally uncorrelated with the percentage of students taking the exams. Because most colleges and universities require either the ACT or the SAT, students who do not take one of the exams are unlikely to go on to attend college. The 1,110 measure, the equivalent of the top 20 percent nationally, is defined by the state of Texas as an indicator of college readiness.

The college-related scores, or higher-end performance scores, are clearly distinct from the TAAS/TAKS scores. The twenty intercorrelations between the TAAS/TAKS and the college scores average 0.27, or about 7 percent shared variance (the highest correlation is between SAT scores and the overall TAAS/TAKS pass rate, 0.48). Interestingly, the college indicators are not highly intercorrelated, except for the correlation between the 1,110+ measure and the average SAT and ACT measures (0.75 and 0.76, respectively). The correlation between ACT scores and SAT scores is only 0.58, which is surprising, since both are intended to measure the potential for students to succeed in college.

The final two measures of performance might be termed bottom-end indicators: attendance rates and dropout rates. High attendance rates are valued for two reasons. Students are unlikely to learn if they are not in class, and state aid is allocated to the school district based, in part, on average daily attendance. Attendance, as a result, is a good indicator of low-end performance by these organizations; the measure is simply the average percentage of students who are not absent. The attendance measure is distinct from the other measures of performance. Its highest correlations are 0.35 with the overall TAAS/TAKS and −0.35 with the dropout rate.

Dropout rates are plagued by serious problems of measurement. Schools have no incentive to determine if a student who does not return to school has dropped out or is attending school elsewhere. Reported dropout rates are widely conceded to be an underestimate. In addition, there are questions about whether or not to count a person pursuing a General Educational Development (GED) test as a dropout. The state of Texas has also changed its measure of dropouts during the period of this study – going from a six-year dropout rate (the average dropout rate for grades 7 to 12) to a four-year dropout rate (grades 9 to 12). Alternative measures of dropouts based on the size of cohort that graduates versus the size of that cohort in earlier years are greatly affected by the high rates of mobility, particularly minority student mobility, of Texas students. Given all these problems, one needs to be skeptical about the results of analysis on dropout rates. For most of the analysis, dropout rates are not included, but, in some cases, dropout rates are one of the better – albeit flawed – indicators of a district's performance dimension: how well the school serves at-risk students. The dropout measure is not highly correlated with the other performance measures; it averages a correlation of only −0.17.

With eleven different performance indicators, we do not intend to subject the reader to a tedious discussion of each performance indicator in every empirical analysis. Rather, for the purposes of validating our major managerial concepts, we use most of the indicators. When our analysis becomes more specialized, we select performance indicators with given characteristics (e.g. high task difficulty, low-end performance, etc.) that provide the best theoretical test of the model.

The production function

Any assessment of public program performance must control for both task difficulty and program resources. For school districts, neither of these types of elements is under the substantial control of the districts themselves, and therefore they can be considered key parts of the vector of environmental forces. Fortunately, a well-developed literature on educational production functions (Hanushek 1996; Hedges and Greenwald 1996) can be used for guidance. Eight variables, all commonly used, are included in our analysis: three measures of task difficulty and five measures of resources.

Schools and school districts clearly vary in how difficult it is to educate their students. Some districts have homogeneous student populations from upper middle-class backgrounds. Students such as these are quite likely to do well in school regardless of what the school does (see Burtless 1996). Other districts with a large number of low-income students and a highly diverse student body will find it more difficult to attain high levels of performance, because the schools will have to make up for a less supportive home environment and deal with more complex and more varied learning problems (Jencks and Phillips 1998). Poor and minority students often lack the in-home learning tools (computers, books, etc.) that are common in middle-class homes. Texas also has a large immigrant population and thus needs to provide programs for students with a native language other than English. Our three measures of task difficulty are the percentages of students who are black, Latino, and low-income. The last-mentioned variable is measured by the percentage who are eligible for free or reduced-price school lunches. All three measures should be negatively related to performance.

While the linkage between resources and performance in schools has been controversial (see Hanushek 1996 and Hedges and Greenwald 1996), a growing literature of well-designed longitudinal studies confirms that, like other organizations, schools with more resources generally fare better (Wenglinsky 1997). Five measures of resources are included. The average teacher salary, percentage of a district's expenditure funded by state aid, and class size (see Molnar *et al.* 1999, Graue *et al.* 2007, and Dee and West 2008) are directly tied to monetary resources. The average years of teaching experience and the percentage of teachers who are not certified (Laczko-Kerr and Berliner 2002) are related to the human resources of the school district. Class size and noncertified teachers should be negatively related to student performance; teacher experience, state aid, and teacher salaries should be positively related to performance.

This set of eight production function variables is used in all analyses conducted with this data set. Since we generally are interested in the role that management plays in organizational performance rather than a full specification of the determinants in education policy, we do not normally discuss the relationships for these control variables. Only when these variables show something unexpected or when they interact with managerial factors to affect performance are they discussed in the text.

The presentation of findings

In the decade of research on public management we have frequently added additional data and developed new measures. As a result, many of the studies have been carried out over different time periods, and sometimes with slightly different measures of management. We have tried to maintain consistency with our published work, so, rather than rebuild an entirely new data set and rerun all the analysis, we have usually opted here to present the original findings. To avoid redundancy in the discussion, we often present abridged tables that show the key relationships. In this manner we avoid focusing on control variables that are not of substantive interest in this project. In a few cases, such as with the analysis of managerial quality in Chapter 4 or the budget crisis in Chapter 6, we present new analysis for two reasons: (1) to present what we think is a better analysis; and (2) to make the text easier to read and consistent with the analysis that preceded it.

Conclusions

There are many possible approaches to exploring the relationship between public management and public organizational or program performance. The approach we have adopted is to build from the inductive, primarily case study, literature to formalize mathematically some of the general relationships that seem to be suggested by the earlier work. The model we have developed may seem simple – perhaps overly simple – in certain respects. For instance, it is comprised in its entirety of four variable clusters: O, M, S, and X. As mentioned in Chapter 1, many of the fine-grained details of public organizational and managerial life do not find a home in this model. Still, as will become clear in the chapters to follow, quite a number of issues and relationships can be investigated through this research program.

In other ways, the model is complex – in particular, in its specification of nonlinear and reciprocal relationships between some variables, as well as in our efforts to begin modeling the multi-level reality of management in networks. For this latter challenge, the work has just begun. This chapter points to some of the issues at stake as well as some of the impediments to systematic investigation, but we do not yet press forward with large-N empirical studies of management at the network level. Rather, we work on the management–performance links at the organizational level, while also taking explicitly into account the important fact that managers of organizations must operate externally as well as internally, and that the outputs and outcomes of their programs can be shaped in important ways by features of the environment with which their units are interdependent. For the former, it is clear, no one empirical study can explore all the relationships and interactions. The demands such an effort would place on a data set would make it impossible to execute any single definitive study. The approach we take, therefore, is to work from the general model, and to explore aspects of it through several related analyses – often via some simplification of the model – in order to focus on one or a few relationships at a time. A number of these are presented in the remaining chapters of this book.

Because of the high and increasing value of the Texas school districts data set, as explained in this chapter, we conduct much of our work by examining performance-related relationships in these roughly one thousand governments over a period of several years. Where appropriate, we supplement these core analyses with findings from some additional empirical settings.

In the next chapter, we begin the empirical exploration by focusing on the externally oriented, networking behavior of top managers. We explain in much more detail the governmental units and the data with which we are working and begin to answer the question of how management shapes results.

NOTES

1. Indeed, Max Weber defined bureaucracy in part in terms of stable decisions over time based upon precedent, thus suggesting reinforcement across certain stabilizing forces. See Gerth and Mills (1958).
2. Some observers might point to another sort of array: the market. The pure neoclassical market setting is characterized by an absence of structural stability, however, aside from some basic rules of the game – such as contract law, barriers to collusion, etc. Markets in the classic sense, in other words, are defined largely in terms of an *absence* of structure among the actors. In practice, of course, markets are often structured to some extent. How structuring and rules affect markets is an important issue of policy design, but we do not address it in this volume. Here we are interested in structured relationships among relevant actors, as these vary between hierarchy and network as the archetypical forms.

3. Beyond the structural variation between hierarchy and network, we also want to take note of other stabilizing elements mentioned earlier as we consider the role of public management. In the initial formulation of our model (O'Toole and Meier 1999), we took structural variation between stable hierarchies and flexible networks into account; but we omitted other stabilizing forces. The model was later expanded to include the latter as well (O'Toole and Meier 2003b), and we work from the broader version of the model throughout this book.

4. An interesting question in management is the degree to which treating it as a vector sum provides a misleading picture by ignoring whether or not management is consistent throughout the organization (Andrews *et al.* forthcoming (b)). The impact of managerial consistency on performance in theory would be positive but one can envision an organization with too much consistency – e.g. groupthink – that would lead to poor performance. Consistency needs to be explicitly modeled; surveying multiple respondents and then averaging the responses (Enticott, Boyne, and Walker 2009) provides no more information than a single-manager survey.

5. The outputs of an organization or program are the immediate consequences of policy and management efforts: bridges built, cases processed, environmental permits issued, etc. Outcomes relate to the eventual impact of policy actions, along with the results of other causal variables, on the ultimate issue or concern prompting the initial policy intervention. An example of an outcome, for which environmental permits would be an output, is cleaner rivers and streams.

6. All these issues can be handled through appropriate conceptualization and methods. Indeed, we address them all in the empirical chapters of this book.

7. This interpretation affects how organizations deal with their environments. That is to say, they can assume some degree of change and build that into the inertial aspects of the organizations rather than treating any environmental change as something new and different.

8. If β were to exceed one, the system would generate positive feedback and eventually explode.

9. Empirically, there is little research on what the stability coefficients are for organizations. A value of 0.99 might well be far more rigid than anything that exists in the real world of organizations.

10. Shocks themselves can have a variety of functional forms and both short- and long-run impacts; with adequate data, all these impacts can be estimated.

11. We realize that sometimes internal management is aimed at changing things – for example, due to slacking, underperformance, etc. Although this recognition suggests that management sometimes has a destabilizing influence, that influence is only in the short run. Once such efforts are successful at fixing organizational problems, management will need to institutionalize the changes via stabilizing structures. We return to the point in the concluding chapter.

12. For a somewhat different way of distinguishing and partitioning managerial functions, see Moore's treatment of managing upward, downward, and outward (1995).

13. It is possible for management to operate independently of the buffering structures. Management can act in a boundary-spanning function to reach out to other organizations or monitor potential changes in the environment. Such functions might even be institutionalized in strategic planning units or units for organizational intelligence.

14. In this exposition, we simplify for the moment by assuming that management knows what it is doing – that is, that management operates with considerable skill or quality, not simply effort. As will become clear later in this book, we consider each managerial function to contain both an effort and a quality component. We introduce and validate a measure of managerial quality in Chapter 4, but the focus here is on effort. An alternative way of thinking about the model at this point is that it contains an assumption of some deliberativeness or choice on the part of management – as to the allocation of managerial effort across the functions of management.

15. Networks can differ from each other in many other ways as well: the number of nodes, the degree of centralization, and numerous other dimensions sketched by those who employ the tools of social network analysis.

16. The 2009 survey was unique, in that the questionnaire included a variety of questions submitted by other scholars.

17. Part of the reforms was a provision that students who did not pass their courses were not allowed to participate in extracurricular activities such as football. The adoption of the reforms and their extensive nature owe a great deal to the leadership of Governor White and his designated reform advocate, Ross Perot. Although some people term these reforms and their impact "the Texas miracle," in reality this set of changes was a twenty-plus-year process that involved significant effort on the part of politicians and school officials. Overall, the state has made substantial progress in educational attainment, but it still has a fair way to go.

18. It is also fair to point out that the Texas school district data set has contributed to several literatures other than the public management research field. These include the study of representative bureaucracy (Keiser *et al.* 2002), the impact of charter schools on public school competition (Wrinkle, Stewart, and Polinard 1999; Bohte 2004), the patterns of organizational cheating (Bohte and Meier 2000), punctuated equilibria in policy settings (Robinson *et al.* 2007), and the investigation of statistical techniques (Bretschneider, Marc-Aurele, and Wu 2005; Wagner and Gill 2005), among others.

19. The various pass rates do not correlate as highly as one might imagine. The intercorrelations between the Anglo, black and Latino pass rates are all in the neighborhood of 0.67, thus suggesting that the overlap is only about 45 percent. The individual scores for race and class correlate more highly with the overall score, because they are subcomponents of it.

3 Public management in interdependent settings: networks, managerial networking, and performance

When people think of what public managers do, often the tasks and responsibilities that come most readily to mind are those tied to the internal functioning of a public organization: motivating staff, organizing tasks, structuring work relationships, handling the budget and other resources such as information technology, appraising individuals' performance, and the like. We begin our empirical examination of public management from another angle: the externally oriented actions of managers as they seek to do their jobs and advance their organization's causes. We do so for two reasons. First, this aspect of public management is often given short shrift in standard accounts, and yet – as explained earlier in this volume – contemporary governance arrangements typically enmesh the actions and objectives of specific public organizations in a web of relations with other actors. Second, in the development of our own research program, we began by studying the external efforts of managers and sought to explore their performance-related implications.[1] Accordingly, in this book we proceed in like manner.

Networks and networking

As noted earlier, public programs and public organizations are often situated in networks – arrays through which many aspects of contemporary governance are handled. Networks are structures of interdependence involving multiple organizations or parts thereof, in which one unit is not merely the formal subordinate of the others in some larger hierarchical arrangement. Networks exhibit some structural stability but extend beyond formally established linkages and policy-legitimated ties. The institutional glue congealing networked ties may include authority bonds, exchange relations, and coalitions based on common interest, all within a multi-unit structure (O'Toole 1997: 45).

Managing in networked settings presents a challenge, not least because public managers cannot be expected to exercise decisive leverage by virtue of their formal position. Influence in larger networks is more difficult to document, predict, and model than it is in relatively simple two- or three-party relationships. If managing in networked settings can be rather difficult, therefore, why do policy makers situate public programs in such arrays?

An extensive research literature developed in North America and Europe contends that implementing programs in interorganizational networks can offer significant advantages. The expertise and/or resources needed to address pressing policy challenges may be spread among multiple organizations and across various sectors. Mobilizing networks of such organizations can sometimes create the right combination of technical knowledge and critical mass of effort. Policy problems also may touch upon several jurisdictions simultaneously: the energy supply is an issue not only for the Department of Energy but also for the Environmental Protection Agency, not to mention the Treasury (balance of payments), the State Department (relations with the Organization of the Petroleum Exporting Countries [OPEC]), and the jurisdictions of various states (drilling in Alaska's North Slope, disposal of low-level nuclear waste in Nevada and elsewhere, etc.). For such "wicked problems" (Rittel and Webber 1973) that have no simple governmental or organizational niche for proper treatment, a multiorganizational networked arrangement may be an appropriate institutional response. Often such multi-actor arrangements are encouraged by the political dynamics of policy implementation and public management. Adding organizational actors to the patterns of policy execution can build support for programs, and public managers often find it useful to engage in regular patterns of interaction with actors outside their organization so as to tap opportunities available by and from others and/ or to fend off potential disruptions and threats to the core organization's operations.

Inducements toward networked arrays, therefore, can be numerous. Sometimes governments formally stipulate that programs have to involve multiple organizational actors. Hall and O'Toole (2000) find that the great majority of new or substantially revised public programs enacted by the US Congress during two different time periods mandated or strongly encouraged the regular involvement of multiple organizations. Pressures to achieve results during implementation often further complicate these arrays. In a companion study to their 2000 article, Hall and O'Toole (2004) explore the interorganizational arrangements specified in regulations, following the enactment of legislation. The pattern is clear: implementation brought even more involvement of additional organizations, along with more complex patterns of interdependence.

Beyond mandates from political leaders, networks of interdependent actors sometimes emerge as a result of the voluntary choices of public organizations and some of those with which they interact. "Collaboration," "public–private partnership," and other like forms of mostly voluntary linkage are now much discussed in the literature of public management (see, for instance, O'Leary and Bingham 2009). In certain cases the networks that emerge consist of complex combinations of mandated (or policy-encouraged) links along with other ties that are mostly or entirely voluntary. These arrays may include public, private, and not-for-profit organizations, perhaps at several different (geographical or scale) levels. Needless to say, the public management challenges in such complex settings can be immense, even though the prospects for significant policy-related problem solving may offer strong encouragement for using such governance structures.

Examining the structure-related impacts on performance of a wide variety of networks is an important long-term objective of public management and public policy research. For reasons of scope and practicality, however, we address systematically only a portion of the relevant research questions here. We do not investigate how network variations across different policy problems, involving public organizations of widely differing jurisdictions, shape performance. The literature of social network analysis provides tools to characterize network variations in many dimensions, but here we would run up against the apples-and-oranges problem of trying to force different organizations, networks, and programs into some sort of common performance metric. For reasons explained earlier in this book, such an approach is best avoided.

We also do not devote substantial space to a full depiction of the networks in which the public managers subject to our empirical investigation operate. Doing so would require detailed data gathering from many actors in each jurisdiction, thus limiting severely the number of cases we could systematically examine. While important work on networks and public management can be undertaken with a study of only a few cases (for instance, Provan and Milward 1995), in such cases it is very difficult to control for other influences, and any observed regularities could be attributed to any number of causal forces.

In this chapter, therefore, we explore a couple of slices of the "networks" question. In particular, we examine the behavior of top managers as they interact with external parties in the course of trying to do their job (for a full treatment of the advantages undergirding this approach, see Meier and O'Toole 2005). Even for managers in similar positions in public organizations of similar types, we can expect their "networking" behavior to vary considerably – in frequency and direction. Networking by managers does not depict the full set of structural relationships in complex networks – for example, regular ties between other actors within the network are omitted – but it is difficult to conceive of how public managers can work in their interdependent environment to shape results unless their behavior includes interactions with others. Since our interest lies in how public managers' actions shape performance, the networking behavior of top managers is a logical focus to address this question.

Most of the coverage in this chapter concentrates on the networking behavior of such managers as they work externally in the interdependent environment of their school districts. (We include some data on networking behavior in other types of public organizations as well to show a general pattern, and provide a concluding summary of other work later in the chapter.) School districts are not the most complicatedly networked of public organizations. Indeed, the very existence of school districts as a special form of special district is due to the pressure in an earlier era to "insulate" education from politics, given the importance of the education function to society.[2] In today's governance settings, however, schools and school districts are interdependent with and relevant to the interests of a variety of other parties in the organization's environment (see Chubb and Moe 1990 and Wirt and Kirst 2005). Accordingly, exploring the relevance of managerial networking to school district performance is an appropriate task. Indeed, if we are able to find influences on performance from managerial networking in rather less networked settings, such a finding would suggest that managerial networking behavior in more thoroughly networked contexts is likely to be even more consequential.

While our focus is mostly on the networking of public managers, we do not ignore the structural aspects of networks. For a portion of our analysis in Chapter 7, we introduce both managerial networking and structural dimensions of the networks in which they operate; there the objective is to explore the independent effects of each upon performance.

Although the coverage here is selective, in the senses just explained, it will quickly become obvious that there is plenty to examine in the impacts of managerial networking on program results. We proceed, therefore, from a relatively straightforward analysis, report the empirical results, and then add further questions and analyses to depict the patterns more completely.

Do public managers network with external parties?

The most straightforward questions have to do with whether public managers engage in networking behavior – and, if so, how, and how frequently? The answers are "Yes," and the pattern and frequency vary by managerial role and the nature of the other parties.

In the case of the more than 1,000 Texas school districts, we have developed a measure of networking behavior on the part of top managers, the superintendents of the districts. Our measure of *managerial networking* is an effort to operationalize our M_2 term in the model – the actions of the manager in the networked environment of a public agency. This work assumes that managers cannot engage in network-like behavior with other actors in the environment without coming into contact with them. Using the Texas school district data set, we asked top managers to rate how frequently, from daily to never, they interact with each of a set of environmental actors (five actors in the 2000 survey, eight actors in the 2002 and 2005 surveys, ten in the 2007 survey, and eleven in 2009): school board members, other superintendents, local business leaders, the Texas Education Agency (the state-level oversight organization), state legislators, federal education officials (2002, 2005, 2007, and 2009 only), parent groups such as parent–teacher associations (2002, 2005, 2007, and 2009 only), teachers associations (2002, 2005, 2007, and 2009 only), police/fire departments (2007 and 2009 only), other local governments (2007 and 2009 only), and non-profit organizations (2009 only). These items have been factor-analyzed, and consistently produce a first factor that is a general networking measure with all positive loadings (at times one factor only is produced).

Table 3.1 displays the means and the factor loadings from the 2007 survey results. A similar pattern obtains for the networking data from other years. It is clear that these top managers do engage in networking behavior with a variety of external actors, though it is also clear that some of these are more frequent interaction partners than are others. School board members are the most frequent contact, but superintendents report weekly contacts with other superintendents, local business leaders, the Texas Education Agency, city/county governments, local police/fire

Table 3.1 Factor loadings for nodes involved in managerial networking, 2007

Node	Loading	Mean
School board	0.5504	4.46
Teachers' associations	0.4778	2.01
Parent groups	0.3863	2.97
Local business leaders	0.6673	3.65
Other superintendents	0.5396	3.93
Federal education officials	0.4530	1.74
State legislators	0.6042	2.42
Texas Education Agency	0.4798	3.13
City/county government	0.7105	3.06
Local police/fire department	0.6272	3.09
Eigenvalue		3.12
N		757

Table 3.2 Levels of interaction are fairly constant over time

Node	2007	2005	2002	2000
School board	4.46	4.44	4.78	4.48
Teachers' associations	2.01	2.09	2.18	NA
Parent groups	2.97	3.02	3.02	NA
Local business leaders	3.65	3.74	3.86	3.86
Other superintendents	3.93	3.89	4.16	3.95
Federal education	1.74	1.81	1.81	NA
State legislators	2.42	2.61	2.31	2.35
Texas Education Agency	3.13	2.61	3.39	3.21
City/county government	3.06	NA	NA	NA
Local police/fire department	3.09	NA	NA	NA

departments, and parent groups. As Table 3.2 shows, however, the relative level of interaction changes little over time. Furthermore, past the first four or five external nodes, the factor scores are relatively insensitive to the number of nodes that are inquired about (see the discussion below). This point is important, since some might argue that one needs to know the full set of interactions before it is possible to understand how managers operate in their networked environment – a hurdle that would make it exceedingly difficult to explore such patterns in hundreds of organizations and with hundreds of managers. The evidence shows, rather, that most of what one needs to know about the general networking pattern exhibited by managers can be educed from information about interactions with the most important, or most frequently contacted, nodes.

A factor score, then, which indicates the extent to which the manager interacts with external parties, is taken as the measure of M_2.[3] The consistent production of a first factor of this sort is strong presumptive evidence that the factor represents a general networking measure.

Discussing this measure is worthwhile, since it plays such an important role in our research. Measurement issues in regard to management more generally are important simply because this research program is one of the most well-developed efforts to create measures of management for use in a large-N quantitative set of performance studies. The argument for this measure of M_2, or managerial networking, as a reliable and valid measure of management activities rests on several grounds. First, the factor analysis of networking items reveals that contact with environmental actors forms a consistent pattern across nodes. Such contacts are all correlated with each other, and always produce a generic first factor with positive loading regardless of how many nodes are included in the analysis.

Second, M_2 is positively correlated with a manager's time estimates of how much of his or her effort is focused outside the organization (as opposed to focused on internal matters; see Meier and O'Toole 2003: 698, note 4).[4] In addition, as explained shortly, the strong results in various linkages to performance with a wide variety of indicators (O'Toole and Meier 2003b: 54, 56) reveal a concept with a great deal of empirical import and external validity.

Third, another way to partially validate the measure of managerial networking is to see if it correlates with other variables where relationships should exist. Superintendents who are more aggressive at managerial networking, all other things being equal, should have a school district that has greater community support, greater school board support, and more parental involvement. Simply stated, more aggressive networking should result in greater support in the external environment. Our survey asked superintendents to rate community and school board support on a five-point scale from excellent to inadequate.[5] The survey also asked for a similar evaluation of parental involvement.

Table 3.3 presents three regressions showing the relationship between managerial networking and support from the school board, the community, and parents. To make sure that any relationships are not the result of better past performance, district poverty, or district resources (teachers' salaries and revenues per student), we control for these factors. More networking is

Table 3.3 Managerial networking improves environmental support

Independent variables	Dependent variables		
	School board support	Community support	Parental involvement
Managerial networking	0.0691 (3.94)	0.1126 (7.09)	0.0764 (4.39)
Past performance	0.0034 (1.94)	0.0073 (4.67)	0.0059 (3.40)
Low-income students	−0.0033 (2.94)	−0.0079 (7.64)	−0.0122 (10.81)
Teacher salaries (000s)	0.0016* (0.24)	0.0193 (3.13)	0.0208 (3.08)
Revenue per student (000s)	0.0239 (1.85)	−0.0204 (1.74)	0.0042* (0.33)
R^2	0.02	0.09	0.10
F	9.37	50.61	55.57
Standard error	0.88	0.80	0.87
N	2,524	2,534	2,529

Notes: T-scores in parentheses. * = not significant at 0.05 level, one-tailed test.

positively associated with support from the school board, support in the general community, and the level of parental involvement. Each relationship contributes additional evidence that we have created a reliable and valid measure of managerial networking.

Fourth, by comparing survey results between two time points – for instance, between 2000 and 2002 – we provide a systematic evaluation of the concept's reliability and validity (Meier and O'Toole 2005). The 2000/2002 assessment reveals that the exact number of nodes included in the measure was not especially crucial; the five-node measure correlated strongly with the eight-node measure (as did the four- and seven-node measures). Similar patterns are found in comparing managers' responses between the more recent surveys. This finding does not mean that scholars can select any set of nodes to create this measure but, rather, that they need to select the most common nodes that occupy a manager's time. Given careful selection, the total number of nodes becomes less relevant; researchers should stress getting information on the most common nodes rather than worrying about information on all nodes.

The 2000/2002 comparisons, along with comparisons between more recent time periods, also reveals that M_2 is very much a managerial choice. At least in principle, measuring interactions does not reveal whether it is the manager seeking to network with actors in the external environment, or whether it is the other actors and/or pressure from external forces that stimulates the networking behavior. Analysis of our data reveals that it is clearly the former. Networking measures for a given organization at the two time points were essentially uncorrelated if the organization had changed top managers. When the same manager was in place in both years, there was a strong positive correlation between the two measures of M_2 (above 0.5 – a notable correlation for a behavioral measure such as this one). It is clear, therefore, that networking itself is driven largely by managers' decisions. It is not an epiphenomenon forced on managers by the external actors (Meier and O'Toole 2005).

There is also evidence that managers' networking style can help to explain the emergence of interorganizational collaborative links, at least during crisis periods. This evidence is also drawn from Texas school districts and their top managers. In a natural-experiment design in the context of Hurricanes Katrina and Rita, we sought to learn if pre-disaster levels of managerial networking were related to the post-hurricane emergence of interorganizational collaboration with particular institutions in the settings of Texas school districts. With appropriate controls, we determined that generalized networking behavior prior to the crisis helps to explain the development of collaborative relationships in response to the disaster, and not simply or primarily contacts with the pre-crisis networking partners (Hicklin *et al.* 2009).

Finally, it is noteworthy that the factor loadings in Table 3.1 and the discussion of nodes in the current chapter include the school board as an "external" node. One might argue that the school board is the primary political principal of the school district and should not be treated as a networked, or networking, partner of the top manager. (Networks, as defined at the outset of the chapter, reference non-hierarchical linkages.) It turns out that the factor scores themselves do not change much, whether or not school board interactions are included in the factor analysis. Nonetheless, our two-year comparison and subsequent work (see O'Toole, Meier and Nicholson-Crotty 2005: 57–8) have found that direct hierarchical linkages might be best treated as separate interactions. While interactions with the school board do correlate with interactions with other nodes, the portion of the school board variance that is uncorrelated with M_2 shows a much different relationship. Unlike top managerial networking with other external actors (see below), superintendent–school board interactions generally demonstrate a negative impact on performance, when one controls for M_2 using interactions with the other nodes. Whether this negative relationship is the result of political meddling in the administrative process or merely reflects an endogenous fire alarm about performance cannot be determined from the data at hand.[6] What is clear, however, is that the school board–superintendent relationship is, in part, of a different form, with different results from the superintendent's normal effort to manage the interdependent environment (see also Meier, O'Toole and Lu 2006).

In short, therefore, we have a good measure of the networking behavior of these public managers. Superintendents vary considerably in their managerial networking, and a considerable amount of such behavior is reported by them. They interact with a variety of external actors, and their behavior seems to be a matter of their own discretionary choice, rather than an activity pressed upon them by their networked environment or other external forces.

Are top managers of school systems unique in this regard? The answer would appear to be "No." With colleagues, we have adapted the networking measure to a completely different set of public organizations: local governments, called local "authorities," in England. The reasons typically offered as to why public managers deal with the network of actors in their organizations' environments are unique neither to the United States nor to school districts. So we should expect to see similar behavior in such settings as English local authorities. Furthermore, top managers are not the only ones who have opportunity and some reason to network in their environment. In our English study, therefore, we have surveyed managers at three organizational levels in these jurisdictions. We surveyed so-called corporate officers, a group that has a perspective on and responsibilities for the organization as a whole; chief officers, who manage the delivery of particular services; and service managers, who are first-line supervisors and have a sub-service view.

Our data were gathered in 2003[7] via an e-mail survey of a sample of 102 English local authorities. The authorities were selected to be representative on a number of background variables. In each authority, questionnaires were sent to three corporate informants, the chief officer, and three managers in each of seven service areas. The total number of potential informants was 2,299, and the number of respondents was 1,026, thus reaching a response rate of 44.5 percent.

We asked the local managers about their interactions with eight different types of external actors: elected members of the authority, user group representatives, trade unions, local business leaders, voluntary sector actors, Members of Parliament, managers in other local councils, and central government officials. This group of actors is roughly equivalent in terms of functions to the nodes about which we have surveyed in the environments of school districts in Texas. Two sets of findings in particular are worth noting in connection with the present discussion. First, as with top managers

Table 3.4 Mean scores for interactions between different groups of officers in English local authorities

	Corporate officers	Chief officers	Service managers
	Mean	Mean	Mean
Elected members	5.07	5.42	4.40*
User group representatives	2.68	3.24	3.03*
Trade unions	2.74	3.10	2.64*
Local business leaders	2.87	2.83	2.27*
Voluntary sector actors	2.87	3.20	3.01*
Central government officials	3.01	3.12	2.68*
MPs	2.16	3.31	2.42*
Managers in other councils	3.61	3.59	3.51

Note: * = significantly different from others at $p < 0.05$.

of school districts, managers in local authorities report interaction patterns that, upon factor analysis, produce a clear first factor on which all the pairs of interactions load positively. Once again, therefore, a general managerial networking measure emerges from the data. Second, the specifics of the interactions vary by managerial level or responsibility. Table 3.4 displays the mean scores for interactions between different groups of local government officers. The most important group of local actors that all three types of managers are likely to interact most frequently with were elected members, with interaction more than once a week for all managerial types. This pattern is to be expected, given the elected members' special relationship with local government and its managerial cadre. By contrast, there was no one group of networking partners with which officers were least likely to interact with. Chief officers were the most likely to interact across all the nodes. Corporate officers, by contrast, are the least likely to interact with others. Two reasons may explain the pattern. Senior managers may spend time managing downward and internally offering buffers within the organization. They are also likely to be focusing their time on non-management issues such as policy development (for more detail regarding this analysis of networking by managers in English local authorities, see Walker, O'Toole, and Meier 2007).

In short, while there are differences in the networking behavior of managers between US school districts and English local authorities, the broad patterns are similar. Clearly, a part of the public manager's function, wherever he or she is located, is managing in and with the interdependent environment. It is also clear that managers with different functions and located at different organizational levels report some differences in the details of their networking activities. Such differences are also to be expected, since different managers face different challenges and responsibilities, as well as different relationships of interdependence with other actors and organizations. The kinds of findings we develop regularly from Texas school districts, then, would seem to be part of a broader pattern for public managers more generally.

We turn now to a particularly interesting question: given that managers interact with some frequency with other actors and organizations in their environment, does this networking carry impacts on the performance of their organizations? Some of the case study literature indicates that the answer may be "Yes," and our model clearly specifies a relationship – indeed, a set of relationships. We explore this important subject next.

Managerial networking and performance

When public managers operate in networked settings, they face many options for action and many strategic choices. Arguably the most important of these is the decision about how much time and energy to work in the networked environment, and in which directions – that is, with which external actors. After all, managers must also consider that efforts might have to be devoted to buffering program activities from the potentially turbulent and uncertain impacts from the interdependent environment. Managers also must devote attention to the internal management of their units. Many other strategic choices confront managers who function in networks, of course, including which issues to raise with others in the network, what positions to take, what style to exhibit, how to balance short-term versus long-term needs, and so forth. The foundational choices, however, are how much and with whom to undertake networking action itself. We concentrate on this topic in the next portion of this chapter.

As noted earlier, school districts are by no means the most thoroughly networked settings in which public managers operate, but there are reasons to expect patterns of interdependence that should carry performance implications.[8] The technical and political demands placed upon school district superintendents encourage them to develop, solidify, and use ties with other important actors in their environments. The most important of these are typically their own school board[9] (the elected body responsible for sketching broad policy for the district), the relevant state-level educational department (a source of primarily formula-based funding that varies in importance from state to state, as well as a unit that issues some regulations that apply to the local districts), state-level legislators (who frame general educational policy), local business leaders (who can play crucial roles in supporting the locally enacted taxing decisions that drive much of school district revenue), and other superintendents (professional colleagues and sources of experience and innovation in the turbulent world of public education). Other parties may also be tied to the operations of school districts, and, as explained earlier, we have surveyed top managers about broader patterns of potential interaction; but the interaction partners just mentioned can be expected to be the most important, and most regularly contacted, in the typical case.

In contemporary American public education, in which funding issues are critical and many ostensibly separate policy problems – e.g. drug abuse, broken families – intrude in highly visible ways in the educational process, schools have become battlegrounds for a range of policy disputes (Chubb and Moe 1990; Meier and Stewart 1991). Efforts to reform schools and influence educational policy are frequently debated and adopted in realms where the school district is only one voice among many. Accordingly, superintendents may have reason to devote managerial energy and effort to understanding and leveraging their networked environment. This network orientation is more extensive in the US context than in most other countries. An Organisation for Economic Co-operation and Development (OECD) (1995: 52) study of fourteen national education systems found that more education decisions had to be made in consultation with others (44 percent) in the United States than in any other Western democracy. US systems were also rated the lowest in terms of local – that is, school district – autonomy.

Superintendents manage their districts – a headquarters office along with sets of schools, which in turn are managed by school "principals" – within this broader constellation of other actors, who may be potentially important as sources of funds, staff, ideas, guidance, other resources, and turbulence. The extent and kind of network to build, maintain, and use is a matter largely under the control of the superintendent.[10]

Managing in the network, then, is an opportunity available to those superintendents who recognize their interdependence and opt to try to manage it actively. To network, in this context, is therefore a key strategic option. Our model suggests that such managerial networking can contribute to performance. What does the evidence show? To answer this key question, we simplify the model in order to focus on the relationship of most importance here.

More specifically, for present purposes we build on an autoregressive function, since we believe that incremental changes in performance are typical for public programs and organizations. Adjustments to performance can be caused by a wide array of forces, including myriad factors in the environment – and also the efforts of managers. Although the general model is

$$O_t = \beta_1(S + M_1)O_{t-1} + \beta_2(X_t/S_e)(M_3/M_4) + \varepsilon_t$$

as explained earlier in the book, we are particularly interested here in probing the externally oriented portion of the model. In particular, we want to isolate the impact of M_2 (where $M_2 = M_3/M_4$) – that is, public management aimed at tapping and leveraging the opportunities presented by the actors in the environment of the core unit, while also protecting the program from hostile or disruptive forces. This means that the basic research issue to be investigated has to do with the second or environmental term in the general model, and in particular with the M_2 specified in that term.

Rearranging terms in the equation yields the following:

$$O_t = \beta_1(S + M_1)O_{t-1} + \beta_2 X_t M_2(1/S_e) + \varepsilon_t$$

The first term in an autoregressive model such as this would surely be the dominant one in empirical settings: current performance can be expected to be heavily driven by past performance. Our primary interest now, nonetheless, is in the second term. We want to know whether exerting managerial skill and effort in the interdependent environment matters for program outputs and outcomes. If it does, the impact of M_2 over more extended time periods can be expected to be considerable, as it feeds into output through each cycle (via the lagged dependent variable) and thus amplifies its impact.

Two options for exploring the second term can be indicated, each simplifying the general model in reasonable ways. One way would be to retain the autoregressive feature as well as the key elements representing managerial networking (M_2) and environmental forces (X), while screening out the other managerial functions as well as the structural stabilizing variable (S). There is no prima facie reason to expect the other aspects of public management within a given case to covary with the managerial networking function, so the term M_1 can be dropped from a simplified model.[11] The S terms, as well, can be omitted for present purposes. While the structural setting matters, the empirical context we are examining consists of a set of managerial cases – Texas school districts – highly similar in most basic structural features. Not only are they all in the same policy sector, they are also the same particular type of program setting, institutional design, and managerial level: system superintendents. By selecting a set of cases in which public managers confront structurally similar settings, structural variation is minimized; and we can initially examine their strategic choices about how to interact in the network without confounding impacts arising from widely differing structural contexts. In later analysis we add structure back into the discussion.

Accordingly, then, a simplified version of the model can be considered:

$$O_t = \beta_1 O_{t-1} + \beta_2 X_t M_2 + \varepsilon_t$$

This equation is simply the one preceding it, after the removal of S and the other managerial form, M_1, as variables. The model in this form is clearly underspecified (it leaves out some important determinants of performance), but the simplification does allow for the testing of important components of the general model.[12] Using this version, we can test the proposition that managerial networking matters for performance. We can also explore whether and how networking managers deal with shocks or perturbations from the environment (X) in fashions different from managers who do not network. These are substantial advantages.

One disadvantage that this version carries, nonetheless, is that, given the degree of dominance that the autoregressive term exerts in the model, detecting the impact of M_2, which appears in the much smaller second term, may be difficult. For this reason, an empirical test involving this form of the simplified model can be considered as a rather stringent one.

Another adjustment could also be useful to examine. This version drops the autoregressive term altogether, in the interest of focusing on the environmental impact itself. Thus:

$$O_t = \beta_2 X_t M_2 + \varepsilon_t$$

Estimating this form means sacrificing some further explanatory power for the purpose of conducting an empirical test more sensitive to the operation of M_2 and its interaction with a matrix of environmental forces.

Both versions are included in the analysis that follows. Despite the fact that these forms of the model omit some influences on program performance, they are not themselves so simple. Each includes a *particular* kind of public management contribution, and each specifies a nonlinear relationship between management and the forces in the networked environment.

Each, in other words, represents a more complex model than the linear, additive versions more typical in multivariate analysis. A linear version of the simplified model depicted in the last equation is

$$O_t = \beta_2 X_t + \beta_3 M_2 + \varepsilon_t$$

Here managerial networking would make a difference, but not by interacting with the set of environmental forces. Similarly, a linear version of the autoregressive simplification introduced above can be depicted in like fashion:

$$O_t = \beta_1 O_{t-1} + \beta_2 X_t + \beta_3 M_2 + \varepsilon_t$$

Estimating these last two equations empirically would constitute a test, generally speaking, of whether managerial networking matters; but the simplified forms of our model – the two equations preceding these two – must also be explored to check for the nonlinear relationships that, we have argued, seem to be called for by the extant case study depictions.

The following hypotheses are the focus of the current investigation.

H1: *managerial networking matters – in a positive direction – for program performance.* School system output/outcome is higher if superintendents exert management effort in the networked environment surrounding them.

H2: *managerial networking matters for how management relates to both educational system inputs and environmental perturbations.* In practical terms, managers in networked settings deal with environmental shocks in different ways from public managers who do not manage in networks. We expect managerial networking to interact in a nonlinear fashion with the vector of environmental forces to which school districts are exposed.

H3: *the way that networking managers tap their surroundings is to exploit opportunities and buffer impediments to program performance.* That is, the form of the nonlinear function can be expected to show managers tapping resources in their networked environments to enhance program performance. To the extent that environmental shocks challenge or threaten program performance, managerial networking – by competent managers – can be expected to protect the core performance bureaucracy from these forces.

We conducted this empirical test of managerial networking and performance on a subset of Texas school districts. The 2000 superintendents management survey provided information about management styles, goals, and time allocations (return rate of 55 percent). Of these, 507 responses were usable in our analysis.[13] We pooled five years of data (1995 to 1999) on performance and control variables to produce a total of 2,535 cases for

Table 3.5 Factor loadings for managerial networking, 2000 survey data

Indicator	Loading
Frequency of contact with school board members	0.60
Business leaders	0.73
Other superintendents	0.67
State legislators	0.68
Texas Education Agency	0.51

Note: Eigenvalue = 2.07.

analysis. All data other than the survey were taken from the data sets of the Texas Education Agency.

Along with the set of production function controls that were outlined in Chapter 2, we must also include a measure of managerial networking in the empirical analyses. In this case, our measure of managerial networking is developed as described above – and with the original five nodes included in the interaction pattern. We asked each superintendent to note how often they were in contact with each of these others, on a six-point scale ranging from daily to never. Superintendents inclined toward networking with the key actors in the district's environment should interact more frequently with all five other sets of actors than should superintendents with a traditional hierarchical (internally focused) management style. A composite networking scale was created via factor analysis (see Table 3.5). All five items positively loaded on the first factor and produced an eigenvalue of 2.07; no other factors were significant.[14] Factor scores from this analysis were then used as a measure of managerial networking or M_2, with higher scores indicating a greater networking orientation.

Clearly, this measure is simplified. It ignores all aspects of networking aside from frequency and direction – for instance, skill, reputation, and a number of strategic considerations.[15] Further, it taps a particular kind of networking activity: interactions of managers in clusters of dyadic interactions. Networks can range considerably in the extent to which they are integrated and the degree to which all actors are directly linked to the full range of others. Even so, the measure taps the effort managers choose to put into managing externally, in the networked environment.[16] Furthermore, the factor-analytic results suggest that the notion of managerial networking as a strategic choice is a coherent concept that makes empirical sense.[17]

Our measure of program output[18] or performance (O) in the present analysis is the percentage of students in each school district who pass state-required, standardized reading, writing, and mathematics tests each year. For the period in question, the examination was the Texas Assessment of Academic Skills. More details on this examination and measure were provided in Chapter 2.

Our strategy of analysis here is to begin with relatively simple models and build up to more complex variants that provide stronger tests of our theory. We start with tests to determine whether management (managerial networking) matters at all in the performance of these school systems (thus testing H1), then move on to tests of whether the relationship of management to performance is nonlinear, and, if so, how (H2, H3). A second, more stringent, set of tests then takes place within an autoregressive model of program performance.

We begin with the linear, additive relationship depicted earlier in one of the equations:

$$O_t = \beta_2 X_t + \beta_3 M_2 + \varepsilon_t$$

In this model the question is whether management matters when one controls for the constraints and resources facing the school district (the vector of X variables). The test of this model, handled via standard multiple regression, appears in Table 3.6. The column designated "Base model" contains all the X variables, and the next column ("Network+") adds the management measure to this equation. The X variables generally predict as expected, with negative relationships for all constraints (percentage of black, Latino, and low-income students), noncertified teachers and class size, and positive relationships for the resource variables (with the exception of state aid). When the managerial networking variable is added to this equation, it produces a strong positive coefficient. Programs characterized by greater managerial networking are programs that generate somewhat higher outputs. Because this management variable is measured as a factor score (mean = 0, standard deviation = 1), virtually the entire range of management falls between +3 and −3. This range suggests that networking by top managers may contribute as much as four percentage points to a district's pass rate, all other things being equal.[19] Although this variable is by no means the most important factor in performance, changes of this magnitude are substantively significant and well worth pursuing. By this test, H1 is supported.

Nonlinear relationships can be tested in a variety of ways. Our theory suggests that management interacts with the resources and constraints in the environment – that it exploits resources and mitigates constraints. One form of that relationship was shown in this equation introduced earlier:

Table 3.6 Management and organizational performance: additive linear estimation

Dependent variable = student exam pass rates

Independent variables	Base model	Network+
Managerial networking	–	0.7035 (4.60)
Resources		
Teacher salaries (000s)	0.4875 (4.49)	0.4665 (4.31)
Class size	−0.3199 (4.83)	−0.3117 (4.72)
Teacher experience	0.2048 (2.10)	0.1943 (1.90)
Noncertified teachers	−0.1874 (5.28)	−0.1873 (5.30)
Percentage state aid	−0.0127ns (1.53)	−0.0173 (2.09)
Constraints		
Percentage of black students	−0.2153 (13.35)	−0.2167 (13.49)
Percentage of Latino students	−0.1099 (10.43)	−0.1091 (10.39)
Percentage of low-income students	−0.1671 (11.12)	−0.1670 (11.16)
R^2	0.58	0.59
Standard error	7.65	7.62
F	294.96	276.07
N	2,534	2,534

Notes: T-scores in parentheses. Dummy variables for individual years not reported.
ns = not significant.

$$O_t = \beta_2(X_t M_2) + \varepsilon_t$$

The classic way to test this relationship is to compare the interactive form to the linear form in the following equation:

$$O_t = \beta_2(X_t M_2) + \beta_3(X_t) + \beta_4 M_2 + \varepsilon_t$$

The key test is whether the vector of coefficients β_2 is statistically significant – that is, whether it adds additional explanatory power to a linear model. The problem with this model is that the interaction terms frequently generate so much collinearity[20] that individual coefficients cannot be precisely estimated. The actual coefficients are important, because we have specific hypotheses about how managerial action affects the environmental variables – that is, it should increase the impact of resources and reduce the impact of constraints.

To test these specific estimates, an alternative approach is necessary. We divide the sample into two parts: districts with high reported networking by top managers (those with scores above 0) and districts with low managerial networking (scores below 0):

Table 3.7 Management and organizational performance: nonlinear impacts

Dependent variable = student exam pass rates

Independent variables	Level of management networking	
	High	Low
Resources		
Teacher salaries (000s)	0.7727 (4.55)	0.2835 (1.98)
Class size	−0.6620 (5.90)	−0.1211ns (1.47)
Teacher experience	−0.1256ns (0.85)	0.4556 (3.51)
Noncertified teachers	−0.1100 (2.20)	−0.2638 (5.30)
Percentage state aid	−0.0189ns (1.39)	−0.0073ns (0.69)
Constraints		
Percentage of black students	−0.1846 (7.20)	−0.2291 (13.49)
Percentage of Latino students	−0.1003 (6.18)	−0.1147 (10.39)
Percentage of low-income students	−0.1966 (8.53)	−0.1537 (11.16)
R^2	0.57	0.61
Standard error	7.60	7.61
F	124.23	176.83
N	1,154	1,380

Notes: T-scores in parentheses. Dummy variables for individual years not reported.
ns = not significant.

$$O_t = \beta_2(X_t) + \varepsilon_t \qquad M_2 > 0$$
$$O_t = \beta_2(X_t) + \varepsilon_t \qquad M_2 < 0$$

The results of these models produced by splitting the sample are shown in Table 3.7. The constraints can be examined first. Our theory suggests that, for high levels of managerial networking, the size, or impact, of each of these should drop in absolute value. Although the coefficients do not change dramatically, in two cases (blacks and Latinos) the hypothesis is confirmed. In one case (low income) it is not. In terms of the four cases of resources (state aid is not significant and can be ignored), three are as predicted. Districts with more networking on the part of superintendents get more out of teacher salaries and reductions in class size and are less affected by noncertified teachers. Teacher experience shows an interesting pattern of significance for the low-networking districts and insignificance for the high-networking districts. While this result ostensibly contradicts our hypothesis, it means that high-networking districts are not affected by having less experienced teachers.

Five of the seven relationships found in Table 3.7 are consistent with our nonlinear, interactive theory of management. Although this pattern might not seem like strong support for the theory, examining the individual coefficients provides additional corroboration. Most of the relationships differ from each other in only marginal ways. The differences between four sets of the relationships are substantial, however. Districts characterized by a high managerial networking style get 2.7 times the impact from higher teacher salaries, receive 5.5 times the impact from smaller classes, get only 42 percent of the negative impact of noncertified teachers, and are not affected at all by inexperienced teachers.[21] Even with the relatively crude test presented here (a simple measure of managing in the networked environment – a deliberately underspecified model), therefore, management does matter; and it matters by interacting with program resources and constraints in predicted directions. H2 (nonlinearity) and H3 (direction of relationships) are supported by these tests.

The pattern of relationships merits some additional comment. Management is about choice and decision making. Quite clearly, managers allocate more time and effort to some constraints and resources than to others. As a result, expecting all resources to become more valuable and all constraints to become less negative may not only be expecting too much, it might also conflict with what the manager is trying to do. In other words, the results may be evidence that managers make strategic networking choices beyond the fundamental ones of "How often?" and "With whom?" An effective manager might well focus on a small number of strategic factors that can be manipulated to get better results, while at the same time accepting some modest negative tradeoffs on less important variables. The relationships in Table 3.7 are consistent with such an interpretation. The negative findings are relatively small, as are a few of the positive findings. Three of the impacts are substantial – those regarding teacher salaries, class size, and noncertified teachers. Getting large positive results on these three variables more than compensates for the modest negative changes on other factors.

Autoregressive models

Because organizations stress standard operating procedures, specialization, and consistency, they tend to be relatively predictable and stable from year to year. They are, as we have explained, autoregressive systems. A stronger and more difficult test of our theory of management in the networked environment involves moving to an autoregressive model in which current performance is determined in part by past performance. Again, our strategy of

Table 3.8 Management and organizational performance: autoregressive and nonlinear models

Dependent variable = student exam pass rates

Independent variables	Base model	Network+	SWAT
Managerial networking	–	0.1719 (1.65)	–
Performance (t − 1)	0.7172 (63.65)	0.7162 (63.48)	0.7042 (63.49)
Resources			
Teacher salaries (000s)	0.3679 (6.75)	0.3704 (6.80)	0.4520 (8.63)
Class size	−0.0752 (1.69)	−0.0750 (1.69)	−0.1913 (4.08)
Teacher experience	−0.1448 (2.38)	−0.1526 (2.50)	−0.1285 (2.10)
Noncertified teachers	−0.0947 (3.95)	−0.0947 (3.95)	−0.1159 (5.30)
Percentage state aid	0.0074ns (1.39)	0.0064ns (1.21)	0.0049 (0.89)
Constraints			
Percentage of black students	−0.0506 (5.19)	0.0593 (5.25)	0.0521 (4.48)
Percentage of Latino students	−0.0412 (5.76)	−0.0413 (5.79)	−0.0475 (6.53)
Percentage of low-income students	−0.0165ns (1.62)	−0.0165 (1.69)	−0.0135 (1.27)
R^2	0.81	0.81	0.82
Standard error	5.18	5.18	2.11
F	1187.17	1069.46	1296.65
N	2,534	2,534	

Notes: T-scores in parentheses. ns = not significant. Classical statistical significance does not apply to SWAT models.

analysis will be the same. First, we examine whether management matters at all; and then we examine whether or not the impact is nonlinear. The autoregressive model analogous to the linear model just estimated – one treating management as simply another additive input – is

$$O_t = \beta_1 O_{t-1} + \beta_2 X_t + \beta_3 M_2 + \varepsilon_t$$

The basic linear model without management is shown in the first column of Table 3.8. The lagged dependent variable dominates the equation, thus strongly supporting our notion that such organizations are indeed inertial systems. All the same, the parameter estimate (just above 0.7) remains at a distance from 1.0, thus indicating that the past does not rigidly determine current performance. The constraints remain negative, though with diminished impact; similarly, the resources remain positive but with smaller impacts. The lagged dependent variable essentially limits the influence of these variables to their impacts on changes from year to year, and this short-term impact by definition must be smaller than a one-shot estimate of impact on a cross-section. Despite the stringent nature of this test, management continues to have a positive impact on performance. For the full range of this variable, management could make a difference of as much as one percentage point *per year* on the pass rate. While this may not appear to be substantial, with the autoregressive model these impacts continue to affect future performance for several years into the future (see Pindyck and Rubinfeld 1991 and O'Toole and Meier 1999).[22] By this stringent test, therefore, H1 is again supported.

Assessing the nonlinear impacts in an autoregressive model is somewhat more difficult, given that the autoregressive term so dominates the equation. The result is that the remaining coefficients are often less stable, so that a standard interaction often has too much collinearity, and dividing the sample could leave too little variance to provide efficient estimates. We do explore the issue via sample splitting (to follow shortly), but we also utilize an alternative approach: the substantively weighted analytical technique (SWAT), a form of exploratory data analysis that allows one to focus on interesting subsets of data (Meier and Gill 2000). We first employ SWAT to examine the question of nonlinearity, and then we explore the question with sample splitting.

Applied to the current case, the logic undergirding SWAT is as follows. If management has a nonlinear/interactive relationship with forces and inputs from the environment, then those units characterized by high levels of managerial networking should operate with a different set of relationships from the average organization. Hypothetically, this suggests that, if one replicated the analysis reported in Table 3.8 with a sample of units but only had those with high levels of networking by superintendents, the regression coefficients would change.

To get at this hypothetical situation, SWAT asks what would happen if the population of units were to contain many more organizations with high levels of managerial networking and many fewer with low levels of such behavior by top managers. SWAT creates such an artificial universe by reweighting cases in the existing sample. Comparing the regression from this sample from a hypothetical population to the sample from the existing population should provide some leverage on whether externally oriented management matters more or in different ways in these sets of situations. In the specific case, we designated those school districts with networking scores above 1.36 (about 10 percent of the total) as having a high level of such activity by management. We used a higher threshold in this situation rather than just the top half, because the autoregressive specification is likely to wash out relatively small differences in management activities. School districts with a managerial networking score below 1.36 were weighted at 0.1

compared to weights of 1.0 for those above this threshold. This process artificially creates a sample that has only one-tenth as many districts in the low category and ten times as many (relatively) in the high managerial networking category. The results of this weighted regression are shown in column 3 of Table 3.8.

The coefficients in column 3 are not parameter estimates (since they deal with a hypothetical universe), but they are informative when contrasted with the ordinary least squares (OLS) regression coefficients because they show how a set of units with a higher degree of networking by managers might use resources differently. The previous results in Table 3.7 suggest that teacher salaries, noncertified teachers, and class size are likely to be the key variables. Most of the SWAT/OLS differences are relatively small, but in two cases – teacher salaries and class size – the differences in coefficients are substantial. In both cases the implication is that programs with more managerial networking get more out of their resources. The SWAT equation stressing high levels of management has a teacher salary coefficient approximately 24 percent larger, and the class size coefficient is 254 percent larger than that for the same variable in the base OLS regression.

The consistency of these two relationships with the same relationships in the nonautoregressive model in Table 3.7 is reasonable evidence that one aspect of management is likely to interact with program inputs from the environment to produce outputs above what would be expected in a strictly linear relationship. Again, H2 and H3 are supported even in the estimations of an autoregressive model.

Finally, for even more evidence on this question, we undertake another analysis by splitting the sample in a couple of fashions. Table 3.9 divides the school districts into five quintiles by level of performance on the TAAS. The top quintile, for example, has a mean student pass rate of 79.2 compared to 73.9 for all districts and 64.8 in the lowest quintile. Care must be exercised in partitioning a sample, particularly when partitioning on the dependent variable, because each subset is designed to be unrepresentative of the entire sample. The prediction levels in Table 3.9 increase dramatically compared to the simple linear, autoregressive estimation in Table 3.8; in the middle three quintiles less than 1 percent of the variance is left unexplained.[23]

Quite clearly, we might have some intuition as to why networking by managers might matter more or less as organizations perform better. The regressions in Table 3.9 show that networking's impact on performance is relatively stable in the middle three quintiles; these estimates are also statistically more reliable than those in Table 3.8. For both the highest- and

Table 3.9 Managerial networking at different levels of educational performance

	Quintiles of performance: 5 = best				
Independent variable	5	4	3	2	1
Past performance	0.6645 (50.70)	0.7189 (187.09)	0.7150 (201.04)	0.7201 (174.85)	0.7330 (42.78)
Managerial networking	0.2792 (2.05)	0.1579 (4.70)	0.1626 (5.99)	0.1766 (5.26)	0.3727 (2.18)
R^2	0.91	0.99	0.99	0.99	0.92
Standard error	2.93	0.75	0.60	0.76	3.71
F	485.13	9,253.65	13,210.42	10,394.95	485.13
N	518	531	484	522	519
Mean dependent variable	79.2	77.5	75.8	71.5	64.8

Notes: T-scores in parentheses. All equations control for the eight control variables used in Table 3.7.

lowest-performing organizations, the management coefficient is much larger.[24] Why might this be the case?

In a smoothly running organization that is attaining adequate performance, the demand for creative management and the opportunities to use that management might be relatively few. An organization interested in optimizing rather than satisficing (or, alternatively, one seeking to change its level of performance dramatically) is more likely to seek out opportunities to exploit inside the organization or in its environment. An aggressive superintendent in this regard might seek a larger bond issue for capital expansion, try new programs for parental involvement, or use traditional resources in nontraditional ways. Seeking higher levels of performance relative to environmental constraints (as these models are set up) requires taking more risk, and management efforts (networking) and skills should come more into play.

For those units at the low end of the performance scale, the function of managerial networking is probably somewhat different but also equally important. These organizations are performing poorly, and that performance is likely recognized by both the district and various actors in the district's environment. In a poorly running unit, perhaps, almost any improvement will get some returns. Good external management in such a situation is likely to matter more, because it compensates for inadequate processes and decisions in other parts of the core organization. Such leadership could also have a salutary impact on internal morale as members see actions being taken that could improve the organization.

Table 3.10 Managerial networking interactions with resources and constraints

Independent variable	Level of managerial networking					
	All	1.0	1.25	1.5	1.75	2.0
Past performance	0.7172	0.6726	0.6431	0.6302	0.5942	0.4732
	(63.65)	(24.08)	(17.00)	(13.92)	(11.34)	(5.65)
R^2	0.81	0.80	0.84	0.82	0.80	0.77
Standard error	5.18	5.17	4.37	4.51	4.45	4.54
F	1,187.17	199.09	148.33	101.87	70.94	31.82
N	2,534	450	260	205	165	95
Mean dependent variable	73.9	74.6	75.5	76.6	76.4	77.3
Mean managerial networking	0.0	1.59	1.91	2.04	2.14	2.35

Notes: T-scores in parentheses. All equations control for the eight control variables used in Table 3.7.

The autoregressive coefficient representing past performance also merits comment. As organizational performance increases, the size of the autoregressive parameter decreases; the parameter in the top quintile is statistically smaller than the estimate for all organizations. This finding suggests that high-performing organizations are less constrained by past performance than are organizations with weaker performance. Because a networking-style management interacts with the environment, as our model expects, this pattern is consistent with tapping opportunities externally and, in the process, reducing organizational rigidity.

This relationship reveals a paradox of organizational management. At the highest levels of performance, stability is a good thing. As performance in an organization declines, stability has less value, simply because the organization is reproducing poor performance. The results of Table 3.9 suggest that stability is greatest exactly when stability is of the least value to the organization.[25]

Table 3.10 looks at the same pattern but in a different way; it presents the results for the districts run by superintendents who rate highly on the networking variable. Since we are interested in probing what happens when managers undertake frequent and extensive networking, we focus on the high-networking cases for special attention here. Subsets of the sample that include larger networking values can be compared with the full set of cases (column 1). The first subset (column 2 in the table) includes only superintendents with networking scores above 1 (or one standard deviation above average) – about 18 percent of all managers. Subsequent regressions, listed in successive columns of the table, raise this standard by 0.25 standard deviations in a series of steps until only the top 4 percent remain (those scoring above 2.0). This incremental process of examination illustrates how the relationships evolve at different levels of networking activity. Because we are selecting progressively less representative organizations, our interpretation should be cautious and avoid assessing patterns where the relationships are not strong. These findings contain all the previous controls, but we show only the relevant coefficients.

As networking by top managers increases, the autoregressive term declines slowly, until the management variable is 1.5 standard deviations above the mean, and then precipitously. This pattern suggests that networking performs its desired function; rather than being trapped by past routines and behaviors, well-networked managers generate more flexibility for their organizations to change. This link should be viewed as the first step in a two-step process of managing the organization overall: first, exploiting the environment to create change in the unit; and, second, then structuring the changes to produce higher performance.[26] Changing the size of the autoregressive component in the model dramatically changes the long-run impact of other variables, because the current values of the independent variables will continue to affect performance in the future by feeding back through the autoregressive term. The finding suggests, therefore, that the influence of managerial networking ramifies forward into the future and can enhance performance substantially in the longer term.

Interpretation and implications

Thus far this analysis has shown that managerial networking is related to performance, but we have not fully demonstrated the process by which managing in the networked environment generates better results. We have several hypotheses. First, management's greater attention to the environment might create buffers from external shocks and thus permit lower-level personnel (teachers, principals) to be more effective. Second, a networking style might encourage a more decentralized internal management approach – an approach advocated by much current education reform literature. Third, the networking might expose the superintendent to innovative programs operated by other districts. Fourth, managerial networking might convince external stakeholders to grant more autonomy to the school district and thus allow the district to exploit the expertise it has. In all four cases, organizations might be able to use resources more effectively.[27] These and other hypotheses for the linkage between networking by managers and performance are all plausible; future research can be designed to evaluate these hypotheses. Indeed, some of them are partially explored later in this book.

The evidence here indicates that public managers need to consider networking outward an important tool of administrative success, not merely a luxury in which to engage if there is extra time. Networkers in our sample spent less time running internal operations than did others, but the tradeoff paid off in results. Nevertheless, managerial networking may not be an unmitigated good. Its contributions to performance may see diminishing returns at higher levels of networking. We explore this issue later in the book. In addition, networking may assist certain goals, and certain stakeholders, more than others. We tackle this subject next.

Distributional consequences

So far, we have seen that managerial networking is a phenomenon that can be discerned in various sorts of jurisdictions, that it helps to shape performance, and that it interacts with selected constraints and resources – the "X" vector – in the interdependent environment in so doing. Consistent with these findings, as implied by our model and as framed in the research literature in the field (and from which the model is developed), the theme of networks, networking, and public management has had a rather positive aura. Networks can assist program and policy delivery, networking can assist performance, and more of both – it is often implied – is a good thing. The bulk of this literature frames the emergence of networks in terms of a tendency or necessity to use multiple linked social actors, often multiple organizational actors, to achieve collective purposes. Corollary attention, unsurprisingly, has been directed at logically related issues, such as how to manage networked arrays, how to measure and improve performance in networked settings, and how to understand network operations through empirical theory. With this attention to networks and management has come an implicit notion among researchers that network development, use, and performance are topics that carry little direct political import –

aside from the obvious point that the performance of networks might itself be of interest to a broader public.

The inadvertently depoliticized analysis of networks in recent research has neglected issues that should be part of the research agenda, however. In this section we outline ways that networks and network management point toward significant political issues.[28] We then focus on one political dimension of networks and their performance: the likelihood that, rather than being neutral producers of collective goods while enmeshed in a broader environment, networking managers respond to the stronger and more politically powerful elements of their surroundings, thus magnifying the tendency toward inequality already present in the social setting. This dynamic – what we call the "dark side" of managing networks – has been largely unexplored by network researchers. Such patterns should not be unexpected, however. The reasons are explicit in longstanding streams of research that have been ignored in the work done thus far on networks. We report some empirical results that give considerable credence to the dark side hypothesis. In so doing, we argue that there is a need for systematic study of the political aspects of networks and their management.

Networks and network management: the functionalist perspective

The standard portrayal of networks attributes the multiactor features of program implementation and management to the demands placed on programs and their administrators. Among the causal factors frequently mentioned as drivers of networked program execution are the increasingly "wicked" character of public problems (Rittel and Webber 1973), the realities of increasingly dense program environments, the expertise-reliant character of modern governance, the requisites of program design in multilevel systems, and the demands placed on program managers in complex settings. Although each of these arguments has a political dimension, the production-focused and partnership-framed perspective obscures political themes with their distributional aspects, instead emphasizing the managerial requisites generated in and for such arrays.

The theoretical claims, parallels, and distinctions among these strands of causal logic represent a complex and somewhat confusing pastiche. The point to be emphasized, however, is that the political interpretation of networks, in terms of their likely causes and consequences, seems largely lost in the analytical picture. Researchers seem to buy into a production logic of one sort or another regarding network formation and operations, and one result is a blindness toward the distributional consequences of network actions.

The point can be put another way. The bulk of research on networks and public management effectively reenacts a network version of the venerable politics/administration dichotomy. This statement holds in two respects. First, instrumental logic is used to explain network patterns, typically with an emphasis on program or clientele needs. This theme gives little attention to certain political drivers of network formation and use that have little to do with program needs and more to do with incentives that can operate on political leadership. Second, researchers typically ignore important political issues about what networks do, how they perform, and how they can be directed toward goal achievement. The modal study of networks and public management recognizes that program results matter for stakeholders. But these results – the dependent variables tapping performance – are treated in a rather sterile fashion, as products of a production system, without attention to distributional aspects or contest between stakeholders. Instead, such studies emphasize management, facilitation, coordination, and related themes. The politics of network performance, in several relevant respects, is virtually ignored.

From other literatures, however, we can sketch three political themes regarding network-associated impacts. One in particular, the last-mentioned below, admits to systematic exploration.

First, while some recognize that additional actors are often needed during implementation to build support for program operations (Pressman and Wildavsky 1984), researchers have not considered the possibility that the use of networks can also be a way of distancing state actors from controversial policy efforts. The choice of networks can be a function not of increasing problem-solving capacity but of authoritative actors dodging difficult or costly responsibilities. Networks can be a symbolic-political choice when there is pressure for state action yet disincentives for the state to address policy problems definitively. This side of the network issue has been absent from systematic investigation, but it is likely involved in the design of institutional arrangements for addressing such policy issues as HIV/AIDS, family planning services, and some aspects of social welfare policy.

Second, networks can have another political effect that has typically been ignored in the research literature: the incorporation of additional perspectives or constraints that shift the policy emphasis during implementation. One way this result can develop is through the dynamics of coproduction.

While it is generally recognized that adding actors increases constraints as well as opportunities, network research has not systematically explored the ways that coproduction can shift the goals and preferences of public programs. Instead, the challenge stemming from the addition of network actors has largely been framed in terms of rendering the pattern less easily managed. The emphasis has been on the complexity of coproduced effort – a coordination problem – rather than the potential shift in the core of what public programs managed through networks actually do. "Adequate management" (Kickert, Klijn, and Koppenjan 1997: 9) is seen as the challenge – one that is best met by more energetic and more talented managerial efforts. Once again, the emphasis is on an instrumental rather than a political point. Adding actors does more than complicate, however; it tilts the balance of power. Determining the scope of involvement shapes the definition of issues and goes a long way toward determining who wins and who loses on policy questions (Schattschneider 1960).

The third way that the addition of network actors can carry political import is through straightforward political pressure. Here the table is tilted again. In this variant, even if production occurs primarily through a core organization, other network parties influence the pattern toward a skewed distribution of program results. In short, a bias in performance can derive both from coproduction as well as from the dynamics of managerial response to pressure from network actors as a core organization responds to its networked environment.

The facts of life regarding public management in a political environment are hardly new to analysts of the twenty-first century. Decades of research have validated the point that agencies and their management must develop support in their setting, and that doing so can mean sacrificing the primary agenda of policy, particularly if it involves social change, in the interests of survival. For instance, Philip Selznick's classic study, *TVA and the Grass Roots* (1949), defines and illustrates the notion of cooptation with vivid exactitude. Cooptation and the difficult tradeoffs it implies have been staples of the analysis of public management and bureaucratic politics for a considerable period. Curiously, however, these basic facts of life seem to have been largely forgotten by enthusiasts of the network perspective. The more public programs are designed to alter the existing order, the greater the threat of the program to those who benefit most from the status quo. A result is heightened emphasis on capturing benefits of the program during execution by those who are best positioned to shape the details of program implementation. By design, moreover, networks are leaner and weaker in the face of larger institutions and significant individual actors in a policy system.

One way of explicating the point has to do with networks, network nodes, and the pattern of exchanges that can be so important in facilitating network action. Virtually all assessments of public management patterns recognize that networks are built around exchanges between the nodes in the network, often with managers framing and brokering the exchanges. An exchange implies that node A provides something to node B, and vice versa, in such a way that the overall aggregation is better off. This positive-sum view of networks and networking overlooks the fact that each node enters the network with a distinct set of goals. Only a portion of these goal sets overlap. Despite the extensive literature on cooptation, the ability of network nodes to shape the direction of public programs has not been carefully investigated. For public organizations that seek multiple goals – that is, all public organizations – the risk is that network interactions will emphasize some goals to the detriment of others. The literatures on interest groups and on citizen participation indicate that network nodes seek greater benefits for goals that are favored by more entrenched interests and downplay efforts that favor disadvantaged clientele.

An empirical test

This last-mentioned aspect of the network politics of program management is amenable to systematic analysis. Do the benefits of managerial networking, documented earlier in this chapter, accrue disproportionately to those who already have more than others? Public school systems are an ideal setting to test this notion, because they display a wide variety of goals and can sit within networked settings. Because schools seek goals that benefit different races and social classes differently, and because networks are more likely to be populated by actors and organizations that already possess political resources, particularly at the critical loci of such networks, our working hypothesis is that managers who expend greater effort in working the network will improve educational performance more for goals that benefit their relatively advantaged clientele than for goals that benefit their disadvantaged clientele.

We used data for five years (1995 to 1999) on the performance of Texas school districts and the set of control variables introduced in Chapter 2. We also used the survey responses we have collected from top managers. The total possible number of cases for this analysis is 2,535. To perform the analyses, we used a simplified version of our model, which asserts a positive relationship between managerial networking and performance, controlling for a set of resources and constraints operating on the organizations. We already knew that managerial networking improves performance; but we also wanted to explore how such positive impacts vary across performance measures that refer to, or are salient for, different school system constituencies that provide part of the networked environment for the core educational organizations. To investigate these questions, then, we used our measure of managerial networking (we used the original five-node factor score for this purpose), as well as the sets of suitable performance measures and appropriate control variables introduced earlier.

The basic hypothesis is that networking contact will contain biases that have distributional consequences for the performance of public organizations. In this case, because we know that participation and interest group action is positively correlated with socioeconomic status, superintendents who network are more likely to be exposed to portions of their networked setting that will seek benefits for the better off or higher-status students rather than for disadvantaged students. We would expect the networking measure, therefore, to be positively correlated with test scores for Anglo students, with ACT test scores, SAT test scores, and the percentage of students who exceed the college criterion on these tests (1,110 on the SAT or its ACT equivalent). We would not expect significant positive relationships for those indicators that reference the performance of disadvantaged students: TAAS pass rates for black, Latino, and low-income students, attendance rates, and dropout rates. These hypotheses are supported by the interest group/participation literature (Zeigler and Peak 1972; Verba and Nie 1972; Salisbury 1984; Scholzman 1984), the urban services literature (Lineberry 1977; Mladenka 1980; Jones 1985), and a substantial literature in education policy (see Tyack 1974, Bowles and Gintis 1976, Kozol 1991, and Meier and Stewart 1991).

Regression estimations were developed for each of the ten performance indicators outlined above. The specification includes all control variables plus the measure of managerial networking. Dummy variables for each year were also included. These were usually jointly significant, reflecting an upward trend in the performance data during this period.[29]

The last column of Table 3.6 displays the results for the overall TAAS pass rate performance. As explained earlier, the adjusted R-squared is approximately 0.59, indicating a reasonable amount of explained variance.

Table 3.11 The impact of network interaction on disadvantaged student indicators

Performance measure	Networking slope	T-score	R^2	N
Latino pass rate	0.4081	1.56	0.36	2,310
Black pass rate	0.2437	0.64	0.37	1,568
Low-income pass rate	0.1168	0.61	0.51	2,518
Dropout rate	−0.0424	2.04*	0.16	2,514
Class attendance	−0.0028	0.18	0.24	2,534

Notes: All equations control for teacher salaries, percentage of state aid, class size, teacher experience, percentage of teachers not certified, percentage of black, Latino, and low-income students, and yearly dummy variables. * = significant at $p < 0.05$, two-tailed test.

Table 3.12 The impact of network interaction on advantaged student indicators

Performance measure	Networking slope	T-score	R^2	N
White pass rate	0.8097	5.31*	0.42	2,506
Average ACT score	0.0670	2.50*	0.38	2,220
Average SAT score	5.0762	3.49*	0.50	1,836
Percentage above criterion	0.5512	2.80*	0.30	2,416

Notes: All equations control for teacher salaries, percentage of state aid, class size, teacher experience, percentage of teachers not certified, percentage of black, Latino, and low-income students, and yearly dummy variables. * = significant at $p < 0.05$, two-tailed test.

Relationships are all in the expected directions and also significant. Of particular interest is the impact of managerial networking, which – as we have seen – shows a positive relationship to TAAS scores. The maximum effect size for this variable is more than four points on districts' overall pass rate. Such an impact – particularly from the top position in the system, one far removed from the core of the educational process – can be seen as substantial, and the impact of management can show impressive results over time.

For the most salient performance indicator, managerial networking contributes to positive results. This result fits with the expectations developed from the research tradition of Selznick and others. How does networking effort play out across the range of performance measures? We ran nine additional regression analyses to determine the answer; the results for those targeting performance for the relatively disadvantaged parts of the educational constituency appear in Table 3.11, while those measures of interest to more powerful parts of the public school networked environment are reported in Table 3.12. Both tables provide summary reports: they include the results for managerial networking but omit the portions of the estimations pertaining to the controls.

Table 3.11 summarizes five direct tests of the hypothesis by showing managerial networking's impact on five performance indicia that matter most to minority constituents, the poor, and/or low performers. The pattern is striking. For each of Latino students, black students, and low-income students,[30] managerial networking does not add to performance with any statistically significant impacts. The same can be said for attendance. All these performance measures are of more interest to marginalized constituencies of the school system network. Only for dropout rates does managerial networking seem to matter. This anomaly may result from the poor quality of the dropout data, however. Data on dropout performance are the least reliable of those analyzed in this study.

Table 3.12 shows the contribution of managerial networking to performance for four indicators relevant to advantaged (that is, top-end and/or Anglo) students. For all, the impact of managerial networking is clearly positive and significant. This is what one would expect if managers engaged in the network are influenced by and attentive to what those with power would prefer. For the Anglo pass rate, average SAT, average ACT, and percentage of SAT above 1,110 (or its ACT equivalent), managerial networking adds to performance. These are all indicators that are of considerable interest to relatively influential or privileged constituencies.

The results overall are clear: the estimations retrieve Selznick's insight with detailed findings. Those parts of a networked constituency that are influential and care about the performance results have managerial networking assisting what they do; those parts dealing with more marginal or less salient issues are less – or not – influenced by managerial networking. Selznick's argument is strongly supported by the findings. It is worth noting that here, as well as for the results to be discussed next, the findings represent distinct impacts from networking, not simply distributional inequities generated in school districts. In other words, the results indicate a set of systematic relationships between networking and distributional impacts. Networking actions generate greater inequalities than the school system would have without network activity.

Further insight as to what is likely occurring in these settings can be gained by taking a more thorough glimpse inside the managerial networking activity reported by the district superintendents. To do so, we replace the overall networking factor scores with the reported degree of networking, respectively, with each node. We enter each node or networking partner into separate

Table 3.13 The impact of network interaction on advantaged student indicators

Interactions with	TAAS	Anglo tests	ACT	SAT	Criterion
School board members	−0.589 (3.39)*	−0.572 (3.33)*	−0.011 (0.37)	−0.87 (0.52)	−0.200 (0.89)
Local business leaders	0.268 (1.72)#	0.450 (2.92)*	0.104 (3.71)*	8.18 (5.48)*	1.093 (5.49)*
Other superintendents	1.011 (5.77)*	0.974 (5.62)*	−0.013 (0.42)	1.20 (0.71)	0.037 (0.16)
State legislators	1.504 (4.21)*	1.170 (4.73)*	0.056 (1.29)	6.33 (2.70)*	0.398 (1.24)
Texas Education Agency	0.631 (3.15)*	0.569 (2.88)*	0.061 (1.72)#	−1.97 (1.05)	−0.256 (0.98)

Notes: T-scores in parentheses. All equations control for teacher salaries, percentage of state aid, class size, teacher experience, percentage of teachers not certified, percentage of black, Latino, and low-income students, and yearly dummy variables. * = significant at $p < 0.05$. # = significant at $p < 0.10$. N = 1,110.

Table 3.14 The impact of individual network nodes on disadvantaged student indicators

	Performance measure				
	TAAS tests for				
Interactions with	Blacks	Latinos	Low-income	Attend	Dropout
School board members	−0.184 (0.44)	0.059 (0.20)	−0.746 (3.43)*	−0.117 (6.97)*	0.049 (2.15)*
Local business leaders	−0.768 (1.95)#	−0.500 (1.91)#	−0.535 (2.75)*	−0.025 (1.66)#	−0.016 (0.80)
Other superintendents	1.180 (2.82)*	0.850 (2.91)*	0.837 (3.80)*	0.078 (4.51)*	−0.057 (2.49)*
State legislators	0.975 (1.59)	0.419 (1.01)	0.307 (0.98)	−0.009 (0.38)	−0.060 (1.81)#
Texas Education Agency	0.556 (1.14)	1.040 (3.11)*	0.733 (2.94)*	0.038 (1.93)#	−0.027 (1.03)

Notes: T-scores in parentheses. All equations control for teacher salaries, percentage of state aid, class size, teacher experience, percentage of teachers not certified, percentage of black, Latino, and low-income students, and yearly dummy variables. * = significant at $p < 0.05$, two-tailed test. # = significant at $p < 0.10$, two-tailed test.

regression analyses that are otherwise specified identically to those performed for the overall networking measure. We explore the impact of interaction with each node on each of the ten performance measures already reported. These additional analyses amount to fifty estimations – ten each for each of the nodes (school board members, local business leaders, and so forth). The results of these analyses are reported in Tables 3.13 and 3.14. The tables omit the findings for the controls in favor of reporting only on the impacts of each of the networking contacts of the school district top managers. Table 3.13 summarizes the findings for the all-pass rate (the most highly salient performance measure) and the advantaged student indicators, while Table 3.14 provides a parallel set of results for the disadvantaged student indicators.

Although we do not have measures of the goals of each of the nodes, in a few cases clear expectations can be inferred. Local business leaders are likely to push for improvements at the elite end of the educational spectrum since their own children are likely to be relatively advantaged in the education system. The Texas Education Agency is most associated with its exam, the TAAS, and it sets standards for students by race and ethnicity. Other superintendents are likely to reflect professional interests, and professional educators in the United States are likely to push education benefits or have ideas for new programs that affect both haves and have-nots. The exact preferences of the political actors – that is, school boards and state legislators – will depend on the composition of their constituencies, and systematic data on the "electoral" constituencies – that is, who voted for the office holder – are not available.

The analyses provide some hints as to what may be going on as top managers of the school districts interact with their environment. While not definitive, the results suggest possible causal links and, thereby, plausible production processes. For business leaders the pattern is especially clear: such contacts help on every measure of advantaged student performance tested and hurt on four out of five measures of disadvantaged student performance.[31] In this case, cooptation is a likely explanation. More contact with business leaders probably exposes top school-district managers to the complaints, concerns, and preoccupations of the local business elite, from whom some support (for instance, for the district's revenue-raising agenda) may be crucial. To the extent that superintendents use their discretion to direct or redirect attention to these matters, some sacrifice to the more marginalized clientele may follow.

Superintendents' interactions with their counterparts in other districts contribute to performance on seven of the ten measures, including on all five measures tapping disadvantaged students' results. What is likely happening here is information sharing and professional assistance to colleagues, thus suggesting that collegial professional interaction can be a route for diffusion of innovations and relatively equitable performance boosts across organizations and governments. Interaction with the Texas Education Agency is also helpful to several measures of performance: three each for the advantaged and disadvantaged groups. Most of these have to do with performance on the TAAS, a subject of obvious concern at the state level. This pattern is consistent with what one might expect from interaction with a regulatory agency – which is, in effect, how the TEA operates.

The more intriguing results are those for the other two external links for the superintendents. Contacts with school board members do not help performance, and for half the measures more networking with school board members impedes performance. The negative impacts are spread across both advantaged and disadvantaged students. Whatever is going on in these contacts, the results do not seem to be aspects of cooptation in the usual sense. For instance, TAAS results for both Anglo and low-income students are negatively associated with more contact with the school board. Somewhat surprisingly, contacts with state legislators show some impacts; these are all positive with regard to performance, and three of the four significant impacts show up on measures tapping advantaged student or generally salient measures.[32]

These findings do not fully demonstrate what is happening as managers engage in networking activity with an array of external parties. They do show, however, that the benefits of this activity are unevenly distributed, and also that these consequences might be traced to contacts with particular actors. Networking with the external world can offer perils as well as prospects, and understanding the political and distributional dimensions of such settings can help to explain what is likely to be produced via networked public action.

Implications

Network researchers have appropriately emphasized the complex and interdependent nature of many of today's public programs and pointed to the challenges faced by public managers who are responsible for concerting policy-relevant action. In implicitly (or otherwise) suggesting that the issues are those of coordination and management alone, however, much of the recent exploration of networks and policy implementation ignores potentially crucial political dimensions of network creation, coproduction, and cooptation. This chapter indicates that these omissions are important and that systematic research on the political aspects of networks and their performance impacts is needed.

The last portion of the analysis in particular makes a strong case that networks and their management are not likely to produce leveraged performance without distributional implications. In a sense, these results validate a venerable theme. As Selznick argued decades ago, administrative units situated in an interdependent political environment must find ways to build support – particularly among those elements of their setting that have the clout and resources to matter to the agency's future prospects. This political dynamic does not disappear when agencies operate in networked contexts; it is probably exacerbated. As we have indicated, however, the point has *not* been a prominent part of the recent and extensive research treatment of networks and public management. In this analysis, it is not only sketched, it is supported with systematic evidence covering hundreds of organizations – and managers – over a several-year period. Treating managerial networking as a cognitive or technical challenge misses the mark, for it obscures the likely tilting of the policy table toward well-established and influential interests. Managerial networking does not eliminate this bias; if anything, it can accentuate it.

In school districts in Texas, at a minimum, managerial networking does boost educational performance, but most improvements accrue to the more privileged portions of the constituency, not to the marginalized ones. Network activity and management matter, but these elements are not ways of overcoming inequities in service delivery. Exposing managers to the pressures of their surroundings, particularly to influential actors with a distributionally related agenda, appears to push them to respond to the most influential portions of the network. Networking in other directions or with other types of actors may produce benefits – or even costs – without catalyzing further inequities as a result, however. Positive, mixed, negative, and zero-sum games are all plausible. The details matter. Managerial networking is not a substitute for politics, nor is it a more sanitized and thereby acceptable form of political activity. It produces the kinds of patterns and dilemmas that social scientists have been documenting for years.

Although the empirical findings presented here are limited to Texas school districts, two reasons suggest that similar patterns would be found in other managerial settings where some networks and networking regularly operate. First, school districts are public organizations with relatively common problems involving the incorporation and management of networks. These findings are most likely to apply to organizations that share the characteristics of school districts: highly professionalized and decentralized organizations with a great deal of managerial discretion. Second, the story told by the data fits longstanding theories about organizations and their environments; in effect, the moral is that we need to think of public management networks in the broader context of organization theory.

Generalizing about managing in the network

Managerial networking, or measures of M_2, have been successfully applied in a number of areas other than Texas school districts. All the studies use regression models similar to those presented in this chapter; all control for a wide variety of other factors that could also influence program outcomes. To retain the focus on the linkage between managerial networking and performance, in our review of such research we do not discuss the control variables but, rather, focus on the relationship between managerial networking and performance.

Donahue *et al.* (2004) use data from the Government Performance Project to examine US state government agencies charged with overseeing human resources activities, and agencies assigned the management of state debt. Managerial networking is measured via contact and the reciprocity of contact with various external stakeholders, such as governors and their staff, legislators and legislative staff, other agencies, etc. For the human resources agencies, they relate managerial networking to subjective perceptions of the quality of personnel hired by the state, and also the level of employee turnover. They find that the quality of the contacts rather than just the volume of the networking positively affects the quality of hires, and that this measure of networking is also associated with low employee turnover rates (Donahue *et al.* 2004: 140).

For the debt administration agencies, managerial networking is measured by the establishment of contacts with financial networks, the use of outside financial advisors, the reliance on negotiated sales (and thus interaction with clientele) rather than the more arm's-length process of auctioning debt, the degree of underwriting training for the staff (which might equally be considered a measure of internal management), and the degree of overall control of the issuance of debt in the state. For outcome variables, they use the percentage of debt issued via competitive sales and the percentage of debt that was sold via requests for proposals (rather than given to a single underwriter). With several measures of managerial networking and two different outcomes, Donahue *et al.* consistently find positive relationships between managerial networking and outcomes, with a majority of the relationships attaining statistical significance.

Meier, O'Toole, and Hicklin (2009) examine the networking behavior of 266 college and university presidents in the United States (for both public and private universities). They create a measure of managerial networking via a factor score that is very similar to the measure used for superintendents. Nine external nodes are included that encompass political actors, other bureaucratic agencies, business and community leaders, and other college presidents. A single factor solution is generated. Greater levels of managerial networking are positively associated with the university's six-year graduate rate, a measure of efficiency often used by state higher education governance bodies. They also investigate efforts to create a more diverse faculty in terms of the percentage of new faculty hires that are African American. In this case

M_2 appears to work for public universities only; the impact of managerial networking is negative for private universities, but the positive impact for public universities cancels this out.

Nicholson-Crotty and O'Toole (2004) apply the model presented in Chapter 2 to 570 municipal police departments in the United States while using the percentage of index crimes cleared as a measure of performance. Index crimes are the crimes that the Federal Bureau of Investigation (FBI) uses to create serious crime indexes for both the nation and for individual jurisdictions. Nicholson-Crotty and O'Toole create a measure of police networking activities, especially related to their community policing activities; in a similar manner to the superintendent's measure, theirs is based on contacts with stakeholders. They find not only that managerial networking correlates positively with the percentage of index crimes cleared but also that it interacts with past performance to generate an even larger impact on performance.

Jacobson, Palus, and Bowling (2010) investigate managerial networking by state government agencies using the 1994 and 1998 American State Administrators Project. Although their primary purpose was to examine management behaviors and how they vary by gender, their findings are directly relevant to the present study. As a dependent variable the authors use whether the agency has adopted a series of government reforms that come under the rubric of the "Reinventing government" initiatives. Basically, these initiatives focus on the use of incentives and the elimination of restrictions on public managers. The authors create four measures of managerial networking: contacts with political principals, contacts with citizens and clientele, contacts with peers, and perception of the contacts initiated with political principals. All these managerial networking variables were positively correlated with "Reinventing government" outcomes, with the exception of contact with other agencies – which was negative. Given that the reinvention movement is generally a politically imposed reform, all these relationships were in the direction hypothesized by the authors.

Andrews *et al.* (2010c) make a direct effort to replicate the managerial networking measure in this chapter, using 69 English local governments for 2002 and 2003. English local governments are multifunctional and have authority over the implementation of most public programs other than health care. These researchers create a networking measure using the same frequency of contact scales as in the Texas studies and inquire about eight nodes, including local and national political actors, other bureaucrats, local stakeholders, trade unions, etc. As reported earlier in this chapter, this study also finds a single, general factor that could be termed managerial networking. Andrews *et al.* find a different and differential impact of networking on overall local government performance (the outcome measure is established by the national government to explicitly assess the performance of local governments across a variety of policy areas), however. They find that poor performance brings contacts from elected officials, and that such contacts serve as wakeup calls to administrators in regard to their level of performance. Local administrators then increase their networking with user groups – an activity that, in turn, has a positive impact on future performance. This cycle of poor performance, wakeup calls from elected officials, networking with user groups and subsequent increases in performance is very similar to that found by Hawes (2006) with Texas education data.

Cohen, Vaughn, and Villalobos (2010) provide additional support for the generality of the networking to performance relationship in their study of the management of the US Office of the President. Explicitly using the management theory in Chapter 2, they analyze more than 300 surveys from individuals who interacted with the president's chief of staff. The dependent variable is the respondents' rating of the effectiveness of the chief of staff. They have an excellent measure of buffering (M_4), with the chief of staff taking the role of guardian of the president's time; they have a separate measure of being accessible that can be an M_2 measure. Both external management variables had a positive impact on how effective the chiefs of staff were rated.

Conclusions

It seems clear that managerial networking contributes to public organizational performance, and not merely for top managers of Texas school districts. The sets of relationships between this facet of management and performance have been explicated with some care here. We have covered considerable ground in this chapter in terms of the externally oriented networking activities of public managers and a set of performance-related impacts of such behavior. Despite this fact, we have not yet concluded our analysis of the M_2 function. We return to some additional aspects of networking later in this book, but first we introduce some additional aspects of management – both because these are interesting in themselves and because they lay the groundwork for further investigations.

NOTES

1. The field of public management initially attempted to distinguish itself from the field of public administration by arguing that it focused on actions at the very top of the organization and, by definition, paid greater attention to the organization's environment. Although we do not see these two fields as separate, this study is central to the concerns of scholars who identify with either of the fields.

2. Needless to say, in reality school districts are anything but insulated from politics.

3. This measure taps managers' efforts to interact with their interdependent environment. It does not reach to, or at least distinguish, efforts to manage at the network level – that is, to manage or orchestrate the full set of interdependent actors en masse. Estimating this aspect of public management is complicated (O'Toole 2000b). As indicated earlier in this volume, we have made efforts to model management at the network level as a part of this research program but do not delve deeply into this set of issues in the current book.

4. Findings in a study of English local government managers, designed around a similarly constructed measure, mirror those obtained from the Texas data set; see Walker, O'Toole, and Meier (2007).

5. The findings presented on this point rely on data from the 2000 survey responses. A more complete exposition is presented by Meier and O'Toole (2003).

6. Work by Hawes (2006) indicates that the fire alarm pattern holds. Low performance at time 1 is associated with greater school board contact at time 2, which is in turn associated with higher performance at time 3. Hawes describes a cycle of political intervention designed to improve performance. We have analyzed a somewhat similar pattern in data on the performance of English local authorities (see Andrews *et al.* 2010c).

7. A similar survey was conducted several years later, in 2008, and the results were generally quite similar.

8. The findings and discussion in this part of the chapter rely on Meier and O'Toole (2001).

9. For reasons explained earlier, for certain purposes the school board can be considered a political principal rather than an external node.

10. Some of the networked relationships are mandatory and imposed from the environment. An instance is the authority given to state auditors to check on fiscal matters. In most cases, however, the superintendent can develop new relationships or seek to alter mandated relationships in such a way as to benefit the district.

11. The actual correlation between managerial networking and interaction with one's school principals (a hierarchical form of management, thus part of M_1), in the data analyzed below, is 0.18, suggesting that, while the two are distinct, they are not contradictory.

12. Underspecification is clearly less of a problem in the autoregressive form of the model, since any omitted variables are likely to affect current outputs via past outputs. Only those variables that affect current outputs but not last year's outputs, therefore, are likely to be a problem. The greatest concern should be whether there are omitted factors that covary with elements included in the model.

13. Districts that responded to the survey were no different from nonrespondents in terms of enrollment, enrollment growth, students' race, ethnicity and poverty, or test scores. There

were slight differences in a few other factors. Respondents had 0.48 more students per class, paid their teachers $200 more per year, but had annual operating budgets of about $100 per student less.

14. In this measure of M_2, we include school boards as an element of the networked environment of the superintendent. We treat school boards as part of the environment in this part of the analysis, since we think that on balance this notion is more appropriate, but we have also performed the entire set of analyses again with M_2 measured only on the other four types of interactions. The results are very similar to those reported here. Omitting boards from the study strengthens the impact of M_2 on performance modestly in the linear versions of the simplified model and weakens slightly the evidence on nonlinearity. The correlation between the two measures of managerial networking is 0.96. The networking factor correlates at −0.27 with time spent managing the district (in contrast to time spent in contacts outside the organization).

15. Later in this book we introduce other measures of management, including managerial quality.

16. Clearly, both "sides" can initiate interactions. Anecdotal evidence suggests that skillful superintendents generally do not wait passively to be contacted, and our later surveys have been designed to distinguish how much of the networking behavior reported by managers was initiated by them. We do so by asking who initiated the last interaction with each of the several nodes. Two findings of note can be summarized here. First, managers do indeed report that they usually initiated the last interactions. Second, as Goerdel (2006) has shown, a measure of managerial networking focused on the managerially initiated interactions shows an even stronger relationship with performance than does the measure used here. We treat this point later.

17. Of course, networking can occur at other levels of the organization, and this measure will underestimate total networking by the organization. Some of the network links are also clearly more important than others, and equal weighting might obscure this. These and other measurement problems are likely to attenuate any relationships found.

18. In policy analysis terms, test scores are an outcome rather than an output.

19. Exactly how managerial networking can influence performance is discussed below.

20. Collinearity refers to a situation in which two or more predictor variables in a multiple regression analysis are highly correlated with each other. In such a situation, the coefficients generated for those variables are typically unstable. When collinearity is high, standard errors are inflated but the estimation is unbiased. Collinearity impedes our ability to develop precise estimates of the coefficients involved.

21. The resource measures should be thought of as general measures of resources from the environment rather than specifically teacher salaries and class size. Access to resources correlates with both teacher salaries and class size, as well as a variety of other factors.

22. The long-run performance of the management variable has a value of approximately 0.6, which means the maximum total impact is approximately 3.6 percentage points – an estimate very similar to the estimate for nonautoregressive models.

23. Only the within-quintile variance is being explained in these analyses. The middle quintiles eliminate a great deal of the between-district variance.

24. As one would expect, the standard errors increase at the extremes, thus suggesting some caution in interpreting the results. We view these findings as suggestive until confirmed by other empirical studies.

25. This finding has implications for management theory and how to manage organizations – that is, in the degree of hierarchical structure that managers should create (Drucker 1967).

26. Management in this situation is both a decision to act and then a match of the strategy with the situation (see Lynn 1984). The decision to act in no way guarantees that the strategy then selected will pay off.

27. Visits to various schools indicate that the process might be that networking behavior is also associated with other behaviors that improve the levels of organizational cohesion. Good and bad schools both frequently have the same programs; the difference is often in the commitment of teachers and administrators to making programs work. Later in this volume, we explore how managerial quality and also the quality of human capital in the system help shape outputs and outcomes.

28. For a complete treatment of this topic, see O'Toole and Meier (2004b). Additional analyses along the same lines have been carried out by Meier, O'Toole, and Lu (2006); and O'Toole and Meier (2006).

29. A few exceptions can be noted. None of the year dummies was significant for attendance. In three other cases – average SAT score, average ACT score, and percentage scoring above 1,110 in the SAT – the dummy for 1996 was not significant, but the succeeding years were consistent with the upward trend.

30. The performance measure is the TAAS pass rate for these subgroups.

31. This summary includes relationships significant at $p < 0.10$.

32. The fourth impact is on dropouts.

4 Managerial quality and performance

Our basic model hypothesizes managerial influences on public organizational and program performance, when managers exert effort on external management as well as when they perform the standard internal functions that comprise managers' responsibilities. Chapter 3 has demonstrated that managers do operate externally – presumably to buffer against negative shocks, and also to exploit resources and opportunities in the organization's environment on behalf of the agency and its programs. Indeed, that chapter illustrated the nonlinear interaction of managerial networking with key resources for school districts. The chapter also showed that managerial efforts outward generate performance dividends, although these are not neutrally distributed to stakeholders; networking can have inequitable distributional consequences. Before we address the subject of internal management (Chapter 5), we need to revisit both managerial functions and introduce an aspect of internal and external management that is implied in the initial model but thus far not incorporated into the empirical analyses: the actual quality of management. We proceed to show that quality not only affects performance but links to managerial networking in interesting, nonlinear ways.

The "M" terms in the model obviously refer to managerial functions that have both a quantity, or degree of activity, aspect as well as a quality component. Our measure of managerial networking, introduced in the preceding chapter, obviously has advantages – including validity and reliability; but it lacks a "quality" component. Managers who network can do so without much talent or perspective; alternatively, they can correctly assess their organization's environment, allocate their networking skills wisely, and tap and/or protect from the most salient forces in the agency's setting. We can expect a considerable range of quality to be present across the individuals managing public organizations. This chapter explores this aspect of public management.

Doing so is important because a basic tenet of public administration is that the quality of public management can make the difference between success and failure in the delivery of public policy results (Lynn 1984). Despite this widespread belief, the notion has rarely been carefully tested. In this part of the book, we develop a measure of managerial quality suitable for certain kinds of empirical settings and then test whether high-quality management contributes positively to public program performance.[1] Public education, an important policy field, once again provides the context for the investigation (Raffel 2007).

This relatively straightforward test of the management quality hypothesis confronts a number of challenges. The notion of managerial quality itself, although often used in teaching, research, and practice, is seldom clarified in a way that facilitates systematic investigation. Difficulties of measurement on this score have also impeded research. In addition, many other influences shape what happens via public programs, so the research needs to take into account these realities. The next sections of this chapter treat these challenges systematically; then our research on the management quality hypothesis is presented and discussed.

The Gordian concept of public management quality

As indicated earlier, the proposition that public management contributes to the performance of government is at the core of a great deal of scholarship; but few systematic efforts have tested for the relationship empirically. The case study and qualitative literature, on the other hand, indicates that good management can be a particularly critical contributor to program success (see, for instance, Doig and Hargrove 1987, Hargrove and Glidewell 1990, Behn 1991, Thompson and Jones 1994, Ban 1995, Riccucci 1995, Cohen and Eimicke 1995, and Holzer and Callahan 1998). Indeed, this body of work suggests multiple and complex channels of managerial influence.

All the same, the conceptual issues are immense. A consideration of management's hypothesized impact on program performance, for instance, must incorporate some attention to the notion of leadership – a theme of substantial importance among researchers. The literature on leadership is huge and complex, however (see Rainey 2009). Rainey and Steinbauer's (1999: 18–19) succinct characterization serves as a daunting reminder of the difficulties of capturing this key notion in a satisfactory and easily measurable form: "[T]he topic of leadership is vast, richly elaborated, and inconclusive. . . Enough listings of desirable leadership skills and qualities could be gathered to build another great pyramid. They vary widely, and none of them can claim conclusive validation."

The growing emphasis on quality – and quality management – in recent years (see Beam 2001) overlaps the attention to leadership in public programs. Interestingly, an examination of this theme also reveals an unresolved tension as to what kinds of broad managerial efforts are likely to be most critical for delivering performance. Much of the attention to quality or excellence in recent years, in the United States and elsewhere, has focused on the value of "entrepreneurial" management for achieving results. The popularity of Osborne and Gaebler's (1992) volume illustrates this point, and the National Performance Review of the Clinton years – a reform effort with direct intellectual ties to the same perspective – reflected a similar emphasis (Gore 1993; see Rainey 2003: 408–11). The new public management, more broadly, emphasizes these themes. Some analysts have seen in these approaches a diminished view of management, however (Lynn 2001), or one, they argue, likely to limit what public agencies can deliver (see Goodsell 1993 and Moe 1994). Terry (2002) in particular contends that administrators perform a key function by executing "conservatorship": preserving established institutional forms and activities that have developed over time and would be difficult to reestablish (for a more elaborate discussion of this point, see O'Toole and Meier 2007).

Indeed, while risk-taking, entrepreneurial activities can sometimes bring benefits, protective, conserving efforts can be especially valuable under other circumstances (see Meier *et al.* 2007). As we have argued earlier, the multiple managerial functions, which likely work through different causal pathways, should all be considered by those who desire to probe the connection between management and performance. Although this general point may be valid, any systematic effort to explore the link between management quality and performance across a large number of cases must confront a nearly intractable measurement challenge. If high-quality public management embraces a multitude of difficult-to-define dimensions and if different strategic approaches and managerial orientations might be appropriate under different difficult-to-specify conditions, how can one test the proposition that good management contributes to good performance across the spectra of cases and circumstances?

The conceptual complexity thus fuels a serious measurement challenge. In the broader literature beyond the public sector, efforts have been made to measure the quality of management (Bloom and van Reenen 2007), but so far the criteria used have not been applied in empirical studies of public management.

With respect to the public sector, for some years now the Government Performance Project has developed comprehensive measures of government management systems via a criterion-based approach. Most of this research effort has been devoted to measures of management itself, and management capacity, rather than managerial impacts, although some relationships between these measures and managerial (intermediate) outcomes have been demonstrated (Donahue, Selden, and Ingraham 2000).

A few additional notes of progress have been sounded in the effort to probe with systematic work the link between elements of public management and ultimate program performance. Wolf (1993) examines subjective assessments of agency leadership, and finds that these are correlated with agency effectiveness. Hennessey (1998) suggests a relationship between public organizational performance and leadership, defined in terms of Bennis's (1993) four competences, on the basis of data from nine offices in two federal agencies. His core argument is that leaders shape organizational culture and, thereby, performance. Attention is directed primarily to reinvention efforts, however, and only secondarily to performance itself. Further, the small number of cases, subjective measurement of leadership features, and lack of controls attenuate the conclusiveness of the work.

Rainey and Steinbauer (1999) have proposed a "theory of effective government organizations" incorporating a number of features that might explain effectiveness. Several characteristics they analyze are part of, or, at minimum, closely related to, public management – including the development of human resources (see Chapter 5), various elements of task design, and, in particular, leadership characterized by certain attributes. Rainey and Steinbauer craft their argument on the basis of a review of existing literature on the likely determinants of effectiveness. While they do no testing, they do "posit" that leadership is likely to "emerge as" among the most important drivers of effectiveness in governmental organizations (28).

Brewer and Selden (2000) report a systematic empirical project based on Rainey and Steinbauer's theoretical argument. They explain a large portion of the variance in federal employee perceptions of organizational performance, as interpreted in rather broad terms, across twenty-three agencies. The model they develop and test includes a leadership and supervision measure, which is positively related to perceptions of performance, although its predictive power is relatively slight. The measure is limited to employee perceptions of how their immediate supervisors rate; and, as Brewer and Selden note, "leadership and supervision may contribute to organizational performance *indirectly*" (704, emphasis in original). Indeed, several other variables they analyze that contribute more to explaining the variance in performance are likely influenced by management as well.

These findings and arguments are provocative, but they are limited in a number of ways and clearly not definitive. Most of the empirical work is cross-sectional, and it is important to test for the impact of public management by incorporating a longitudinal dimension as well. Most of the measures of performance are perceptual and/or intermediate, and thus may be biased, given that the respondents are evaluating their own performance (see Meier and O'Toole 2010). In addition, the measurements developed thus far capture only a limited part of the concept of quality management as it has been understood by scholars.

If characterizing and measuring managerial quality is challenging, even more demanding is the task of doing so for individuals in specific managerial positions. The general task of individual performance appraisal in the public sector has been notoriously difficult to conduct (Kellough 2006; see also Murphy and Cleveland 1995). The approach adopted in the present investigation does not resolve the host of issues under dispute, but it does rely on decision making by knowledgeable political principals in contact with the particular managers whose impact is being analyzed here. To be precise, the method relies on assessments revealed in salary determinations. This approach might seem ironic, since when individual performance appraisals are used in public agencies to determine pay – so-called "pay for performance" systems – researchers have consistently noted serious flaws (Ingraham 1993; Rainey 2009). Under certain conditions and with certain caveats, we argue below, decisions about pay can provide a defensible indirect measure of management quality, particularly given the conceptual and measurement difficulties associated with developing a more direct yet still feasible alternative (for a similar approach to measuring quality at the middle manager level, see Johansen 2008).

In the next section, we sketch our general approach to measuring managerial quality in the kinds of settings that will be analyzed later: public education via the Texas school districts data set. Our focus is once again on the top managers there: school superintendents. We propose an aspect of managerial salary as a reasonable proxy measure for testing the management quality hypothesis. We then develop the specifics of our empirical measure and finally model our tests of school system performance. We then show how managerial quality can interact with managerial networking to avoid problems of diminishing returns.

Measuring superintendent quality

As outlined above, what is needed from public managers seems to vary by program, agency, time, and context. Any simple measure of the quality of management, therefore, is likely to be biased.[2] Those in the best position to know and evaluate what and how managers are doing are knowledgeable observers in the local setting at the time, particularly those with access to information about managerial behavior, organizational morale, environmental demands, and performance results. The strategy in this study is to tap into the judgments of just such a set of individuals who observe the managers – school system superintendents – on a day-to-day basis: members of the school board.

Rather than seeking attitudinal judgments by the school board on management quality (thus merely moving the problems of definition from researchers to practitioners), we assume that actions reveal evaluations. Each school board makes an annual assessment of the superintendent's performance and then sets his or her salary for the following year. In that determination, we think that management quality plays a role – not an exclusive role, but a role nonetheless. Similarly, deciding the compensation to offer a new superintendent contains an inherent quality assessment.

Quite clearly, political principals face limitations in judging managerial quality – in particular, limitations in access to relevant information. For governmental jurisdictions that perform only one policy function, these limits are less severe. To the extent that political leaders in such situations are interested in attending to the quality of management in their jurisdictions, they know where to look and are undistracted by competing or overlapping responsibilities. School districts are among the governmental jurisdictions fitting this stipulation.

Furthermore, isolating on the managerial quality aspect of a superintendent's salary is facilitated by several characteristics of the market for superintendents. That market can be characterized as competitive with substantial information. School district managerial talent is mobile within the state (and somewhat mobile across states). While some superintendents remain for extended periods in one locale, most individuals typically move through several districts as they pursue their careers. With few exceptions, positions are filled after open searches that are often conducted with the assistance of a search firm. Superintendents seeking to move (the average tenure in Texas is approximately 5.3 years) will know the salary paid to the previous superintendent and can access an extensive state database on the district and its characteristics. Similarly, the hiring district will have extensive information about how the candidate's current district (or school, if it decides to hire a principal) has performed, and assessments of an individual superintendent candidate's management ability are relatively easy to obtain via the established network of school board members. In short, a manager with a good track record is likely to have several options, so that a school district seeking to hire such a manager will need to offer a premium, all other things being equal. There are no regulatory floors or ceilings regarding compensation. The sheer range of salaries in the study ($35,000 to $205,228 in 1999 [mean = $74,400; standard deviation = $24,087]) supports the notion that market dynamics are at work.[3]

Salary premiums operate within a salary structure that recognizes basic understandings about the job, however (see Ehrenberg, Chaykowski, and Ehrenberg 1988a, 1988b). First, the most significant determinant of salaries, both normatively and empirically, is the size of the district; as the size of the job expands, salaries increase proportionately. Second, human capital factors such as education, experience, and training will result in additional adjustments to salaries. Third, personal characteristics of the individual are likely to affect salaries. Particularly relevant are such factors as race, ethnicity, and gender. Although discrimination might play a role here, some districts, such as large inner city districts, will prefer a minority superintendent for political reasons. Fourth, because the relationship between salaries and performance can be expected to be reciprocal – that is, superintendents could also be rewarded for performance in the past – a control for prior school district outputs is needed.

Our strategy of analysis is to take variables measuring each factor that should influence the manager's salary and use them to predict the manager's actual salary. The residual from this equation – that is, the variance in salary not accounted for by job size, human capital, personal characteristics, and past performance – will contain the assessment of managerial quality (for a similar residuals-based measure in a different context, see Palmer and Whitten 1999: 629). This measure is quite clearly a messy one, since the residual contains all those factors not included in the model – such as the ability to sell oneself, experience and renown as a football coach, physical characteristics and other irrelevant factors, as well as the assessment of quality. The impact of this measurement error will attenuate any relationships between the quality measure and organizational outputs, however (Carmines and Zeller 1979; Bollen 1989: 159–67). The measurement error, as a result, creates a bias in favor of null findings.

Measuring managerial quality

How might a superintendent, a single manager at the top of the hierarchy, actually affect student performance? In the last chapter we discussed how external efforts on the part of top managers might shape organizational outputs and outcomes, and in the next chapter we examine some of the details of how internally directed management can contribute. Here we note several causal paths, some internal to the organization and others partially external. Our interactions with superintendents, administrators, and teachers suggest several ways that top managers can boost performance. First, superintendents can recruit, train, and reward talented mid-level administrators (school principals) and teachers. Of particular importance is recruiting individuals who share organizational goals in regard to student standards and approaches to education. Second, superintendents, like all organizational leaders, can motivate employees to invest greater effort in the organization. Superintendents do so by providing and communicating a vision for the organization. They can also generate greater commitment by handling the inevitable problems that arise in the environment; in particular, they can provide political cover for teachers and administrators. Third, superintendents can affect the student learning environment by mandating the adoption of specific educational reforms. The list of possible reforms is endless, and reforms need to be matched to the specific needs of the students and the skills of teaching faculty. Part of this matching process relies on the management ability of the superintendent. Fourth, superintendents can contribute to the predictability and reliability of the system for those who operate within it. They can provide stable processes and avoid the disruptions of policy churn (Hess 1999) and other activities that interfere with the process of educating children.[4] Finally, superintendents can acquire more resources for the organization. While most of these resources will then appear in the district's budget, some may be intangible – for instance, the goodwill of local business leaders or the support of parent groups.

To generate the residuals-based measure of managerial quality, we use a relatively common salary model from the literature (see Ehrenberg, Chaykowski, and Ehrenberg 1988b). The dependent variable is the logged annual compensation for the superintendent. The log transformation is used to ease the problem of skewed data resulting from the large salaries associated with Texas's megadistricts. The log transformation also permits the relationships to be interpreted as elasticities. This salary figure includes only the official base salary; it omits the perks some districts offer, such as club memberships, cellphones, and transportation benefits that are not reported to the state of Texas.

Three district characteristics are included as independent variables: the district's total budget, tax rate, and average revenue per student; all three variables are logged. Total district budget is our measure of district size, which should be the strongest predictor in the model. The tax rate is included because some earlier work contends that superintendents are rewarded for keeping taxes low (Ehrenberg, Chaykowski, and Ehrenberg 1988b). Revenue per pupil is a measure of wealth; certain districts will pay higher salaries simply because they can afford to do so. For some districts this decision is a matter of civic pride.

Four human capital characteristics are included: experience as a superintendent, tenure in the current job, age, and the possession of a doctorate. The first three variables are measured in years; salaries should increase both with total experience as a superintendent (most of this experience will have been in other districts) and time in the current job. Age is commonly included in models such as these, even though it is considered a surrogate for experience, which is already in the model.[5] In terms of education, virtually all superintendents have a master's degree (98 percent), so the most salient distinction is the possession of a doctorate, which should be positively related to salary.

Three personal characteristics are included: whether the superintendent is female, black, or Latino. The predicted signs for these variables are ambiguous, depending on whether a district might see it as an advantage to hire a superintendent with a given demographic. Data on salaries, district characteristics, human capital, and personal characteristics were provided by the Texas Education Agency from their administrative database.

Finally, we include the previous year's test scores in the model. Because we think perceived managerial quality is affected by prior performance, and because quality then affects future performance, over time there is reciprocal correlation. We cannot control for prior test scores without adjusting for this endogeneity, or the quality measure's impact will be biased downward. The appropriate method is to purge the reciprocal causation via an instrumental variables technique. We do this using six student characteristics and district resources (percentage of black, Latino, and low-income students, teacher salaries, class size, and instructional funding) as instruments; the purged measure of prior performance is then included in the model. Five years (1995 to 1999) of data are used in the model, and dummy variables for

Table 4.1 Determinants of superintendent salaries

Dependent variable = logged annual compensation

Independent variable	Slope	Error	T-score
District characteristics			
Logged budget	0.1641	0.0017	95.07
Logged tax rate	0.0272	0.0161	1.69
Logged revenue/pupil	0.0683	0.0092	7.45
Human capital			
Past experience	0.0022	0.0003	7.94
Current job tenure	0.0009	0.0002	3.63
Doctorate	0.0532	0.0045	11.79
Age	0.0004	0.0002	1.95
Personal characteristics			
Female	0.0025	0.0009	2.85
Black	0.0941	0.0183	5.16
Latino	−0.0165	0.0081	2.03
Past performance	0.0009	0.0003	3.16
R^2	0.78		
Standard error	0.1251		
F	1193.92		
N	5,127		

Note: Coefficients for individual years not reported.

individual years are included to account for the general increase in salaries over this time period.

The results of the salary model appear in Table 4.1. The predictive ability of the model (78 percent) compares favorably to other models in the literature; and, with one exception, all the variables are in the predicted direction.[6] That exception is the tax rate, which has a slight positive association with salary rather than a negative relationship, thus indicating that superintendents are not systematically rewarded for keeping taxes low. Although the relationships in the model are interesting in terms of both personnel management and educational policy, discussion of them is beyond the scope of the present investigation. The objective of this part of the analysis is merely to remove as many "non-quality" factors from the superintendent's salary as possible. The regression residuals are then standardized (converted to a mean of zero and a standard deviation of one) for use in the subsequent analysis. Because salaries are set before the school year begins, the quality measure has a natural one-year lag in its relationship to current organizational performance. As a consequence, any relationships that are found can be attributed to quality influencing performance rather than district performance influencing boards' decisions about superintendent compensation.

Modeling performance

Our measure of management quality can now be related to educational performance. Given the preliminary nature of such a measure in public management, this effort might be viewed as an attempt to determine if the measure has external validity – since managerial quality should affect organizational performance when one controls for the resources and constraints on the core organization. The section first identifies the control variables in the model and then discusses the measures of organizational performance.

Control variables

As discussed in earlier chapters, any assessment of organizational performance must control for both the difficulty of the job faced by the organization and the resources in its possession. We use the well-developed literature on educational production functions for guidance and include the same set of control variables used in Chapter 3. These eight variables are three measures of task difficulty and five measures of resources.[7] These are used strictly as controls, to make sure that any findings we have relative to management quality are robust to the inclusion of factors normally linked to educational performance.

Performance measures

This chapter incorporates eleven different performance indicators in an effort to determine if management quality affects a variety of organizational outputs. The most salient is the student pass rate on the Texas Assessment of Academic Skills.[8] Our measure is the percentage of students who pass all (reading, writing, and mathematics) sections of the TAAS.

Four other TAAS measures are also useful as performance indicators. TAAS scores for Anglo, black, Latino, and low-income students are included as measures of performance indicators. TAAS scores are linked most directly to basic skills and performance levels for all students. Many parents and policy makers are also concerned with the performance of school districts regarding college-bound students. Four measures of college-bound student performance are used: the average ACT score, the average SAT score, the percentage of students who score above 1,110 on the SAT (or its ACT equivalent), and the percentage of students who take either test. As mentioned in Chapter 2, Texas is one of the few states where both the ACT and the SAT are taken by sufficient numbers to provide reliable indicators of both.

The final two measures of performance might be termed bottom-end indicators: attendance rates and dropout rates. Dropout rates, while it is conceded that they contain a great deal of error, are frequently also used to evaluate the performance of school districts. The official state measure of dropouts is the annual percentage of students who leave school from eighth grade onward.

Findings

The first school district performance measure assessed is the overall TAAS score; these results are presented in the first two columns of Table 4.2. The proposed measure of managerial quality is positively and significantly related to school district performance. Since the measure is standardized, and thus ranges between approximately −3 and +3, these equations suggest that the maximum impact of quality management is approximately 5.3 points on the TAAS. Although management quality is clearly not the most important factor in determining test scores, in substantive terms 5.3 points is a meaningful amount of change (the standard deviation of TAAS scores is approximately 12.5). To check for omitted variables bias, we ran regressions with forty-one additional variables, without affecting the findings here. These variables included additional student characteristics, budget expenditures in various categories, teacher assignments, and additional measures of district wealth.

To explore a bit more how management quality might work through other factors known to influence performance, a second regression in Table 4.2 adds three variables: parental involvement, community support, and student attendance. Parental involvement and community support were assessed via a superintendents' survey; because they reflect the impressions of the superintendents, these measures might contain some bias.[9] All three new measures are positively associated with organizational performance; in the case of student attendance, the relationship is a strong one. Including these factors in the model reduces the size of the management coefficient.

Table 4.2 The impact of management on performance: standardized tests

Dependent variable = TAAS pass rate

Independent variable	Slope	T-score	Slope	T-score	Slope	T-score
Management quality	0.8866	7.76*	0.4888	3.23*	0.8334	5.13*
Managerial networking	–		–		0.6418	4.27*
Parental support	–		0.3984	2.01*	–	
Community support	–		0.9572	4.51*	–	
Student attendance	–		3.7705	20.90*	–	
R^2	0.59		0.67		0.60	
Standard error	8.00		6.78		7.51	
F	574.29		298.36		264.25	
N	5,126		2,498		2,502	

Notes: Coefficients for annual dummy variables are omitted. Equations also control for teacher salaries, state aid, class size, teacher experience, noncertified teachers, and the percentages of black, Latino, and low-income students. * = significant at $p < 0.05$.

These relationships suggest that some of the impact of quality management operates through increasing community support and parental involvement.[10] Even with the addition of the attendance and support scores, however, management quality as defined in this study has a significant and positive effect on the overall performance of the organization.[11]

This final regression in Table 4.2 includes the managerial networking measure from Chapter 3 (four nodes). Networking is uncorrelated with the managerial quality measure ($R^2 = -0.01$), and thus both positively influence organizational performance. The size of the coefficient changes only because the networking measure is survey-based, and thus the third equation reflects the missing data from survey nonresponse. Controlling for networking has little impact on the strong positive relationship between quality and performance. Because both measures have a mean of zero and a standard deviation of one, they can be directly compared to each other. The impact of managerial quality is about 30 percent larger than the impact of managerial networking on the TAAS scores.

A measure of managerial quality should be general; it should be related to a wide variety of organizational outputs. The relationship should, of course, vary across different measures of outputs, because some problems are likely to be more sensitive to the quality of management in the organization. As problems become more intractable, for example, one would expect that

Table 4.3 Management quality and other measures of performance

Performance measure	Slope	T-score	R^2	N
Latino pass percentage	0.4832	2.53[*]	0.38	4,243
Black pass percentage	0.7014	2.68[*]	0.38	2,965
Anglo pass percentage	0.8700	7.60[*]	0.41	5,053
Low-income pass percentage	0.8998	6.17[*]	0.50	5,093
Average ACT score	0.0817	3.94[*]	0.36	4,248
Average SAT score	3.1534	2.85[*]	0.50	3,516
Percentage above 1,110	0.6535	4.23[*]	0.29	4,682
Percentage tested	0.0113	0.05	0.12	4,601
Dropout percentage	−0.1241	8.21[*]	0.16	5,026
Class attendance	0.0866	7.49[*]	0.24	5,126

Notes: All equations control for teacher salaries, instructional expenditures per student, class size, teacher experience, percentage of teachers not certified, percentage of black, Latino, and low-income students, and yearly dummy variables. [*] = significant at $p < 0.05$.

management would matter less, simply because what the organization could do to solve such problems is more limited.

Table 4.3 presents the regression coefficients for management quality and the ten additional performance indicators. Each equation also controls for all the variables included in the first regression in the table.[12] The performance of the managerial quality variable can be appropriately characterized as stunning. For nine of the ten additional performance indicators, management quality is significantly related to performance in the predicted direction (the exception is the percentage of students who take college boards). This pattern of relationships, along with those in Table 4.2, amounts to strong evidence that the residual-based measure of managerial quality is tapping at least in part some aspects of how well superintendents manage their districts.[13]

We also replicated the results of Table 4.3 and included the managerial networking variable. For all the dependent variables but black pass rates and the percentage of student who took either the SAT or the ACT, the relationships were statistically significant and in the correct direction. As one final robustness check, we reestimated the equations with a lagged dependent variable. Such a test is stringent, since it requires managerial quality to have an impact over and above last year's scores – in short, to continue the improvement that generated the higher salary in the first place. Table 4.4 reports an abridged set of results, which show that managerial quality maintains a statistically significant impact for five of the outcome indicators – Anglo

Table 4.4 Management quality in an autoregressive specification

Performance measure	Slope	T-score	R^2	N
TAAS pass rate	0.1049	1.39	0.84	5,125
Latino pass percentage	0.0782	0.50	0.59	4,398
Black pass percentage	0.3811	1.82*	0.56	2,850
Anglo pass percentage	0.1742	2.16*	0.68	5,037
Low-income pass percentage	0.1293	1.20	0.73	5,083
Average ACT score	0.0435	2.24*	0.47	4,018
Average SAT score	1.4379	1.59	0.68	3,216
Percentage above 1,110	0.3853	2.68*	0.38	4,632
Percentage tested	−0.0441	0.21	0.33	4,485
Dropout percentage	−0.0843	6.19*	0.32	5,024
Class attendance	0.0150	2.17*	0.73	5,125

Notes: All equations control for teacher salaries, state aid, class size, teacher experience, percentage of teachers not certified, percentage of black, Latino, and low-income students, and yearly dummy variables. * = significant at $p < 0.05$.

pass rates, ACT scores, college boards above 1,110, dropouts, and attendance. If the criterion is relaxed to a 0.10 with a one-tailed test, given the direction specified, the results for the overall TAAS rate, the black pass rate, and SAT scores are also significant in the correct direction.

Managerial quality and managerial networking: diminishing returns?

At the outset of this chapter we noted that our measure of managerial networking focused only on the quantity of the networking, not on the quality of the networking. The creation of a management quality measure provides us with the opportunity to investigate further the relationship between managerial networking and organizational performance. What, for example, is the *functional form* of the link between management and performance? Our model specifies some hypothesized relationships, and we have seen that there is evidence in support of some of its clearest notions. What about the details, though? One possibility, of course, is that the two are linked in a straightforward linear fashion over the full range of the management variables: additional increments from management, or various types of management, may add some regular and fairly constant amount of outputs or outcomes. Alternative possibilities, however, are myriad. The relationship might be curvilinear; or there may be diminishing returns; or there may be some critical managerial contribution, past which point performance accelerates more rapidly. Alternatively, the relationship might be exceedingly complex, in which case plotting a management-versus-performance curve might encompass twists and turns of confusing sorts. Sketching the possibilities de novo would produce graphic patterns reminiscent of so many serpents lying in the sand – some stretched out lazily and signaling simple forms, others arching and wiggling across the sand (for a complete exposition of this analysis, see Hicklin, O'Toole, and Meier 2008).

In the initial formulation of the model, we explicitly suggested some nonlinearities – in particular on managerial networking externally into the interdependent environment, and specified nonlinearities with respect to resources and constraints in the organization's setting. A careful further examination of the model and its features suggests that other nonlinearities may also be expected, however. These have to do with, for instance, opportunity costs and potential tradeoffs across different managerial tasks; the potential for diminishing returns from management; and the role that even internal resources, particularly those related to personnel, can play in providing a partial support or substitute for explicit top managerial effort.

This section focuses on one particular managerial responsibility – managerial networking, or managers' interactions externally in support of the public organization and its tasks – in order to explore the nature of the functional form between this aspect of management and organizational performance. The empirical work presented thus far has demonstrated overwhelming support for the positive effect of networking (M_2) on performance. More networking is correlated with an increase in performance, when controlling for resources and constraints in the environment as well as selected other managerial influences. Networking seems to be the gift that just keeps on giving. With the extant evidence, it could be concluded – rather implausibly, granted – that managers who want to increase performance should devote as much time as possible to externally oriented networking.

Does this inference make sense, though? Are there times and circumstances when it is probably better to network less, perhaps in the interest of fulfilling another managerial requisite? Is it possible for managers to devote too much time to managing the external environmental – to the detriment of the organization's performance? Could the benefits of networking be contingent on the characteristics or talents of individual managers? Could organizational characteristics affect this relationship? First we explore the reasons to anticipate a possible nonlinear relationship, and then we outline a number of contingencies that might affect this relationship.

Resources, time, and the managerial balancing act

There are reasons to expect that very high levels of networking may have diminishing, or perhaps even negative, effects on organizational performance. Most of the literature on the benefits of networking focuses on how managers form relationships with other organizations and stakeholders to secure benefits, fend off disruptions, and identify opportunities. Managers often network with others in an effort to attract and acquire more resources for the organization. The environment and the relevant network actors do not have infinite resources, however. While managerial networking should result in considerable payoffs much of the time, there could be a limit to these payoffs – meaning that at some point there is nothing, or, at least, less, to gain from more external interactions.

A related point has to do with opportunity costs. Managers must perform functions internally within their institution, not just outside. At some point, the time spent on trying to extract the last bit from resources or buffer the agency from all potential disturbances could have been better spent elsewhere. The formal model sketched in Chapter 2 implies some sort of balancing between managerial responsibilities without specifying how and when the tradeoffs actually appear. More precisely, the model does not specify the relationship between M_1 (core internal functions) and M_2 (external, or networking, management). Although there is no reason to believe that these two functions are necessarily a zero-sum effort – with a full tradeoff at the margin between the two – managers who spend most of their time on one component to some neglect of the other may generate performance setbacks, or, at least, suboptimal results.

Regardless of whether the limits on the benefits of networking come from increasing difficulty in tapping opportunities/fending off perturbations from the environment, or from tradeoffs among the multiple functions of management,[14] the consequence should be the same: at higher levels of managerial networking, still more networking could be expected to produce little in the way of positive performance payoffs for the organization. This relationship can be tested with an hypothesis: *the relationship between networking and performance is nonlinear, with diminishing returns at the higher levels.*

We might also consider contingencies. Although we expect that, in the aggregate, higher levels of networking will have diminishing effects, some managers and certain public organizations may be able to ensure that time spent networking continues to result in steady performance dividends, even at higher levels of networking. Drawing on the two explanations as to why the relationship may be nonlinear, we can speculate on what types of managers and organizations may be able to avoid diminishing returns.

Indeed, we have already noted two dimensions of such managerial activity as networking: a "quality" or skill component, along with the "quantity" or effort aspect. The original model does not specify the relationship between these two elements, but it seems reasonable to expect that one influences the functional form of the other. The most straightforward way of interpreting the relationship would be that management quality mitigates the otherwise expected diminishing returns hypothesized above.[15] Second, the model clearly suggests that aspects of "management" and aspects of personnel/staffing perform some overlapping functions. Each, accordingly, should be considered for generating nonlinear relationships for managerial networking.

If the explanations for the general, hypothesized nonlinear relationship sketched above are correct, a highly skilled manager might be able to avoid negative returns to networking by being just active enough in the organization's environment to gather the crucial benefits feasibly available. This expectation is grounded in a basic rational choice framework, which suggests that managers are likely to try to assess when the "costs" of networking (in terms of time spent and opportunities forgone) can no longer be expected to be outweighed by the benefits that they expect to reap. The best managers should be more adept at weighing the costs and benefits, and they will therefore be the most efficient with their time, thus avoiding spending too much time in the networked setting, presumably at the expense of other managerial possibilities that also contribute to performance.

This chapter has demonstrated that managers vary considerably in quality, and the abilities of individual managers can have a strong impact on their behavior and their organization's performance. For the best managers, therefore, we may find that this nonlinear effect disappears – a relationship we test with a second hypothesis: *the relationship between networking and performance is positive and linear, when controlling for managerial quality.*

The second explanation as to why increased networking may not always be positively related to performance centers on the tradeoffs made by top managers when choosing to apportion time and effort between internal and external management. Organizations obviously need a certain amount of the former to function properly – what Woodrow Wilson (1887) referred to, in a household analogy, as the "management of the fires and the ovens."

Neglecting these managerial requirements can be expected to result in poor performance. Managers must find the right balance in splitting their time so that internal needs are not neglected and external opportunities are sufficiently exploited. Organizations may differ, however, in the extent to which these tradeoffs bind tightly. Some managers may be able to hire and use administrative staff to take care of straightforward but important internal managerial functions, thus freeing up the top manager to spend more time externally. These staff become managerial capacity – the ability to take action if opportunities arise. If a manager has an executive staff that can coordinate some of these internal management functions (and so an aspect of M_1 – a subject explored more systematically later in this book), significant tradeoffs may be obviated (see Chapter 6). This line of reasoning leads to additional hypotheses: *the relationship between networking and performance is nonlinear for those organizations with fewer administrative staff*; and *the relationship between networking and performance is positive and linear for those organizations with more administrative staff.*

Our argument about the diminishing marginal returns of networking can be tested by simply adding a squared value of networking to our basic equation, with the expectation that the slope for the linear term will be positive and the slope for the squared term negative. For the empirical analysis, we use once again the Texas school districts data set. Our analysis includes our survey data from superintendents as conducted in 2000. To these survey responses, we added eight years of data (1995 to 2002) from the Texas Education Agency.[16] Because this analysis involves a pooled time-series approach, we included dummy variables for the individual years (fixed effects) to deal with serial correlation. We then assessed the degree of heteroskedasticity with pooled diagnostics, and found the levels well within acceptable limits.

Our measure of performance is the percentage of students in a district who passed all (reading, writing, and mathematics) sections of the TAAS. For managerial networking we use the four-node factor score derived from the survey responses. We also include the same measure of managerial quality that was introduced in the preceding empirical analysis. Two sets of hypotheses specify that the nonlinear relationship between networking and performance is conditioned by another variable: administrative capacity. Administrative or management capacity can be measured in a straightforward manner; it is simply the percentage of employees who are classified as central office staff (see Chapter 6). This measure includes assistant superintendents and staff positions such as the business manager, the human resources function, and others, but it excludes staff assigned at the school

Table 4.5 The nonlinear relationship between networking and performance

Dependent variable = student pass rates on TAAS

Independent variables	Linear		Nonlinear	
	Slope	T-score	Slope	T-score
Managerial networking	0.883	7.54	1.970	4.21
Managerial networking squared	–		−0.232	2.40
R^2	0.611		0.612	
F	271.93		245.59	
N	4,182		4,182	

Notes: All equations control for teacher salaries, state aid, class size, teacher experience, percentage of teachers not certified, percentage of black, Latino, and low-income students, and yearly dummy variables. F-test for added variable yields F-statistic of 5.176 and probability of < 0.0165.

level (principals, counselors, etc.). Our eight usual controls, resources and constraints from the environment, are also included in all analyses.

Table 4.5 provides the abridged regression results for the linear and non-linear estimation of managerial networking's impact on performance (control variables not shown). Because managerial networking is a factor score, it has a standard deviation of one; therefore, a one standard deviation change in managerial networking is associated with a 0.883 percentage point increase in TAAS exam pass rates. Over the full range of this variable, this effect size translates into a maximum possible impact of approximately 4.7 percentage points on a district's pass rate for this time period. The impact is both statistically and substantively significant. This result is similar to analyses presented earlier for different time periods.

Table 4.5 displays the results for the nonlinear estimation of managerial networking – that is, it includes a value for networking squared. As predicted, the linear term is positive and significant and the squared term is negative and significant. This pattern represents a classic case of diminishing returns. The slope for managerial networking can be calculated for any value by simply taking the first derivative of the equation and substituting in values. Since the variable's range was rescaled to be positive and runs from 0 to +5.3, the slope is steepest at low levels of networking. At a networking value of 0 (the least amount of contact with other nodes), a one-unit change in networking is associated with a 1.97 point increase in the TAAS pass rate. The impact gradually declines until a networking value of 4.25, where the slope is zero – that is, additional networking above this value does not

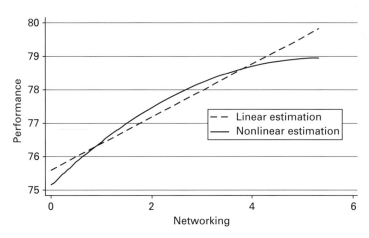

Figure 4.1   Linear and nonlinear relationship

contribute anything further to performance. In the aggregate, therefore, and as the first hypothesis states, the relationship between managerial networking and performance is clearly nonlinear. Figure 4.1 depicts the patterns for the linear and also the more accurate nonlinear estimations graphically. For the latter, the "serpentine" relationship arches gracefully.

We then test the second hypothesis – that, when one controls for quality, the nonlinear relationship is expected to disappear. Table 4.6 presents the findings for the test of this hypothesis. Here it is apparent that the squared term is not significant, although it remains negative. The size of the networking coefficient itself is similar to that in the previous model, meaning that, even when we control for quality, networking is still a significant predictor of performance; managerial networking and managerial quality contribute distinguishable and positive impacts on performance. We no longer see the diminishing returns, however.

Why, exactly, does the nonlinear relationship disappear when we control for quality, as Figure 4.2 shows? Are better managers able to network more effectively (so that they always see returns), or are they able to network more efficiently (they avoid networking to the point where they see diminishing returns)? A simple look at the data can help to answer this question. Whereas the networking variable for the entire sample ranges from 0 to 5.3, the range of networking for the best managers (those managers in the top 5 percent on the quality measure) reaches a maximum value of only 4.32. The highest-quality managers limit their network activities before they generate negative returns. This fact lends some support to the idea that

Table 4.6 Nonlinear effects of networking, controlling for quality

Dependent variable = student pass rates on TAAS		
Independent variables	Slope	T-score
Managerial networking	1.519	3.27
Networking squared	−0.144	1.50
Managerial quality	0.691	5.60
R^2	0.624	
F	235.58	
N	4,114	

Notes: All equations control for teacher salaries, state aid, class size, teacher experience, percentage of teachers not certified, percentage of black, Latino, and low-income students, and yearly dummy variables. F-test for added variable yields F-statistic of 31.35 and probability of $F < 0.001$.

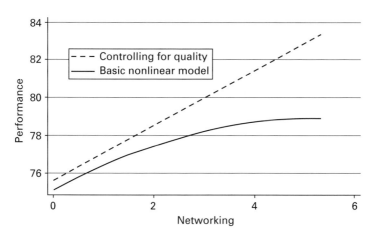

Figure 4.2   Controlling for quality

better managers are more efficient, or at least more perceptive, with the ability to gauge when additional time spent in the networked environment may not garner substantial payoffs.

Organizational differences

To evaluate the third and fourth hypotheses, on the impact of central office staff size on the management–performance relationship, we split the sample into two groups to test for how the presence of administrative human

Table 4.7 Nonlinear effects of networking on performance: impacts of the relative size of central administrative staff

Dependent variable = student pass rates on TAAS		
Independent variables	Smaller central staff	Larger central staff
Managerial networking	1.382 (2.38)	2.978 (2.03)
Networking squared	−0.199 (1.70)	−0.412 (1.28)
R^2	0.69	0.43
F	203.27	18.12
N	2,256	829

Notes: All equations control for teacher salaries, state aid, class size, teacher experience, percentage of teachers not certified, percentage of black, Latino, and low-income students, and yearly dummy variables. T-scores are reported in parentheses.

resources centrally can affect the relationship between networking and performance. We are interested in whether managers who have a greater management capacity as indicated by a larger central administrative staff are able to spend more time networking without seeing the diminishing returns that are present for the sample as a whole. Again, the basic logic is that, when top managers can take advantage of internal help to share in some of the responsibilities, the superintendent is thereby freed up to spend more time on external management that also can reap performance dividends.

Table 4.7 presents the findings for these hypotheses. The two groups into which the sample is split are: those organizations with a leaner administrative staff (operationalized as the percentage of administrators in the district who work in the central district office) and those with a more bulky central administrative staff. The data for this variable has a mean of 1.88 percent. Because the mean is near to two, we split the sample so that the districts with 1 percent or fewer are in the "low central staff" category, and those districts with 3 percent or more are included in the "high central staff" group. We analyzed each subset via multiple regression to see whether the nonlinearities related to central staff and the management–performance question are as hypothesized.

Our results mostly support these two hypotheses. The relationship between networking and performance is nonlinear[17] for superintendents of those districts with fewer administrators in the central office (and thus capable of a lower level of "substitute" or supportive M_1 to assist the top manager), but for districts with more central administrators (and thus a

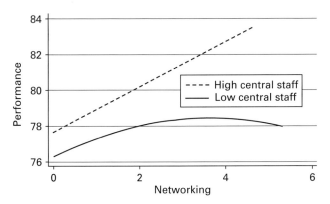

Figure 4.3   Differences by size of central staff

higher M_1 capacity) the relationship between networking and performance is positive, linear, and substantively larger. Figure 4.3 offers a picture of the differences in these relationships, with the former "serpent in the sand" displaying a rather marked curvature, while the latter slithers straight ahead.

This set of findings offers some real evidence that the effect of networking on performance may be contingent on the administrative capacity inside the organization, not merely the effort and skill of the networking top manager. The impacts of public management, in turn, are functions of the activities and skills of multiple managers; and the behavior of one person (or, in this case, the effectiveness of the behavior of one person) may be affected by the presence and activity of other managers in the organizations – in part through processes of adaptation, delegation, and backstopping.

Generalizing the management quality measure

Managerial quality measures have been successfully applied in a number of areas other than Texas school districts. All the studies use regression models similar to those presented in this chapter; all control for a wide variety of other factors that could also influence program outcomes. To retain the focus on the linkage between management and performance, we do not discuss the control variables but, rather, focus on this key relationship. The managerial quality studies cover the broadest range of organizations, including Columbian local governments, federal government agencies, state agencies, the executive office of the US president, and even major league baseball teams (although this last-mentioned group is obviously not a set of *public* organizations). Given this wide range of cases, what "quality" means will vary a great deal. In a developing country, for example, one would not expect the market to generate an intrinsic measure of managerial quality; more rudimentary measures of quality will be used.

Avellañeda (2009a, 2009b) uses the basic theoretical model and applies it to municipal governments in Columbia. Given the location in a developing country and given that local government in Columbia is not highly professionalized, her works suggests that the concept of quality is highly portable to different public sector contexts. Her studies cover forty cities over a several-year period of time. The measure of mayoral quality – the top manager is the elected mayor of the city – includes both level of education and prior service at the local government level. While these would not be impressive indicators of quality in a developed country, there is substantial variation on these features in Columbian municipalities. Avellañeda (2009b) has as her dependent variable the percentage of eligible children who actually attend school; education is a municipal function in Columbia. Despite an extensive set of control variables to deal with structure, politics and elections, socio-demographics, and even citizen displacement by armed groups, she finds that mayoral education and experience are both positively correlated with educational outputs – although the impact is significantly dampened in areas with the presence of armed guerrilla groups. Avellañeda (2009a) relates mayoral quality to the ability to collect greater levels of local property taxes and per capital social spending. Again, the presence of local armed groups has a dramatic negative effect on the positive relationships she finds between managerial quality and program outcomes.

Jacobson, Palus, and Bowling (2010) examine state-level administrators and the adoption of new public management reforms (essentially the use of incentives and the limitation of restrictions on managers). Their purpose is to estimate a model that incorporates both internal management and managerial networking rather than to create a measure of managerial quality; they also find that the manager's level of education is positively related to the adoption of these reforms, however.

Petrovsky (2006) examines federal agencies using the Program Assessment Rating Tool. PART scores, which were discussed briefly in Chapter 1, are an effort initiated by the George W. Bush administration to evaluate federal agencies and programs by using employees of the Office of Management and Budget (OMB) to do the evaluations. Petrovsky's strategy is to pull out the management element of the PART scores and use this as a measure of managerial quality for the agency. There are twenty "Yes" and "No" management questions scored by OMB personnel that focus on various quality aspects of the agency's management. He then uses as a dependent variable a separate performance score created in a similar way that focuses on goal attainment, efficiency, and a series of other factors. Petrovsky finds a consistently strong positive correlation between management quality and agency performance even after correcting for a partisan bias variable.

In a somewhat different type of study using the basic management model, Hill (2009) attempts to determine the impact of managerial turnover on performance using a pooled time-series analysis of North American major league baseball teams. As part of the analysis, Hill creates a reputation-based measure of managerial quality. His analysis with an extensive set of controls shows that managerial quality matters for two measures of performance: whether the team scores more runs than expected and whether the team wins more games than predicted (Hill 2009: 565).

Cohen, Vaughn, and Villalobos (2010), using the formal theory specified in Chapter 2, examine the management practices of the chief of staff in the US Office of the President. Their dependent variable is how effective the chief of staff is as rated by a survey of experts in the administration. Although they present two variables – the chief of staff's experience and the chief of staff's working relationship with the president – as stability measures, both are very similar to the quality measures in the Columbian mayors study. Both measures of experience/quality are positively related to the perceived effectiveness of the chief of staff.

Conclusions

The analyses in this chapter offer three principal contributions. First, we develop and apply an uncommon measure of public management quality, thus fleshing out an aspect of managerial influence that is implicit in our model but that was not tapped directly with our examination of managerial networking. The application of the quality measure relies on avoiding an underspecified model for explaining salary variations, as well as on the notion that the mobility, information, and compensation for managers in the empirical setting approximate the labor market assumptions of neoclassical economics. We have argued that both conditions hold here. To the extent that these conditions do not hold, in fact, we would expect null results. This chapter, therefore, offers an innovative, albeit indirect, overall measure of public management quality. The most important limitation here has to do with the specialized nature of the measure, or, at least, its restricted applicability. Most settings of interest do not approximate the required conditions, although investigations of some other situations – certain additional educational systems (see Johansen 2008), some public authorities, or quasigovernmental entities, for instance – might be able to use and perhaps improve on the approach taken here.[18] Tapping public management quality in many other circumstances, however, will require tackling more directly some of the tough issues about what quality means, how it is related to leadership, and from what sources the requisite quality judgments can be derived.

Second, this research offers the fullest rigorous test to date of the proposition that public management quality contributes positively to performance. The results are clear and convincing. If the assumption is made that the measure of quality is valid, then the almost completely consistent results across eleven measures of performance are firm evidence indeed.[19] That these results obtain despite any likely measurement error for management quality creating a bias toward null findings is particularly striking. With all the appropriate controls for the educational setting, the quality of superintendents' management makes a difference. Whether the focus is on pass rates, dropout rates, or the performance of specialized groups of students, such as those from low-income families or those aiming to attend college, management matters considerably. This set of results is even more striking given that the focus here is on only one managerial position – that of superintendent – at the top of the district's organizational structure. Since almost all school systems include additional managerial layers – at a minimum, school principals – the overall impact of management is probably even higher (see Johansen 2008).

The relationship of management quality to performance is also likely to be complex. The impact of management quality appears to be partially channeled through the mobilization of parental and community support. In addition to contributing directly to operations, then, and to dealing with political principals and external regulatory authorities, managers appear to contribute to performance by mobilizing the efforts of others who have allied interests in delivering results at the local level.

Third, managerial networking contributes positively to performance, but the returns diminish at higher levels of networking. This finding is consistent with our notions that managers apportion time and effort *across* managerial functions, presumably because multiple contributions are needed, and the distribution of managerial time and effort is likely driven in part by managerial assessments of marginal returns to performance. It is also consistent with a conceptualization of public management as goal-directed activity aimed at coordinating people and resources to produce public value. Almost any model of the manager as an intendedly rational actor would imply a consideration of just such tradeoffs.

Even more interesting is the additional set of findings concerning the functional form of this relationship. How does managerial quality mediate the relationship? As the results displayed in Table 4.6 and Figure 4.2 attest, skillful managers are able to avoid diminishing returns; and additional evidence suggests that they do so, at least in part, by economizing on their investment in external interactions – thereby avoiding too much of a good thing. High-quality management thus contributes directly – and also via its influence on the shaping of at least one important, externally directed management activity.

These findings are also consistent with the argument supporting the model, but it is helpful to note that they focus only on the behavior and influence of the top manager. The justification for the model, plus virtually the entire literature of the field, indicates that contributions of additional actors supporting the management function should also matter. While we do not test this proposition directly, we do so obliquely by examining the extent to which central staff capacity supportive of top management can reduce the internal/external tradeoff for school district superintendents. The findings (Table 4.7 and Figure 4.3) support the argument that central staff can buttress performance by supporting and contributing to internal management, thereby eliminating – or, at least, substantially reducing – the need for top managers to balance their internal and external responsibilities. By contrast, low central staff capacity can mean not only diminishing returns but, past a certain point, negative returns on performance from additions to external managerial effort. Bulking up with central staff should not be considered mere administrative padding, however; staff do entail fixed costs, and these need to be considered in managerial decisions. When we incorporate a full set of controls regarding resources and constraints, though, our analyses show that significant staff capacity is supportive of performance, and some of this contribution is apparent in the way that *others*, particularly top managers, are able to add performance value. Substantial central staff capacity alters the pattern of the externally conjured "serpent in the sand."

All these findings are consistent with themes developed by astute observers and analysts of public management. That public management quality matters, of course, is hardly news to specialists in public management and public policy. The field of public administration has developed a rich literature arguing for this notion; but to find management quality influencing performance directly, and consistently, in a data set spanning hundreds of governments over a several-year period is particularly persuasive evidence. While this chapter reports in detail on only one set of administrative units – and in one policy field, at one level of government, and, in fact, at only one level of management within that set – it indicates clear support for theoretical arguments that have been articulated for years by scholars and practitioners in the field. Any who doubt the importance of management and managerial quality for what can be delivered by public education in the United States should note the implications of this analysis for identifying a critically important point of leverage: in Texas, at a minimum, public management quality itself, not simply influences such as district spending or students' home circumstances, makes a difference. Furthermore, the consistent support for the importance of managerial quality in a number of other recent studies far removed from education in Texas suggests the general nature of the relationship.

In many respects, the results of this set of investigations are suggestive. Considerable additional work is warranted. The links between public management in its various additional guises and the results of interest to multiple stakeholders need to be explored more thoroughly, as is done in other chapters of this book. Even more work needs to focus on settings beyond those of public education. Considering the issues in the broadest possible context will require additional conceptual, theoretical, and measurement advances. More complex models need to be considered, as a part of this agenda. In addition, the implications for public managers themselves need to be unpacked more fully. In short, even if it can now be argued with persuasive evidence that the quality of public management shapes policy outputs, most of the important challenges remain to be addressed.

NOTES

1. Much of the material covered in this chapter has been presented by Meier and O'Toole (2002). We have redone the analysis to include managerial networking in the equations and have also included analysis by Hicklin, O'Toole, and Meier (2008).
2. Alternatively, it might be tautological: good management is whatever seems retrospectively to have produced good results – a special problem when perceptual measures of both management and performance are used (see Wolf 1993).

3. Since 1999 superintendent salaries in the large districts have approached $400,000.

4. In the next chapter we analyze another stability-relevant theme: personnel and managerial stability, and how these influence performance.

5. The two are moderately correlated, but the relationship is not strong enough to pose a collinearity problem.

6. In analyses in subsequent chapters in which managerial quality is included as an hypothesized influence on performance, we use a measure calculated in the same way. Recalculating the residuals-based measure with other, more recent, time series data produces an even higher predictive ability in the salaries' equation.

7. The number of candidates for inclusion in education production functions is virtually limitless. Because many of the variables measure the same thing or relatively similar things, collinearity in these models is a problem. As a result, some variables may have an inappropriate sign. Because our concern is with having sufficient controls in the model rather than estimating the precise impact of each control variable, we are less concerned with collinearity.

8. In a 2000 survey of superintendents by the authors, 45.5 percent of superintendents rated TAAS scores as their top priority; no other goal was endorsed by more than 13 percent of superintendents. An additional 46.8 percent of superintendents rated TAAS scores as "very important." Surveys in later years show an even higher priority for TAAS or its replacement.

9. The specific question asked the superintendent to rate parental involvement and community support on five-point scales that ranged from excellent to inadequate. This 2000 survey had a 57 percent response rate, thus reducing the total number of cases for analysis.

10. A path analysis of the results of this second analysis shows that 72 percent of the impact of management quality is direct, with the other 28 percent indirect through community and school board support.

11. Note that we are limiting our analyses to linear specifications in this portion of the chapter. We recognize that our measure of managerial quality is likely to be controversial. To provide focus on the management quality measure, therefore, we have opted for relatively simple models of management. As explained early in this book, we believe that management operates in a contingent and nonlinear manner conditioned by structural context. Some of the chapters include analyses involving more complex models of management.

12. When community and school board support are included in the equations, the results are similar, except that the impact of management on black TAAS scores is no longer significant.

13. The n-size varies for these equations because the state reports results only when five or more students per district meet the category. Some districts, for example, do not have sufficient minority students to generate results.

14. The most likely answer of all is: from both.

15. The relationship between managerial quality and performance is not subject to these diminishing marginal returns and has a strictly linear relationship.

16. The difference in years reflects when the original analysis was done. Replicating all the analysis with 1995–2002 data produced similar results.

17. The squared term is significant only at the 0.10 level.
18. We believe that this approach will work for other management positions subject to competitive markets for which measures of program performance are available. Municipal agency heads such as fire chiefs, police chiefs, and public works heads may fit these conditions in some jurisdictions.
19. Alternatively, if one views this empirical study as a check on external validity, as explained earlier, the results are highly encouraging.

5 Internal management and performance: stability, human resources, and decision making

We have now seen evidence that managerial networking helps to shape organizational performance and also that the quality of management makes a difference for outputs and outcomes. We have explored these matters first in this book because we tackled them early in our research program. Much of what public managers do involves activity and decisions within the organization, however. This set of possible managerial efforts is represented by the M_1 term in our model introduced in Chapter 2:

$$O_t = \beta_1(S + M_1)O_{t-1} + \beta_2 X_t/S_e(M_3/M_4) + \varepsilon_t$$

In the model, the term seems straightforward enough, but that appearance can be deceptive. The reason is that most of what has conventionally been treated as public management consists of various aspects of internal management – management within and of the organization – rather than actions directed externally. The forms of internal management are myriad. They include the various aspects of managing people, or human resources management – such as hiring, orienting new personnel, classifying positions, defining jobs, retaining and promoting people, disciplining and even firing employees, counseling staff, crafting training and development programs, handling grievances and other complaints, resolving interpersonal disputes, dealing with issues of diversity, and much more. Internal management also involves many other functions, including managing and allocating budgets, operating financial management systems, structuring and restructuring work units and tasks, motivating personnel, shaping the culture of the organization, and – in some organizations – using performance data to help manage various of these other managerial operations.

Internal management, in short, is not a simple and undifferentiated function but, instead, encompasses the bulk of the managerial functions mentioned in Chapter 1. It would probably be a job of a lifetime, or even more than that, to try to estimate the independent and combined effects of all these varied and complex aspects of internal management on public organizational performance. No researchers have taken on this Herculean task; and, even if some do, chances are that they would have modest success at best. What we have done is to tackle three limited and yet substantively significant parts of internal management to explore its performance results: maintaining organizational stability, managing human resources, and making effective decisions.

We explore these aspects of internal management because of their obvious importance in virtually all organizations. Given the kinds of organizations involved in public education and the nature of our core data set, we can expect the internal management of school districts to be a critical element in their overall performance. Three aspects of internal management can be distinguished. One is the longevity, or stability, of staff and management in an organization. For various reasons, sheer stability in terms of the human capital in an organization might be expected to boost performance (but see Meier and Hicklin 2008). A second is the quality of human capital in the organization and its effective management. Quality and the management of it should contribute to results, for obvious reasons. After all, it is not only the quality of top management overall that can be important, but also the quality of the workforce – and the efforts to develop it. A third aspect is the ability to make good decisions, particularly when faced with major problems. To examine this situation, we analyze what school districts do when faced with a budget crisis. What actions do they take to limit the impact of budget cuts on organizational performance?

These matters do not completely cover the full range of internal management issues and challenges, of course, and they certainly do not reach many other aspects of internal management that can be important in public organizations.[1] Exploring them should nonetheless provide some insights regarding the role of internal management in helping to shape results.

Stability, change, and the performance of public organizations

Ideas swing wildly in and out of fashion; take, for instance, the notion of stability in administrative organizations. For decades conventional wisdom simply assumed that stability contributes to public management performance. Such core bureaucratic features as standard operating procedures, regular structure, incremental decision making, and fixed rules are emblematic of the persisting features of such organizations. At least since the early years of the last century, scholars linked stable patterns to efficient functioning. As explained in Chapter 2, stability has often been seen as virtually the *sine qua non* of bureaucracy (Gerth and Mills 1958: 228).[2]

The literature on public management in recent decades has heavily emphasized the contrary themes of organizational change, adaptability, entrepreneurship, and reform, however. The term "bureaucracy" has become equated with stodgy, hidebound, and inefficient operations. Much emphasis among recent proponents of good government has been on ways to escape from or banish bureaucracy (Osborne and Plastrik 1997) – and move toward alternative forms and processes.

In this section of the chapter, we begin a systematic empirical exploration of the link between an aspect of stability and public organizational performance. We use the Texas school district data set to do so. We establish a basis for this inquiry by reviewing features of the relevant literatures, clarifying the core concept, and narrowing the empirical focus to one aspect of stability: constancy in personnel.

Stability and public management: an out-of-fashion statement

Our analysis of personnel stability in public organizations can be put into a broader context: the general role of stability in administrative systems. Few ideas these days seem as retrograde as the quaint notion that stability can be helpful in the world of public management. One need only look as far as the high-visibility "Innovations in government" project supported over many years by the Ford Foundation and centered at the Kennedy School of Government at Harvard. Similarly, the National Performance Review during the Clinton–Gore years emphasized the advantages of freeing agencies from the heavy hand of extant structures and processes. Successive waves of administrative reforms have stressed different and sometimes conflicting "solutions" to a broad set of managerial challenges, with the common premise that a disruption of existing patterns was beneficial (Light 1997). The impetus for innovation is just as lively within particular policy fields. Educational policy, for example, has emphasized curricular changes, the introduction of new technologies, the recruitment of new teachers, and new kinds of teachers, along with an assortment of organizational and incentive-based experiments ranging from high-stakes testing to merit pay to charter and magnet schools (Elmore 1997). Nothing seems hotter than novelty.

Scholarly experts in public management have similarly pushed themes that critique stability. Organizational change, organizational development and renewal, planned change, and, of course, the range of efforts to spark a new public management in many countries have been of intense interest to researchers, particularly those desirous of "breaking through bureaucracy" (Barzelay and Armajani 1992). Research has followed the manifold governmental efforts to innovate and reform, with particular attention to determinants of innovation and how to develop and institutionalize change (for a review of these themes and some of this literature, see Rainey 2003, especially 355–89; for a comparative cross-national consideration of NPM, see Barzelay 2001). While innovation has produced considerably less than its strongest proponents claim (Light 1998), the emphasis remains clearly positive (see Altshuler and Behn 1997). Some work has been influential among practitioner and research audiences alike (Osborne and Gaebler 1992), and additional dimensions of the innovations theme continue to be advocated (Behn 2001). Stability, in contrast, rusts at the bottom of the public manager's toolbox.

Despite the attention given to change, reform, and entrepreneurship, some dissents can be heard. Terry (2002) has critiqued the perspectives sketched above and argues strongly, instead, for the importance of "administrative conservatorship," whereby administrative leadership cultivates and protects the core competences, values, and institutional elements of agency life that are accumulated over extended periods. Administrative executives, Terry indicates, are "*conservators* because they are entrusted with the responsibility of preserving the integrity of public bureaucracies and, in turn, the values and traditions of the American constitutional regime" (Terry 2002: xv, emphasis in original; see also Spicer and Terry 1993).

Distinct but similar arguments have been offered by a disparate set of scholars. The Blacksburg group has emphasized the importance of a long-term "agency perspective" that may serve as a guarantor of the public interest (Wamsley *et al.* 1990). Kaufman, particularly in his classic *The Forest Ranger* (1960), shows administrative routines and ingrained patterns of oversight to be important "centripetal forces" that lend coherence to an otherwise chaotic policy setting rife with opportunities for atomistic decision making.

Indeed, motivating the study reported here is the notion that stability is not necessarily the bane of those committed to high performance, but can offer opportunities for enhanced program achievement. Although this proposition had been a truism of standard organization theory (see Perrow 1986), it seems to have become lost in the rush to embrace entrepreneurial notions of public management, the enactment of innovations of all sorts, and various forms of reinvention and change.[3]

Stability in administrative systems

As we have observed several times, administrative systems are fundamentally inertial: once put into operation, they tend toward stability. Earlier we noted that stability means, quite simply, constancy in the design, functioning, and direction of an administrative system over time. Administrative stability can be seen along a number of related but distinguishable dimensions.[4]

Structural stability: the preservation of organizational features over time. Structural stability itself is multidimensional and includes such elements as size, formalization, differentiation, span of control, and so forth.

Mission stability: the consistency over time of the goals of an administrative unit. When bureaus are asked to change course with frequency, they may experience disruptions. One of the distinctive features of public agencies, furthermore, is that their mission is for the most part externally determined (Wilson 1989): policy changes, as established by political executives, legislatures, and/or judicial determinations, exert profound impacts on the missions of agencies and therefore on the stability these units experience.

Production or *technology stability*: Lynn, Heinrich, and Hill (2000) contend that governance systems are characterized by a mode of production or type of technology, and that altering the form of production essentially shifts governance arrangements.[5] Analysts of public administration have long been aware of the importance of agency technology, particularly "core technology" (Thompson 1967).

Procedural stability: Related to production but distinct from it is the set of rules, regulations, and standard operating procedures used in a public agency. Units pursuing the same missions with similar technologies sometimes develop quite different procedures for getting the job done. Welfare-to-work programs illustrate this variation across the United States and even across offices within a given state (Sandfort 1999). Stable procedures create opportunities for coordinating action across large numbers of individuals without overwhelming their capacity (Allison 1971).

Personnel stability: The types of stability mentioned above all deal with features of the administrative system. Bureaucracy, according to Weber, is characterized by career employees, so an additional element of stable administration is the people who occupy positions within the organization. If the positions and/or their relationships shift over time, a system experiences instability. Even if the structural and procedural aspects remain constant and the goal of a public agency persists, however, changes in the personnel themselves can represent an important variety of instability.

Personnel stability

Personnel stability is the focus of empirical analysis in this section of the chapter. Selection criteria, motivation, and agency incentive systems have often received scholarly attention (Ban and Riccucci 2002). The stability of the personnel over time has been much less frequently explored, though. One reason may be the classic view that individuals within the system are "career" bureaucrats.[6]

Leadership stability has been a concern, however; a point of persistent tension between US politicos and career appointees is the relative impermanence of the former, who constitute, in the famous phrase of Heclo (1977), a "government of strangers." Turnover among politicos has exacerbated the difficulties involved in building competence, mutual trust, and long-term commitment (see Dunn 1997).

Other aspects of personnel instability have received some attention recently. A few jurisdictions have abandoned commitments to lifetime merit appointments in favor of flexibility and responsiveness; the state of Georgia, for instance, no longer offers job protection to new employees. At the national level, analysts have noted that careers in public service have become more varied. Those seeking such careers, particularly individuals with advanced degrees in public affairs, now work in the private and nonprofit sectors as well as in government; they are much more likely to change agencies, organizations, and even sectors several times over the course of a career (Light 1999). While these flows of human resources can bring fresh perspectives to public organizations, they may also engender complications.

Personnel experts sometimes express concern about burnout-generated turnover (Golembiewski 1990). In public education itself, personnel shortages in key fields such as mathematics and science have made headlines in recent years, and teacher burnout has been the object of policy change in a number of jurisdictions. Educational system administrators have been increasingly difficult to recruit for extended tours of duty (Hess 1999). Ironically, then, even as public management and public education press for change, concerns have been raised about the performance consequences of personnel instability.

In this section we explore this issue by estimating models of how personnel stability influences school district performance in Texas. We are interested especially in two forms of personnel stability: the durability of top-level public managers and the retention of front-line teaching professionals.

Why should either type of stability matter? Top managers navigate in a complex environment; they need time to learn the basic demands of the job. Assessing the surroundings, both inside and outside the administrative system, can take time. Even the most skillful managers can be expected to improve efficacy by learning their institutional, political, resource, personal, and administrative contexts. Time also permits other stakeholders to ascertain top management's intent and style. Over an extended period, and particularly among managers who do high-quality work, this familiarity can breed trust. Top managers who have developed reputations can use longevity to exercise power.[7]

Stability alone, of course, is not management's sole contribution to program performance. The quality of management exhibited by a given manager can be expected to have an impact. Moreover, the sheer degree of managerial activity devoted to monitoring and negotiating the external environment can also pay off, as we have seen earlier. Accordingly, the analysis reported below considers these additional dimensions of management as well as the issue of stability.

Front-line professional workers, particularly in so-called "street-level bureaucracies" (Lipsky 1980) that deal with unpredictable needs and demands from clients, can also benefit from longer periods on the job. Extended time in high-stress front-line positions can lead to burnout and departure, of course; but, for those who endure, the multifaceted skills acquired in the "trenches" can make a significant difference in performance. Classroom teaching surely fits this pattern. Veteran teachers learn how to juggle the many tasks involved in delivering high-quality instruction. They gradually see how to translate pedagogical theories into workable practices in their own particular setting. They also can learn over time how to sort through the distractions that can absorb energy and attention during a school day. They will have developed experience with difficult cases and multicultural nuances. Many of these craft-like skills, developed through years of experience, are only partially transferable to other districts with different mixes of students and different curricula. Sheer time in position in a local setting can help.

These characterizations offer a rationale for the hypothesis that personnel stability on the part of both top-level managers and front-line workers can assist in delivering program outputs. In the next subsection we place this stability hypothesis into our more general model of public management and public program performance.

Modeling the impact of stability

In considering the hypothesized impact of personnel stability – and stability more generally – upon the performance of an administrative system, we begin with our general model:

$$O_t = \beta_1(S + M_1)O_{t-1} + \beta_2(X_t/S_e)(M_3/M_4) + \varepsilon_t$$

In the model, the Ss are composites of the various kinds of stability outlined earlier: structural stability, mission stability, and so forth. More stability means that current operations in an agency have more impact on future performance – that is, the larger the impact of the autoregressive term and the smaller the impact of the second, or "environmental," term.

Although we expect many kinds of stability to matter for public agencies, the focus here is on personnel stability, or S_P. Other aspects of stability within public organizations, such as school systems, are also worthy of investigation, when appropriate measures for them are available.[8] "Personnel stability" itself is something of an abstraction, in that different kinds of personnel can exhibit different degrees of stability. This analysis focuses on personnel stability for two kinds of system employees: top system managers (school district superintendents) and front-line workers (teachers).

Although the model treats stability as something separate from public management, it is clear that management itself influences personnel stability. In certain important respects, therefore, personnel stability is another aspect of M, or management – primarily internal management, or M_1. Since the terms S (including S_P) and M_1 are additive and thus substitutable in our formalization of the theory, it makes no difference for estimation purposes as to whether we regard personnel stability as stability or as management. Clearly, it is both.

In analyzing the impact of personnel stability on performance, we also include our measures of managerial quality and managerial networking; we already have seen considerable evidence that they shape outputs and outcomes. Since probing for multiple nonlinear impacts of personnel stability via a single research design is impractical, we simplify the model further for present purposes by retaining stability only in the first term of the model. The upshot is a deliberately underspecified model designed to explore some of the issues raised in the general formulation. With these adjustments, the model reduces to

$$O_t = \beta_1(S_P + M_Q)O_{t-1} + \beta_2(M_2X_t) + \varepsilon_t$$

The particular interest in this investigation is personnel stability – both of top managers and of front-line workers. Since the autoregressive form means that a large part of any variance is likely to be explained by the lagged dependent variable O_{t-1}, it can be difficult to pick up the influence of other variables. Accordingly, we test both this model and a further simplified form that excludes the lagged dependent variable:

$$O_t = \beta_1 S_P + \beta_2 M_Q + \beta_3(M_2X_t) + \varepsilon_t$$

Both equations are used in the analysis here. Our usual set of eight appropriate controls, represented by X_t, a vector of environmental forces, is included in the analysis.

Once again we use data drawn from a set of Texas school districts. We incorporate superintendent responses from our initial survey and pooled five years (1995 to 1999) of data on performance and control variables to produce a total of 2,535 cases for analysis.

Personnel stability can be a recurring issue in such districts. School district managerial talent is mobile within the state (and somewhat mobile across states). While some superintendents remain for extended periods in one locale, most individuals move among several districts as they pursue their careers. Further, districts themselves seek to replace their superintendents for various reasons. This movement inevitably means instability at top managerial levels; those in the system must adjust to a new top manager and that person's influence on a range of district decisions. Indeed, shifts in the top managers often trigger other personnel changes near the top, among deputies, assistant superintendents, principals, and so forth. The average tenure of superintendents in Texas is 5.3 years in their positions; their mean tenure within the district in any capacity is 8.7 years.

Stability in the teacher corps should matter as well. Inexperienced teachers are likely to be less effective as they engage in trial-and-error searches to determine which of their academic skills actually matter in the classroom. The teacher shortage in particular specialties compounds the difficulty. To recruit new teachers on a regular basis, at the very least, school systems must devote significant budgetary resources to human resources management.

Some systems find it necessary to take particularly sizable and costly efforts; the Houston Independent School District, for instance, employs a recruiter in Moscow, Russia. The average period of teacher experience in Texas school districts is 11.6 years.

Measures of personnel stability

We examine two measures of personnel stability: one for school district superintendents (managerial stability) and a second for school district teachers (teacher stability). Managerial stability is simply the number of years the superintendent has been employed by the district *in any capacity*.[9] Teacher stability is measured as the percentage of teachers employed by the district during the preceding year who continue to work for the district this year. In other words, teacher stability is measured as 100 minus the year's turnover rate. The mean for this variable is 85.1 percent with a standard deviation of 8.1.[10] For both measures, higher scores mean more stability. Interestingly, the two forms of stability are unrelated to each other empirically (the correlation is 0.09), thus suggesting that different forces shape personnel patterns in these two loci.

Other measures

Two measures of public management are included as potential explanatory variables in this analysis: managerial quality and managerial networking. Both measures have been introduced in earlier chapters. Eight control variables, all introduced earlier, are included; three are measures of task difficulty and five measures of resources.

We use ten performance measures in this portion of our analysis: the overall student pass rate on the Texas Assessment of Academic Skills, TAAS scores for Anglo, black, Latino and low-income students, three measures of college-bound student performance (average ACT score, average SAT score, and the percentage of students who score above 1,110 on the SAT (or its ACT equivalent)), along with attendance rates and dropout rates.

Findings

The first line of analysis here focuses on explaining the overall TAAS pass rate. Table 5.1 displays abridged results of regression analyses for two

Table 5.1 The impact of management on performance: standardized tests II

Dependent variable = TAAS pass rate

Independent variable	Slope	T-score	Slope	T-score
Managerial networking	0.6846	4.58*	0.1977	1.96*
Management quality	0.9182	5.57*	0.1732	1.56
Stability – teachers	0.1374	5.53*	0.0511	3.05*
Stability – managers	0.0739	4.51*	0.0251	2.27*
Lagged pass rate	–		0.7083	55.04
R^2	0.61		0.82	
Standard error	7.43		4.99	
F	239.58		678.43	
N	2,503		2,503	

Notes: Coefficients for annual dummy variables and control variables (teacher salaries, state aid, class size, teacher experience, noncertified teachers, and the percentages of black, Latino, and low-income students) are not shown. * = significant at $p < 0.05$, one tailed test. Time period = 1995–9.

models, the first omitting the autoregressive term and the second including it.[11] The tables omit the coefficients for the control variables.

In each equation, both measures of personnel stability are positively and significantly related to school district performance. The impact of teacher stability is slightly more than that for managerial stability in both cases. While clearly not the most important determinant of districts' standardized test performance, both kinds of stability contribute to the explanation.

Since the measure of teacher stability in the sample ranges between 44.4 (55.6 percent of a district's corps of teachers departed in one year)[12] and 100 (zero turnover), the maximum impact of teacher stability is considerable: more than 7.6 percentage points on a district's pass rate, if the equation without the lagged dependent variable is used, and almost three percentage points even in the much more stringent autoregressive specification.[13]

Managerial stability also contributes to district performance. Here the measure is in years of experience in the district; since the range in the data set is forty-one years, the maximum impact of this feature is less but still worth noting: approximately three percentage points or one percentage point on the pass rate, respectively, depending on whether the equation excludes or includes the lagged pass rate. Since the two elements of stability are uncorrelated, the combined maximum impact of stability could amount to almost eleven percentage points.[14] Considering the short shrift given such unglamorous organizational features as stability in recent years, these positive performance impacts are quite remarkable. Clearly, some enhancement in outcome is due to the leverage gained by retaining those who know the system and applying their talents to the educational and managerial tasks at hand.

In addition, management itself is positively and significantly related to district performance on pass rates. In the first equation reported in Table 5.1, both measures of management boost performance, beyond the impact attributable to personnel stability. Since both management measures are standardized and thus range between approximately −3 and +3, these equations suggest that high-quality management's maximum impact is approximately 5.5 points on the TAAS, and managerial networking's maximum impact is approximately 4.1 points. Even while taking into account the stability impacts, therefore, management quality and networking influence district pass rates. For the equation including the lagged dependent variable, managerial networking continues to have a positive and statistically significant impact while management quality has the correct sign but just misses the 0.05 threshold for statistical significance.

Taken as a whole, the analyses reported in Table 5.1 constitute evidence that management and stability affect school district performance. The fact that even the autoregressive form of the production function continues to show the importance of personnel stability as well as management is a particularly impressive demonstration.

The overall pass rate on the TAAS exam is an important and salient measure of school district performance, but not the only one. Table 5.2 presents the regression coefficients for the four stability and management variables for the nine additional performance indicators. Table 5.3 repeats the same analyses but with the inclusion in each case of the lagged dependent variable.

The results in Table 5.2 support our theoretical arguments regarding stability and confirm the importance of management as well. Of the thirty-six coefficients reported, all but three are properly signed; approximately two-thirds are statistically significant.[15] In every analysis, one or more of the stability and/or management variables are statistically significant. In seven of the nine additional analyses, one or both measures of personnel stability are statistically significant; in eight of the nine analyses, the same can be said for one or both of the management measures. *Both stability and management contribute positively to performance in statistically significant ways in all but three estimations.* This pattern is strong evidence that personnel stability contributes to educational performance,

Table 5.2 Management, stability, and other measures of performance

Performance measure	Management		Stability		R^2	N
	Networking	Quality	Teacher	Manager		
Latino pass percentage	0.5394 (2.07)*	0.7722 (2.74)*	0.0634 (1.37)	0.0659 (2.36)*	0.36	2,283
Black pass percentage	0.4920 (1.29)	0.5691 (1.47)	0.3417 (4.54)*	0.1093 (2.93)*	0.37	1,548
Anglo pass percentage	0.7728 (5.20)*	0.7986 (4.88)*	0.1347 (5.44)*	0.0781 (4.79)*	0.45	2,475
Low-income pass percentage	0.2693 (1.42)	0.9401 (4.48)*	0.1345 (4.20)*	0.1265 (6.07)*	0.52	2,492
Average ACT score	0.0445 (1.64)	0.0932 (3.14)*	−0.0072 (1.41)	0.0018 (0.64)	0.36	2,196
Average SAT score	3.7900 (2.59)*	3.6348 (2.28)*	0.8699 (2.96)*	0.1592 (1.05)	0.50	1,814
Percentage above 1,110	0.3743 (1.89)*	0.7481 (3.40)*	0.0636 (1.81)*	−0.0185 (0.86)	0.30	2,387
Dropout percentage	−0.0368 (1.76)*	−0.1014 (4.40)*	−0.0006 (0.17)	−0.0016 (0.71)	0.16	2,483
Class attendance	−0.0015 (0.10)	0.0655 (3.89)*	0.0120 (4.71)*	0.0000 (0.02)	0.24	2,503

Notes: T-scores in parentheses. All equations control for teacher salaries, instructional expenditures per student, class size, teacher experience, percentage of teachers not certified, percentage of black, Latino, and low-income students, and yearly dummy variables. * = significant at $p < 0.05$, one tailed test.

Table 5.3 Management, stability, and performance: autoregressive estimation

Performance measure	Management		Stability		R^2	N
	Networking	Quality	Teacher	Manager		
Latino pass percentage	0.2787 (1.32)	0.3523 (1.56)	0.0148 (0.39)	0.0377 (1.68)*	0.58	2,216
Black pass percentage	0.2640 (0.87)	0.3989 (1.29)	0.1254 (2.02)*	0.0519 (1.73)*	0.59	1,490
Anglo pass percentage	0.3110 (2.85)*	0.1909 (1.59)	0.0576 (3.16)*	0.0336 (2.82)*	0.71	2,467
Low-income pass percentage	0.2028 (1.47)	0.1580 (1.03)	0.0700 (2.99)*	0.0543 (3.56)*	0.75	2,491
Average ACT score	0.0346 (1.35)	0.0631 (2.27)*	−0.0055 (1.11)	0.0001 (0.05)	0.45	2,091
Average SAT score	1.0705 (0.87)	1.3360 (1.01)	0.4979 (1.94)*	0.0893 (0.72)	0.67	1,655
Percentage above 1,110	0.2458 (1.33)	0.4301 (2.09)*	0.0498 (1.51)	−0.0134 (0.67)	0.39	2,366
Dropout percentage	−0.0134 (0.72)	−0.0669 (3.27)*	−0.0014 (0.45)	−0.0006 (0.31)	0.34	2,483
Class attendance	0.0013 (0.14)	0.0126 (1.25)	0.0066 (4.36)*	0.0004 (0.44)	0.71	2,503

Notes: T-scores in parentheses. All equations control for teacher salaries, instructional expenditures per student, class size, teacher experience, percentage of teachers not certified, percentage of black, Latino, and low-income students, a lagged dependent variable, and yearly dummy variables. * = significant at $p < 0.05$, one tailed test.

and also clearly supports the notion that management itself matters, aside from the personnel impacts captured by stability.

Table 5.3 shows the coefficients for the nine autoregressive analyses. Picking up the impacts of independent variables is quite difficult in such cases; the results further support the importance of personnel stability, however. Here thirty-four of the thirty-six coefficients are correctly signed, and all equations show one or more of the independent variables as statistically significant. Half the personnel stability coefficients are statistically significant, and two-thirds of the nine equations show personnel stability in some form as statistically significant. The management measures do not perform as well, particularly managerial networking (see Chapter 3 on the distributive aspects of M_2). Nonetheless, management influences performance in positive and statistically significant fashions for one-half of the ten performance measures. Indeed, if the criterion for statistical significance is relaxed to $p < 0.10$, twenty-five of the forty coefficients in the autoregressive estimations are significant. Given the stringency of the tests used to produce the results displayed in Table 5.3, and given the range of performance indicators considered, the results are noteworthy – especially regarding personnel stability.

Some of the details clearly deserve more careful attention and further analysis; one example can suffice. The analysis for pass rates among black students indicates that a maximum of almost seven points in a district's pass rate can be explained by teacher stability, *even controlling for the lagged dependent variable*. This level of impact for a regular cadre of teachers on such students is phenomenal. It may be that students from particular family backgrounds or certain circumstances are especially sensitive to stability among the role models and mentors in their midst at school,[16] or perhaps experience matters in adjusting pedagogy to the needs of individual students. If so, policy makers and educational administrators would do well to attend to some of these differential impacts.

In short, the results of this study support the notion that personnel stability can be an important determinant of public organizational performance, at least for education; and that the impact of stability can be particularly strong for certain measures and/or clients of public organizations. Given the presumed importance of teachers themselves in the educational process, that stability among teachers would be more important than that at the level of top management in school districts makes sense; and, indeed, the strength of the relationship between stability and performance for teachers exceeds that for district superintendents in most but not all of the ten estimations.

Nevertheless, stability at the top seems often to matter as well. This finding is noteworthy for at least two reasons. First, superintendents are insulated from the classroom, so to be able to demonstrate such impacts on performance from this level in the organization constitutes a particularly telling result. Second, other relevant aspects of management are already controlled for in the analysis. In particular, managers' activity in the network of external parties is already taken into account, as is management quality. It would appear, then, that managerial stability per se can be helpful.

This finding should be treated with appropriate caution. Sometimes organizational change can be a good thing, especially in underperforming organizations. The results here pertain only to personnel stability; they cannot necessarily be generalized to all forms of stability, though they certainly render the broader stability hypothesis more intriguing. The evidence, furthermore, does not support a sweeping castigation of all personnel changes. The stability-related findings hold after controlling for managerial quality. They surely do not buttress any argument that bad managers (or, for that matter, poor teachers) should be retained merely to keep things constant. Further, the value of personnel stability might actually lie in part in the abilities of experienced, knowledgeable, and widely respected people – both teachers and superintendents in the case of school districts – to initiate and implement some of the right kinds of changes at the right time.[17] All in all, then, these findings support carefully framed arguments for personnel stability but do not promote an uncritical conservatism.

Nonlinear relationships

All findings reported thus far involve linear estimations for the full set of school districts. We are interested in exploring nonlinear elements as well, however, since both the theory and some earlier analyses indicate that these can be expected when dealing with public managerial and related relationships. Nonlinear impacts can be assessed either via interaction terms or by examining relationships with different subsets of the sample. Here we explore nonlinear relationships among the independent variables via physical controls – that is, by partitioning the data set.

We divide the school districts into quartiles four different times – by values of each of the key independent variables successively (that is, management quality, managerial networking, teacher stability, and managerial stability) – and examine changes in the impacts of the other independent variables on performance.[18] For each quartile of partitioning and each of the independent variables, we calculate the regression coefficients for the other variables. The coefficients can then be graphed, as in Figures 5.1 to 5.4. Each figure shows the full set of coefficients for each quartile of the partitioned

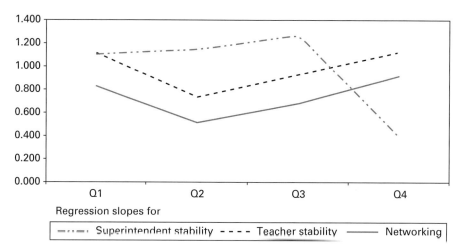

Figure 5.1   The interaction of management quality with networking and stability: quartile regression coefficients

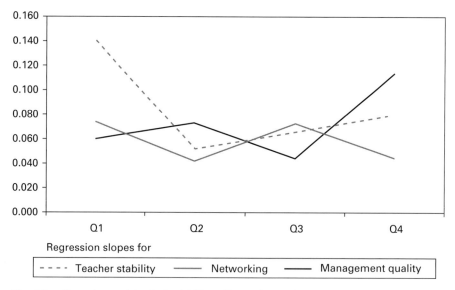

Figure 5.2   The interaction of superintendent stability with teacher stability, management quality, and networking

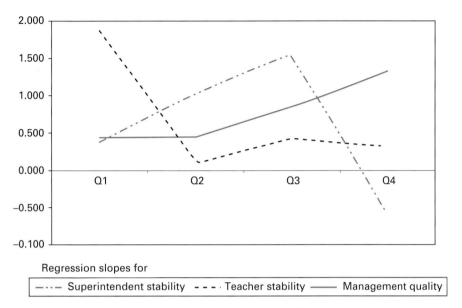

Figure 5.3   The interaction of networking with management quality and stability

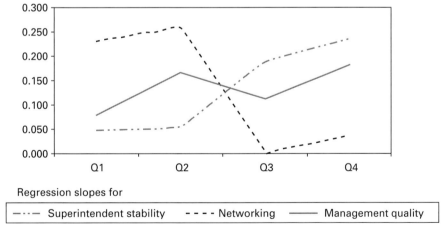

Figure 5.4   The interaction of teacher stability with superintendent stability, management quality, and networking

variable: twelve coefficients in each figure. To illustrate, in Figure 5.1 the solid line shows the size of the networking coefficient for each quartile of the management quality variable. For the lowest quartile (those near the bottom in managerial quality), the coefficient is 0.83; for Q_2 the figure drops to 0.52; for Q_3 it rises to 0.675; and then it climbs to 0.921 for Q_4. This generally U-shaped pattern means that networking matters more for those highest and lowest in managerial quality.

The figures, taken as a set, confirm the expectation of nonlinearity. Fully linear relationships would show (roughly) identical and constant coefficients on each graph – four horizontal and nearly equivalent lines at some height reflecting the impact of that variable. For all four management and stability variables, nonlinearity is clearly evident. Even in the case reflecting the most consistency of impact (Figure 5.1), the size of the superintendent stability coefficient varies by 332 percent from lowest to highest. In the cases of quartiles of managerial networking (Figure 5.3) and teacher stability (Figure 5.4), the shifts in strength are substantially more dramatic.

Second, some of the relationships are particularly interesting. Explicit comparisons of these results with the model do not constitute definitive tests, since the tests involve some simplification of the original formulation. All the same, one expectation sketched earlier – that more stability would mean a greater impact from the first term of the model and lessened impact from the second – is supported in the case of teacher stability (Figure 5.4): more stability is accompanied by a dropoff in the impact of networking. When managerial quality is high, the impact of networking and teacher stability is high, but management stability is less important (see Figure 5.1). This pattern fits with the notion that the best managers may be able to leverage more from their own actions and the other variables they can influence, directly or indirectly. Management quality, in turn, seems to matter more when superintendents engage in a great deal of networking in their environments (Figure 5.3; see also Chapter 4). The interaction of teacher stability with management quality is also interesting: the former has its greatest impact at very low and high levels of managerial quality (Figure 5.1). Conversely, teacher stability is far less important when networking is high (Figure 5.3). These illustrations are only a few of the ways that management and stability interact. Probing these interactions and the practical and theoretical reasons for them is fertile ground for future management scholarship. The findings here also suggest that practical strategies focused on any single aspect of management are likely to be contingent on the entire matrix of activities under examination here.

Conclusions about stability

Stability has received little attention in recent times from management gurus. The vaunted virtues of entrepreneurship and reengineering, change and reinvention, are the coins of today's reformist realm. The best thinking about public management over the decades offers justification for considering this issue afresh, however. Administrative arrangements are autoregressive systems, and change certainly entails costs as well as possible benefits. The model we have developed suggests that stability in public programs is a dimension worthy of systematic investigation and that it could shape performance for the better.

Stability takes on many forms in administrative systems. We have explored just one of these, personnel stability, and its impact on educational performance. We have also incorporated an explicit consideration of other aspects of public management. Our analyses reconfirm the importance of the other aspects of management while offering substantial support for the notion that personnel stability at both managerial and front-line levels contributes positively to performance. The findings regarding stability are persuasive in a number of respects. They are unambiguous on the most important and salient performance indicator, persist in analyses of many other measures of performance, and can even be documented in most autoregressive estimations. Further, the examination of interactions among the independent variables of management and stability indicates that not only do the variables matter, the relationships between them are nonlinear and complex. The model contends that management actions are likely to be contingent on stability. This empirical evidence suggests that the impact of management actions on performance is likely to be contingent on the full range of management decisions and how the various features interact.

Although we have referred to "management" and "stability" variables, in an important sense all four have to do with public management. The latter two reference an aspect of what is usually referred to as personnel management. Unlike items such as jurisdictional wealth or student characteristics, personnel stability derives from the administrative system itself and those who comprise it. While not totally in the control of school district leaders, these variables are susceptible to influence by the individuals who make decisions about how such organizations are run. In a real sense, therefore, all four variables tap aspects of public management.

This point is worth an explicit mention because, taken as a whole, the set of four independent variables accounts for an impressively large slice of educational performance in Texas school districts. For those who would say that public management constitutes, at best, a tiny part of the explanation as to why programs work as they do, we would say: look to education in Texas for a rather dramatic rebuttal. We expect that, as additional scholars develop similar, theoretically informed indicators of management in other public organizations, the results will be similar.

This investigation might seem to amount to a fairly comprehensive exploration of the issues in question. This section of the chapter reports on the role of four public management variables in shaping educational performance, uses ten performance measures, includes numerous controls, tests for relationships with and without the autoregressive form, and unpacks interactive effects. In these respects, the study offers convincing evidence. It is nonetheless important to emphasize that the results are but partial findings regarding a broader and more complex set of issues.

Indeed, as emphasized at the outset of the chapter, personnel stability is merely one theme even within the realm of internal management. We next turn to a second set of HR issues: the quality of human capital in an organization and its effective management.

The human side of public organizations

Attracting and developing skilled and motivated people at all levels is a core function in the management of public organizations' human resources. McGregor admonished students of management to take note of the "human side of enterprise" (1960; see also 2006).[19]

Of all the internal managerial functions, the management of public organizations' human capital is surely one of the most important and often discussed (see Light 2008). Indeed, today's frequent references to the federal government's "human capital crisis," the attention devoted to HR strategy by the US Comptroller General (see, for instance, Walker 2001), and the arguments of a number of scholars that human resources management is critical all amplify the theme (Ingraham, Selden, and Moynihan 2000; Bilmes and Neal 2003; Breul and Gardner 2004; Kellough and Nigro 2006).

Within the United States, the great majority of public employees pursue their careers at the local level, and far and away the vast majority of these – more than 6.7 million – work in the field of public education, especially elementary and secondary education (Nigro, Nigro, and Kellough 2007: 4–5, 8). Here we examine the impact over a several-year period of human capital and its management on the performance of Texas school districts, while controlling for a range of additional influences – other resources, constraints, and managerial variables – that also might shape outputs and outcomes. This study appears to be the first systematic empirical exploration of this sort in the literature on public management in attempting to isolate the link between human capital and performance in a set of several hundred public organizations.

We proceed by placing this investigation in the context of our model of how public management helps to shape program results. We then sketch the theoretical background that serves to support our focus on human capital and its management as a key HRM function, and of internal management generally. We then describe our measures, provide some evidence for the reliability of our measure of public human resources management, and report the results for the estimations of human capital on organizational performance.

Human capital management and the model

Our full public management model is complex. We proceed here as we have been doing thus far: testing portions of the model, often through partial and simplified specifications. Because all the public organizations in this study are school districts, we are going to assume that the major structural/ stability factors (other than the management-related personnel stability measures) are essentially constant and can be dropped from the model, thus resulting in the following:

$$O_t = \beta_1(M_1)O_{t-1} + \beta_2(X_t)(M_3/M_4) + \varepsilon_t$$

We then initially drop the autoregressive term in the model, to avoid missing significant long-term relationships simply because the lagged dependent variable can overwhelm small but significant influences. We estimate the model both with and without the lagged dependent variable, however. In addition, following earlier simplifications, we convert the (M_3/M_4) ratio into M_2:

$$O_t = \beta_1(M_1) + \beta_2(X_t)(M_2) + \varepsilon_t$$

Because our concern is internal management, we simplify further by moving from an interactive model in the second term to one that is linear. This step eliminates a portion of the relationships that are anticipated by the full model. The simplification is justified, however, to focus attention on the relationships of particular interest in this investigation. The nonlinearities theorized regarding the relationship between external management, on the one hand, and the opportunities and constraints in the organizational environment, on the other, have already been partially examined. The linear version of the last equation is

$$O_t = \beta_1(M_1) + \beta_2(X_t) + \beta_3(M_2) + \epsilon_t$$

The result is a relatively simple linear model that will permit us to assess the impact of the internal management of human resources on organizational performance while controlling for the environment and other managerial factors. We also estimate a second set of models with a lagged dependent variable to simulate the autoregressive nature of most organizations.

Theorizing about the content of M_1

An extensive literature emphasizes the importance of the "human side" of public organizations (for reviews and analyses, see Shafritz *et al.* 2001 and Nigro, Nigro, and Kellough 2007). The recent high-visibility study of "management capacity" in the Government Performance Project theorized that human resources management is one of four key management "subsystems" linked via leadership and driven toward higher performance by a system of managing for results (see Ingraham, Joyce, and Donahue 2003, Ingraham 2007, and in particular Selden and Jacobson 2007).

A recent argument based in part on formal theory concludes that the personnel function in government is the most critical one for those concerned about results that comport with the "core governmental values – judgment, balance, rationality, and accountability" (Bertelli and Lynn 2006: 131; see also 103–31). A conceptual and empirical literature on business organizations also contends that HRM generally, and especially employee development efforts, can be important contributors to organizational performance (for literature reviews and conceptual contributions, see Wood 1999 and Jacobs and Washington 2003; for empirical findings supportive of this theme, see Koch and McGrath 1996 and Li 2000). Indeed, some economic analyses have emphasized the importance of human resources (see Ellingsen and Johannesson 2007, Lazear and Shaw 2007, and Pfeffer 2007), and some empirical work has been conducted on public education with regard to teacher labor markets and sorting (Lankford, Loeb, and Wyckoff 2002; Boyd *et al.* 2003), and the impact of teacher quality on student achievement (Rivkin, Hanushek, and Kain 2005). These studies do not explore management or the performance of school districts as organizations, however.

For all these reasons, it seems reasonable to expect the component of M_1 that has to do with human resources management to be related to performance. Of course, even this narrowing of the subject distills a rather large set of managerial practices and responsibilities. For the purposes of our empirical analysis, we focus on what we regard as the core indicia of what should be expected from a successful managerial program in the field of human resources: evidence of talent at the top of the organization, mid-level managerial quality, skilled and capable front-line people, and the quality of programs in place to provide professional development. These are all elements of human capital and its management. We have developed a separate measure for top managerial quality, of course, and the detailed discussion of that facet was provided in Chapter 4.

Sample and measures

Once again we use the Texas school district data set and our 2004/5 survey of school district superintendents. For this version of the survey, the return rate was 61 percent.[20] Pooling four years (2004 to 2007) of data on performance and control variables produces a total of 2,400 usable cases for analysis. Missing data on individual items reduces this number somewhat in individual equations.[21]

We use our measure of managerial networking as developed earlier in this book and used frequently throughout. One adjustment made in the analysis in this section is that we use the factor score of interactions for the four possible interaction nodes aside from interaction upward with the school board. The school board interaction can be considered a principal–agent link and is included in the equations reported here as a separate measure. We also employ our validated measure of managerial quality, and we use both measures of personnel stability developed in the present chapter.

We also employ the usual eight control variables, and we focus in this section on the same ten performance measures already introduced in the first part of the chapter.[22] What remains to be explained is the measure of human capital management.

Our measure of human capital management taps what should be present as a part of successful human resources management: the attraction and development of the organization's human capital. Success in this aspect of management should produce high-quality managers and front-line workers – teachers in these highly professionalized organizations – and should also

Table 5.4 Measuring the quality of human capital: factor loadings

Indicator		Loading
Quality of experienced teachers		0.74
Quality of professional development		0.65
Quality of principals' management skills		0.75
Our people can make any program work		0.67
Recommend subordinate as superintendent		0.39
Eigenvalue	2.12	

see in place an effective professional development program. Although many other aspects of HRM could be examined, including the nature and quality of strategic planning for HR needs, we focus here on the core: the talent of the people and the quality of professional development available to them.

Based on our assumption that internal management will result in the development of the human resources of the organization, five survey items were used to tap the quality of this aspect of internal management.[23] Superintendents were asked to rate the quality of principals' management skills, the quality of experienced teachers, and the quality of professional development available on a five-point scale from "Excellent" (5) to "Inadequate" (1). Principals are the key line managers of the organization and generally are the chief operating officers of the individual schools. Teachers, of course, are the primary production personnel of any school system. Superintendents were also asked to agree or disagree with two statements, "With the people I have in this organization, we can make virtually any program work" and "I am quite likely to recommend a subordinate for a superintendent position in another district," on four-point scales from "Strongly agree" to "Strongly disagree." The first question taps into a growing view in education policy that schools are successful because they have effective human resources rather than because they adopt specific programs (Meier *et al.* 2006). The second seeks to determine if the superintendent is developing the skills of mid-level managers.

Our measurement strategy is to use factor analysis to extract the common core concept of human capital from these five indicators. The results of the factor analysis are shown in Table 5.4. The five items all load positively on the first factor, accounting for 42.4 percent of the total variance. No other factor meets the standard criterion of significance by producing an eigenvalue of 1.0 or greater. The factor loadings show strong correlations between

Table 5.5 The reliability of the human capital measure

Correlation of 2004/5 and 2006/7 measure	0.51	N = 467
Correlation 2005–2007 if same manager	0.60	N = 327
Correlation if managers change	0.33	N = 145

the indicators and the overall factor, except for the willingness to recommend an employee as a superintendent elsewhere.

The measure has some limitations, as it emphasizes the quality of human capital and only somewhat its management. We do not have many details regarding just how top management applied HR strategies and tactics to build its stock of human capital. The question on professional development does tap explicitly an aspect of management's responsibility, and the fact that it loads reasonably well on the factor suggests that the measure reflects aspects of human capital and also its management.

While the individual items and the factor scores show some face validity, before using the variable in any statistical analysis we should demonstrate whether or not the concept is reliable. We can make some assessments of this because the 2004/5 survey questions that were used to construct the index were repeated in a 2006/7 survey of superintendents. This second source of data means that we can gain some leverage on the reliability of the measure over time. To the extent that management develops human resources, we would expect these human resources to have some relatively lasting impact on the organization. In short, we would expect a positive correlation between the two measures. Further, we would expect this correlation to be even higher if the same superintendent headed the system in both years, simply because management practices are less likely to change if the same person remains as superintendent.

Table 5.5 presents these findings. For the 467 districts that responded to both surveys, the correlation of the human resources measure across time was a robust 0.51 – fairly strong for perceptual measures over a two-year period. When the analysis is restricted to those superintendents who held the same position in 2004/5 and 2006/7, the correlation jumps to 0.60. For those districts that changed superintendents between these two years, the correlation drops to 0.33. The pattern is consistent with the notion that the store of human capital both reflects the efforts of the top manager (the superintendent) and is also embedded in the processes and structures of the organization, so that the gains from good management are not lost immediately when the top manager leaves.

Table 5.6 The impact of human capital on organizational performance

Dependent variable = student exam pass rates

Independent variables	Slope	T-score	Slope	T-score
Human capital	1.7332	9.42*	0.4182	3.54*
Managerial networking	0.3556	1.73*	−0.0564	0.38
School board contact	−0.5490	2.72*	−0.1842	1.26
Management quality	0.5591	3.35*	0.2823	2.34*
Management experience	−0.0117	0.71	0.0046	0.38
Personnel stability	0.2096	9.42*	0.0386	2.34*
Previous year's pass rate	–	–	0.7042	46.41*
R^2	0.72		0.85	
Standard error	7.30		5.27	
F	354.98		761.51	
N	2,380		2,379	

Notes: Coefficients for annual dummy variables and control variables (teacher salaries, state aid, class size, teacher experience, noncertified teachers, and the percentages of black, Latino, and low-income students) are not shown. * = significant at $p < 0.05$, one tailed test. Time period = 2004–7.

Findings

We first report the impact of human capital on the most salient performance measure: the all-pass rate on the standardized, statewide examination (the TAKS). The first two columns of Table 5.6 display the full estimation for the model developed above, without the lagged dependent variable and with the pass rate as the dependent variable. The other two columns show the results when the autoregressive term is added to the first model. In the former case, and leaving aside the key variable of interest for the moment, all the other management measures aside from management experience are related to performance, and in the direction expected theoretically and on the basis of earlier work. In addition to these relationships, human capital contributes positively to the test results, and the relationship is highly significant – with a T score above nine. Interestingly, as well, the effect size for this variable is substantial. Since the measure is a factor score with an effective range of −3 to +3, the maximum effect size is more than ten percentage points on the pass rate. This result suggests a substantively important impact.

The estimation including the lagged dependent variable has some of the variables dropping out of statistical significance, as would be expected given the high hurdle that would have to be surmounted to show performance impacts controlling for the preceding year's pass rate. Management quality, which can be considered a measure tapping top-level human capital, and front-line workforce stability continue to have impacts on performance, however. Our human capital factor score remains significant and contributes positively to districts' pass rates. Although the effect size is smaller in this estimation than the previous one, it is worth bearing in mind that in the autoregressive equation the estimated impact of the variable should be considered as building into the base from one year to the next, and thus reverberating forward over time. In a several-year period, this model shows, this aspect of human resources management has a substantial effect on the statewide standardized exam performance. This finding is striking, particularly since a considerable portion of the human capital was already in place during the preceding period. The fact that this variable is shown to be substantively as well as statistically significant in an autoregressive equation and with numerous management and other controls included speaks to the importance of human capital and its management for delivering public policy outcomes. The strong finding in the equation with the lagged dependent variable suggests that it is likely that causality works in the direction we have hypothesized, rather than the reverse.[24]

The overall pass rate on the statewide exam is an important performance result, but the organizations in question are expected to achieve other educational results as well. Tables 5.7 and 5.8 show summary results for the nine other performance measures sketched earlier in this chapter. The tables include only coefficients and T-scores for the estimated impacts of HRM, but the full model was used to develop the results. Table 5.7 displays the results for the model without the lagged dependent variable, while Table 5.8 shows the findings for the autoregressive estimations.

As the results in Table 5.7 demonstrate, human capital has a performance-improving impact in all nine instances (a negative influence on the dropout rate counts as an improvement). Results for subgroups of students taking the TAKS – black, Latino, Anglo, and low-income students – all benefit from better human resources management. Latino students benefit even more than the others. Similar results can be seen for the other dependent variables. For example, the maximum effect size for SAT scores is more than thirty points. High-end performance also improves with better human resources and their management; the percentage of students achieving college-ready

Table 5.7 The impact of human capital on alternative indicators of performance

Performance measure	Slope	T-score	R^2	N
Black TAKS pass rate	1.5366	4.31*	0.40	1,433
Latino TAKS pass rate	2.1036	8.51*	0.50	2,139
Anglo TAKS pass rate	1.5019	8.99*	0.60	2,336
Low-income TAKS pass rate	1.7028	9.29*	0.37	2,391
Attendance	0.0826	5.61*	0.27	2,400
Dropouts	−0.1203	2.32*	0.28	2,317
ACT scores	0.1007	3.27*	0.43	2,125
SAT scores	6.3842	4.02*	0.40	1,742
College-ready percentage	0.9950	4.41*	0.35	2,232

Notes: All equations control for the five management variables, teacher salaries, per student instructional funds, class size, teacher experience, percentage of teachers not certified, percentage of black, Latino, and low-income students and yearly dummy variables. * = significant at $p < 0.05$, one tailed test.

Table 5.8 The autoregressive impact of human capital on alternative indicators of performance

Performance measure	Slope	T-score	R^2	N
Black TAKS pass rate	0.9231	2.93*	0.54	1,379
Latino TAKS pass rate	0.8263	4.05*	0.67	2,117
Anglo TAKS pass rate	0.4053	3.17*	0.77	2,333
Low-income TAKS pass rate	0.4778	3.55*	0.67	2,387
Attendance	0.0147	1.85*	0.78	2,400
Dropouts	−0.0617	1.47	0.46	2,296
ACT scores	0.0709	2.52*	0.54	2,044
SAT scores	2.2582	1.74*	0.62	1,641
College-ready percentage	0.7436	3.59*	0.46	2,196

Notes: All equations control for past performance, the five management variables, teacher salaries, per student instructional funds, class size, teacher experience, percentage of teachers not certified, percentage of black, Latino, and low-income students, and yearly dummy variables. * = probability $p < 0.05$, one tailed test.

test scores increases a maximum of nearly six percentage points of students tested. By any measure, the overall pattern constitutes an impressive set of results.

Table 5.8 shows the results for the nine additional performance measures when including lagged dependent variables in each equation. In eight of these cases, or nine out of ten overall, human capital is related to improved performance. For all four subgroups of TAKS-taking students, human capital boosts results. Positive results are also estimated for attendance as well as high-end performance. In none of the cases are there negative performance impacts; the result for dropouts is not significant. Given the difficulty of attaining significant results in autoregressive estimations, and particularly since the districts' human resources at any time are likely to be partially tapped in the preceding period (see Table 5.5), these results again provide support for the proposition that good human resources and the skillful development of them can pay important performance dividends.

Implications

Everyone "knows" that internal management contributes to the policy outcomes produced by public organizations. Conventional wisdom, intuition, and considerable quantities of theoretical argument all support this proposition. A great deal of the case study literature also lends plausibility to the notion. In this part of the chapter, we have developed a measure for one important aspect of internal management – the quality or talent of the people involved in delivering results, along with the quality of the development program designed to enhance the contributions of these people. This slice of internal management – the strength of an organization's extant human capital – omits a great deal of what public managers do to support performance inside the organization, but it does tap a key dimension of the internal management.

Even when controlling for several other aspects of management, including some that have to do with external management (such as managerial networking), we find that the strength of the human resources of the organization provides a substantial performance payoff. The results are found across a wide array of performance measures, and they remain for almost all the measures when controlling for past performance. The evidence provides especially strong support for the proposition that the "human side" contributes to tangible, measurable results.

Moreover, the impacts of this aspect of internal management appear to be distributed broadly across stakeholders. Human capital helps on the most widely noted performance measure, but it also helps for important subgroups of the population – including more disadvantaged students. Human capital also assists in the performance of the top-end students as well. Given the importance attached to human resources and their management in the literature on management, including public management, this pattern of findings is certainly not surprising. Given the absence of systematic empirical research on the question, though, the results here are important.

In recent years much attention has been devoted to an emphasis on marketizing the context for public services and incentivizing their management. The results from these 1,000 plus governments, however, suggest the need for public organizations to invest in their people, at both front-line and managerial levels, as a major priority. The findings also support the value of significant development programs as a part of HRM. These implications point toward treating the human capital of public organizations as a long-term asset to be built and nurtured, rather than as a set of somewhat interchangeable individuals who must simply be surrounded by the inducements implied by such innovations *du jour* as performance contracts.

This analysis nonetheless provides only a starting point for the exploration of internal management and its links to performance. Even regarding the management of human capital, substantial additional research is warranted. Longitudinal designs with multiple time points could further clarify the questions of whether and to what extent reciprocal causation might be present. Analyses in fields other than public education can determine whether the performance-related impacts of human capital and its management hold in other kinds of public organizations and in other policy domains. Education is, after all, an especially human-capital-intensive function. Other types of highly professionalized public organizations, especially those with substantial front-line discretion, may operate similarly; but the performance impacts may vary with the extent of specialized education and training, along with the degree of decentralized discretion allocated to or near the street level. In addition, it will be important for researchers to study the relationship between human capital and performance in very different kinds of settings from school districts for yet another reason. For some public functions and in some contexts, when the long-term reinforcement of extant production patterns may not be the preferred approach, the effective management of human capital may be more, or less, important – or, at least, differently influential.

This human capital aspect of HRM, furthermore, is only a part of the broader array of HR-related challenges of interest to researchers in public management. A number of other elements can be expected to contribute to organizational outcomes as well. These might include HR planning, the allocation of job responsibilities across positions, the rules and culture regarding labor relations, and numerous other facets. Moreover, of course, the management of financial resources, the crafting of structural arrangements, and many more elements of managers' internal responsibilities still await systematic study.

In short, how to understand fully the internal management of public organizations and its impacts on program performance remains a daunting but important research question. Even with regard to the narrower question of how human capital management shapes results, we are only partially down the road to an answer. The human side of public organizations is clearly important, but we are far from a full and general understanding of just how, where, and when.

Making high-quality decisions

The most fundamental part of internal management is making decisions (Simon 1997). Examining the quality of decision making in a large-N quantitative study is extremely difficult, since many decisions are context-specific and can be studied only by a more in-depth analysis. What is needed is a decision context that is relatively similar across organizations in settings offering the ability to track how managers respond to the decision event. This section examines just such a context – how organizations respond to a large budget cut. Budget reductions require organizations to make decisions about resources, personnel, and programs – and to do so while trying to protect the core performance of the organization. How decisions are made in response to an exogenous shock might not be similar to day-to-day decision making, but it does provide an opportunity to observe decisions when the decisions actually matter.[25]

A budget cut is one type of what scholars term an environmental shock: any sort of disruption emanating from outside the administrative system and buffeting the core organization. Some such shocks can be anticipated and protected against, but, no matter how elaborate its buffering apparatus, any public organization – as an open system – experiences shocks on occasion. Shocks can be negative or positive; even an unexpectedly happy budget decision approved by political leaders can constitute a perturbation to the system and can have disruptive impacts, at least in the short term, as managers and others devote time and attention to handling the largesse.

Especially important and potentially dangerous to performance, however, can be negative environmental shocks.

We focus for present purposes on negative budgetary shocks – significant cuts in the budgets for operations. Some likely budget cuts can be anticipated, and some can even be avoided. On occasion, however, major budget cuts constitute unexpected shocks to the system. For school districts in Texas, the site of our empirical analysis, school funding is heavily but not exclusively formula-driven. A formula would seem to be a metric with a highly predictable result, but, even here, shocks are possible and do occur. The state-level formula producing intergovernmental funding decisions, and thus a part of the district budget, is heavily driven by enrollment and by legislative willingness to provide the funds; both can be unpredictable. The statewide budget for intergovernmental assistance in education also faces a budgetary ceiling; therefore, the revenue received by any given district is only partially a function of its own enrollment; it is also shaped by the relative growth (decline) in enrollment in the state's other districts. Needless to say, such changes cannot be anticipated in any detail. Additionally, locally raised revenue, on which part of the budget is based, is mostly derived from the property tax. Here too disruptions can enter the system. Major industrial plant closings in a jurisdiction can cause property values, and thus property tax revenue, to fall abruptly. Property tax reassessments can also quickly alter the revenue picture. Sometimes such shocks are imposed or driven by political choices, such as popular votes via referenda in some states or the decision by Michigan in 1994 to eliminate the property tax as a source of school funding. In short, negative budgetary shocks can be expected from time to time; and it is an important function of management to mitigate their impacts and help the administrative system to recover in the face of such exigencies.

It can often be the case, in other words, that a relative *lack* of change in outcomes or an *absence* of fluctuation constitutes a subtle signal of managerial success and achievement. To the extent that managers succeed in helping to maintain production in the face of unhappy surprises and adversity, sometimes even invisibly so, the contributions of management to performance can be essential and far from trivial. Sometimes a placid pattern of results constitutes a major managerial achievement. Such an event constitutes, in effect, a managerial version of Sherlock Holmes' famous exchange in Arthur Conan Doyle's story "Silver Blaze" (Conan Doyle 1894: 50):

Gregory (a Scotland Yard detective): "Is there any point to which you would wish to draw my attention?"

Holmes: "To the curious incident of the dog in the night-time."

Gregory: "The dog did nothing in the night-time."

Holmes: "That was the curious incident."

Estimating the degree of managerial impact in such cases is a particularly difficult task, since doing so involves dealing with a counterfactual: little or nothing seems to have happened, but what would have happened had management not intervened? Still, it is apparent that sometimes, when performance dogs do not bark, that result constitutes a curious incident indeed – one that may signal a key sort of managerial success.

Management's contribution to performance in this situation functions as a recovery operation that might (partially) return the system to regular performance despite the environmental shock. In the remainder of this analysis we focus on exploring whether and how management decisions (M_1) mitigate negative budgetary shocks.

Since many of the internal actions of managers are unobservable and cannot be directly estimated via a large-N analysis such as the one undertaken in this study, we pursue the M_1 impact indirectly, albeit carefully. We first estimate the extent to which, if at all, shocks have their amplitude reduced in the organizational system in terms of performance results. We then examine reported managerial goals and internal budgetary and staff allocations to see if the evidence indicates that managerial decisions directed at such allocations have been aimed at protecting core functions from disruption.

In the present analysis, our data are drawn almost entirely from the Texas Education Agency. For one portion of the work we also use 2002 survey responses of school system superintendents. The response rate was 60 percent, with sampled districts very similar to the universe of districts. All other analyses are conducted with a data set containing eight years (1995 to 2002) of data on performance and control variables, for a maximum of 8,329 cases for analysis.

Measuring shocks

To estimate budget shocks, we follow Rattsø (1999), who examines shocks to national economies. We regress total school district revenues (logged) on their logged values for the prior year.[26] This regression essentially estimates what school district revenues would be if past trends continued. We then designate as "shocks" any year-to-year reductions in school district budgets that exceed 10 percent of the previous budget. A total of 730 budget shocks occurred in this eight-year period, thus affecting approximately 8.8 percent of the cases. Although for our purposes the minimum shock is set at a 10 percent reduction, the budget shocks could be much larger, and actually averaged 18 percent. We have also performed sensitivity analyses by adjusting the designated minimum cut that would constitute a shock for the purposes of analysis, and the results do not affect the basic findings of the analysis. It is important to note that the autoregressive estimation *incorporates past budget patterns.* This means that a district with a growing budget will suffer a 10 percent plus loss from that growing trend. A district with a flat budget would see a real drop of 10 percent. By measuring the shock relative to past expectations, the Rattsø technique focuses on the unpredictable element in budget cuts. In all equations here, a budget shock of 10 percent or more is converted to a dummy variable. We are confident that this measure isolates the shock component because the models also control for a variety of expenditures. The coefficients for the variable, therefore, estimate the impact of the shock while controlling for the level of resources.

Dependent variables and controls

We also employ the usual eight control variables, and we focus in this section on the same ten performance measures already introduced in the first part of the chapter. We deal with serial correlation with a series of year dummy variables. Heteroskedasticity was well within acceptable ranges.

Findings

Our first question is to ask what the impact of a budget shock of 10 percent or more is on the performance of the organization. Table 5.9 provides a regression of overall TAAS rates on a budget shock while controlling for the other resources and constraints of the organization. The results in the first two columns are surprising. A budget shock has only a modest impact on the organization's performance; it results in only a drop of one half-point in TAAS performance, all other things being equal, and this relationship is statistically significant only if we use our directional hypothesis and then use a one-tailed test of significance at the 0.10 level. The remaining control

Table 5.9 The impact of a 10 percent or greater budget shock on organizational performance

Dependent variable = student exam pass rates

Independent variables	Slope	T-score	Slope	T-score
Budget shock	−0.5006	1.62ns	−0.4938	1.59ns
Lagged budget shock	–	–	−0.9956	3.05
Control variables				
Teacher salaries (000s)	0.6616	12.31	0.6596	12.28
Class size	−0.3450	8.91	−0.3578	9.19
Teacher experience	0.0783	1.62ns	0.0826	1.72
Noncertified teachers	−0.1371	7.84	−0.1386	7.92
Percentage state aid	−0.0123	2.81	−0.0136	3.09
Percentage of black students	−0.2332	27.52	−0.2329	27.50
Percentage of Latino students	−0.1035	18.66	−0.1031	18.59
Percentage of low-income students	−0.1485	19.32	−0.1472	19.13
R^2	0.61		0.61	
Standard error	7.66		7.66	
F	820.09		773.71	
N	8,321		8,321	

Notes: Dummy variables for individual years not reported. ns = not significant at $p < 0.05$. Time period = 1995–2002.

variables in the model show the predicted relationships. (The findings are also robust to the inclusion of a set of management variables.)

Because student performance is highly autoregressive (the same students are tested every year), it might take more than one year for a negative impact to show up. The third and fourth columns of Table 5.9 include a one-year lag for the budget shock. The results show a *small but statistically significant negative impact* of the budget cut in the second year, approximately one percentage point on the TAAS. Additional estimations with longer time lags show no further impacts.

The ability of school districts to take a 10 percent or better budget cut and produce performance results that drop only a small amount is an interesting finding. This is clearly a case of a sizable cut, and the interesting story is the dog that did not bark, let alone bite. The most plausible explanation has to do with management. Public organizations are open systems, but they are also actively managed – that is, they are not blown along at the whim of environmental winds. They adopt procedures to dampen environmental threats, and they can also take actions internally to ameliorate the effects of unpleasant shocks from the environment. Budget shocks should be no

Table 5.10 The impact of budget shocks on other indicators of performance

Dependent variable	Slope	T-score	R^2	N
Black pass rates	−0.6232	0.77	0.49	4,870
Latino pass rates	0.0424	0.08	0.46	7,477
Anglo pass rates	−0.5101	1.66#	0.45	8,202
Low-income pass rates	−0.1609	0.41	0.56	8,252
Attendance	−0.0147	0.45	0.22	8,324
College board exams rate	−1.3930	2.06*	0.14	7,449
SAT scores	−2.7372	0.74	0.46	5,742
ACT scores	−0.0885	1.45	0.38	6,909
Percentage above 1,110, SAT	−1.2834	2.84*	0.30	7,525

Notes: All equations control for teacher salaries, per student instructional funds, class size, teacher experience, percentage of teachers not certified, percentage of black, Latino, and low-income students, and yearly dummy variables. * = significant at $p < 0.05$, two-tailed test. # = significant at $p < 0.10$, two-tailed test. Significant second-year effects were found for Anglo students and for the percentage above 1,110.

exception to this rule, as the budget process is often fraught with crises of either economic or political origin (Rubin 2005).

Table 5.9 shows the impact of the budget shock only on the primary performance indicator for Texas school districts. Nine additional regressions were run on the other performance indicators to determine if budget shocks had any other impacts, or if perhaps the shocks affected some portions of the organization rather than others. Table 5.10 shows the abbreviated results of these regressions. In three cases, we find statistically significant negative impacts of a 10 percent or greater budget shock on the organization: Anglo test score results, the percentage of students who take one or both of the SAT and ACT exams, and the percentage of students who score above 1,110 on the SAT or its ACT equivalent. TAAS pass rates for blacks, Latinos, and low-income students, as well as attendance rates and ACT and SAT mean scores, show no discernible impact (similar null results occur with a lagged shock variable). The budget-shock impact on Anglo TAAS rates remains at the marginal level of about one-half point and now just crosses the threshold of significance at the 0.10 level (or the 0.05 level with a one-tailed test, not an especially stringent test with 8,000 plus cases). A one-year lag of the shock on this variable shows a slightly larger negative impact of 0.9 points (results not shown). The impact on college-bound students appears greater. Approximately 1.4 percentage point fewer students take either the ACT or the SAT (in the first year), and those students who score above 1,110 drop by about

Table 5.11 Superintendent priorities: what is your primary goal for improving your district?

Goal	Percentage
Student TAAS scores	70.3
College preparation	24.4
Bilingual education	3.1
Vocational education	1.7
Extracurricular	0.6
Athletics	0.3

N = 650

1.3 percentage points (in the first year, and a significant second-year drop of 0.8 points [equation not shown]). These two impacts are likely cumulative; fewer students take the exam and those who do score lower. Although a 1.4 percentage point drop from the average of 62.8 percent taking the exams is not large, a 1.3 percentage point drop and a 0.8 percentage point drop from the 19.0 percent who score above 1,110 is a sizable reduction.

Why might such a pattern occur whereby one set of performance indicators is generally unaffected by a major budget reduction while others are? One explanation might be that management seeks to protect those organizational outputs that are more highly valued – that is, part of their core mission (Thompson 1967). Although it might be argued a priori that the emphasis on standardized tests in Texas will be valued more highly than other outputs, the results from a 2002 survey of Texas school superintendents (see Table 5.11) provides unequivocal evidence. Superintendents were asked to rank-order their goals among six different areas: TAAS, college-bound students, vocational education, bilingual education, extracurricular activities, and athletics. Fully 70 percent of superintendents listed TAAS as the top goal for their district. The results of Tables 5.9 and 5.10, therefore, are consistent with the view that superintendents protected their primary goal at the expense of some degradation in the achievement of secondary goals.

Goals convey intentions; they do not tell us how superintendents are actually able to keep a large budget cut from affecting their primary performance goal. Indeed, prior research on the public management of cutbacks offers at least three broad possibilities. One, developed by researchers focusing on local government management, indicates that managerial choices under fiscal stress can be fairly unpatterned and unsystematic (Pammer 1990; Bartle 1996). Another is that cuts might be

Table 5.12 The nonbarking dog: the relationship between a budget shock and instructional expenditures

Dependent variable = logged total instructional expenditures			
Independent variables	Slope	T-score	P
Intercept	0.1849	28.15	0.0000
Budget shock	−0.0518	10.83	0.0000
Lagged expenditures	0.8803	158.14	0.0000
R^2	0.75		
Standard error	0.12		
F	12,707.20		
N	8,328		

absorbed in politically more acceptable ways, especially by spreading the pain – for instance, by across-the-board cuts ostensibly affecting all parts of the organization and stakeholders equally (Levine 1978, 1980). A third option, suggested in the preceding paragraphs and explicated in the literature on organization theory, would be for managers to make selective and perhaps subtle, even if difficult, choices regarding budgetary and staffing decisions so as to minimize negative performance impacts. Unfortunately, much of the earlier research contains little if any systematic information on performance effects.

We have sought to rectify this omission here, as Tables 5.9 and 5.10 document. Further, we can try to sort through the different managerial possibilities by tracing some of the choices made to deal with budget shocks – in particular, by examining management's internal budgetary reallocations in the wake of the shock, and also certain personnel data. For instance, one obvious option for management is to absorb most or all of the budget cut in areas that are not directly related to the organization's core function: the instruction of students. As a first step, Table 5.12 examines the allocation of funds to instruction. Because the total expenditures of each district are logged and we control for last year's expenditures on instruction, the shock coefficient indicates that a 10 percent or greater budget cut resulted in only a 5.2 percent reduction in instructional funds. Bearing in mind that the criterion for a shock was a budget cut of 10 percent or more, the actual drop in revenues for the "shocked" districts was 18.4 percent, meaning that superintendents were able to shelter instructional expenditures from approximately 72 percent of the impact of an across-the-board cut.

Table 5.13 Redistributing funds to core functions: percentage point reductions in allocations

Function	Gain/loss	T-score	R^2	N
Instruction	1.119	6.36[*]	0.35	8328
Central administration	0.265	3.91[*]	0.72	8328
Campus administration	0.337	8.85[*]	0.57	8328
Physical plant	0.484	9.22[*]	0.61	8328
Nonoperating expenses	−2.167	11.10[*]	0.34	8328

Notes: All regression equations estimated with a lagged dependent variable. [*] = $p < 0.05$.

A second look at the budgeting actions of superintendents can be found in Table 5.13. We took the percentage of the overall budget allocated to five functions – instruction, central administration, school administration, physical plant, and nonoperating expenditures – and examined the impact of the budget shock on these percentages while controlling for the expenditures in the previous year. These results clearly demonstrate the privileged position of instructional expenditures in the districts' internal budgetary decisions. Bearing in mind that these districts are operating with a smaller total budget, we note that the 5.2 percent decrease in instructional expenditures (in Table 5.12) actually means that the percentage of all funds allocated to instruction increases by 1.1 percentage points (Table 5.13). Administration and physical plant percentages go up, but this essentially means that they absorb less than a 10 percent cut (although more than the 5 percent in instruction). The major loser in the reallocation is nonoperating expenses (capital expenditures, debt service, and community services), with a reduction of 2.2 percentage points. This is a substantial cut, since nonoperating expenditures average only about nine percentage points in the school districts' budgets.

Squeezing out the frills and capital expenditures is unlikely to be enough to cover the shortfall, however. Texas superintendents have extensive personnel powers that they can use. Teachers work on annual contracts, and superintendents can opt not to offer a contract for the next year or to offer a contract at the same salary. Table 5.14 illustrates two personnel approaches that districts facing a major budget cut use. The first regression predicts average teacher salaries with teachers' salaries in the previous year and the budget shock. The significant negative coefficient indicates that teacher salaries in the examined districts actually drop by $278 in the year of the

Table 5.14 Reducing core costs: teachers' salaries and class size

	Dependent variable	
	Teacher salaries	Class size
Intercept	3.629	0.925
Budget shock	−0.278 (5.14)	0.073 (2.11)
Lagged dependent variable	0.923 (244.41)	0.917 (242.51)
R^2	0.88	0.88
Standard error	1.39	0.87
F	29,908.92	30,203.83
N	8,323	8,329

budget crisis. As a point of comparison, over this eight-year time period teacher salaries in all districts increased by approximately $1,329 per year. A portion of the budget deficit, therefore, is made up by offering lower average salaries to teachers. This can be done by offering continuing teachers the same salary and replacing teachers who leave with cheaper, less experienced teachers (teacher turnover averages 16 percent per year in the state).

The second equation in Table 5.14 examines class size in the same way. Districts hit with a budget shock responded by allowing their class sizes to increase slightly, by 0.07 students per teacher. Although this is not a large change, it should be viewed in terms of the general trend during this time in Texas, when student-to-teacher ratios declined from 13.4 to 12.4. In combination, these two results suggest that districts replaced fewer teachers (and some may have actually terminated teachers), thus permitting class sizes to increase, and at the same time held the line on teachers' salaries.

Managers obviously take multiple actions to render budgetary canines somnolent. A related strategy is to alter the composition of the instructional personnel. Table 5.15 examines the percentage of employees who are teachers, teachers' aides, and instructional support staff (audio-visual assistants, etc.). Although Table 5.13 shows that the percentage of funds allocated to teaching increased, Table 5.14 illustrates again that this is effectively a result of instructional funds declining at a lower rate than for other types of funding. The percentage of teachers in the budget-impacted districts does not change from one year to the next – evidence consistent with zero growth in total teaching positions. At the same time, the percentage of teachers' aides declines by 0.3 percentage points and the percentage of support staff declines by 0.13 percentage points. Although these are relatively small

Table 5.15 Reducing core support tasks: instruction, aides, and support staff

Dependent variable = percentage of staff assigned to

Function	Gain/loss	T score	R^2	N
Teaching	−0.036	0.31	0.72	8,329
Support staff	−0.125	2.21*	0.69	8,329
Teachers' aides	−0.312	2.52*	0.62	8,329

Notes: All regression equations estimated with a lagged dependent variable. * = $p < 0.05$.

Table 5.16 Seeking less expensive core personnel

Dependent variable = percentage of teachers in various functions

Function	Gain/loss	T score	R^2	N
Regular education	0.871	4.95*	0.71	8,329
Special education	−0.191	2.26*	0.69	8,329
Compensatory education	−0.377	3.29*	0.55	8,329
Vocational education	0.041	0.60	0.68	8,329
Bilingual education	−0.182	2.43*	0.87	8,329
Other education	−0.210	3.56*	0.64	8,329

Notes: All regression equations estimated with a lagged dependent variable. * = $p < 0.05$.

reductions in absolute terms, the changes should be contrasted with a 20 percent growth in support staff and a 17 percent growth in teachers' aides over the years examined. In short, additional funds are saved by reducing the number of "less" essential personnel.

Finally, an organization facing fiscal constraints is likely to recognize that their core personnel vary in skill and cost. Although school districts might like to think of all teachers as fully interchangeable, in practice teachers are specialists in a given curriculum, and some of these specializations are in short supply. The state of Texas faces a large shortage of qualified bilingual education instructors, and many districts pay a bonus to newly hired bilingual teachers (or offer a higher pay scale for these professionals). Table 5.16 provides an analysis of the percentage of teachers that fall into six categories (regular education, special education, compensatory education, vocational education, bilingual education, and other). Quite clearly, these results are consistent with a strategy of responding to budgetary shocks by seeking out or concentrating on less expensive teachers. A district facing a budget shock sees a 0.87 percentage point increase in regular education instructors but a 0.19 percentage point decline in special education teachers, a 0.38 percentage point decline in compensatory education teachers, and a 0.18 percentage point cut in bilingual education teachers (the "other" teacher category also declines, but the composition of this residual category is too diverse to determine if such teachers are more or less likely to be better paid). Because these shifts appear in the context of a constant number of teachers (see Table 5.15), the implication is that, as bilingual or other more expensive – i.e. special education – teachers leave, they are replaced by less expensive regular education teachers.[27]

Through a variety of stratagems that can be documented with some care, therefore, managers make a series of decisions that, in the short term, insulate the most highly valued organizational tasks from the potentially negative impacts of budgetary shocks. The effort was made to keep teachers in the classroom, even if class size had to grow a little bit and even if the district could afford only a lower-cost teacher (regular education rather than bilingual or special education). In the short term, at least, the performance-related results are clear: core performance is protected as much as possible, some other goals are subtly deemphasized, and for the most part the managerially crafted system is tweaked in order to deamplify or detour sizable shocks from having their full effect on public education.

Implications

We have shown in a sample of 1,000 public organizations over an eight-year period that, when faced with significant budgetary shocks, these units make a series of internal management decisions that absorb the unpleasant event without experiencing much if any performance decline. These findings are valid for many but not all performance metrics, and they document short-term impacts only. Interestingly, few if any declines are seen in delivering results on the most salient organizational goal, and also on bottom-end performance measures. The organizations and their managers appear to be successful at generating desired outcomes on priority matters and for the most disadvantaged clientele. The results constitute evidence that internal management is fairly effective in shaping performance. In this set of cases, in effect, the budgetary dog did virtually nothing in the night-time. That pattern of findings constitutes not only a curious array of results but also one that contains encouraging news for those interested in the link between public management and performance. A virtual lack of impact can be taken as strongly hinting at effective management. Considering these results, we conclude that, despite a sizable shock delivered to school systems via the "X" term, internal management (M_1) is rather successful at propping up the steady delivery of outcomes by making a series of key allocation decisions.

The analyses arrayed in Tables 5.12 to 5.16 considerably strengthen the inference that managers operate systematically to make tough choices with the objective of protecting the most valued outputs and outcomes. In these cases, school system superintendents worked to insulate instructional resources from unexpected cuts, redistributed resources within the diminished total budget to help instruction at the expense of ancillary tasks and also important but less immediate capital needs, and managed the teaching corps – and its compensation – in the interest of similar objectives. By attrition and salary constraints, an emphasis on core teachers instead of support staff and aides, and a focus on employing standard classroom instructors instead of specialized teachers, they managed their organizations toward success – as measured by a focus on performance in the core business of the organizations.

The emphasis here, however, is on internal management. Tried-and-true core managerial functions, such as careful budget management and the management of human resources, are tools that public managers use to craft policy-relevant results. These are not blunt instruments – like so many clubs wielded to keep the budgetary dogs at bay. Rather, delicate and often almost invisible tweaks of a set of managerial systems can be used to fashion success in the midst of troubled times. Not only does POSDCORB live; its injunctions receive partial validation on the basis of performance.

Lest the lessons of this study appear overly optimistic and also excessively managerialist, however, two caveats should be entered. First, there are some losers when budgetary shocks hit. Interestingly, the evidence suggests that top-end and/or more privileged students fare the worst in response to substantial budgetary shocks. While those concerned with equity might regard this pattern as better than its obverse, it does demonstrate that managers cannot turn budgetary mastiffs completely into sleek greyhounds. To the extent that the public prefers, and ultimately benefits from, higher-end achievement such as a college-ready student body, sizable cutbacks entail costs.

Second, managers are able to handle a substantial portion of the potentially deleterious cutbacks through a series of short-term choices. The findings reported here do not speak to long-term consequences, however.

The analyses show that managers are able to cope rather well, but what happens beyond short-term coping is an important and so far unanswered question. Clearly, repeated budgetary shocks are likely to show substantially greater negative impacts on performance. Even isolated shocks may carry larger long-term consequences, particularly on some aspects of educational performance – bilingual or special education, perhaps, or advanced work by high-performing students. The protective moves visible in the school districts studied here provide some clear benefits, but they may also function, in effect, as initiating a process of eating the seedcorn: weakening the educational system's infrastructure so that it becomes progressively more difficult over time to maintain effective performance. These matters too deserve careful investigation.

Generalizing the impact of internal management

Internal management actions, both by themselves and via their contributions to stability, have been successfully linked to performance in a number of settings other than Texas school districts. All the studies use regression models similar to those presented in this chapter; all control for a wide variety of other factors that could also influence program outcomes. To retain the focus on the linkage between management and performance, we do not discuss the control variables but, rather, focus on key relationships between management or stability and performance.

In a specific application of the management model presented in Chapter 2, Donahue *et al.* (2004) examine US state agencies that oversee human resources and state agencies that manage the fiscal debt of the state and its programs. For the HR agencies, they measure M_1 in terms of the degree of program decentralization, the extent of formal reporting on personnel matters, and the extent of workforce planning. They find that both decentralization and the extent of workforce planning positively affect the quality of personnel hired (this is measured in terms of managerial perceptions) while the degree of formal reporting is associated with lower levels of employee turnover (Donahue *et al.* 2004: 140). For debt management agencies, Donahue *et al.* (134) measure M_1 via a survey that assesses how much control the agency has over capital improvement plans in the state, their enforcement powers over the use of bond-raised funds, and the agency's control over the repayment life of the debt. The agency outputs are the percentage of bonds issued via competitive sales and the percentage of bonds sold via requests for proposals; both measures should be associated with lower interest rates for debt. Although the M_1 measures do not have much impact on competitive sales, they do have a strong positive impact on the percentage of bonds covered by requests for proposals (142).

Meier, O'Toole, and Hicklin (2009) examine the managerial practices of 266 public and private universities in the United States. They create an internal management measure that is a factor analysis of how the university president allocates his or her time. Using scales similar to the managerial networking scales in terms of frequency, the president's interactions with thirteen different individuals or groups within the university are assessed. A two-factor solution is found. One factor indicates a very hierarchical managerial style, whereby actions are taken almost exclusively through direct subordinates – that is provosts, deans, and department chairs. The other factor is a more fluid internal management style that includes interactions with a far larger variety of individuals and resembles more a network-like approach than a strict hierarchical orientation to management. The study includes two performance measures: the six-year graduation rate (the percentage of new first-year students who graduate within six years) and the percentage of new faculty hires who are African American. A hierarchical management style is positively associated with six-year graduation rates but had no impact on the effort to hire more African American faculty members. In contrast, a more networked internal management style is positively associated with increases in faculty diversity but is unrelated to the six-year graduation rate. In short, one approach to internal management appears to generate efficiency benefits while a different management style is associated with greater equity.

Roch, Pitts, and Narvarro (2010) study a specialized aspect of internal management in their analysis of public schools in the US state of Georgia from 2002 to 2005. The outcome they explore is whether the individual schools pursue school disciplinary policies that are punitive (out-of-school suspensions, expulsions, etc.) or ameliorative (in-school suspensions, assignments to alternative schools, etc.). Their internal management measure is based on human resources and, essentially, is a measure of how well the demographic composition of the teaching force and the administrators reflect the demographics of the student body, using a Euclidian distance measure. In essence, this measure taps how successful the HR managers have been in recruiting a diverse workforce. Roch, Pitts and Narvarro find that this measure of internal management is associated with more ameliorative disciplinary actions, especially in the case of teachers.

Roch and Pitts (2010) extend this work on Georgia schools by examining the differences between public schools and charter schools. Charter schools are schools funded by the state of Georgia but not subject to the extensive rules and regulations that affect public schools. The idea is to free up these schools to be innovative and let them compete for students with each other and public schools. Roch and Pitts argue that charter schools are managed in a distinctly different way from public schools. They are generally headed by entrepreneurs who have a strong commitment to a specific education philosophy and who recruit teachers and administrators who share this philosophy. In short, such organizations rely on value congruence rather than hierarchy to manage the organization. This strong emphasis on value congruence in terms of educational philosophy, the authors argue, means that some key HR variables for public schools will no longer matter in charter schools. Again, the authors focus on race, but in this case they have two dependent variables: ameliorative disciplinary policies and the performance of minority students on the Georgia state standardized tests. For public schools, the authors find, as in the previous study, that the diversity of the faculty is positively associated with ameliorative disciplinary policies and also that it is positively associated with minority student test scores. For charter schools, however, these relationships are insignificant – a finding that allows the authors to conclude that the strong goal orientation of charter schools, an internal management factor, squeezes out other values in the implementation of educational policy.

Pitts (2009) also pursues this line of management research but focuses on federal government agencies, using the 2006 Federal Human Capital Survey (a large survey of federal employees with over 200,000 respondents). Pitts creates an internal management index (M_1) designed to tap the organization's commitment to diversity management in terms of goals and actual implementation. He then relates this measure of internal management to a dependent variable that asks respondents to rate how well their work group performs, and a second dependent variable that measures job satisfaction. Pitts finds a strong positive association between internal management (M_1) and perceived job performance. He also finds this aspect of management is positively correlated with job satisfaction, so it might indirectly affect other organizational processes and outcomes though increases in job satisfaction.

The studies by Pitts and colleagues fall into a research genre termed "representative bureaucracy." This literature documents when and under what conditions attempts to create a workforce representative of the population results in changes in program outcomes. The literature is not considered part of the public management field, but the basic premise – that managerial efforts to build human resources of a specific type will generate a predictable set of program outcomes – is a premise that is part of the public management agenda. We do not review this extensive literature here; we should note, however, that the basic relationship (that internal management affects performance) has been found for child support enforcement agencies in Missouri (Wilkins and Keiser 2006), local police forces in urban counties (Meier and Nicholson-Crotty 2006), the federal Equal Employment Opportunity Commission (Meier, Eller, and Pennington 2005), and the Federal Housing Administration (Selden 1997), as well as in public schools data, both nationally in the United States and in the state of Florida (Meier and Stewart 1991).

Nicholson-Crotty and O'Toole (2004) use the basic management model in Chapter 2 to study 570 municipal police departments in the United States. They create an internal management variable by using survey measures that include both structure and the development of human resources. The fourteen items produce a single internal management factor that they designate as M_1. As a dependent variable, the authors use the clearance rate for indexed crimes; these are the serious crimes that the FBI uses to calculate crime rates in the United States. The internal management measure has a positive impact on crime clearance rates; it also interacts with past performance and generates additional impacts via this autoregressive interaction.

Jacobson, Palus, and Bowling (2010) use data from the 1994 and 1998 American State Administrators Project; this is a large survey of state administrators that asks a range of questions about these managers and how they perform their jobs. Although their objective is to examine management behaviors and how they vary by gender, their findings are relevant for this study. As a dependent variable they measure how extensively "reinventing government" initiatives were implemented. Reinventing government is a general reform of the new public management that seeks to bring more business management techniques and more incentives into public management. The authors find a negative relationship between the extent of time spent on internal management (regular day-to-day operations) and the adoption of these reforms. The negative relationship is expected, because these reinventing reforms are being pushed by outside political actors, and the management measure taps into an internal rather than an external focus for management.

Andersen and Mortensen (2010) take the O'Toole and Meier notions on the stability aspects of internal management as the starting point and ask whether stability per se is an advantage for organizations. Their organizations are Danish schools, and they include a measure of resource stability in a large production function that predicts the performance of 140,000 school children on standardized tests. They find that stability in resources contributes positively to student performance over and above the level of resources or the change in resources.

Cohen, Vaughn, and Villalobos (2010) explicitly use the formal theory specified in Chapter 2 to study the management of the US Office of the President. They have more than 300 surveys concerning ten different individuals who served as chief of staff to the president. The respondents are all individuals who held positions of authority in the administration, and they were asked to rate the effectiveness of the chief of staff. The authors have two different measures of internal management: whether the chief of staff adopted an administrator role (rather than a policy role) and an assessment of the chief of staff's advice. Both measures of internal management were positively associated with the respondents' assessment of performance.

In a variety of other investigations, therefore, and in numerous other empirical settings, the effectiveness of various aspects of internal management in shaping organizational outputs and outcomes has been demonstrated. The pattern of findings is quite consistent with the more detailed research results reported here from the Texas school districts data set.

Conclusions

This chapter has examined three elements of internal management: creating stable personnel, managing an organization's human resources, and making decisions in the face of a significant budget cut. In systematic analyses we have shown that, for public organizations, the stability of the workforce contributes to performance, as does the management of the organizations' human capital. In addition, basic internal management decisions can be used to limit the harmful effects of negative shocks to the organization. In several additional ways, therefore, management matters – either directly, as with human resources management or budget decisions, or indirectly, as with the stability of personnel. These findings do not reach to still other aspects of internal management, but they do suggest that managerial actions directed inward as well as those (discussed earlier in this book) that are directed externally shape results.

In the next chapter we build on our notion of shocks introduced above to examine more fully how management might shape outcomes when the system comes under stress, primarily from unanticipated perturbations to the organization. We ask if organizations can take actions that permit them to weather crises. In particular, we examine the role of management capacity and the development of buffering capacity.

NOTES

1. Sargent (2009) examines other internal management issues, such as goal setting, budget efficiency, employee training, and technology adoption.
2. This portion of the chapter is adapted from the analysis presented by O'Toole and Meier (2003b).
3. Overgeneralization should be avoided with regard to the impact of stability on performance. In this chapter we argue that stability can be helpful, and test one aspect of this idea against evidence; but we expect the overall impact of stability, as well as of certain types of stability, to be contingent. We are exploring some of the contingencies in additional research.
4. Recently Andersen and Mortensen (2010) have considered an additional aspect of stability beyond what is included here: the stability of resource allocation. Based on Danish public educational data, and consistent with the argument of the present chapter, they find that budgetary stability helps organizational performance.
5. Their primary term for this set of features is "treatments," by which they mean "primary work or core processes or technology" (Lynn, Heinrich, and Hill 2000: 15).
6. Despite the stereotype of bureaucracy as unchanging, substantial personnel turnover exists, and it varies greatly across public organizations (Kellough and Osuna 1995).
7. Such stability can also reduce policy churn – the adoption of frequently changing reforms without leaving sufficient time for implementation. Policy churn is identified by Hess (1999) as a major problem affecting urban school system performance.
8. Structural stability is largely constant across the entire sample examined in this study. We are pursuing some additional aspects of stability in work not reported here.
9. As a result, the measure taps both stability and an aspect of capacity – the latter in the sense of knowledge about the organization.
10. Turnover in organizations varies widely. School districts are similar to other public organizations in the level of turnover (see Meier and Hicklin 2008).
11. We assessed the normal problems of serial correlation and heteroskedasticity in pooled models. We include individual dummy years to control for the changes in variables from year to year. Diagnostics showed only marginal levels of heteroskedasticity that should not affect the results.
12. This level of exceedingly high turnover could be a behavioral symptom that, in turn, is driven by other causes. Several of the most plausible sources of turbulence are included in the model via the set of controls; obviously, idiosyncratic factors are not. Since the focus of this research is to explore the influence of the impact of

management and stability on performance, not to explain turnover per se, the issue is not pursued further here.

13. We also reran the analysis for a much larger sample: all 1,000+ districts in Texas. Given the five-year time series, this exploration amounts to a 5,000-case data set. Doing so requires dropping two independent variables derived from the survey: managerial networking and managerial stability. In this estimation, teacher stability maintained its impact and is statistically significant. The impact of management quality also continues to appear.

14. For the autoregressive form, the comparable figure is approximately 4 percent. Although this result may not seem overwhelming, the autoregressive term means that an increase in performance today grows the base for future increases as well, via the lagged dependent variable, and therefore improvements reverberate forward into the future. If the improvements continued indefinitely, the total impact would be 13.3 percentage points, relatively close to the 11 percentage points without the lag.

15. Including the analysis for overall TAAS pass rate results in totals of thirty-seven properly signed coefficients out of forty, with more than two-thirds statistically significant.

16. The sensitivity of black student TAAS performance to personnel stability at school seems more general. Note the enhanced impact of managerial stability as well, surely an influence at some remove from most students' day-to-day educational experience (Tables 5.2 and 5.3).

17. Note in this regard, for example, the function of M_3 in our theoretical model.

18. For these analyses, the performance indicator used is the overall TAAS pass rate. The estimations omit the lagged dependent variable but include all other controls.

19. This section treats human resources and their management seriously but is not designed to explore McGregor's advocacy for so-called "theory Y" over "theory X" (or vice versa). The analysis in this section draws on that presented by O'Toole and Meier (2009).

20. We also use the 2006/7 survey in Table 5.5; that survey had a response rate of 67 percent. Districts responding to the surveys were no different from nonrespondents on key variables such as enrollment, enrollment growth, students' race, ethnicity and poverty, or test scores.

21. In addition, performance measures (the dependent variables) are reported for school districts only if the district had performance data on five or more students. For certain measures, such as the black pass rate on the statewide standardized exam (white suburban districts) and SAT scores (more Texas college-bound students sit for the ACT instead), some districts have no performance data reported.

22. As of 2003 the TAAS had been replaced by the Texas Assessment of Knowledge and Skills. The results of the two examinations correlate very highly, nonetheless.

23. These items were asked on the 2004/5 survey. They were also repeated on the 2006/7 survey. The results are presented in Table 5.4 and the actual values used are from the 2004/5 survey.

24. To investigate further the causal direction, we conducted a panel version of Granger causality analysis. The results were ambiguous, and we could not rule out reciprocal causation for this and the other nine indicators. Measures at two time periods, particularly with different respondents for some of the time periods, did not provide enough leverage to sort this out statistically.

25. The analysis here draws from that presented by Meier and O'Toole (2009a).

26. This estimate is carried out on the panel so that the individual estimate for a district is based on its entire history in the data set. The key estimation question is whether to estimate one set of parameters for the entire data set or use individual parameters for each district. While in theory this distinction is important, in practice the results are correlated at 0.96. For efficiency purposes, therefore, we used the estimates based on a single set of parameters rather than more than 1,000 sets.

27. It might be supposed that managerial quality should have something to do with organizational responses to negative budgetary shocks. Analysis of the data shows no significant effect of quality. This finding is not especially surprising, given the salary-based quality measure used in this data set. The top managers are likely to be rewarded for what they do on a day-to-day basis, and budgetary crises do not occur with great frequency.

6 Nonlinearities in public management: the roles of managerial capacity and organizational buffering

Chapter 5 mentioned that, in the classic Sherlock Holmes tale "Silver Blaze," Arthur Conan Doyle's famous detective infers an important finding lurking behind an apparent non-event.[1] Similarly, in the last section of the previous chapter we built from something that did not happen – in this case, a very limited negative impact on public program performance even in the face of sizable and negative budget shocks from the environment – to highlight ways that public managers are able to protect their organizational systems from unanticipated and unpleasant disruptions to maintain performance in the face of adversity. Because managers made a series of decisions that reflected key priorities and long-term goals, the "dog that didn't bark" in this latter instance was a set of school systems that did not appreciably suffer – at least in the short run.

This chapter follows the earlier analysis, at the intersection of public management and organization theory, to explore a more general process that bureaucracies use in the face of potentially disruptive circumstances. We first examine the question of whether and how the presence of managerial *capacity* in public organizations might provide protection or support for public agencies facing environmental battering. Apart from the day-to-day efforts on the part of managers to encourage efficient and effective production, in other words, we ask if reserve capacity has positive impacts on performance. Can capacity be activated in times of crisis to protect the organization? This is the first core research question explored here. Chapter 5 offered a crisis response that entailed a series of decisions that are highly specific to school districts. Our purpose is to determine if more general principles hold that could be applied to other organizations.

The role of managerial capacity is examined as one of the nonlinear relationships in our theory. Essentially, we expect managerial capacity to interact with environmental shocks to lessen their impact. After examining two kinds of environmental shocks – budget cuts and a natural disaster – we proceed to probe additional nonlinear aspects of our managerial theory: the relationship of managerial capacity and networking together as they affect performance and the more general nonlinearities of organizational buffering in the context of our theory. In all four cases we take the nonlinear aspects of our theory seriously and seek to determine a set of interactions or different nonlinear specifications to establish which best fits the experiences of these organizations.

Managerial capacity and budget cuts

Several recent research efforts have moved public management to the central concern of organization theory – performance (Kelman 2008) – by offering evidence that public management and public managers make a difference in delivering the outputs and outcomes of public organizations (see, for instance, Lynn, Heinrich, and Hill 2001, Meier and O'Toole 2001, 2003, O'Toole and Meier 2003b, 2004a, 2004b, Donahue *et al.* 2004, Ingraham and Lynn 2004, Andrews, Boyne, Law, and Walker 2005, Brewer 2005, Chun and Rainey 2005, Martin and Smith 2005, Boyne *et al.* 2006, and Hicklin, O'Toole, and Meier 2008). Such varied managerial features as networking behavior, strategic stance, and the stability of managerial and front-line personnel are linked to stronger performance. What of the relative size, or capacity, of the managerial cadre, though? The relative size of the management cadre is important theoretically because it is a fashionable target for journalists and management consultants who condemn bureaucracy. This chapter seeks to bring some empirical evidence to bear on this popular nostrum.

Management capacity has attracted interest from public management researchers and practitioners, and efforts have been made to develop data on the relative capacity of different governmental agencies and different units of government (Ingraham, Joyce, and Donahue 2003). These data have not thus far been tied clearly to information about program outcomes, however. The present chapter taps an important aspect of managerial capacity across a large number of public organizations, and estimates the impact of capacity in mitigating the negative performance repercussions of downward exogenous shocks.

Capacity as managerial potential

Protecting public organizations and programs from disruption is a core managerial function (for a classic depiction, see Thompson 1967; or, more recently, O'Toole and Meier 2003a), even if the emphasis in recent literature has been on the proactive and entrepreneurial aspects of public management. Protection and defense are important, even if currently underemphasized, aspects of management; and evidence has been offered on behalf of the role of these elements in contributing to performance. Studies of strategic management explore a "defender" approach to dealing with the organizational environment (Miles and Snow 1978), and defenders can outperform other strategic stances in some settings (Meier *et al.* 2007). Personnel stability, including managerial stability, also contributes to outcomes (see Chapter 5). Most significantly for present purposes, subtle managerial efforts internally can protect the core organizational tasks from performance disruptions. The idea here is akin to the notion of "disturbance handler," as characterized by Mintzberg (1973). Even if environmental (budgetary) shocks enter the organization and threaten to wreak havoc, managers are far from impotent; they can reallocate staff and resources toward the highest-priority tasks within the organization and continue to deliver results with minimal disruption (see Chapter 5), at least for a while and at least within some limits.[2]

There are, accordingly, theoretical and empirical reasons to explore the various ways that public managers either buffer or dissipate negative shocks. This subject links the theoretical interest of public administration in organizational constraints with the organization theory focus on performance (Kelman 2008). The issue is important in practice as well, since no public organization, no matter how well supported and how protected from its environment, is immune from unpleasant and often unanticipated shocks.

In the present section we move beyond the aspects explored in earlier studies to examine whether managerial capacity per se can mitigate the impact of substantial budgetary shocks (for a recent review of the literature on capacity, including the complex ways that the concept has been used, see Christensen and Gazley 2008). Ingraham, Joyce, and Donahue (2003) observe that the notion of "capacity" has been defined in varied ways (see also Malysa 1996) but is typically considered a concept with multiple dimensions (15). As they indicate, "By *capacity,* we mean government's *intrinsic ability* to marshal, develop, direct, and control its financial, human, physical, and information resources" (15, emphasis added in the latter instance). Ingraham, Joyce, and Donahue then go on to stipulate four "key levers" that, they argue, drive or feed into capacity. We build from their general definition but treat the "levers" aspect more abstractly.

In particular, these researchers reference governments' "intrinsic ability" to get things done, and this framing of the concept draws one's attention not to actual operations but to the "potential" or "reserve" available for handling the varied tasks of management. Management capacity, therefore, is not management effort or practice but, rather, what *could be* mobilized if needed. An analogy drawn from the field of physics comes from the distinction between kinetic and potential energy, the former constituting energy in operation or execution, the latter the possible energy available in a system.

How might the management capacity of an administrative system be assessed? The answer is not obvious, since capacity cannot be directly and operationally observed; it constitutes a potential for action rather than action in practice. Capacity, moreover, probably has multiple dimensions, and there is no real evidence regarding which aspects might be most important and under which circumstances. Accordingly, we work from a general notion that reaches to potential that could be mobilized in varied ways. The relative size of the administrative corps of a system should tell us something of the capacity of that system, but some of the administrative personnel have regular line responsibilities and are not easily mobilized or deployed to deal in nonroutine ways with the challenges raised by sizable budgetary shocks. Our empirical study focuses on school districts, and so we consider the relative size of a district's central office staff as a rough measure of the management capacity in the organization. Central staff have regular responsibilities, but in the typical educational system the central office is the locus for financial planning, human resource analysis, data gathering, and system leadership. Central administrators would be more likely to have organization-wide views and also be less likely to be solidly booked with running day-to-day operations. These perspectives and related functions are those that, we could expect, are crucial for maximizing the operational capacity of the system in times of stress (see Yukl 2006: 364 ff.). Accordingly, we consider whether this measure of managerial capacity of school districts can contribute to performance when budgetary crises threaten.[3]

Central office staff are obviously not dead weight in such administrative systems. Under normal circumstances, they are occupied with a variety of tasks, including manifold analytical functions as well as efforts to diagnose and address chronic problems facing the organizational system, whether legal, political or production-related. One example of this last-mentioned type of chronic challenge, for the case of school districts, would be efforts to devise programs to improve student attendance. Doing so would probably boost performance on other indicia over the longer term. In a sense, however, our conceptualization of management capacity considers central staff as representing a kind of (partial) slack in the managerial resources available for near-term production, and thus as a potential for action that may not be fully realized except under relatively unusual circumstances – when tasks can be reassigned and central staff can directly address immediate performance-related needs. Indeed, the central office (headquarters) is also the location where one might expect some slack in human resources, such as it is, to be stockpiled – if there is any conscious effort to build such slack into the system. The logic of storing slack in administrative capacity is based on the notion of flexibility, innovation, and relative payoffs. Adding a single person to a line production position is likely to increase production by a marginal amount, but that person is unlikely to be usable for other functions should the need arise. Similarly adding a person as a line administrator could well improve day-to-day responsiveness, but these skills would not necessarily be transferable in times of emergency. Storing slack within the central office provides the greatest flexibility, however, because a central manager can be moved from seeking grants one week to assessing the profitability of food services the next week to an emergency fill-in for a line manager the next. Theoretically, organizational slack of this sort is best stored at the managerial levels, where it translates into increased management capacity.

Earlier research and theorizing on slack can help to clarify this notion. Thompson (1967) and Galbraith (1973; see also Pfeffer and Salancik 1978) argue that slack can serve as a buffer to help organizations absorb and survive the effects of shocks. Slack is therefore conceptualized as resources that can, if needed, be mobilized as inputs for the technical core during turbulent times. Cyert and March (1963) point out that slack can also be seen as resources available on behalf of innovation (see also Doig and Hargrove 1990: 3). Organizations with slack are likely to be more innovative – particularly so when the slack is managerial. Innovative organizations are more likely to sustain their level of performance when shocks occur given their orientation of seeking new ways of dealing with problems. Organizational slack, therefore, including managerial slack, should be positively associated with performance in organizations experiencing shocks.

A reduced model of management and performance

To consider the role of managerial capacity in assisting administrative systems in recovering from negative environmental shocks, we rely on a simple model. Since we are seeking answers about how management capacity, rather than specific managerial functions such as internal management or external networking, might carry implications for performance, we model the situation even more straightforwardly than is the case in our model introduced in Chapter 2. Here we start with a measure of managerial capacity (M_c) and a set of environmental forces (X) that are related to organizational performance (O):

$$O_t = \beta_1 M_c + \beta_2 X_t + \varepsilon_t \tag{6.1}$$

We want to separate out from this environmental term (X) some shock to the system; we call it X':

$$O_t = \beta_1 M_c + \beta_2 X_t + \beta_3 X'_t + \varepsilon_t \tag{6.2}$$

From this general linear model, we add a bit of complexity based on what is suggested in some of the qualitative literature. Specifically, we would expect management, or some forms of management such as managerial capacity, to interact with the environmental shock and reduce the impact of the shock on the organization. Specifically, we operationalize the following model, which includes such an interaction:

$$O_t = \beta_1 M_c + \beta_2 X_t + \beta_3 X'_t + \beta_4 M_c X'_t + \varepsilon_t \tag{6.3}$$

Essentially, the argument that managerial capacity, once mobilized, can mitigate environmental shocks suggests that β_3, the coefficient for the shock, should be negative but that β_4, the coefficient for the interaction term, should be positive and of such a magnitude as to cancel out the negative impact of the shock.

Sample and measures

The present analysis uses data drawn entirely from the Texas Education Agency for eight years (1995 to 2002) for a total of 8,329 cases for analysis. Missing data on individual items reduces this number somewhat in individual equations. We are interested, then, in budgetary shocks, managerial capacity, and their performance consequences, while we control for a set of other influences. Each of these variables is introduced in turn.

Measuring shocks

Our budget shock measure, introduced in Chapter 5, follows Rattsø (1999), who examines economic shocks to national economies. We regress total school district revenues (logged) on its logged values for the prior year. As explained in the preceding chapter, this regression essentially estimates what school district revenues would be if past trends continued. We then designate as "shocks" any year-to-year reductions in school district budgets that exceed 10 percent of revenues. A total of 730 budget shocks occurred in this eight-year period, thus affecting approximately 8.8 percent of the cases. In all equations here, a budget shock of 10 percent or more is converted to a dummy variable.

Managerial capacity

To deal with a shock to the organization, one would expect managers to mobilize the available managerial capacity to analyze the nature and extent of the shock and design strategies for mitigating the impact on the organization. Without some surplus capacity, one would expect that the reallocating of managerial time to deal with the shock would result in lower performance in the short term, as managers – particularly line managers – neglect their day-to-day duties in order to deal with the shock. Our measure of managerial capacity is the percentage of school district employees engaged in central office administration. This includes the superintendent, assistant superintendents, the basic administrative support staff (budgeting, personnel, etc.), and any centralized analytical capability. Capacity measured this way is relatively common in the empirical studies of organizations (Dalton *et al.* 1980). Texas school districts are exceptionally lean in terms of administration. The average district during this time period had only 1.89 percent of total employees allocated to central office administration, with a standard deviation of 1.42. Nine out of ten school districts had between 0.71 percent and 3.54 percent central administrators.

Performance indicators

A preliminary analysis incorporated ten different performance indicators in an effort to determine how budget shocks affect a variety of organizational outcomes. The results in the analysis indicated that, for most of the performance measures, managers were able to reallocate funding and staff in ways that resulted in no statistically significant reductions in performance. For three of the ten measures there were negative performance impacts in the year in question and/or in the following year (see Chapter 5).[4] We focus in this section entirely on these three indicators – the Texas Assessment of Academic Skills, the percentage of students who took either the SAT or the ACT, and the percentage of students who score above 1,110 on the SAT (or its ACT equivalent). Since these measures cover both the core task of the organization and the more difficult high-end objectives, they should provide a good overall view of how the organization deals with shocks.

Control variables and methods

We include the eight control variables used in earlier models. These variables are all commonly used in education production functions (Todd and Wolpin 2003). Assessments of the equations showed serial correlation, so a set of dummy variables for individual years has been included in the analysis as an adjustment. Pooled diagnostics for heteroskedasticity show only modest evidence of heteroskedasticity; estimation with robust standard errors generates results similar to those presented here.

Findings

Our first question is to ask what the impact of a budget shock of 10 percent or more is on the performance of the organization. Because organizations are highly autoregressive systems, they might be able to shrug off the impact of a shock immediately by short-term adaptations but absorb greater losses as a result in future years. The analysis in Chapter 5 revealed that budget shocks affected the organization in the first and second years but had no impacts in the third and fourth years. Accordingly, we include both the initial shock to the organization and a shock that is lagged by one year. Table 6.1 provides a regression of overall TAAS rates on a budget shock while controlling for the other resources and constraints of the organization. A budget shock has only a modest impact on the organization's performance in the first year; it results in only a drop of one-half of a point in TAAS performance, all other things being equal, and this relationship is statistically significant only if we use our directional hypothesis and a 0.1 one-tailed test of significance. The impact of the shock in the second year is much stronger, however, and clearly significant (a drop of about one percentage point in the TAAS pass rate).

The impact on examination pass rates, particularly the delayed impact, is clearly an important finding. Given how important school districts' performance on this metric is considered, it seems clear that, despite short-term efforts to

Table 6.1 The impact of a 10 percent or greater budget shock on students' state examination performance

Dependent variable = student TAAS exam pass rates

Independent variables	Slope	T-score
Budget shock	−0.4938	1.59
Lagged budget shock	−0.9956	3.05*
Control variables		
Teacher salaries (000s)	0.6596	12.28*
Class size	−0.3578	9.19*
Teacher experience	0.0826	1.72*
Noncertified teachers	−0.1386	7.92*
Percentage state aid	−0.0136	3.09*
Percentage of black students	−0.2329	27.50*
Percentage of Latino students	−0.1031	18.59*
Percentage of low-income students	−0.1472	19.13*
R^2	0.61	
Standard error	7.66	
F	773.71	
N	8,321	

Notes: Dummy variables for individual years not reported. * = significant at p < 0.05, one-tailed test. Time period = 1995–2002.

protect the educational system from disruption, they are not completely successful. School system superintendents overwhelmingly identify TAAS performance as their highest priority (see Chapter 5), and budget shocks certainly impede that objective.

Table 6.2 shows the impact of a 10 percent or greater budget cut on the other two performance indicators – the percentage of students who take either of the two standard national college entrance examinations and the percentage of students who score above 1,110 on the SAT or its ACT equivalent. For the former, the estimation shows that a budget shock reduces the test taking rate by approximately 1.39 percentage points in the first year – a sizable drop. This reduction in the performance criterion may be due in part to efforts to maintain and protect other key educational activities. There is no statistically significant impact of the budget shock in the following year, however. The second set of regression results reported in the table show that the percentage of students who score 1,110 or above on the SAT – a level designated by the state of Texas as "college-ready" – drops by approximately 1.28 percentage points in the first year of the budget hit

Table 6.2 The impact of a 10 percent or greater budget shock on the performance of college-bound students

Independent variables	Take SAT/ACT test		Score 1,110+	
	Slope	T-score	Slope	T-score
Budget shock	−1.3918	2.06*	−1.2819	2.84*
Lagged budget shock	−0.6173	0.86	−0.7977	1.68*
Control variables				
Teacher salaries (000s)	0.3529	3.04*	0.4749	6.23*
Class size	−1.4456	15.66*	0.1535	2.51*
Teacher experience	0.9479	8.90*	0.1444	2.05*
Noncertified teachers	−0.0061	0.16	−0.1118	4.30*
Percentage state aid	−0.0224	2.27*	−0.0608	9.36*
Percentage of black students	0.0329	1.81*	−0.0024	0.20
Percentage of Latino students	0.1437	11.46*	0.0037	0.45
Percentage of low-income students	−0.3617	20.11*	−0.2545	21.42*
R^2	0.14		0.30	
Standard error	15.18		10.07	
F	71.00		189.56	
N	7,449		7,526	

Notes: Dummy variables for individual years not reported. * = significant at $p < 0.05$, one-tailed test.

and then another 0.8 percentage points in the next. The total impact on the college-ready student cohort is a matter of real concern. On average, only 19 percent of students meet this criterion; a drop of 2.08 percentage points over two years, therefore, translates into an 11 percent drop in students meeting this criterion.

Table 6.3 examines whether managerial capacity can mitigate the impact on the TAAS pass rate of a 10 percent or greater budget cut. Because we are estimating the shock in both the first year and the second year, we add the interaction of managerial capacity with both these shocks. The estimations control for all variables included in Table 6.1, but only the relevant coefficients are presented. The intuition about an interaction term is that the slope of a relationship (between shocks and performance) changes contingent on the value of some other variable (management capacity). To see how this occurs, we illustrate using the impact of the shock in the first year. To do this we need both the shock coefficient and the interaction coefficient:

$$O = -1.24 \text{ shock} + 0.28 \text{ (shock} \times \text{capacity)}$$

Table 6.3 The impact of a 10 percent or greater budget shock on students' state examination performance

Dependent variable = student TAAS exam pass rates

Independent variables	Slope	T-score
Budget shock	−1.2411	2.42*
Lagged budget shock	−2.2501	4.28*
Management capacity	−0.0089	0.11
Management capacity times budget shock	0.2813	1.63*
Management capacity times lagged budget shock	0.5027	2.90*
R^2	0.61	
Standard error	7.64	
F	661.02	
N	8,319	

Notes: Equations also control for teacher salaries, class size, teacher experience, noncertified teachers, percentage state aid, percentage of Latino students, percentage of black students, percentage of low-income students as well as dummy variables for individual years. * = significant at $p < 0.05$, one-tailed test.

If we rearrange the terms, we get an equation that tells of the impact of the budget shock – that is, the slope – at any level of managerial capacity:

$$O = (-1.24 + 0.28 \text{ capacity}) \times \text{shock}$$

Various values can be substituted into this equation to calculate the effect of a shock at a stipulated amount of managerial capacity. For example, an organization with only 0.71 percent central office staff (the tenth percentile) would suffer a reduction of about 1.04 in the TAAS pass rate that first year. In contrast, a well-staffed central administration of 3.54 percent (the ninetieth percentile) would suffer a negative impact of only 0.26 points – a result that is itself not statistically significant.

For the second year of the shock, a similar set of calculations can be made. The equation for the slope is

$$O = -2.25 \text{ lagged shock} + 0.50 \text{ (lagged shock} \times \text{capacity)},$$

or

$$O = (-2.25 + 0.50 \text{ capacity}) \times \text{shock}$$

To illustrate, then at the tenth percentile we would see a drop of about 1.89 percentage points, and at the ninetieth percentile the result would be –0.48 percentage points.

Two important calculations can be made with these relationships. The first is to estimate where the slope of the line becomes zero and thus the shock has no impact on the organization at all. This can be done by taking the first derivative of the expression with respect to shocks and setting the result equal to zero. For the first year of the shock, this occurs when central office staff exceed 4.41 percent of total employment (about 5 percent of the cases); for the second year of the shock, the respective value is 4.48 percent, or essentially the same level. One can also take the formula for the confidence limits and calculate when the slope ceases to be statistically distinguishable from zero (or statistically significant, in layperson's terms). For the first year of the shock, that occurs when management capacity exceeds 0.764 percent (well below the mean); for the second year of the shock, this occurs at 2.38 percent central adminis-tration – a level exceeded by 24 percent of all school districts. In short, greater management capacity appears to mitigate the negative impact of budget shocks on the TAAS, and the level of capacity is well within the range of existing organizations.

What about management capacity's impact on what budget shocks do to the number of students undergoing college testing? The first two columns of Table 6.4 show the results of a regression constructed in a fashion parallel to that for the TAAS pass rate. For this performance measure, the shock has no impact in the first year if the management capacity measure reaches 4.01 percent of total staff – a value exceeded in 7 percent of the districts. In the second year, districts with a central staff larger than a mere 0.34 percent experience no negative, lagged impacts from the budget cut. Almost all the districts – 97.9 percent – have this minimum level of managerial capacity. The slope ceases to be statistically different from zero in the first year at a managerial capacity value of 2.49 percent (23 percent of the districts), and in the subsequent year at central staff size of 0.33 percent and above (98.1 percent of the districts).

Finally, the last two columns of Table 6.4 report the results for the percentage of students scoring above 1,110 on the SAT or its ACT equiva-lent. The budget shock has no effect in the first year when central staff are 3.70 percent or more of the total district employment (9 percent of all districts) and no effect in the second year when managerial capacity equals or exceeds 1.21 percent (64.2 percent of all districts). The slope ceases to

Table 6.4 The impact of a 10 percent or greater budget shock on the performance of college-bound students

Independent variables	Take SAT/ACT Test		Score 1,110+	
	Slope	T-score	Slope	T-score
Budget shock	−2.7284	2.18*	−3.0814	3.51*
Lagged budget shock	−2.9939	2.30*	−2.7196	3.21*
Management capacity	−0.7496	3.40*	−0.8213	5.65*
Management capacity times budget shock	0.6801	1.32	0.7359	2.07*
Management capacity times lagged budget shock	1.2044	2.24*	1.1732	3.16*
R^2	0.14		0.30	
Standard error	15.17		10.05	
F	61.14		163.66	
N	7,449		7,526	

Notes: Equations also control for teacher salaries, class size, teacher experience, noncertified teachers, percentage state aid, percentage of Latino students, percentage of black students, percentage of low-income students as well as dummy variables for individual years. * = significant at $p < 0.05$, one-tailed test.

have an impact distinguishable from zero at managerial capacity values of 2.63 percent (20 percent of all districts) and 1.39 percent (54.3 percent of all districts) for the first and second years, respectively. In short, higher levels of managerial capacity can indeed mitigate the negative performance-related impacts of sizable budget cuts for all three indicators examined.

Implications

In the era of new public management, bureaucracy is an epithet frequently used to criticize public organizations. Such a narrow view of bureaucracy overlooks the need for governments to have the capacity to respond to problems as they occur. This section has examined how organizations respond to budget cuts and finds that a little "bureaucracy" might be a good thing.

In a sample of 1,000 public organizations over an eight-year period, the evidence indicates that, when faced with significant budgetary shocks, some units absorb a good deal of the unpleasant event without experiencing much, if any, performance decline. Some sacrifices to performance do, nonetheless, occur. This section has explored the impact of managerial capacity in mitigating the impacts of budget shocks on the most vulnerable outcomes of public education systems.

The most obvious findings are straightforward. In these instances, the analysis shows that managerial capacity interacts with substantial budget shocks and reduces their impacts. At sufficiently high levels of managerial capacity – the level depends on which year and which performance measure – the administrative systems are protected from any performance drop. Such impacts are defensive only – that is, bureaucracy can mitigate the negative impact of budget cuts; as might be expected, it cannot turn them into a positive outcome for the organization.

Earlier research in this book demonstrated that management, including internal management, can indeed contribute to performance. In most of those studies, the decision-making and/or behavioral moves of managers add value. In this section, by way of contrast, the evidence supports the notion that latent or potential managerial resources – managerial capacity – can be mobilized to blunt the impact of negative shocks on public organizations. In terms of the model tested (Equation (6.3)), managerial capacity can be considered an aspect of M_1 feeding, when active and mobilized, into S. Our measure of this reserve "army" of management is the relative size of the central office staff. Although front-line workers in educational systems are absolutely critical for delivering results, it is logical for there to be a kind of latent performance bonus associated with central staff. The actions and the analytical effort on the part of a centrally positioned staffer, once mobilized to protect the system from the effects of a shock, might well be felt at the margin in many parts of the larger organization – for instance, in multiple classrooms and multiple schools.

Thus far, we have emphasized the contribution that managerial capacity can make to performance. We have done so by focusing particular attention on the impact, or non-impact, of budget shocks. Concentrating on shock events and their consequences allows us to see in full relief the positive aspects of carrying such capacity in administrative systems – some sort of stabilizing mechanism, perhaps, that maintains the organizational ship on course despite budgetary gales or even hurricanes. This interpretation is accurate as far as it goes – but also incomplete. If only the subject of managerial capacity were so simple. Unfortunately, capacity can cut both ways. It is worth looking closely in Tables 6.3 and 6.4 at the coefficients for managerial capacity alone – that is, the impact of capacity on performance in the absence of a budget cut. Table 6.3 shows that, with regard to pass rates on the statewide standardized exam, managerial capacity does not constitute a drag on the system in "normal" times, and this finding is both interesting and substantively significant. Table 6.4 offers a different story for the high-end performance metrics associated with college-bound students, however. For each of these measures, managerial capacity is negatively related to results for systems not experiencing sizable budget shocks.[5]

The result suggests, in other words, another key decision that should be considered by public managers: how much to protect performance against shock, on the one hand, versus how much to seek to maximize performance during more typical times, on the other. A second key decision is how much to stress basic performance versus top-end college goals. There is no generally applicable optimal point in this balancing act. The choices made by managers in particular places and at particular times are likely to be a function of several considerations – including the history of and expectations regarding large budget cuts and other shocks, the relative salience of various performance criteria, and the value placed on maintaining core production in difficult times or boosting performance during the more usual periods.

In a sense, these results and their implications might seem sensible, even expected. They certainly offer a performance-related rationale for crafting some degree of slack into administrative systems, and that is a far cry from other motivations sometimes attributed to bureaucrats – such as the argument for budget (or discretionary budget) maximization sketched by some public choice theorists.

The findings also suggest that, to the extent that slack is being built into such organizations, it makes sense to locate it in a central office, rather than (for instance) at the front line. The marginal degree of help in assisting performance potentially available from a central analyst or manager, once mobilized, is likely to be greater in terms of system results than the marginal benefit from an additional skilled instructor – even though a cadre of the latter is absolutely essential for educational excellence (Hanushek, Kain, and Rivkin 1998).

This section provides some performance-tested validity to the idea that managerial capacity generates results and raises questions about some of the injunctions of the so-called new public management, which emphasizes lean administrative systems and the market-oriented management of programs. Such arrangements may carry advantages on occasion, but they are likely to provide little assistance or protection when budgets become tight or unstable. Rather, mobilizing managerial help to shift capacity into actuality can provide results that the latest NPM innovations would be likely to miss.

Managerial capacity and natural disasters

Managerial capacity appears to mitigate negative budget shocks. Is it possible to generalize about the role of managerial capacity with regard to other shocks?[6] After all, managers and organizations must sometimes cope with sizable negative shocks that land without notice inside the organizational system and simply have to be handled. A classic case of just such an eventuality occurred on the US Gulf Coast in 2005, when two major hurricanes descended upon the same region within weeks of each other and caused massive destruction and considerable loss of life. Aside from those who were required to deal swiftly with the emergency needs of the moment (the police, fire and rescue, disaster relief, public health, and other such programs and agencies) many additional organizations and their managers had to manage major shocks stemming from the hurricanes and their aftermath – perturbations that had penetrated their organizations and posed substantial managerial challenges.

Public organizations and public managers, in short, sometimes face the "fire and rain" (to borrow singer-songwriter James Taylor's imagery) from a major unanticipated disruption and have to seek to mitigate its negative impacts. In this section, we examine via a natural experimental design how the performance of a large set of public organizations – public school districts – in the Gulf Coast region was affected by the hurricanes of 2005. We also explore the key question of whether and how aspects of management capacity were able to reduce or eliminate measurable disruptive impacts.

On August 29, 2005, Hurricane Katrina slammed into the Gulf Coast near the Louisiana–Mississippi state line. An estimated 1,900 deaths were attributed to Hurricane Katrina and the subsequent flooding; property damage was estimated at $81.2 billion. The flooding of New Orleans and subsequent problems resulted in a mass evacuation of Louisiana residents. Included in these evacuees were 46,503 students (plus their families) who were relocated to Texas and enrolled in Texas public schools. Of these students, a total of 35,091 remained in Texas schools until the end of the 2005/6 school year.[7]

While coping with the widespread devastation from Hurricane Katrina and the relocation of thousands of students and their families, the people of the Gulf Coast region took a second blow – this one from Hurricane Rita. The storm made landfall near the Texas–Louisiana border on September 24, 2005. Although only seven fatalities were attributed directly to the hurricane, the hurricane caused some $10 billion of property damage. Many damaged facilities were schools in east Texas. The evacuation itself shut down most schools in the Gulf Coast region; and, because schools further inland served as evacuee centers, these schools were also closed for a period of time. A total of 243 Texas school districts were closed for, on average, six days, with some districts closed for five or more weeks.

The two hurricanes created two distinct natural experiments in terms of how public organizations respond to environmental shocks. First, many districts received an influx of students from Louisiana. Given that Louisiana public schools are generally perceived to be inferior to the Texas schools, and given the poor urban areas that sent evacuees to Texas, the general perception was that Texas schools received an unexpected flood of students who were not likely to perform well in class and who, in addition, were living with multiple challenges resulting from their evacuee status. Many struggled with health, housing, and other difficulties. Second, many districts were then closed for a week or more, thus creating the need to adjust curricula and lesson plans to the shortened time period.

The important theoretical aspect of these two environmental shocks is that they both penetrated to the technical core of the organization – that is, the teaching of students. Many environmental shocks can be screened out (as indicated in the second term of our model) as management seeks to buffer or as stabilizing forces dampen the environmental shocks. For example, a law such as the "No child left behind" act with its massive reporting requirements might be handled by special reporting units rather than the schools themselves. In the present case, there was no way to avoid the arrival of new students or the closing of schools. The addition of new students or the cancelling of class days directly affected the production processes – that is, the schools and classrooms – of the school district. This logic suggests that we then seek information on how school districts mitigated the impact of the two hurricanes, and that we do so by focusing on the first term of the model, the internal management and structural elements.

Data and measurement

The units of analysis are all Texas school districts with 500 or more students.[8] The smaller districts are excluded from study here because these units often have highly fluctuating test data (our dependent variable measuring performance) that are overly sensitive to the handful of students who are examined. In such cases, the ability to control for past performance is limited, and so the estimation of how much an intervention event affected performance may be biased or inefficient. The 703 school districts included in the study range widely on a variety of dimensions, including student composition (race, ethnicity, etc.), resources, setting (urban, rural, suburban), and performance.

"X": measuring the environmental shock

Two measures of environmental shock are used in this analysis. First, the "Katrina student influx" shock is tapped by using the percentage of the student body in a school district that was composed of Katrina evacuees at the end of the 2005/6 school year (thus, measured in late spring 2006). The year-end count is used rather than the initial count, because students often moved from temporary districts to "permanent" districts in Texas as parents became employed. A total of 424 out of the 703 districts in the study enrolled Katrina evacuees as students, with a range from 0 to 5.42 percent of the district's total enrollment; these districts contained 99.8 percent of all Katrina evacuees enrolled in Texas public schools (see Table 6.5). Of those districts receiving students, the average evacuee enrollment was 0.47 percent of the overall total; but, as the standard deviation shows, the distribution is positively skewed.

Second, the shock due to Rita is measured by the total number of days the school district was closed because of the impact of the storm. (Rita caused a number of Texas system closures, but Katrina, for which the brunt of the impact occurred considerably further to the east, caused few Texas district closures.) Table 6.5 shows that 243 districts were closed approximately one week (5.14 days), but that the standard deviation indicates a positively skewed distribution. Twenty-eight districts were closed more than two weeks. Logic suggests that the relationship between days missed and student performance is likely to be subject to a threshold effect. Missing a single day

Table 6.5 Organizational shocks: Hurricanes Katrina and Rita

Relocated students as percentage of enrollment	
Mean	0.28
Standard deviation	0.52
Low	0.00
High	5.42
Mean of impacted districts	0.47
Days of school missed due to district closure	
Mean	1.36
Standard deviation	3.34
Low	0.00
High	29.00
Mean of impacted districts	5.14

of class is unlikely to cause major problems for teachers or students. To account for such a threshold, we recalculated this variable to include days missed only if the period of closing constituted more than one week of school – that is, six or more days; sixty districts met this criterion.[9]

The two environmental shocks affected some of the same districts. Of those districts in the study, 20 percent were hit by both shocks, while 67.1 percent were hit by at least one of the shocks.[10] Because these measures of the shocks sustained are somewhat collinear and because we attempt to explain the response to the shocks via interactive effects, we estimate the impact of the shocks both separately and together in the same equation. The results are highly similar, although the impact of Katrina students is lessened by its collinearity with the Rita/days measure.[11]

"O": outcome measures

There are many ways to evaluate the success of public school systems. By one relatively low standard, the schools were a clear success; 46,000 students were absorbed and damaged schools reopened. A more interesting assessment is how the shocks affected district scores on the Texas Assessment of Knowledge and Skills. Because the "official" TAKS pass rate, known as the accountability subset, permits students to be excluded from the test if the student is enrolled in special education, has limited English skills, or has not resided in the district for a sufficient time period, we do not employ the official rate in our analysis. Rather, we use the pass rate for *all* students in the district. This is especially important in picking up the impact of the Katrina students, since many of them might have changed districts after the late October deadline and thus be excluded from the accountability subset. Because the overall pass rate we use includes all students, the pass rates are lower than those officially used to rate and evaluate districts. For the 2005/6 school year, the average TAKS pass rate when all students are included was 66.4 percent with a standard deviation of 10.9; the all-pass rates are normally distributed and range from thirty-one to ninety-six.

Many other performance indicators used to assess schools are not particularly valuable in the present study because the measures are not likely to be sensitive to environmental shocks or were not collected in time. College preparation indicators such as SAT or ACT scores, for example, are not available for approximately one year after TAKS test results are released; in addition, performance on such indicators reflects only the age cohort that is taking the test in any given year. Two other possible performance indicators are available: the "commended" pass rate and school attendance. The commended pass rate is based on a much higher test score; to illustrate, in the average district only 9.9 percent of students passed all tests at the commended level of performance. Because this measure is affected by a much smaller number of students and the overwhelming majority of students do not meet this standard, the influx of students and the missed days is unlikely to have much impact. Attendance results are tightly clustered, with a mean of 95.9 percent and a standard deviation of 0.7. This lack of variation means that finding impacts for any variables, including the hurricanes, will be difficult. Although the analysis therefore focuses primarily on the TAKS results, we also note in passing any impacts on these two other measures.

Control variables

Our theory specifies an autoregressive model, and that fits well the logic undergirding the notion of environmental shocks. Our analysis, therefore, includes the 2005 TAKS pass rate in all models that estimate 2006 performance impacts.[12] The post-hurricane TAKS results are thus assessed relative to the pre-hurricane TAKS results (a before–after research design). Although such an estimation controls for the history of the school district by incorporating it in this lagged dependent variable, other changes in school district resources or constraints could also affect performance for 2006. To control for these factors, we include our five measures of resources and three measures of constraints. All eight of these measures are change, or

Table 6.6 Environmental shocks and student performance: the impact of students and missed class days

Dependent variable = all-students TAKS pass rate			
Independent variable	Slope	Slope	Slope
Students	−0.479* (1.84)	–	−0.437* (1.68)
Days missed	–	−0.138* (2.36)	−0.131* (2.23)
Lagged pass rate	0.928* (80.47)	0.928* (80.58)	0.928* (80.70)
Change in			
Teacher salary	0.000 (0.98)	0.000 (0.85)	0.000 (0.91)
Instruction funds	0.136* (1.65)	0.137* (1.67)	0.134 (1.64)
Black students	0.139 (0.84)	0.020 (0.13)	0.129 (0.79)
Latino students	−0.149 (1.32)	−0.179 (1.59)	−0.163 (1.45)
Low-income students	−0.005 (0.13)	0.008 (0.22)	−0.006 (0.17)
Class size	−0.654* (2.98)	−0.758* (3.42)	−0.732* (3.31)
Teacher experience	0.069 (0.40)	0.089 (0.52)	0.064 (0.37)
Noncertified	−0.034 (1.09)	−0.035 (1.14)	−0.032 (1.02)
R^2	0.91	0.91	0.91
Standard error	3.21	3.21	3.21
F	735.05	737.55	672.53
N	703	703	703

Notes: T-scores in parentheses. * = significant at $p < 0.05$, one-tailed test. Time period = 2005/6.

differenced, measures – that is, they measure the change in the variable from 2005 to 2006. All the impact of the variables' levels – e.g. if resources act as a stock of capital rather than a flow – should be reflected in the lagged dependent variable.[13]

Findings

Table 6.6 presents our findings for the impact of the two environmental shocks on the Texas school districts. These shocks are estimated separately (columns 1 and 2) as well as simultaneously in the same equation (column 3). The third column with both shock measures included in the model shows that a one percentage point increase in Katrina students (as a percentage of the student body) is associated with a drop in the TAKS all-pass rate scores of 0.437 percent ($p < 0.05$, one-tailed test). Although some of this drop might have been the result of the originally enrolled students not doing well as the result of more crowded classes and other factors, this effect size is the equivalent of 43.7 percent of Katrina evacuees failing the TAKS (in contrast to the statewide average of 33.6 percent). The maximum total impact of Katrina students on district performance, based on the maximum of 5.42 percent evacuee students, is approximately 2.4 points on the TAKS pass rate.[14]

The missed class days variable has a similar negative and statistically significant impact on TAKS scores. Each additional day (above five total days) that schools were closed is associated with a decline in TAKS scores of 0.131 percentage points on the pass rate. Based on the largest value of days closed (twenty-nine), the maximum impact on performance in districts suffering from closed schools is estimated to be approximately 3.1 points.[15] The remaining factors in the equation are generally consistent with past research. Clearly, the autoregressive term dominates the equation; it especially does so given the limitation to districts with 500 plus students. This point is reflected in the extremely high coefficient of determination accounting for 91 percent of the variance in 2006 TAKS scores. Of the differenced measures, only class size reaches the 0.05 level of statistical significance; an increase in class size from 2005 to 2006 was associated with a (predictable) drop in TAKS scores.

Estimating the performance results of the hurricane shocks raises the important theoretical question of how the districts responded to the shocks and whether there were factors that could have (or in some districts did) mitigate(d) these negative results. An analysis of the residuals from the equations in Table 6.6 confirms that the hurricane-impacted districts include both positive and negative residuals; some districts were able to take one or both shocks and still outperform expectations. East Chambers Independent School District, for example, was closed for twelve days and had slightly more than 1 percent of its study body as Katrina students, yet the district scored 6.9 percentage points above the regression line.

The parsimonious theory of public management that we use implies that districts might mitigate shocks in one or more of three fashions: through the stabilizing effects of structural (and other) elements, the operations of management in supporting and reinforcing performance-related operations, and/or the inertia that carries established practices forward into the future (past performance). The easiest explanation to consider is that for past performance. Prior performance is already in the model as part of the autoregressive estimation; for past performance to matter more than it does in Table 6.6, it would have to interact with either or both of the shock variables in such a manner that high-performing districts would be less affected by the shock than low-performing districts. We tested this idea (analysis not shown), but the impact of past perform-ance as interacted with the two shocks was not sufficient to overcome the negative impacts.

If high levels of prior performance do not limit the negative impact of environmental shocks, then structure and management are the two logical possibilities. Based on the previous study of budget cuts, managerial cap-acity is a logical candidate in this regard. Greater central management capacity permits a set of decisions to be made concerning how to evaluate the incoming students,[16] which schools can be assigned the evacuee stu-dents, what resources have to be shifted to the needed schools, how one can restructure curricula to make up for missed days, and what resources need to be procured from outside the district. By using central management to make these decisions and perform these tasks, the district does not pull school-level personnel away from the day-to-day operations of the district.

To measure central management capacity, which represents a structural resource that might mitigate the performance impacts of negative shocks, we use the percentage of total staff that are assigned to central office adminis-tration. The mean for the current set of districts is 1.34 percent, with a standard deviation of 0.63.

To determine if management capacity afforded by central structure can mitigate the negative impact of either or both of the unexpected arrival of students or the missed school days, we interact this variable with each of the hurricane shocks. These results are presented in Table 6.7.

Such interactive models induce a fair amount of collinearity and funda-mentally change the interpretation of coefficients. The standard errors normally used to determine statistical significance need to be recalculated as the marginal impact of the shocks is determined given the level of managerial capacity. To illustrate, the slope for days of school closure now depends on the value of managerial capacity, and this can be deter-mined by taking both the slope for the days and the interaction term (from column 3):

$$-0.222 \times \text{days} + 0.095 \times (\text{days} \times \text{administration})$$

Grouping the terms gives us

$$[-0.222 + (0.095 \times \text{administration})] \times \text{days}$$

Table 6.7 Administrative capacity can overcome the impact of environmental shocks

Dependent variable = all-students TAKS pass rate

Independent variable	Slope	Slope	Slope
Students	−0.901 (1.60)	–	−0.864 (1.53)
Days missed	–	−0.233 (1.54)	−0.222 (1.47)
Central administration	0.381* (1.71)	0.454* (2.30)	0.328 (1.46)
Students × administration	0.442 (0.96)	–	0.434 (0.94)
Days × administration		0.101 (0.78)	0.095 (0.73)
Lagged pass rate	0.929* (80.80)	0.928* (80.73)	0.928* (80.81)
R^2	0.91	0.92	0.92
Standard error	3.21	3.20	3.20
F	617.58	619.18	531.84
N	703	703	703

Notes: T-scores in parentheses. * = significant at $p < 0.05$, one-tailed test. Equations also control for change in teacher salaries, per student instructional funds, class size, teacher experience, noncertified teachers, black students, Latino students, and low-income students.

We can then use this equation to draw a line that will show the impact of a day of school lost at various levels of administrative capacity (see Figure 6.1). This figure, which also displays the 95 percent confidence limits, indicates that, at low levels of administrative capacity, the impact of missing a day of class is negative and statistically significant. As the level of central administration increases, however, this negative impact becomes less, and it becomes statistically indistinguishable from zero at approximately 1.0 percent of central administrators. The slope equation can be set equal to zero to get a point estimate of when the negative impact ceases – that is, has a slope of zero; this occurs when central office administration is equal to 2.33 percent of total employment. The equation actually shows a positive slope at very high levels of central administration, but this can be ignored for two reasons: these values are not statistically different from zero, and only a small percentage of districts have central administration percentages that are high (forty-eight of the 703). The logical conclusion is that, as central administrative capacity grows, it gradually eliminates the negative impact of the environmental shock on performance.[17]

Table 6.7 also shows that central management capacity has a similar impact on the shock of Katrina evacuee students (see also Figure 6.2). The impact of evacuee students is strongly negative and statistically significant at

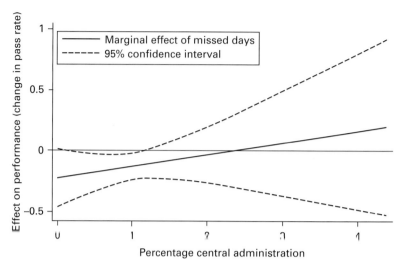

Figure 6.1   The marginal impact of missed school days contingent on managerial capacity

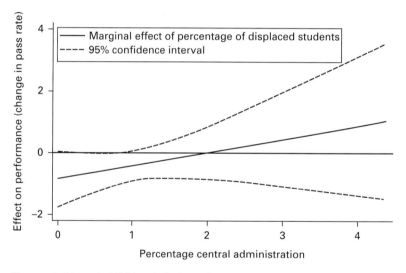

Figure 6.2   The marginal impact of Katrina students contingent on managerial capacity

low levels of managerial capacity but declines in impact as central administration increases. The point prediction of zero impact is estimated to be approximately 1.99 percent central office staff (fairly similar to the days impact). Again, the positive slope predictions are never statistically different from zero, and cover only ninety-three of the 703 total districts. In short, central management capacity appears to mitigate the negative impacts of the hurricanes.[18]

Implications

Natural disasters are a different type of shock from budget cuts because there is no advance warning. As such, a natural disaster is a rigorous test of the management capacity hypothesis. Indeed, the two hurricanes did reduce the overall level of TAKS scores in the district (either by the influx of students or the school closures). Management capacity interacted with these shocks, however, and was able to reduce their impact on performance. In short, management capacity operated as organizational slack and had an important nonlinear impact in crisis situations.

Management capacity in non-crisis times

The previous two sections have demonstrated the crucial role of managerial capacity in dealing with budget cuts and major shocks to the organization such as a natural disaster. In both cases, managerial capacity had nonlinear impacts to mitigate the negative consequences of the shock. These findings raise the question of whether or not managerial capacity is also useful in other management efforts and if the impact continues to be in nonlinear interactions with other factors. One potential candidate for such a set of relationships is managerial networking, a management activity that has demonstrated substantial impact on performance. This section investigates whether managerial capacity can enhance the impact of networking.[19]

The literature often emphasizes the necessity for – and benefits of – networking efforts, but effective managerial action entails costs as well. Various reasons thus suggest the plausibility of the idea that the performance-related effects of managerial networking are likely to be contingent on the capacity of the managerial cadre to perform or assist with such functions.

This point can best be seen by considering what managers typically do when they interact with others in their networked environment. Most public managers face an environment with myriad potential actors who might be useful to the "core" organization and/or might seek to impede the organization in its effort to attain its goals. These actors, in turn, are frequently linked with yet others (Scharpf 1993, 1997).

Public managers face the prospect of sorting through a potentially large series of interactions with other actors, individual and corporate. Some interactions are sure to be mandatory; some are voluntary; and some contain elements of both. Certain interactions may be one-shot, but, in the longer term implementation of policy, managers would need to take into account repeat pattern formulations (see Stoker 1992). The manager must decide which external actors to engage; how to indicate this intention and initiate contact; and, if engagement takes place, what strategy to take. Any such externally oriented action entails some opportunity costs; managers cannot do everything at once. There may also be some networking interactions in which both (all) actors will, on average, be better off; some zero-sum patterns; and some negative-sum interactions in which the strategy will be to limit losses.

In any of these, the manager has to convince the other actor(s) to engage and to cooperate – that is, to contribute positively to the manager's organization or program. While success might occasionally be achieved through sheer persuasion, the manager typically must bring something to the interaction. Such inducements might be in the form of monetary resources, superior information, or the capacity to take action if some consensus is reached. By "bearing gifts" in these exchanges, the manager can offer something of value to induce the other actor(s) to participate. In principle, therefore, the payoff from managerial networking will be contingent in part on the creativity a manager displays in identifying attractive options (a form of capacity), the inducements that the manager brings to the interaction (resources), and the ability to convert the results into concrete gains (another aspect of capacity).

This formulation implies that managerial networking – that is, making contacts with key actors in the environment for the purposes of identifying and implementing mutually acceptable, even attractive, jointly determined decisions – will depend on the resources, broadly construed, that the manager possesses. Managerial capacity can be expected to be one crucial resource needed to operate effectively in an interdependent environment.

Sorting through such complicated institutional terrain and making the most appropriate strategic moves, therefore, calls for a considerable amount of informational and cognitive capacity (Simon 1997). In complex public management settings, this requirement can perhaps be met via managerial capacity. Greater managerial capacity can contribute to the choice among interactions in which to engage, and how. Nor is this all; engaging the right partners in an appropriate way does not ensure successful completion. Greater managerial capacity can be used to implement whatever agreement occurs in the networking process. An environmental actor might even be more willing to participate if he or she perceives that the manager has the ability to transform the network discussions into reality.

This conceptualization of managerial interactions suggests that managerial capacity more broadly conceived can be expected not only to boost performance on tasks amenable to managerial influence but also to enhance the value to the core organization of managerial interactions in the interdependent environment. Managerial capacity, in short, can be viewed as the potential to analyze and evaluate relationships with environmental actors and the potential to implement any decisions that result from those interactions.

Modeling the impact of managerial capacity

We begin with several aspects of public management. Substantial earlier research in this volume and elsewhere has shown positive contributions to organizational outcomes from managerial networking in the environment of public organizations, while interactions between political principals and top managers were negatively related to results. The work has also shown that managerial quality positively influences performance, as does a key aspect of personnel management: retaining experienced employees and thereby maintaining stability in human resources. Our opening argument generates the expectation that management capacity should also contribute. These several aspects of management and their expected relationships, therefore, yield the following (with several of our usual managerial functions relabeled here for ease of interpretation in the current analysis, and with the use of a simplified linear additive model for the other managerial functions already explored):

$$O_t = \beta_1 M_2 + \beta_2 M_u + \beta_3 M_q + \beta_4 M_p + \beta_5 M_c + \varepsilon_t \tag{6.4}$$

where

O_t is some measure of organizational outcome at time t,

M_2 represents external networking efforts by managers,

M_u is a measure of managerial interactions upward with political principals,

M_q is a measure of managerial quality,

M_p is personnel stability,

M_c represents management capacity,

ε is an error term, and

β_1 to β_5 are estimable parameters.

Equation (6.4) is insufficient, for two reasons. First, it lacks a vector of control variables that represent the environmental forces that must be taken into account in explaining outcomes. Adding such a vector, represented by X_t to designate a set of such forces as they operate at time t, yields the following:

$$O_t = \beta_1 M_2 + \beta_2 M_u + \beta_3 M_q + \beta_4 M_p + \beta_5 M_c + \beta_6 X_t + \varepsilon_t \qquad (6.5)$$

Second, our argument is not that managerial capacity adds in a linear manner to the performance of an organization; other studies have demonstrated that it does in some cases (Meier, O'Toole, and Hicklin 2010; O'Toole and Meier 2010). Rather, we are interested in whether managerial capacity can be the gift that managers bear – that is, the resources that make interactions with environmental actors more successful. The question, therefore, requires estimating the specification in Equation (6.6) that includes an interaction between managerial networking (M_2) and managerial capacity (M_c) as indicated by the new multiplicative term in the model:

$$O_t = \beta_1 M_2 + \beta_2 M_u + \beta_3 M_q + \beta_4 M_p + \beta_5 M_c + \beta_6 X_t + \beta_7 M_2 M_c + \varepsilon_t \quad (6.6)$$

If the inclusion of this new term adds additional explanation to our models, then we can conclude that managerial networking interacts with managerial capacity. More precisely, we are expecting the slope coefficient for the interaction (β_7) to be positive.

Data and measurement

For the empirical portion of this study, the units of analysis are all Texas school districts. In this analysis we include eight years of performance data (1995 to 2002) and supplement these with data from an original management survey. The survey had a 55 percent response rate, and when combined with the archival data produces 4,114 total cases for analysis. Missing data on one of the performance indicators reduces the total number of cases to 3,798 in that case.[20]

A pooled time-series analysis such as this one needs to be concerned with violations in the assumptions of multiple regression, particularly serial correlation and heteroskedasticity. Assessments of the equations showed serial correlation, so a set of dummy variables for individual years was included in the analysis as an adjustment. Pooled diagnostics for heteroskedasticity showed only modest evidence of heteroskedasticity; estimation with robust standard errors generated results similar to those presented here.

"M": the management variables

Managerial networking. This variable (M_2) seeks to measure the reported behavior of school district top managers as they interact with the important parties in the district's environment. Our measure, introduced in Chapter 3, is a factor score that indicates how frequently superintendents interact with four key environmental actors.

Management capacity (M_c) is operationalized as the percentage of employees who are located in central office administration (as opposed to school administration). The mean percentage of central office administrators for all districts in this study is only 1.89 percent, with a standard deviation of 1.43.

Managerial quality (M_q) is a validated measure based on the residual from a model explaining salaries of district superintendents. We replicated that analysis for the years 2000 to 2002 and created a measure for 1995 to 2002.

Managing upward is measured as the frequency of interaction with school board members, on a scale ranging from daily to never.

Personnel stability. Two aspects of personnel stability are included. *Managerial stability* seeks to measure constancy in top leadership; it is simply the number of years the superintendent has been employed by the district *in any capacity. Workforce stability* is the percentage of teachers employed by the district during the preceding year who continue to work for the district.

"O": outcome measures

This study incorporates three different performance indicators in an effort to determine how public management affects a variety of organizational outcomes. The performance indicators are selected to illustrate a range of functions that the school districts perform: the overall student pass rate on the Texas Assessment of Academic Skills, the percentage of students who score above 1,110 on the SAT (or its ACT equivalent), and attendance rates.

We also include the three constraint variables and the five resource variables that are contained in previous models.

Table 6.8 How the interaction of managerial networking and managerial capacity affects organizational performance

Dependent variable = student exam pass rates

Independent variables	Slope	T-score	Slope	T-score
Managerial networking	1.1425	9.25	0.9045	4.62
Managerial capacity	0.0075	0.08	0.0204	0.22
Networking × capacity			0.1294	1.57
School board contact	−0.7894	5.76	−0.7897	5.76
Management quality	0.7223	5.88	0.7185	5.85
Management experience	0.0573	4.64	0.0571	4.63
Personnel stability	0.1548	9.04	0.1551	9.06
R^2	0.64		0.64	
Standard error	7.13		7.12	
F	341.43		326.14	
N	4,114		4,114	

Notes: Equations also control for teacher salaries, class size, teacher experience, noncertified teachers, percentage state aid, percentage of Latino students, percentage of black students, percentage of low-income students as well as dummy variables for individual years. Time frame 1995–2002.

Findings

As noted above, the statewide standardized test, TAAS, is considered the education system's primary indicator, and it is used to evaluate the performance of both the superintendents and the school districts in Texas. Table 6.8 provides two regressions for this dependent variable. On the left side is the regression without the interaction term, and on the right the interaction between management capacity and managerial networking is included.

First, it is apparent that, leaving aside the influences of networking and managerial capacity, the other management measures included in both specifications have their expected impacts; all these additional slopes are statistically significant. We omit detailed discussion of these in order to focus attention on the primary relationships under consideration here.[21]

With regard to the results reported in Table 6.8, note that on the left, by itself, managerial capacity has no impact on student TAAS performance.

In interpreting the interactive results on the right, care must be taken, because the multiplicative nature of the interaction often creates relatively artificial T-scores (they compare to a zero point that may be well outside the range of the data). As a result, the equation has to be rearranged to calculate the slopes if the contingent relationship is to be illustrated. In essence this process shows that the impact of managerial networking will vary depending on the value of managerial capacity. It is also necessary to recalculate the standard errors to determine if the impact of the interactive relationship is statistically significant at these various levels.[22]

To determine the impact of managerial networking, the zero-order coefficient (0.905) and the interacted coefficient (0.129) both have to be taken, as follows:

Networking slope $= 0.905 + 0.129$ (capacity)

First we can illustrate the problem with direct interpretation of the uninteracted slopes in an equation such as this. The formula above says that, when capacity is zero, the slope of networking's impact on TAAS performance is 0.905, or a one standard deviation change (M_2 is a factor score) in networking is associated with an increase of 0.905 percentage points on the TAAS, all other things being equal. This is the equivalent of the zero-order slope listed in the table; but, since there are no school districts with no central office administrators, this part of the relationship is well beyond the range of the data. The best way to interpret the interactive slope is to include representative values of capacity and then calculate the slope of networking at those levels of capacity. We do such a calculation using the mean value of capacity, as well as values one standard deviation above the mean and one standard deviation below the mean. These calculations produce the following results.

Level of capacity	Slope for networking
0.46	0.964*
1.89	1.149*
3.32	1.333*

* $=$ significantly different from zero, $p < 0.05$.

At low levels of managerial capacity (0.46 percent of central office staff), therefore, a one standard deviation increase in networking is associated with an increase of 0.964 points on the TAAS, but at high levels of capacity (3.32 percent of central office staff) a similar increase in networking is associated with an increase of 1.333 points – or about a 38 percent increase in relative impact. Although a 1.33 percentage point increase might not seem like a great deal, this result is for a one standard deviation change in networking. Since this is a factor measure with an effective range from −3 to +3, the total impact at this level of managerial capacity could be as large as eight percentage points – a substantively important amount.

Although our concern is not how networking influences the impact of managerial capacity on performance, the equations show some interesting results in this regard. A similar assessment for managerial capacity, which is not statistically significant on the left-hand side regression, shows the following.

Level of networking	Slope for capacity
−1.0	−0.109
0.0	0.149
+1.0	0.278*

* = significantly different from zero, $p < 0.05$.

Capacity has no impact on TAAS performance except at high levels of networking, where its impact is statistically significant but not especially large. The networking measure ranges as high as +3, however, so this impact for a small number of districts will be considerably larger. The overall conclusion from Table 6.8 is that managerial capacity enhances the positive impact that networking has on performance; and, at high levels of networking, managerial capacity also has a positive impact on TAAS performance, all other things being equal.

Student attendance is crucial to school districts but is not easy to influence, given that many student absences are the result of illness or other factors outside the control of the student or the school district. At the same time, school districts spend substantial time trying to influence the portion of attendance that is under the control of the student. Table 6.9 uses the same format as Table 6.8 to show the interaction of managerial capacity and networking and their impact on student attendance. It is noteworthy that, on the left hand equation, both managerial networking and managerial capacity have significant, positive impacts on performance.

Table 6.9 How the interaction of managerial networking and managerial capacity affects organizational performance: attendance

Dependent variable = student attendance rates

Independent variables	Slope	T-score	Slope	T-score
Managerial networking	0.0730	5.67	0.0380	1.86
Managerial capacity	0.0975	10.12	0.0994	10.28
Networking × capacity			0.0190	2.21
School board contact	−0.1281	8.93	−0.1282	8.97
Management quality	0.0506	3.95	0.0500	3.90
Management experience	−0.0012	0.93	−0.0012	0.95
Personnel stability	0.0126	7.05	0.0126	7.07
R^2	0.26		0.26	
Standard error	0.74		0.74	
F	69.58		66.70	
N	4,114		4,114	

Notes: Equations also control for teacher salaries, class size, teacher experience, noncertified teachers, percentage state aid, percentage of Latino students, percentage of black students, percentage of low-income students as well as dummy variables for individual years.

Calculating the slopes for managerial networking at different levels of managerial capacity reveals the following impacts.

Level of capacity	Slope for networking
0.46	0.047*
1.89	0.074*
3.32	0.101*

* = significantly different from zero, $p < 0.05$.

The impact of managerial networking essentially doubles as the level of management capacity increases from one standard deviation below the mean to one standard deviation above the mean. This finding makes a great deal of intuitive sense. While networking can create pressures or generate ideas for how to deal with truancy problems, actually dealing with the problems requires some capacity to act, and that capacity is almost always lodged at the central office level.[23]

Performing the same set of calculations for managerial capacity at different levels of managerial networking shows the following:

Level of networking	Slope for capacity
−1.0	0.080*
0.0	0.099*
+1.0	0.108*

* = significantly different from zero, p < 0.05.

Table 6.10 How the interaction of managerial networking and managerial capacity affects organizational performance: college readiness

Dependent variable = percentage scoring above 1,110 on SAT				
Independent variables	Slope	T-score	Slope	T-score
Managerial networking	0.7471	4.33	0.2196	0.73
Managerial capacity	−0.7589	3.98	−0.8114	4.22
Networking × capacity			0.3166	2.12
School board contact	−0.2146	1.12	−0.2216	1.16
Management quality	0.6733	3.88	0.6649	3.83
Management experience	−0.0182	1.07	−0.0184	1.08
Personnel stability	0.0783	2.89	0.0766	2.83
R^2	0.32		0.32	
Standard error	9.60		9.60	
F	84.36		80.81	
N	3,798		3,798	

Notes: Equations also control for teacher salaries, class size, teacher experience, noncertified teachers, percentage state aid, percentage of Latino students, percentage of black students, percentage of low-income students as well as dummy variables for individual years.

Again, the interaction shows that the impact of managerial capacity on absenteeism increases when the superintendent engages in more effort to manage externally in the network. The relative increase from low to high (35 percent) is not as large as it is for the networking increase contingent on capacity (118 percent), but the impacts are strong and statistically significant at all levels.

The college board scores variable (see Table 6.10) has a different relationship for managerial networking and performance in the noninteracted equation. While managerial networking is strongly related to performance in a positive direction, the relationship for managerial capacity is negative and significant. Our experience in interviewing superintendents suggests that the negative relationship for capacity, in part, reflects tradeoffs that superintendents have to make. Resources committed to central office administration are resources that cannot be committed to other programs, particularly to programs that enhance the performance of the best students. Although the choice might not always be so stark as whether to hire an advanced placement calculus teacher or an attendance officer instead, once such hires are made they create a path dependence in the short term, since the individuals are not fungible.

The interactive relationship shows that increases in managerial capacity have a dramatic impact on the influence that networking has on the college boards indicator, specifically the following.

Level of capacity	Slope for networking
0.46	0.366*
1.89	0.819*
3.32	1.272*

* = significantly different from zero, $p < 0.05$.

The impact of managerial networking at high levels of managerial capacity is more than three times that at lower levels of capacity. The effect sizes here are large, as the mean value of the dependent variable is 18.8 – which means that an increase of 1.272 percentage points is a 6.8 percent increase in the proportion of students meeting this criterion (over a range of −3 to +3, this impact is clearly substantial for this subset of districts).

The results for managerial capacity, which has a negative relationship with college-bound performance, are somewhat different, but follow the same pattern.

Level of networking	Slope for capacity
−1.0	−1.128*
0.0	−0.811*
+1.0	−0.494*

* = significantly different from zero, $p < 0.05$.

Managerial capacity's negative impact drops by approximately 56 percent as the level of managerial networking is increased from one standard deviation below the mean to one standard deviation above the mean. The relationship remains statistically significant at this level, but becomes statistically insignificant when the level of networking approaches two standard deviations above the mean.

Implications

Our theoretical discussion argued that managerial networking and management capacity should be expected to interact, with networking having enhanced positive impacts on organizational performance at greater levels of capacity. Further, we expected to see such impacts across organizational outcomes: for any given level of networking activity, enhanced capacity should allow managers to leverage more organizational benefit from external interactions. Identifying interaction partners and types of interactions, engaging productively with promising external opportunities, negotiating joint agreements, and implementing the results of any bargains reached should all be more effectively accomplished with enhanced central capacity.

The findings confirm these expectations. For arguably the most important measure of performance, pass rates on the statewide examination, the impact of managerial networking increases as capacity increases −38 percent across the range examined. The interactive effects for the other dependent variables tested are even greater. The networking slope more than doubles at higher capacity for school attendance – a result that fits with how we might expect networking to contribute to this outcome. Interestingly, while capacity itself negatively influences college-bound performance at many levels of networking – a pattern probably reflecting the opportunity costs of capacity for this outcome – greater capacity dramatically boosts the contribution of networking to college-bound performance.

Nonlinearity and buffering: applying Occam's razor

The previous three sections of this chapter examined nonlinearities in public management with a focus on managerial capacity. Capacity at high enough levels was able to mitigate the deleterious impacts of budget cuts and natural disasters. Capacity also interacted with managerial networking in nonlinear ways to influence performance. These findings raise the question as to whether there might be a generic process by which capacity protects the organization from turbulent aspects of the environment that might harm the organization. To address this broader question, we return to our general model of management and develop a measure of buffering. We then seek to determine if the nonlinear predictions of our theoretical model hold in the real world.

From the extensive empirical work documenting cases of public organizations operating in complex and turbulent environments – settings in which the organizations are charged with carrying out policy objectives as they face interdependence with other actors, including organizational and political ones – it seems clear that two broad classes of forces can contribute to protecting, insulating, or mitigating impacts on the organization from the external environment: structural or procedural elements that help secure an administrative system, on the one hand, and managerial contributions to protection, on the other (see O'Toole and Meier 2003a: 112).[24] As a shorthand, we refer to any of these influences that reduce the impacts of environmental forces on organizational or performance results as buffers, and we refer to the dynamic of reducing such influences as buffering.

Whether structural or managerial (or both), several types of buffering functions can be envisioned. Various particular forms of adaptive response have been shown to be used in organizations to protect core tasks from environmental perturbations, including the development of organizational subunits to handle any uncertainty and instability generated externally (see, for instance, Fennell and Alexander 1987). Indeed, even the development of interorganizational linkages can be a means of buffering core organizational activities (Miner, Amburgey, and Stearns 1990).

If the variety of buffering forms are framed at an abstract level, the protective mechanism or effort could serve as a blockade insulating the administrative system from external shocks up to, but not past, a particular size (much like levees around New Orleans), or a selective filter allowing some but not all external influences through the apparatus (a legislative affairs office for contact with public officials), or a dampener reducing the amplitude of any external influences (O'Toole and Meier 2003a: 113–14; see also Lynn 2005: 38–9). Modeling the impacts of such different forms of buffering would mean taking into account several rather distinct forms of insulation, as explained in the discussion of buffering in Chapter 2, each with its own somewhat different effect on the administrative systems in question. Indeed, some public organizations might employ simultaneously several different kinds of buffering devices or effort. Investigating all such buffers would be a useful task, but modeling and estimating the impacts of buffering across many such organizations requires some simplification.

We return to our base model presented in Chapter 2:

$$O_t = \beta_1(S + M_1)O_{t-1} + \beta_2(X_t/S_e)(M_3/M_4) + \varepsilon_t \qquad (6.7)$$

where

O is some measure of outcome,

S is a measure of stability, denoting structural, procedural, and other elements that support unperturbed production,

M denotes management, which can be divided into three parts:

M_1 – management's contribution to organizational stability through additions to hierarchy/structure as well as regular operations,

M_3 – management's efforts to exploit the environment,

M_4 – management's effort to buffer environmental shocks,

X is a vector of environmental forces,

ε is an error term,

the other subscripts denote time periods, and

β_1 and β_2 are estimable parameters.

Where does buffering, as we have defined it, appear in the model? Our conception of buffering is similar to Lynn's (2005: 45) idea of moving buffers out into the interface with the environment. Hence, buffering is present as the denominator of the second, or environmental, term:

$$\beta_2(X_t/S_e)(M_3/M_4) \tag{6.8}$$

or, after rearranging,

$$\beta_2(X_t M_3)/(S_e M_4) \tag{6.9}$$

This term models the impact of the set of environmental forces X_t on outcome O_t. The impact can be leveraged by managerial effort (M_3) or buffered by the combined impacts of stabilizing forces (S_e), such as structure, as well as managerial influences aimed at protecting the production system (M_4). Note that this model simplifies by treating the buffering function in mathematical terms solely as a dampener. This reciprocal function ($1/S_e M_4$) essentially reduces the size of the impact that an X or environmental variable can have (hence the division into X), by dampening the impact over time. Eventually, other functional forms can be formally specified and tested, as we draw once more from the extensive case study literature, but this particular version is a useful first step. It is the "$S_e M_4$" denominator as a whole, then, that serves as the model's term for buffering.[25]

In Chapter 3 we noted that the two terms related to managing the environment could be combined where $M_2 = M_3/M_4$.[26] Thus M_2 incorporates all efforts to manage externally in the environment, in contrast to managing the organization, M_1:

$$O_t = \beta_1(S + M_1)O_{t-1} + \beta_2(X_t/S_e)(M_2) + \varepsilon_t \tag{6.10}$$

Although much of our preceding work has used this combined M_2 term in a series of analyses that demonstrate that managerial networking can be effective and that its impacts can be nonlinear, as the model indicates, they have not addressed four fundamental elements of the model. We have not proposed and validated a measure of M_4,[27] the efforts of managers to buffer the environment; we have not incorporated the structural elements of stability; we have not addressed whether the M_2 measure contains the M_3 and M_4 elements or whether there might be other elements of M_4 that have yet to be measured; and we have not addressed the hypothetical functional form specified in their model – that is, the reciprocal function.

This section addresses three of these questions. First, we propose a measure of environmental buffering that encompasses both structural and managerial activities. Second, we incorporate this measure into an explanation of organizational performance that includes several other management and stabilizing factors as well as measures of resources and constraints. Third, we then brave Occam's razor[28] to determine if the complex nonlinear relationship specified by theory is the most appropriate functional form, or if a simpler estimation will provide equally good results. With regard to the fourth question, we make the assumption that, because previous measures of M_2 did not specifically address the buffering function, prior analysis does not explicitly include buffering actions. The model can thus be expanded to contain both M_2, composed of actions seeking environmental opportunities, and M_4, an explicit buffering function.

Measuring buffering

An organization's effort to buffer environmental influences is likely to be accomplished through a complex combination of structures (along with associated procedures)[29] and managerial actions (Meyer and Rowan 1977; Miner, Amburgey, and Stearns 1990: 690; Sorenson 2003). Faced with a turbulent environment (for a classic treatment, see Lawrence and Lorsch 1967) or one that is relatively stable but hostile, organizational leadership has two options. First, decision makers could establish structures (S_e) that interact with the environment to absorb the environmental pulses, and in the process shelter the organization's core technologies (Thompson 1967). In business firms, these structural elements would include organizational units that deal with inventory control for inputs or post-production marketing and distribution of outputs. In a public organization, such structural features might include special legislative affairs or public affairs units designed to handle requests from outside the organization, or an emergency response unit such as a SWAT (special weapons and tactics) team or Delta Force. For school districts, the organizations examined here, the response to the children of migrant workers provides an excellent illustration of buffering. The Houston Independent School District begins the school year with about 176,000 students, with enrollment then peaking at 210,000 in November. To buffer its schools from this turbulence, HISD has created student intake units to conduct immediate assessments of the students (language, grade level, special needs) and assign them to appropriate classes. These bilingual assessment units operate as what Lynn (2005: 41) terms "absorbed slack," and thus process the environmental influx and allow schools to continue to function in regular ways.[30]

Second, management itself could engage in a set of buffering activities. Management might decide that certain environmental events or influences will be ignored, while others will require the intervention of top management, and still others should be programmed for response by specific units – say, an accounting office primed to handle external audits or other challenges regarding expenditures. School systems sometimes establish their own police forces to deal with security and crime problems rather than rely on the double environmental shock of a crime and the arrival of an outside police force. Such a unit allows management to set procedures for dealing with minor crimes without involving local law enforcement. This buffering component of management (which is termed M_4) might be an ancillary function of management's effort to interact with the environment (M_2) – that is, while seeking external opportunities, managers can also identify negative or threatening forces. We can consider including both aspects of management, therefore, in the model eventually specified here.

Because the buffering function itself is a combination of both structure and management, we opt for a unified measure of overall buffering (in lieu of trying to separate out the two processes), stipulate operational definitions of each, and then simultaneously test these concepts and the various ways they could combine. This simplification then allows as a first step a validation of the measure of buffering as dampening, and an effort to probe how it affects performance. If this effort is successful, future research will permit an examination of exactly how the buffering process is developed and operated.

How might we get an organizational measure of buffering? If we start with the basic principle that organizations are autoregressive systems – that what they do today reflects what they did yesterday – then an examination of how autoregressive processes respond to novel events should be useful. Consider the following simple autoregressive system:

$$O_t = \beta_1 O_{t-1} + \beta_2 X_t + \varepsilon_t \qquad (6.11)$$

where O is the organization's outcome[31] and X is some type of environmental shock, whether positive or negative from the standpoint of performance.

One unit of any "X" variable affects output by β_2 in the current year; but, because this output then becomes part of the production base of the organization (O_{t-1}), the impact of one unit of X in the second year becomes $\beta_1\beta_2$. Subsequent years see additional impacts, with the size of each year's impact declining in what is termed a geometrically distributed lag. Although a buffering process could operate either on the X term through β_2 or on the O_{t-1} term via β_1, in this assessment our attention focuses on the latter.

Let us assume that there are two organizations, one with an autoregressive parameter of 0.9 and another with an autoregressive parameter of 0.7. Let us further assume the occurrence of some environmental disturbance that has an impact of Y on the organization. The following illustrates the impact that this Y-level disruption has on the two organizations in future years.

Parameter	Year 0	Year 1	Year 2	Year 3	Year 4	Year 5
0.9	Y	0.9Y	0.81Y	0.73Y	0.66Y	0.59Y
0.7	Y	0.7Y	0.49Y	0.34Y	0.24Y	0.17Y

Even five years later, all other thing being equal, the environmental disturbance retains nearly 60 percent of its impact for the first organization but has fallen all the way to a 17 percent impact in the second.[32] In organization-theoretical terms, we think of the first unit as tightly coupled internally; any disturbance, however slight, will reverberate through the organization for a substantial period of time (see Meyer and Rowan 1977 and Powell and DiMaggio 1991).[33] The second organization is more loosely coupled internally (probably decentralized but with absorbed slack; see Lynn 2005: 41); events dissipate more quickly over time. This is the pattern that one would expect to see if the organization had established structures and used managerial processes to buffer or reduce the impact of environmental events or forces over time.[34] Loose coupling permits an organization to make a mistake and correct that mistake without endangering the organization (Lynn 2005: 49). In this way it lessens the threat of environmental shocks on the entire organization. This view is consistent with that of Meyer and Rowan (1977: 341), who suggest that organizations "tend to buffer their formal structures from uncertainties of technical activities by becoming loosely coupled."

How might we get an estimate of the impact of such buffering or loosely coupled internal structure on program performance? A simple autoregressive estimation will not work, because this coefficient essentially uses a panel of this year's and last year's performance for many organizations, and it is not possible, as a result, to get an organization-specific estimate with only two points. Because we have several years of prior data, our solution is to use the historical data on each of the organizations to establish a baseline measure of buffering in a subsequent period. Since our analysis here investigates the years 1995 to 2002, we use data from 1986 to 1994 for each organization to estimate this buffering process (incorporating therefore both structural and managerial aspects). This approach allows us to have an a priori estimate of buffering that is independent of the actual data used in the study. The specific buffering measure correlates output (TAAS scores) at time t with output from time t+1 for the 1986–1994 period.[35] This correlation coefficient is transformed into a buffering measure by subtracting it from 1.0 so that larger numbers indicate greater levels of buffering (looser coupling) and lower levels indicate less buffering.

Three aspects of this measure merit discussion. First, the measure is essentially a system component rather than an event component. It seeks to assess the organization's response to the environment in general rather than in relation to any one specific event or type of external event. It is quite likely that certain events might generate much greater effort at buffering, depending on their salience and centrality for the organization in question. At the same time, a systematic buffering element is likely to play a role even in these one-time unique occasions, because systemic buffering obviously provides some of the experience and capacity to deal with the more idiosyncratic incidents.

Second, the measure is focused on outcomes. We are interested in explaining the policy performance of systems rather than, for instance, their internal operations. For that reason, the buffering measure directly taps how an administrative system is or is not protected from having its production – in terms of results – shaped over time by reverberations from earlier events.

Third, the measure opts for parsimony in the composition of the measurement – that is, it is a single measure generalized from past behavior and does not attempt to separate out the individual influences of structure and management. We use this strategy because we are interested in probing the complex functional forms in our model of management.

Our strategy of analysis is to make some simplifying assumptions in the model and proceed to test this notion of buffering as dampening, and its various functional forms, in a step-by-step process. We start with the base model in Equation (6.7) and regroup the elements in the second term of the model to cluster stability and M_4 together as follows:

$$O_t = \beta_1(S + M_1)O_{t-1} + \beta_2(X_tM_3)/(S_eM_4) + \varepsilon_t \qquad (6.12)$$

In this model, buffering generates a highly complex reciprocal relationship that interacts with M_3 and X_t (that is, $S_e M_4$ is divided into X_tM_3). We then simplify this model by focusing solely on the second term of the model, thus eliminating the autoregressive term as in Equation (6.13).[36] The rationale is that the current investigation focuses entirely on how environmental influences (the X vector) shape performance and may be mitigated by buffering. These elements of the model all appear in the second term.

$$O_t = \beta_2(X_tM_3)/(S_eM_4) + \varepsilon_t \qquad (6.13)$$

Because (6.13) is a highly nonlinear form, we investigate whether the relationships are actually this complex. To do so, we move to the simplest possible option: a linear additive model for all variables. Equation (6.14) displays this linear model, and also includes another term (M, operationalized below) to represent any other relevant management influences:

$$O_t = \beta_1M + \beta_2X_t + \beta_3M_3 + \beta_4(S_eM_4) + \varepsilon_t \qquad (6.14)$$

(6.14) becomes the basis for the first model that we test. The exact model to be tested is based on measures developed earlier, particularly a measure of M_2 used in place of M_3:

$$O_t = \beta_1M + \beta_2X_t + \beta_3M_2 + \beta_4(S_eM_4) + \varepsilon_t \qquad (6.15)$$

This model now contains a direct test of whether buffering, the last-listed term in (6.15), contributes to performance. Then we add to this model in a series of incremental steps to determine if more complex forms of the relationships are warranted. First, we determine if including a reciprocal relationship for buffering adds any additional information to the analysis, by estimating Equation (6.16):

$$O_t = \beta_1M + \beta_2X_t + \beta_3M_2 + \beta_4(S_eM_4) + \beta_5(1/S_eM_4) + \varepsilon_t \qquad (6.16)$$

Because a linear relationship is simpler and more direct, our approach to testing is to employ Occam's razor as a selection criterion – that is, of two competing explanations the simpler one is to be preferred unless the more complex explanation adds significantly to our knowledge. From this perspective, therefore, both the linear and the nonlinear terms (β_4 and β_5) should be included in the same equation. Because the theoretical model contains not only a reciprocal function but also an interaction, we also test Equation (6.17), which includes an interaction of buffering with managerial networking (M_2), and Equation (6.18), which interacts the reciprocal function with the environmental variables (X).

$$O_t = \beta_1 M + \beta_2 X_t + \beta_3 M_2 + \beta_4 (S_e M_4) + \beta_5 (M_2/S_e M_4) + \varepsilon_t \tag{6.17}$$

$$O_t = \beta_1 M + \beta_2 X_t + \beta_3 M_2 + \beta_4 (S_e M_4) + \beta_5 (X/S_e M_4) + \varepsilon_t \tag{6.18}$$

Data and measurement

We use eight years of data (1995 to 2002) from the Texas Education Agency on organizational performance, resources, student composition, and other relevant factors and results from our 2000 survey. Because this is a pooled time-series analysis, we included dummy variables for the individual years to deal with serial correlation. We then assessed the degree of heteroskedasticity with pooled diagnostics and found the levels well within acceptable limits.

Our measure of buffering, as explicated in the preceding section, is unity minus the correlation of school district outcomes for the period 1986 to 1994. Given that the primary statewide standardized test (the TAAS) is the central outcome in the state's performance appraisal system, we calculated the buffering measure for that outcome and used it as a measure of buffering in equations using TAAS or other outcomes as the dependent variable. The final measure has a mean of 0.49 with a standard deviation of 0.20; it ranges from 0.03 (a very tightly coupled system, with reverberations important over time) to 0.999 (a school district well protected from the impacts over time of environmental disturbances).

"O": outcome measures

Buffering might well be an approach used to protect some goals and not others. This study incorporates ten different performance indicators in an effort to determine how public management affects a variety of organizational outcomes: the overall student pass rate on the Texas Assessment of Academic Skills, TAAS scores for Anglo, black, Latino and low-income students, the percentage of students who took either of the college board exams, the average ACT score, the average SAT score, the percentage of students who scored above 1,110 on the SAT (or its ACT equivalent), and attendance rates.[37]

"M": management variables

We take in a full set of managerial variables, including managerial networking, managerial quality, managing upward, managerial stability, and workforce stability.

"X": environmental factors

We include the standard production function controls used in earlier models: percentage of black, Latino, and low-income students, class size, teacher salaries, state aid, noncertified teachers, and teacher experience.

Findings

The linear model estimates for the specification in (6.15) with the dependent variable as the most prominent outcome measure – the overall TAAS pass rate – are found in Table 6.11. The buffering variable is positively related to overall performance, even controlling for a series of management variables (M) as well as a set of variables covering a series of resources and constraints (X). The inclusion of these controls supports the conclusion that buffering itself matters rather than some combination of positive environmental factors. Although the unstandardized coefficient looks large, the range of the buffering variable is between zero and one, so this slope indicates a maximum impact of 3.2 percentage points on the TAAS. In comparison, this size represents approximately half the possible impact of that attributable to the managerial networking variable. Although our concern is with the buffering measure, the other relationships for the management variables are consistent with earlier research: each variable is statistically significant, and all of them except contact with the school board are positively associated with performance.

Table 6.12 presents abbreviated information from nine additional regressions, each representing the model specified in Equation (6.15) and one for

Table 6.11 The impact of buffering on organizational performance

Dependent variable = student exam pass rates

Independent variables	Slope	T-score	p-value
Managerial buffering	3.2223	5.25	0.0001
Managerial networking	1.1810	9.58	0.0001
School board contact	−0.7912	5.79	0.0001
Management quality	0.6939	5.73	0.0001
Management experience	0.0571	4.64	0.0001
Personnel stability	0.1532	8.98	0.0001
R^2	0.64		
Standard error	7.10		
F	345.04		
N	4,114		

Notes: Equations also control for teacher salaries, class size, teacher experience, noncertified teachers, percentage state aid, percentage of Latino students, percentage of black students, percentage of low-income students as well as dummy variables for individual years.

Table 6.12 The impact of buffering on alternative indicators of performance

Performance measure	Slope	T-score	R^2	N
Black TAAS pass rate	13.0681	7.23*	0.48	2,503
Latino TAAS pass rate	2.9283	2.73*	0.45	3,745
Anglo TAAS pass rate	2.5750	4.26*	0.50	4,068
Low-income pass rate	4.8122	6.08*	0.58	4,087
Attendance	0.3847	5.94*	0.25	4,114
Percentage taking college boards	4.8069	3.38*	0.12	3,776
ACT scores	−0.3265	2.60*	0.39	3,522
SAT scores	−10.9686	1.54	0.48	2,902
Percentage college-ready	1.5563	1.72	0.32	3,798

Notes: All equations control for the five management variables, teacher salaries, per student instructional funds, class size, teacher experience, percentage of teachers not certified, percentage of black, Latino and low-income students and yearly dummy variables.
* = significant at $p < 0.05$, two-tailed test.

each of the other dependent variables. The top four lines deal with the impact on TAAS scores for various subsets of students. In each case, greater buffering is associated with higher student scores. The pattern of these coefficients is interesting. Without question, the greatest impact of buffering is for African American students – an impact five times larger than the relationship for Anglo students. Similarly, the impact for low-income students is substantially larger than that for all students; the Latino impact, while only marginally larger, is still greater than that for Anglos. This pattern of results suggests that buffering is particularly valuable for the least advantaged of the organizations' clientele – a finding that is especially interesting given that managerial networking tends to be associated with gains for more advantaged groups (see the analysis in Chapter 3).

Buffering also has additional impacts, as a glance at the other relationships in Table 6.12 attests. Attendance is a basic minimum performance indicator that is focused on disadvantaged rather than well-off students. Although attendance does not vary a great deal and is difficult to affect, buffering is positively related to attendance. We suspect that, if attendance rates were analyzed by race, some larger relationships would appear for non-Anglo groups. For the more elite measures, on the other hand, buffering does not do as well. It is associated with more students taking college boards, but it is also associated with *lower* scores on the ACT. Neither SAT scores nor the college-ready percentage is significantly related to buffering. Again, these relationships could be interpreted as consistent with the notion that buffering benefits the more disadvantaged clientele. Expanding the number of students who take the college boards is a policy that benefits students who would not otherwise go on to college.

Having established that buffering is associated with organizational performance, we turn to determining if the functional form specified by the theory is correct. Table 6.13 adds the reciprocal of the buffering variable to the ten equations represented in Tables 6.11 and 6.12, thus summarizing ten estimations for Equation (6.16), one for each performance measure. If the reciprocal functional form were to add explanatory power, over and above a linear specification, we should find that the coefficients for this reciprocal variable are statistically significant. In seven of the ten cases, the reciprocal relationship fails to attain the 0.05 level of statistical significance. If the case of SAT scores with the negative relationship is dismissed, there are only two cases for which the nonlinear form appears to contribute: low-income pass rates and attendance. In both cases the relationship is not strictly linear, but the increase in the overall level of explained variation is minimal. The linear coefficient holds up better than the nonlinear version. An overall conclusion, then, should be that – in trimming with Occam's razor – the relationship between buffering and organizational performance is linear rather than nonlinear.[38]

Table 6.13 tests a simple reciprocal relationship, while the full theory specifies that buffering as a reciprocal relationship interacts with managerial

Table 6.13 Buffering: is the relationship linear or reciprocal?

Performance measure	Linear		Reciprocal	
	Slope	T-score	Slope	T-score
Overall TAAS pass rate	2.2877	2.13*	−0.1934	1.06
Black TAAS pass rate	13.3745	3.51*	0.0591	0.09
Latino TAAS pass rate	4.4454	2.00*	0.3307	0.78
Anglo TAAS pass rate	0.9695	0.92	−0.3294	1.85
Low-income pass rate	7.1709	5.18*	0.4855	2.07*
Attendance	0.9084	8.03*	0.1084	5.64*
Percentage taking college boards	6.5834	2.27*	0.3805	0.70
ACT scores	−0.3426	1.32	−0.0034	0.07
SAT scores	−52.1820	3.58*	−8.1818	3.23*
Percentage college-ready	1.4133	0.76	−0.0305	0.09

Notes: All equations control for the five management variables, teacher salaries, per student instructional funds, class size, teacher experience, percentage of teachers not certified, percentage of black, Latino and low-income students and yearly dummy variables.
* = significant at $p < 0.05$, two-tailed test.

Table 6.14 Does the interaction with M_2 add explanation to a linear model?

Performance measure	Networking	Buffering	Ratio	T-score
Overall TAAS pass rate	1.9468*	3.1950*	−0.3199	2.88*
Black TAAS pass rate	0.0948	13.1852*	0.2337	0.78
Latino TAAS pass rate	1.7959*	2.9230*	−0.5877	3.03*
Anglo TAAS pass rate	1.6782*	2.5435*	−0.1876	1.73
Low-income pass rate	1.2212*	4.7917*	−0.1714	1.20
Attendance	0.0908*	0.3841*	−0.0067	0.57
Percentage taking college boards	0.3583	4.8161*	0.0971	0.39
ACT scores	0.1893*	−0.3369*	−0.0315	1.45
SAT scores	−0.6654	−10.4876	3.1806	2.69*
Percentage college-ready	0.3205	1.5781	0.1927	1.20

Notes: All equations control for the five management variables, teacher salaries, per student instructional funds, class size, teacher experience, percentage of teachers not certified, percentage of black, Latino and low-income students and yearly dummy variables.
* = significant at $p < 0.05$, two-tailed test.

networking and/or environmental resources and constraints, as indicated in Equations (6.17) and (6.18). Table 6.14 shows abridged results from ten regressions that include an interaction term between the reciprocal and the managerial networking variable. Because this equation also includes linear

Table 6.15 Does buffering interact with resources in a reciprocal manner?

Performance measure	Resources	Buffering	$X/S_e\,M_4$	T-score
Overall TAAS pass rate	1.1810*	3.1165*	−0.0003	0.13
Black TAAS pass rate	0.7132*	14.0069*	0.0023	0.29
Latino TAAS pass rate	0.3863	5.3821*	0.0069	1.30
Anglo TAAS pass rate	1.2284*	1.6955	−0.0023	1.06
Low-income pass rate	0.8097*	7.5907*	0.0073	2.59*
Attendance	0.0749*	0.9529*	0.0015	6.46*
Percentage taking college boards	0.6006*	7.1153*	0.0063	0.95
ACT scores	0.1124*	−0.4044	−0.0002	0.35
SAT scores	7.2452*	−50.9109*	−0.1011	3.25*
Percentage college-ready	0.7871*	1.8649	0.0008	0.20

Notes: All equations control for the five management variables, teacher salaries, per student instructional funds, class size, teacher experience, percentage of teachers not certified, percentage of black, Latino and low-income students and yearly dummy variables.
* = significant at $p < 0.05$, two-tailed test.

terms for both networking and buffering, these coefficients are reported in the table as well, in case the interaction achieves statistical significance at the expense of inducing collinearity in the other parameter estimates. In only three cases – overall TAAS scores, the Latino TAAS rate, and SAT scores – is the interaction term statistically significant. In all three cases, the sign of the ratio interaction coefficient is the opposite of the two nonlinear terms (one indicator of collinearity),[39] the size of the coefficients is not large, and the coefficients of determination increase only marginally (not shown). A conservative interpretation of the results in Table 6.14 is that the relationship between networking and buffering regarding performance is linear rather than a more complex nonlinear interaction.

The other possible nonlinear interaction is with the "X" variables representing external resources and constraints (Equation (6.18)). Because there are eight such X variables, and a set of eight interaction terms would generate an excessive number of coefficients, we converted and simplified the interaction term by first regressing performance on the eight environmental factors and saving the predicted values. This step creates a vector that contributes the full amount of explained variation to the dependent variable. Then we ran ten regressions, one for each of the dependent variables, with the complete set of independent and control variables and included an interaction term between this new resources vector and the reciprocal of the buffering measure. These results are reported in Table 6.15. Again, the findings are not impressive enough to conclude that the nonlinear inter-action term is a superior specification to the linear additive specification, at least for this set of data. Only three of the interaction terms meet the minimum level of statistical significance, and only one of these, for attend-ance, appears to add anything more than a minimum level of explained variation.

By examining the functional form of the buffering relationships in com-parison with a linear additive model, we find that the nonlinear estimations produce some interesting individual results but are not demonstrably super-ior to the linear additive ones. In such a circumstance, the principle of Occam's razor holds that the simpler linear models are to be preferred. This finding does not mean that these relationships are linear or noninteractive in all circumstances. For instance, in this analysis we have not probed subsets of the sample to determine if high performers or low performers operate in a manner different from the median organization (see Chapter 4). Nor have we examined different or unusual combinations of the resources and con-straints provided or imposed by the environment (turbulent or stable environments) to see if selected configurations might produce different results regarding the functional form among these variables. All the same, the results here do indicate that the rather more complicated specification entailed in the full model is not necessary in at least some important empirical cases.

Implications

In this section, we have treated buffering as a combination of managerial efforts and structural features that limit the impact of environmental forces on public organizations' performance over time. Rather than differentiating the micro-details of managerial buffering activities, which could be quite subtle and varied, or the structural forms that buffers might take, we have developed a buffering measure that is designed to tap all these by encom-passing the results of buffering over a several-year period *prior to* the period under direct examination. Developing such a measure has been particularly helpful, in that it does not rely on the details of structural form or managerial action but, instead, gathers their accumulated influences into a single measurable term – one that can be tapped for many organizations. We have used the measure to estimate the impacts of buffering, and also to explore some theoretical expectations about the functional form of its influence.

The results provide not only some support for the model's assertions but also some Occam-guided negative findings. A key bottom line is that buffering can help performance. In seven of the ten linear estimations, this conclusion is supported. In only one of the ten equations does buffering have a statistically significant impact in the direction of impairing performance. This general support for the buffering function appears in a set of well-specified models that contain five other management influences and eight controls for resources and constraints. These control variables rule out many alternative explanations for performance fluctuations, such as socioeconomic differences among the districts or personnel and management activities. It seems clear, therefore, that the protection of organizational production from potentially disturbing influences can be an important function for those who care about performance, even if "protection" sometimes comes at the price of missed opportunities to tap new resources or acquire new support or jurisdiction. To put the point another way: public organizations can benefit both from protecting their operations internally – for instance, by stabilizing their personnel in front-line and managerial positions (note the full estimation sketched in Table 6.11 as an example) – and also by insulating internal operations from externally generated perturbations.

The results of these analyses offer more than a simple brief for the advantages of buffering, however. For school districts in Texas, buffering clearly helps improve performance as measured by criteria pertaining, or of most interest, to disadvantaged students. It helps little or not at all for those who are advantaged. This distributional dimension of the results is striking, and highly interesting as well. In an analysis reported in Chapter 3, we showed that managerial networking also carries distributional consequences, but with a pattern opposite to that found here for buffering. Networking by top managers in school districts benefits the most advantaged students and does little for those at the other end.

The results of this study also raise questions about the functional form through which buffering operates. The model tested here includes complexity: a reciprocal for buffering, plus interactions with both managerial behavior (networking) and external forces (resources and constraints). The empirical results show only limited and sporadic support for these features over the considerably more straightforward linear form, however. The latter represents the notion that buffering serves as a simple input to production. If a linear functional form can be regularly shown to be just as efficient in explanation as one incorporating the nonlinearities and reciprocal, these features of the model should be rejected.[40]

Capacity: an English example

With one exception, neither management capacity nor buffering has been used in other studies, so much evidence on the generality of the Texas findings is not yet available. One study of management capacity and its interactive effect does exist, however. Andrews *et al.* (2009) examine the negative impact of unexpected immigration on the performance of local governments in England using the national government's evaluation score for local governments. Immigration was a significant shock. The number of immigrants who came to the United Kingdom with the expansion of the European Union was seventeen times the anticipated number, and the influx overwhelmed the services of some local governments. Andrews *et al.* create a capacity measure based on central office bureaucracy similar to that for Texas school districts, and find that local governments with greater management capacity are able to mitigate this negative impact of immigration so that the end result is no longer statistically significant.

Capacity, buffering, and performance: concluding thoughts

In earlier chapters we explored management's performance-related effects as managers work externally and internally, and we demonstrated that – apart from sheer activity or effort – managerial quality also matters. In this chapter we have extended the analysis of managerial and organizational influences on policy outcomes. In doing so, we have paid sustained attention to some so-called nonlinearities – in these cases, the possibility that managerial capacity might interact with other features of the system to protect against performance declines or enhance the value of another managerial function. We have also explored the impact of organizational buffering on performance.

In several analyses, we have shown that managerial capacity – reserves of management or potential managerial effort – can provide performance improvements. It can do so when unexpected and negative jolts hammer the organizational system, as when budget cuts or natural disasters strike with little warning. In such instances, capacity can partially or even fully mitigate the otherwise expected dips in performance. Part of the value of such capacity, therefore, is protective or defensive. Capacity can also leverage additional results from already established and potentially valuable managerial functions. In the case analyzed here, managerial networking's value to the organization and its clientele is enhanced as capacity is expanded.

Managerial capacity is not costless; adding capacity means providing funding for what sometimes may seem to be excess staff or forgoing funding for alternative activities. Having some such capacity also produces the performance-related benefits documented in this chapter, however. These can be demonstrated most readily by exploring the nonlinear relationships that have been the focus of particular attention here.

Our base model points toward an additional sort of nonlinearity, which we have also examined in the chapter. The "S_eM_4" in the denominator of the second, or environmental, term of the model represents a combination of the structural and the managerial elements of organizational buffering. In this chapter we have developed a measure for this aspect of the system and analyzed its performance-related effects. Here we found, as extensive theoretical literature expects, that buffering aids performance. We found relatively little evidence in our empirical data, however, that it does so in the nonlinear way that the model stipulates. At this point, therefore, and without substantial additional research, we cannot conclude that the model's specification of how the buffering function operates is correct.

What we can conclude, nonetheless, is that capacity and buffering provide additional aids as public organizations and their managers seek to deliver results. In yet further ways beyond those sketched in earlier chapters, managerial and organizational features contribute to the production of public services.

NOTES

1. The section draws from the presentation by O'Toole and Meier (2010).
2. Huge and continuing shocks, whether budgetary or otherwise, would take their toll, theoretically, but there are no existing studies of this in public management literature.
3. Other measures of managerial capacity might consider education levels, skills sets of managers, or even years of experience.
4. There were no statistically significant losses in any of the ten performance measures in the third or fourth years.
5. In some preliminary analysis, we find that increased staffing of the central office leads to some tradeoffs likely to benefit more disadvantaged students at the expense of students

with greater advantages. The relative size of the central office staff is positively associated with increased student attendance and negatively associated with drop-out rates, and these are both desired outcomes. There is also a negative relationship between central office staff and the percentage of teachers the district employs in gifted programs. In essence, there appears to be a clear tradeoff: build managerial capacity if the goal is to help the disadvantaged students or build specialized teaching capacity if the goal is to improve the performance of high achievers.

6. This section draws from the presentation by Meier, O'Toole, and Hicklin (2010).

7. All data are from the official records of the Texas Education Agency.

8. Using the entire set of 1,043 districts, including the smaller ones, has only modest impact on the results. In this case, the weaker of the two influences, the "Katrina" coefficient (explained shortly), fails to attain statistical significance (the direction and final results still hold). The results for the "Rita" coefficient remain unchanged.

9. The results using all the days were very similar but were affected more by collinearity, since many of the Katrina evacuee districts were closed for the Rita evacuation but did not sustain physical damage that would have prevented them from opening the following week.

10. Here we count as districts affected by one or both shocks any district with a non-zero value for enrolling Katrina evacuee students or sustaining a period of at least six days of closure due to Rita.

11. The hurricane-impacted districts are not appreciably different from those not affected. Both the Katrina and the Rita districts actually had lower revenues per pupil but higher teacher salaries (for Katrina) and larger class sizes. These differences are in part a result of the hurricane-impacted districts being in the region of the state where wages are likely to be higher.

12. The equations in all tables were also estimated using a three-year average of prior TAKS scores rather than just the previous year. The three-year average tends to underestimate the district's record, because the TAKS was a new exam created in 2003, and there is a positive trend in overall scores as districts and students got used to the new exam. The results of this estimation were generally the same as those presented but showed a slightly larger impact from the hurricane, because it underestimated the prior performance of the district.

13. The hurricane-affected districts did not do better as the result of an influx of aid. Instructional expenditures per student go up by $645 in districts impacted by Katrina (versus $658 for all districts) and $533 in the Rita districts (versus $661 for all other districts). The influx of additional state or federal funds was overwhelmed by the total number of new students who arrived.

14. The impact of Katrina might have been larger, but the majority of evacuee students were distributed in a ring of school districts in the Houston metropolitan area that are generally fairly high-performing and are known for talented instruction. The districts with Katrina students, for example, had a TAKS pass rate of 62.8 percent in 2005 compared to 61.1 percent for all other districts. They achieved this despite having lower revenues per pupil ($8,643 versus $8,945) and higher student to teacher ratios (14.3 versus 12.7).

15. The use of the TAKS exam as the most sensitive performance indicator is corroborated by the results for the commended pass rate. The respective coefficients for the model in column 3 for that equation were −0.184 for the Katrina students and −0.039 for the days

missed. Both were significant but only at the 0.10 level. The commended rate impact of both shocks is about one-third the size of the impact on the overall TAKS pass rate. The attendance equations show no impact for the missed class days, and a coefficient of – 0.034 for the Katrina students (significant at the 0.10 level). The attendance impacts are tiny and thus need not be considered in detail.

16. Hurricanes aside, many of the districts regularly receive a large number of students after the start of the school year because the families of migrant workers return to Texas after working harvests further north. These evaluation systems are generally administered by central management in order to avoid disrupting the schools.

17. The findings are not the result of districts with greater central office capacity simply being wealthier districts. The correlation between central office bureaucracy and property tax wealth per student is 0.03 (not significant). There is a positive correlation between revenues per student (which include state and federal funds) and central office bureaucracy of 0.26, but for districts with 1,500 students or more this correlation is an insignificant 0.04. The measure is the percentage of employees in the central office bureaucracy, which is likely why the measure is unrelated to district wealth.

18. We also examined how personnel stability affects the impact of the hurricanes, and found relatively similar results (see Meier, O'Toole, and Hicklin 2010).

19. This section draws from the presentation by Meier and O'Toole (forthcoming (a)).

20. The TEA does not report data if fewer than five students are in the category. In some smaller school districts this might mean that fewer than five students take the college boards, and thus the percentage of students scoring above 1,110 on the SAT or its ACT equivalent will be missing.

21. The same pattern holds generally for the estimations with attendance and high-end performance, as reported in Tables 6.9 and 6.10. A few of the management coefficients there are not significant.

22. Calculating the slopes is relatively simple and is illustrated in the text. Calculating the standard errors for the marginal standard errors is more complicated and requires using the variance–covariance matrix from the regression (see Brambor, Clark, and Golder 2006). If the formula for the conditional slope is represented by

$$\text{slope} = \beta_1 + \beta_2 Z$$

where Z is the interacted variable, then the standard error at any point in the regression line can be calculated by taking the square root of $[\text{var}(\beta_1) + Z^2\text{var}(\beta_2) + 2Z\text{cov}(\beta_1\beta_2)]$.

23. Texas school districts generally require the schools to keep track of attendance and do the routine follow-ups. More elaborate programs focused on truancy are generally housed in the central office. One district, for example, works with local law enforcement agencies to have police visit the homes of absent students to let the parents know of an unexcused absence. This district also has a program through which, on a given day, law enforcement officers routinely stop all school-age children visible in public places during school hours to determine why they are not in school.

24. Of course, these two are related. Management can undertake actions that build or alter structural features of the organizations, for instance.

25. As indicated below, we do not develop separate measures for each of the "S" and "M_4" terms of the model. The measure used here is one for the entire buffering term,

encompassing both elements. The model's incorporation of the buffering concept suggests that its impacts on performance are likely to be similar across outcomes. It may nonetheless be that some kinds of performance, affecting certain kinds of groups, are more or less sensitive to the impacts of organizational buffering. This notion is not included in the general theoretical argument being examined but is analyzed empirically.

26. This argument is theoretical rather than empirical – that is, we have not demonstrated that the measures of these concepts actually combine in this way, nor have we demonstrated that the measures cover the full extent of the two concepts (see below).

27. Nor have we proposed and validated a measure of M_3, the efforts of managers to tap or exploit the environment.

28. *Entia non sunt multiplicanda praeter necessitatem*, or "No more things should be presumed to exist than are absolutely necessary." The principle is attributed to William of Ockham, a fourteenth-century philosopher and logician.

29. For the remainder of the chapter we refer to the combination simply as structure.

30. Such structures can buffer other events. When 5,000 students arrived at HISD in September 2005 as the result of relocations from Hurricane Katrina, they were assessed and assigned in the same manner.

31. The logic works whether the "O" variable is defined either as outputs or outcomes.

32. All things are not equal, of course, because new environmental events enter this system every year. More recent events could swamp the later-year impacts of this initial event, depending on their size.

33. Coupling could actually be considered on two dimensions: the extensiveness of the interdependent links with the environment and reverberation through time. Here we focus on the latter and assume the former as a constant. For the empirical part of the analysis in this book, this assumption is reasonable, since the full sample of organizations are structurally alike and similarly specialized.

34. There can be both internal and external drivers of the autoregressive parameter. We assume that the main source of influence over variations in the parameter, among organizations of similar structure and function, is the set of externally generated influences – the "Xs" of the model – during the preceding cycles.

35. Essentially, we estimate over 1,000 regression equations, one for each school district, to produce these estimates.

36. Some of our management and structural variables contain an element of this internal dimension. The choice is between leaving out management elements that are more general or including them even though they might operate within the organization.

37. We considered using dropouts as a performance measure, but the state of Texas made one significant change in the dropout measure during this time period so that early dropout rates are not comparable to later ones. Accordingly, we omitted this measure from the analysis.

38. We also experimented with a quadratic estimation, and got similar results.

39. As an illustration, Table 3.12 shows that networking is positively and significantly related to SAT scores while Table 6.14 produces a negative and insignificant coefficient.

40. This section of the chapter has offered such tests of certain portions of that model and has raised questions regarding functional form. We are a long way from clearly rejecting – or accepting – such theoretical expectations in toto, however. For one thing, Chapter 3

has shown evidence of other nonlinearities supportive of certain complexities in functional form – interactions between managerial networking and some external influences, to be precise. A prudent additional step, therefore, would be to concentrate on additional analysis of selected resources in the environment, those showing nonlinear relationships with managerial networking, to see if these also interact with buffering. For another, as suggested earlier, different portions of the sample may behave differently (high or low performers, for instance), and interactions can be probed systematically in this regard as well.

7 Public management in intergovernmental networks: matching structural networks and managerial networking

In this book on public management and performance, we began by noting the importance of networked relationships among organizations as a key part of contemporary public managers' institutional settings. We also explored at length the question of how what managers actually do shapes the results of public programs. We have analyzed managerial networking behavior, among other aspects of management, but thus far we have not assessed how networked structures themselves – as distinct from the networking behavior of managers – shape policy outputs and outcomes. To put it in terms of the elements of our model, we have unpacked several elements of "M" but largely ignored the structural aspects of the core organization's environment – an aspect of the "X" term.[1]

The reasons for this focus were explained in Chapter 2, and it should be clear from the extensive reliance of our empirical exploration on the Texas school district data set that researchers inevitably face real limitations in fully exploring structural influences with such a sample. School districts internally look much like each other in structural terms, so the range of variation is quite limited. Moreover, sketching the full networks in which they may operate would require labor-intensive data gathering among many actors in each of the more than 1,000 districts in the sample. The task is not practical without large amounts of time and resources for extensive fieldwork.

Nonetheless, with data now available it is possible to begin an effort to integrate the structural aspects of such networks with the behavioral networking efforts of top managers. We can do so because the fiscal ties between the districts and other levels of government are themselves structural, and data are available that allow us to establish whether these relatively stable intergovernmental relationships – these funding-based network links – affect performance in a manner that is distinct from the networking behavior – the M_2 – of the managers.

This chapter offers such an examination. While it certainly does not cover the full terrain of how structural networks can shape results, it does show some of the complex causal patterns that are part of today's managerial setting.

Public management and the intergovernmental landscape

In the United States, intergovernmental programs have become more the rule than the exception. Most "national" public initiatives are implemented with active involvement by states and/or localities, and a large portion of US-based state programs – varying by state, to be sure – are in reality state-local efforts. The principle of federalism and the political realities of program adoption and execution provide a heavy tilt toward collaborative intergovernmental arrangements under most circumstances (O'Toole 2000a). Of course, the significance of intergovernmental programs is not limited to the United States, and many other nations also confront the challenges and opportunities of managing public purposes across governmental lines. In particular, with the gradual emergence of the European Union as an important contributor to governance in multilevel systems, the theme of public management in intergovernmental settings is acquiring renewed importance.[2]

The crucial role of public management in such programs has been recognized by specialists in intergovernmental relations, who have emphasized the rise of "intergovernmental management" as the core of intergovernmental relations more generally (Wright 1990). This is not to say that management is everything in such programs. The politics of intergovernmental relations matter greatly, and the details of program design can be critical. With due caution regarding the hazards of overgeneralization, the management of intergovernmental programs should be of central interest to scholars of governance in the twenty-first century.

Although the theme of intergovernmental management has been emphasized as a key part of the contemporary policy environment, theoretical work on this topic has been slow to develop. The specialty is descriptively rich, with many studies of the efforts and intricacies of what managers do when they work across governmental boundaries and how important the details can be (see, for instance, Agranoff 1986, Gage and Mandell 1990, and Agranoff and McGuire 2003). The field has not managed to integrate these insights into a theoretical perspective that can offer testable generalizations, however, or links to allied theoretical developments on the burgeoning subject of governance (Lynn, Heinrich, and Hill 2001). A review of the subject of intergovernmental relations some time ago remains valid on this point: Beam, Conlan, and Walker (1983) point to the descriptive strengths but theoretical weaknesses of this line of work (see also O'Toole 1990). In this chapter, we use our work on management and performance to begin a systematic examination of the role of public management in executing intergovernmental public programs.

Intergovernmental ties as networked relations

As we have made clear earlier in this book, an increasing body of scholarship argues, and in some cases demonstrates, that public management often takes place in and on networks of actors rather than solely within the confines of a single, hierarchical public bureaucracy framed in a dirigiste state (Hufen and Ringeling 1990; Scharpf 1993; Bressers, O'Toole, and Richardson 1995; Klijn 1996; Bogason and Toonen 1998; O'Toole 1998; Peterson and O'Toole 2001). In networked settings, program success requires collaboration and coordination with other parties over whom managers exercise little formal control. Many of these complex arrangements are required or strongly encouraged by policy makers, others emerge through mutual agreement among organizations or other partners who find that mutual interests are served by working together on a regular basis.

Networked arrays may include some combination of: agencies (or parts of agencies) of the same government; links among units of different governments; ties between public organizations and for-profit companies; public–nonprofit connections; and more complex arrangements, including multiple types of connections in a larger pattern. Networks can range in complexity from simple dyads, at one pole, to bewilderingly complex arrays entailing dozens of units, at the other (see, for instance, Provan and Milward 1991). Beyond the issue of size or complexity, networks can vary greatly on many other dimensions. Clearly, examining "networks" and public management in any comprehensive sense requires investigating a great number of research questions, network dimensions, and levels of analysis (for a preliminary sketch of a research agenda, see O'Toole 1997).

One aspect of networks and public management worthy of close examination is the intergovernmental component. Several reasons justify such a focus. Intergovernmental ties are frequent, and intergovernmental links are among the most common networked connections during the execution of public programs (Hall and O'Toole 2000). Second, intergovernmental components of networks per se have generally not been a focus of empirical studies of networks and public management, so it is worthwhile to explore whether this aspect of networked public management offers particular insights. Third, given the generally atheoretical nature of much work conducted on intergovernmental management, an effort to consider the topic through the lens of recent network studies offers the prospect of some much-needed theoretical leverage.

Intergovernmental ties involving public organizations could take one or more of several forms. Service agreements in intergovernmental regulations, for instance, are reasonably common. Perhaps the most frequently occurring, and clearly among the most important, are regular ties triggered and sustained by intergovernmental aid, particularly grants-in-aid. Intergovernmental grant programs involve one or more "donor" government(s), and governmental agencies, in regular interaction with one or more "recipient" government(s) and agencies (Pressman 1975). Donor units offer incentives for recipients to undertake certain initiatives with certain emphases, and typically attach some regulatory "strings" as a condition of aid. Recipient units may have their effective program costs trimmed substantially by grants, even though entering into the bargain means dealing with the preferences of the donor and the conditions of support, usually on a regular basis. Such programs create dependences, and also increased probabilities and scope for public action. Over time, the intricacies of program management require diplomatic, fiscal, and other forms of managerial skill and effort (for a classic depiction of the subtle forms of intergovernmental influence in grant programs over time, see Derthick 1970). In short, examining networked patterns of intergovernmental aid provides an opportunity to begin an exploration of the intergovernmental dimensions of public management.

Intergovernmental networks and public education

We explore intergovernmental management here in the field of public education. Public education is not among the most highly networked public service production and delivery sectors (Tyack 1974). Nevertheless, this policy arena has developed into a significantly more complex and interdependent setting. Schools are now venues for the delivery of a host of associated services or regulatory programs, from public health (vaccination programs, the prevention of sexually transmitted diseases) to substance abuse, to the prevention and control of child abuse, to the achievement of nutritional objectives, to the reduction of adolescent violence, to civil rights, and to the improvement of life chances for disabled children. The "core" educational function has been surrounded by and insinuated into a panoply of other public objectives, and in turn a host of other organizations have become involved in the day-to-day functioning of school district activities. Funding and curriculum strength as well as program innovations depend in part upon school district support from – and, in some circumstances, coproduction with – other important stakeholders in other school districts, in the business community, among community groups, and from elsewhere. School districts, in short, typically operate within a network of other organizations and actors that influence their students, resources, programs, goals, and reputation.

While this chapter concentrates on the most important intergovernmental links in school districts' networked environments, we do not ignore the significant components of managers' networking activity involving other external parties as well. Managerial networking more generally is taken account of in the analysis reported below, but the regular ties of school districts with their other governmental partners receive systematic attention. This study can be viewed, then, as an extension of earlier theoretical and empirical work with the addition of an explicitly intergovernmental (and, as will be explained, structural) component.

School districts can have regular ties with a variety of external parties. Among the most important are links with other levels of government. The key intergovernmental link for school districts in most US states is with the state-level department of education. Typically, state education agencies do not become directly involved in the provision of educational services. In recent years, however, they have overcome the political support for local independence of the educational function and begun establishing and monitoring accountability standards (Wong 1999). States – through their state education agencies – are a critical source of funding for most school districts (again, the extent and type of state support varies considerably from state to state), and they also enforce some regulations, primarily about attendance and graduation requirements but also in connection with the certification of teachers. More frequently they administer statewide standardized tests and evaluate districts on the basis of them. The reliance of school districts on state departments of education for significant funding and some direction on the educational function means that state education agencies are a particularly central actor in districts' intergovernmental networks on a continuing basis.

Nationwide, state agencies provide significant funding for public education. About one-third of all state-level expenditures went to education nationwide in 2000 (Wulf 2002: 271), with 60 percent of this amount provided intergovernmentally to local governments, primarily school districts. The proportion of local educational spending deriving from state sources varies between virtually all (as in Hawaii, where no local taxes are used and only a tiny fraction of the overall total comes directly from the federal government) and barely more than 10 percent of the total (New Hampshire) (Council of State Governments [CSG] 2002: 486–7).[3]

One additional intergovernmental fiscal link can be significant: school districts' interdependence with the federal government, particularly the US Department of Education. Unlike in some countries, the US national government is involved in the public education function only in relatively peripheral ways. Even so, the Department of Education is not a minor player in the environments of at least some school districts. Overall, approximately 12 percent of the total national budget for elementary and secondary public education derives directly or indirectly from the federal government.[4] Although this figure is not overwhelming, neither is it trivial. More importantly, the degree of national support varies considerably from district to district. In some cases, particularly districts with large federal military bases, national funding can provide an important supplement to state-level aid and local own-source revenue.

In this chapter, we focus on these fiscal ties between school districts, on the one hand, and the state and national educational funding agencies, on the other. In effect, we examine the fiscal networks of school districts. Districts raise a major portion of their own revenue, but most school districts also depend on ties with other levels of government – especially state education departments – for an important slice of their budget. Management in the school districts receives primary attention. We are interested in seeing how the degree of fiscal reliance on these other parties in the educational network of school districts is connected to management and its relationships to educational performance.

The network theme: structure and behavior

Sometimes, the word "network" has been used as a loose metaphor for the interdependence characteristic of governance. Other analysts mean the term to refer to relatively stable interorganizational structures, and they use the concepts and tools of sociology to dissect these and build empirical theory. Yet other researchers focus primarily on networking: the actual connections made between or among actors operating in some social space.

We avoid the metaphorical use of the term here, but we are interested in the other two aspects of the network theme. Relatively stable arrays of interdependent organizational actors are characteristic of the intergovernmental system. When grant programs continue over multi-year periods, units develop elaborate formal understandings with each other, and the networked sets of institutional actors approximate a structurally identifiable cluster. (It is worth noting the use of images such as "picket fence federalism" to describe US vertical links between or among donor and recipient agencies that jointly administer public programs; see Wright 1988.) For present purposes, in our treatment of intergovernmental relations and the management of public education, we refer to this feature as the structural network. Regardless of whether and how often actual interaction can be observed between the linked entities, an ongoing fiscal link clearly defines part of a structural relationship between the units involved.

In addition, managers may also be active in their networked environment in efforts to build support for programs, attract partners for cooperative effort, and fend off challenges from other actors. Some of these efforts may in fact take place in concert with others involved in a structural network, some may involve other dyads and other network actors – sporadically or regularly. We refer to the set of these moves, which are in principle observable, as the behavioral network, and the efforts of managers to be active in this way as managerial networking.

Typically, researchers do not distinguish carefully between structural features of networks and behavioral manifestations of networking. Both signal some connection, perhaps interdependence, with other actors in a public organization's environment. These aspects may operate somewhat independently of each other, however, and we view it as important to take both into account in any comprehensive understanding of the network theme in public management. Intergovernmental management, in particular, involves a consideration of both.

This study represents a first effort at combining structural and behavioral networks. Accordingly, it raises a number of issues related to the substantive area under consideration – educational policy – including what the relative impacts of different funding sources are. Our primary focus is on management and performance, however, and exploring these other issues is beyond the scope of this book.

Intergovernmental networks and public management: a formal treatment

In this chapter we begin once again with our model, but concentrate on only its second term by deliberately underspecifying the full set of relationships we have hypothesized, as follows:

$$O_t = \beta_2 (X_t/S_e)(M_2) + \varepsilon_t$$

The intergovernmental structural dimension can be considered part of the environment, designated as X_i, and included as a separate term:

$$O_t = \beta_2 \big((X_i)X_t'/S_e\big)(M_2) + \varepsilon_t$$

Here X_t' simply refers to the portion of the X_t vector besides the intergovernmental structure – that is, all other environmental forces impinging on the local government. These include a wide variety of resources (for example, the extent of local wealth) and constraints (the task difficulty of educating the children of a particular community; a school system educating a more diverse or impoverished student population confronts a larger challenge). We simplify further by not designating the stability relationship as a reciprocal one:

$$O_t = \beta_2 X_i X_t' S_e M_2 + \varepsilon_t$$

This leaves us with a highly complex four-way interaction between the environment, intergovernmental structure, stability, and management. The best test to determine if the relationships actually fit a four-way interaction is with a set of nested hypothesis tests that contrast various interactions with strict linear additive models. Doing so would require us to include not just the four additive terms and the four-way interaction, but also four three-way interactions and six two-way interactions. Such a set of tests puts a great deal of stress on a data set by generating massive collinearity, and would likely make pinpointing the precise relationships extremely difficult. To provide a first step in assessing the linkage between the intergovernmental environment and the various forms of management and stability, we further simplify the model to one with interactions between intergovernmental structure and the remaining terms only.

$$O_t = \beta_2 X_i \big(X_t' + S_e + M_2\big) + \varepsilon_t$$

which can be transformed to the following equation to be estimated:

$$O_t = \beta_2 X_i X'_t + \beta_3 X_i S_e + \beta_4 X_i M_2 + \varepsilon_t$$

In terms of actual testing, we have two measures of intergovernmental structures, two measures of management, and two measures of stability, in addition to several environmental variables. This simplified model probably gives up a fair amount of explanatory power by omitting the lagged dependent variable in particular.

Although the model has been simplified in the last equation, the relationships continue to incorporate a number of features we expect to find for public management in networked settings. Behavioral networking is explicitly incorporated, and in the analyses that follow we add our measure of managerial quality as well. In addition, the "S" term, as indicated above, represents a set of stability-inducing forces. Earlier we incorporated managerial and personnel stability, and we retain these elements here. The X_t term represents a vector of environmental forces, and we include several of the most important of these in the analyses as well. From the X_t term, which had been relatively undifferentiated beforehand, we extract two aspects of the intergovernmental system for closer examination and denote them with X_i. Both variables represent financial dimensions of the intergovernmental environment. The first is the dependence on funds from other levels of government, especially those from state governments, and the second is the diversity of school district funding sources. The degree of dependence on state and national funders renders a school system's environment more network-like in structural terms. We interpret school systems with high dependence on intergovernmental aid as being situated in a more networked setting than those that are self-funded. State aid is the primary kind of such support, and we incorporate a measure of dependence on state aid into our treatment of structural stability in the analyses below.[5] In other words, dependence on state aid taps what we are calling structural networks, as distinct from the managerial networking we also examine.

In terms of the intergovernmental network itself (beyond the dependence on state aid), another feature for school districts that should tap the degree of structural complexity facing districts and their managers is the extent to which a school district's financial support is provided by a diversity of sources in the network rather than merely one funder. Some districts might derive virtually all their financial resources from their own-source revenues. These, presumably, are the most independent of other networked partners, in that they exert their own taxing authority rather than being dependent on decisions of others.

Others might derive considerable financing from the state or the federal government. These may be advantaged, in a sense, in having an additional source of funds; but the management challenges in dealing with own-source and intergovernmental funding streams, and the uncertainties connected to the latter, render managerial networking (and perhaps other managerial functions) more important. Those school districts with financial support stemming in substantial measure from more than one intergovernmental funding stream would seem to face more challenging and, potentially, more uncertain network environments. For these reasons, the sheer diversity of funding across the intergovernmental network can also be expected to be related to the requisites of intergovernmental management. Dependence on state aid, in short, and dependence on a more diverse and thus complex intergovernmental network are features of the interdependent environment that should be related to school district management, and also to performance.

The units of analysis

Our data are drawn from the 1,000 plus Texas school districts. District superintendents were sent a mail questionnaire on management styles, goals, and time allocations (return rate 55 percent with 507 usable responses). We pooled five years (1995 to 1999) of data on performance and control variables to produce a total of 2,535 cases for analysis. All nonsurvey data were from the Texas Education Agency.

Our measures can be discussed in terms of parts of the model: management (M); elements of stability (S_e); the vector of environmental forces (X'); intergovernmental structures (X_i); and program outcomes (O), or performance. These items are covered in this order.

"M": management

Two measures of public management are included as potential explanatory variables in this analysis: managerial quality and managerial networking. We treat them both here as elements of the M_2 term in our simplified model but leave them distinct in our efforts to develop estimations. *Managerial quality*, as reported in Chapter 4, is based on the residual from a model explaining the salaries of district superintendents. A second measure of management is included, as well: *managerial networking*. To measure the behavioral networking activity of school superintendents, we use the factor score from the reported interactions with five sets of actors from the organization's environment: school board members, local business leaders, other school superintendents, state legislators, and the TEA. The managerial networking measure and the managerial quality measure are uncorrelated with each other ($r = -0.01$).[6]

"S_e": stability

We incorporate two aspects of personnel stability in this study, as developed in Chapter 5. *Managerial stability* is simply the number of years the superintendent has been employed by the district *in any capacity. Teacher stability* is measured as the percentage of teachers employed by the district during the preceding year who continue to work for the district. For both measures, then, higher scores mean more stability. Data on managerial stability were obtained from the survey respondents; data on teacher stability were provided by the Texas Education Agency. Although these measures are treated as stability features here and in the subsequent discussion, they can also be considered aspects of management – what is usually referred to as personnel management. While not totally under the control of school district leaders, these variables are susceptible to influence by the individuals who make decisions about how such organizations are run. In a real sense, therefore, all four variables tap aspects of public management.

X_i environment: the intergovernmental dimension

School districts differ substantially in terms of their structural network contexts, and we focus on the intergovernmental aspect of this structure: their dependence on state aid and their dependence on a diversity of funding. Dependence on state aid is measured by the percentage of total school district funds that originate from the state. The average district receives 51.5 percent of its funds from the state, but the range is from 0 to 100 percent (allowing for rounding errors). We dichotomize this variable with a median split, designating districts with more than 58 percent of state aid as highly dependent on state aid. For the diversity of funding measure, we take the percentages of state, local, and federal funds and squared them. This number is then subtracted from 10,000. A score of zero means that the district received all its funds from a single source; higher scores indicate greater diversity, with a maximum possible score of 6,733 (if funds came equally from each of the sources). The mean diversity measure is 4,334 with a standard deviation of 1,217, range 198 to 6,358. We again use a median split, with district scores above 4,735 designated as more diverse. A district with a score of 4,735 might have approximately 4 percent federal funds, 66 percent state funds, and 30 percent local funds, although many other combinations are possible.

X'_t: control variables

Any assessment of public program performance must control for both task difficulty and program resources. For school districts, neither of these types of elements are under the substantial control of the districts themselves, and therefore they can be considered key parts of the vector of environmentally influenced X' forces represented in the model. We use the usual set of three measures of task difficulty and five measures of resources, as employed several times already in this volume.

"O": performance measures

Finally, for measures for O, or performance (outcomes), we use ten different performance indicators in an effort to determine if intergovernmental network structures influence how public management and personnel stability affect a variety of organizational processes. We continue to employ the all-pass rate on the Texas Assessment of Academic Skills, as well as four other TAAS measures: TAAS scores for Anglo, black, Latino and low-income students are included as measures of performance indicators. Three measures of college-bound student performance are used: average ACT score, average SAT score, and the percentage of students who score above 1,110 on the SAT (or its ACT equivalent).[7] The final two measures of performance might be termed bottom-end indicators: attendance rates and dropout rates. Dropout rates, although it is conceded that they contain a great deal of error, are frequently also used to evaluate the performance of school districts. The official state measure of dropouts is the annual percentage of students who leave school from eighth grade onward.

Findings

Our strategy for testing the simplified model is to conduct regression analyses that seek to explain the performance measures across the districts for all ten performance measures available while also distinguishing simple and complex intergovernmental networks for each analysis. This latter step allows us to see how all the sets of relationships differ between more and less interdependent intergovernmental network settings (and more and less diverse intergovernmental funding sources). This last aspect of the approach helps, in particular, to probe for nonlinear relationships – a central aspect of the model and one often difficult to analyze systematically. Nonlinear impacts can be assessed either via interaction terms or by examining relationships with different subsets of the sample. The former, while elegant, is often plagued by severe collinearity problems that prevent meaningful interpretation of coefficients. Accordingly, we explore nonlinear relationships among several of the management and intergovernmental-structure variables here via physical controls – that is, by partitioning the data set. Given the large number of regression analyses required to examine the full range of educational performance (ten dependent variables) and the fact that we are using two different measures to tap intergovernmental network structure, we partition the sample in a straightforward fashion: each specification is run with estimations developed separately for the top and bottom halves of the sample, based upon intergovernmental network structure.

Forty separate regressions have been run. First, using dependence on state aid as our measure of intergovernmental structure, we have sought to explain outputs and outcomes on each of the ten performance measures. Since the sample is split into high and low state aid districts for each of the ten measures, these analyses represent twenty estimations. The state aid measure of intergovernmental structure was then replaced with the measure tapping diversity of funding, and all twenty analyses were rerun. These forty sets of results are displayed in Tables 7.1 to 7.8; to provide overviews of the patterns embedded in the accumulation of so many results, we have summarized the most important tendencies in Tables 7.9 and 7.10. For the sake of emphasis on the sets of relationships of interest, we report here only the results for the management and stability variables; the same control variables were used in each analysis – all eight controls explained earlier were included, as were dummy variables for each year of the time series.

With regard to the management- and personnel-stability-related variables, a first general point is that the hypothesized positive relationships between management and personnel stability, on the one hand, and performance, on the other, are clearly supported. While the relationships and their strength vary depending on which aspect of performance is considered, the overall pattern is unambiguous for settings reflecting both higher and lower quantities of intergovernmental network structure. Tables 7.1 to 7.4 report on the twenty regression analyses that included state aid as

Table 7.1 Management and dependence on state aid

Dependent variables = TAAS pass rates for						
	All students		Black students		Latino students	
	State aid		State aid		State aid	
	High	Low	High	Low	High	Low
Networking	0.713*	0.574*	0.326	0.669*	0.702*	0.376
	(0.217)	(0.211)	(0.647)	(0.435)	(0.408)	(0.343)
Quality	0.678*	1.030*	0.164	0.692*	0.882*	0.774*
	(0.249)	(0.221)	(0.719)	(0.424)	(0.453)	(0.361)
Teacher stability	0.176*	0.089*	0.338*	0.280*	0.096*	−0.005
	(0.035)	(0.035)	(0.113)	(0.099)	(0.067)	(0.065)
Management stability	0.097*	0.060*	0.167*	0.091*	0.113*	0.035
	(0.025)	(0.022)	(0.068)	(0.040)	(0.045)	(0.035)
R^2	0.62	0.61	0.29	0.52	0.33	0.42
N	1,246	1,222	705	818	1,119	1,133

Notes: All equations control for teacher salaries, instructional funding, percentage of black students, percentage of Latino students, percentage of low-income students, class size, teacher experience, noncertified teachers, and individual year dummy variables. Numbers in parentheses are standard errors. * = significant at $p < 0.10$, one-tailed test.

Table 7.2 Management and dependence on state aid II

Dependent variables = TAAS pass rates for				
	Anglo students		Low-income students	
	State aid		State aid	
	High	Low	High	Low
Networking	0.948* (0.222)	0.457* (0.202)	0.293 (0.270)	0.254 (0.276)
Quality	0.374* (0.256)	1.017* (0.211)	0.771* (0.311)	1.116* (0.289)
Teacher stability	0.156* (0.036)	0.106* (0.034)	0.168* (0.044)	0.084* (0.047)
Management stability	0.111* (0.025)	0.060* (0.021)	0.136* (0.031)	0.120* (0.029)
R^2	0.45	0.47	0.52	0.54
N	1,226	1,214	1,246	1,212

Notes: All equations control for teacher salaries, instructional funding, percentage of black students, percentage of Latino students, percentage of low-income students, class size, teacher experience, noncertified teachers, and individual year dummy variables. Numbers in parentheses are standard errors. * = significant at $p < 0.10$, one-tailed test.

Table 7.3 Management and dependence on state aid: college aspirations indicators

Dependent variables

	ACT scores		SAT scores		Above 1,110	
	State aid		State aid		State aid	
	High	Low	High	Low	High	Low
Networking	0.076*	0.007	3.53*	2.74*	0.528*	−0.126
	(0.040)	(0.037)	(2.24)	(1.87)	(0.279)	(0.281)
Quality	−0.019	0.159*	−3.36*	6.45*	−0.098	1.283*
	(0.046)	(0.039)	(2.51)	(2.01)	(0.327)	(0.295)
Teacher stability	−0.004	−0.006	1.40*	0.08	0.053	0.099*
	(0.007)	(0.008)	(0.42)	(0.41)	(0.046)	(0.053)
Management	−0.002	0.007*	0.05	0.32*	−0.031	0.008
stability	(0.004)	(0.004)	(0.24)	(0.19)	(0.032)	(0.029)
R^2	0.35	0.33	0.47	0.56	0.24	0.36
N	1,097	1,068	869	921	1,216	1,138

Notes: All equations control for teacher salaries, instructional funding, percentage of black students, percentage of Latino students, percentage of low-income students, class size, teacher experience, noncertified teachers, and individual year dummy variables. Numbers in parentheses are standard errors. * = significant at $p < 0.10$, one-tailed test.

Table 7.4 Management and state aid: low-end indicators

Dependent variables

	Attendance		Dropouts	
	State aid		State aid	
	High	Low	High	Low
Networking	0.007 (0.021)	−0.042* (0.023)	−0.080* (0.031)	−0.007 (0.029)
Quality	0.064* (0.024)	0.061* (0.024)	−0.108* (0.036)	−0.099* (0.031)
Teacher stability	0.017* (0.003)	0.004 (0.004)	−0.006 (0.005)	0.004 (0.005)
Management stability	0.000 (0.002)	0.001 (0.002)	−0.002 (0.004)	−0.001 (0.003)
R^2	0.29	0.23	0.16	0.20
N	1,246	1,223	1,246	1,203

Notes: All equations control for teacher salaries, instructional funding, percentage of black students, percentage of Latino students, percentage of low-income students, class size, teacher experience, noncertified teachers, and individual year dummy variables. Numbers in parentheses are standard errors. * = significant at $p < 0.10$, one-tailed test.

Table 7.5 Management and funding diversity

Dependent variables = TAAS pass rates for

	All students		Black students		Latino students	
	Diversity		Diversity		Diversity	
	High	Low	High	Low	High	Low
Networking	0.586*	0.912*	0.111	1.052*	0.438*	0.760*
	(0.196)	(0.229)	(0.447)	(0.655)	(0.336)	(0.343)
Quality	0.567*	1.144*	−0.591	1.440*	−0.113*	1.412*
	(0.233)	(0.231)	(0.488)	(0.599)	(0.395)	(0.402)
Teacher stability	0.159*	0.132*	0.487*	0.225*	0.143*	0.017
	(0.038)	(0.033)	(0.105)	(0.110)	(0.069)	(0.064)
Management	0.091*	0.038*	0.079*	0.143*	0.128*	−0.025
stability	(0.022)	(0.025)	(0.042)	(0.067)	(0.036)	(0.044)
R^2	0.63	0.58	0.44	0.30	0.39	0.34
N	1,279	1,220	865	681	1,185	1,095

Notes: All equations control for teacher salaries, instructional funding, percentage of black students, percentage of Latino students, percentage of low-income students, class size, teacher experience, noncertified teachers, and individual year dummy variables. Numbers in parentheses are standard errors. * = significant at $p < 0.10$, one-tailed test.

Table 7.6 Management and funding diversity II

Dependent variables = TAAS pass rates for

	Anglo students		Low-income students	
	Diversity		Diversity	
	High	Low	High	Low
Networking	0.514* (0.200)	1.112* (0.224)	0.058 (0.246)	0.685* (0.294)
Quality	0.635* (0.238)	0.920* (0.226)	0.679* (0.293)	1.052* (0.298)
Teacher stability	0.137* (0.038)	0.142* (0.033)	0.141* (0.047)	0.135* (0.044)
Management stability	0.107* (0.022)	0.033* (0.024)	0.159* (0.027)	0.072* (0.032)
R^2	0.47	0.42	0.57	0.45
N	1,226	1,199	1,278	1,209

Notes: All equations control for teacher salaries, instructional funding, percentage of black students, percentage of Latino students, percentage of low-income students, class size, teacher experience, noncertified teachers, and individual year dummy variables. Numbers in parentheses are standard errors. * = significant at $p < 0.10$, one-tailed test.

Table 7.7 Management and funding diversity: college aspirations indicators

Dependent variables

	ACT scores		SAT scores		Above 1,110	
	Diversity		Diversity		Diversity	
	High	Low	High	Low	High	Low
Networking	−0.009	0.121*	4.86*	1.33	−0.060	0.906*
	(0.035)	(0.042)	(1.79)	(2.45)	(0.233)	(0.331)
Quality	0.094*	0.094*	2.66	4.26*	1.067*	0.495*
	(0.042)	(0.042)	(2.10)	(2.44)	(0.281)	(0.337)
Teacher stability	0.000	−0.009*	0.57*	1.26*	0.038	0.096*
	(0.008)	(0.007)	(0.42)	(0.43)	(0.047)	(0.052)
Management	0.007*	−0.006*	0.40*	−0.10	0.038	−0.079
stability	(0.004)	(0.005)	(0.18)	(0.26)	(0.025)	(0.036)
R^2	0.29	0.45	0.51	0.50	0.31	0.31
N	1,146	1,046	1,005	805	1,238	1,145

Notes: All equations control for teacher salaries, instructional funding, percentage of black students, percentage of Latino students, percentage of low-income students, class size, teacher experience, noncertified teachers, and individual year dummy variables. Numbers in parentheses are standard errors. * = significant at $p < 0.10$, one-tailed test.

Table 7.8 Management and funding diversity: low-end indicators

Dependent variables

	Attendance		Dropouts	
	Diversity		Diversity	
	High	Low	High	Low
Networking	−0.026* (0.019)	0.037* (0.023)	−0.062* (0.029)	−0.013 (0.030)
Quality	0.033* (0.023)	0.072* (0.024)	−0.100* (0.034)	−0.078* (0.031)
Teacher stability	0.011* (0.004)	0.014* (0.003)	0.003 (0.006)	−0.004 (0.005)
Management stability	−0.001 (0.002)	0.000 (0.003)	−0.002 (0.003)	0.000 (0.003)
R^2	0.29	0.23	0.20	0.15
N	1,279	1,220	1,277	1,202

Notes: All equations control for teacher salaries, instructional funding, percentage of black students, percentage of Latino students, percentage of low-income students, class size, teacher experience, noncertified teachers, and individual year dummy variables. Numbers in parentheses are standard errors. * = significant at $p < 0.10$, one-tailed test.

Table 7.9 Summary of results: state aid

	High	Low	Neither
Networking	8	1	1
Quality	3	7	0
Teacher stability	7	1	2
Management stability	5	2	3

Notes: Comparison of slopes for districts with a great deal of state aid with those with less aid. Figures are which slope is larger. Neither is coded if neither coefficient is significant or if they are equal. Median splits on all, including federal aid.

Table 7.10 Summary of results: funding diversity

	High	Low	Neither
Networking	2	8	0
Quality	2	7	1
Teacher stability	5	4	1
Management stability	7	1	2

Notes: Comparison of slopes for districts with a great deal of funding diversity with those with less aid. Figures are which slope is larger. Neither is coded if neither coefficient is significant or if they are equal. Median splits on all including federal aid.

the measure of intergovernmental network structure. Of the eighty coefficients reported in these tables – twenty each for behavioral networking by top managers, top managerial quality, teacher stability and management stability – fifty are statistically significant and in the expected direction, and only two are statistically significant in the opposite direction.[8] Based on the binomial probability distribution, the probability of a set of relationships this consistent is less than one in a million. When state funding is replaced by our measure for funding diversity, fifty-six of the eighty relationships are significant in the predicted direction, four in the opposite direction. Again, the probability of this pattern of relationships if the actual data were random is less than one in a million. Overall, management – measured via both behavioral networking and quality – as well as personnel stability certainly improve educational systems' performance.

Second, although there are, clearly, general patterns, the degree of explanation varies across the performance measures. This point holds whether the sample is split by state aid or funding diversity. Our ability to explain the variance in a number of performance measures is quite good, although the level of explanation for the so-called "low-end" performance measures is modest. For equations explaining attendance and dropout rates, the R^2 ranges between 0.15 and 0.29. The equations concerning dropouts are particularly unimpressive (unlike for the other performance measures, this one looks better as scores decline; accordingly, coefficients indicating contributions to performance should be negatively signed), and a probable reason is the quality of dropout data, as explained above. For both low-end measures, additional factors are surely important in driving results. Keeping students in school and getting them to attend on a regular basis are particularly challenging issues when students are beset with other problems, such as substance abuse, family difficulties, and the like. That the low-end equations leave most variance unexplained is not surprising. We include and discuss these results below but concentrate particular attention on the other eight equations.

Third, the relationships in different intergovernmental settings clearly differ; in short, management interacts with intergovernmental structures to generate nonlinear relationships just as the model predicts. In the remainder of this discussion, we concentrate on how managerial and personnel stability impacts vary by intergovernmental network type.

We consider the results in Tables 7.1 to 7.4 first. An interesting finding is that managerial networking is more important for performance in districts that receive more state aid. The criterion for the judgment of a difference was simply whether one coefficient was larger than the other, subject to the constraint that at least one of the pairs of coefficients had to be statistically significant. In eight of the ten measures the coefficients for managerial networking are greater for the high-aid half of the sample; in one case – TAAS pass rates for black students – the opposite is the case.[9] In some of the cases the difference is substantial. The effect size for networking in improving Latino students' state exam pass rates in high-aid districts is a maximum of more than four points, whereas the impact for low-aid districts is not statistically significant.[10] An impact of four points might seem relatively small, but over the long term increases of this magnitude can make a real difference. The impact of managerial networking is even greater on pass rates for Anglo students in the high-aid part of the sample: a maximum of about 5.7 percent; in the other half of the sample the relationship is still positive but is less than half the size.

Networking efforts on the part of managers generally pay greater dividends if another government, in this case the state, is a major source of resources. Higher state aid means that districts are more dependent on a key partner in their structural network. Major financial benefits for the district may be contingent on managers' treating the issue of intergovernmental support seriously, and external managerial effort does contribute more to results. In this case, good behavioral networks mimic structural networks.

A second pattern is discernible in Tables 7.1 to 7.4. Personnel stability also tends to matter more for performance in those settings more dependent on state aid. The relationship is particularly clear for teacher stability. For seven performance measures, teacher stability contributes more in the high-aid districts, whereas for only one – high SAT performance – is the pattern reversed. For two performance measures, ACT scores and dropout rate, teacher stability is significant for neither half of the sample. In some instances, such as the all-students' TAAS pass rate, the teacher stability impact for the high-aid districts is twice as large.

The pattern across the performance measures is similar for management stability, although the results are a bit less straightforward. For five cases, the high-state-aid half of the sample gets a bigger impact on performance from superintendents' stability than does the low-aid half; in two cases, the pattern is reversed. Three cases do not involve statistically significant impacts of management stability on performance, although two of these are the instances focused on the low-end measures.

Personnel stability helps educational performance more in the more heavily networked settings – at least, as measured by districts' dependence on the primary source of intergovernmental aid. This pattern is especially interesting. Often the characterization of networks and network management suggests that stability and networking are somehow opposed. Either stability impedes the entrepreneurial networking often endorsed by network enthusiasts, or networking promises to break through the rust of overly entrenched bureaucracy. The findings reported here point toward a more intriguing pattern: that stability – at least of personnel – and intergovernmental network dependence interact positively with respect to program outcomes. Stability in at least some forms may be a platform on which managers and others can build effective performance in heavily networked settings.

Another way of characterizing the findings is that personnel stability may compensate for, and be especially important in dampening, some of the disruptiveness of structurally less stable (more networked) settings. A second possibility is that personnel stability allows the manager to turn network interactions into repeat games, thus allowing each side to build trust and make credible commitments. This characterization is close to what researchers report as typical in instances of intergovernmental cooperative agreements. If so, to treat stability in general and networked patterns as somehow at odds would be a distortion. It may be especially important for public managers in networked intergovernmental settings to work to build sufficient stability into their contexts so as to be able to operate effectively – or to find ways of balancing the compensating advantages and disadvantages of various kinds of stability and instability for delivering results. This set of findings is generally consistent with a theme articulated by Milward and Provan (2000: 370), who have emphasized that, in networked settings, stability in certain senses may be valuable for effective performance.[11]

One other pattern is worth noting from Tables 7.1 to 7.4. Management quality matters most in settings with less fiscal dependence on the intergovernmental network. This relationship obtains in seven of the ten pairs of regressions; in three, including the two sets of low-end performance analyses, the relationship is reversed. It is not immediately clear why management quality should matter more in the more structurally homogeneous districts, although here the school systems must learn to rely more on their own fiscal resources or transactions – a kind of "fend for yourself" aspect of intergovernmental relations. The relationship is striking in some instances, not least the results for standardized state test performance for Anglo students; quality matters here for both high- and low-aid districts, but for the latter its impact is nearly triple. (The maximum effect of quality for districts heavily reliant on state assistance is about 2.2 percentage points on districts' pass rate but about 6.1 percentage points for the other half of the sample.)

Top managers of high quality may be particularly influential in more "standard" settings – those contexts best approximating the hierarchical and structurally stable environments that public management scholars and practitioners have been assuming for decades. If so, perhaps if high-quality managers become trained for the more networked world of many contemporary public programs, they could have greater impact in more challenging program contexts. Considering these results in conjunction with the personnel stability findings discussed above also suggests that, as settings become more network-dependent, sheer managerial (and others') stability – longevity in the system, chances to learn the lie of the land – starts to trump managerial quality. Such a conclusion is plausible when it is considered that, in less structurally stable surroundings, knowing the contacts and history of how to get things done may be a particularly prized (and scarce) asset for managers, as well as others.

Another possibility is that more diverse networked program contexts are inherently less manageable, so the impact of managerial quality is tempered in such circumstances.[12] If so, the structural context for public management may be important in ways that need to be considered by analysts and practitioners. The findings reported in Tables 7.1 to 7.4 are summarized in Table 7.9. Overall, these findings support the theoretical notions contained in our simplified specification.

Tables 7.5 to 7.8 display the results, excluding the control variables, for the same set of analyses, with our measure of funding diversity replacing that for the extent of reliance on state aid. Funding diversity measures how much a school district turns to multiple sources of aid (federal, state, and own-source) to support itself. The measure taps not the extent of reliance on funding from the intergovernmental network or any of its components – which would be a measure of fiscal dependence – but, rather, the extent to which a district has to juggle a multiplicity of significant funding streams. We are measuring something like the complexity of the intergovernmental funding network. Splitting the sample between low- and high-funding-diversity segments reflects a structural distinction between simpler and more complex structural settings for trying to manage the education of students.

Tables 7.5 to 7.8 contain the coefficients for the funding diversity regressions, while Table 7.10 summarizes the findings. The more a district's funds are concentrated in one source – any source – the more important managerial networking and managerial quality are to performance. For networking, eight of the ten pairs of regression results point in this direction. For managerial quality, seven sets of regressions indicate that greater impacts of quality are associated with less diverse funding arrangements.[13] In a number of cases, the differences are quite large. In one, the Latino student pass rate on the statewide test, quality is actually negatively related to performance for "complex" districts, although the slope is small, while it has a substantial positive impact for the low-funding-diversity half of the sample (a maximum impact of approximately 8.5 percentage points).

Funding homogeneity seems to allow top managers to focus their networking and have a chance to produce better results. When funding diversity is high – that is, when the funding network is complex – managers presumably have to be effective in spreading themselves and their efforts over more nodes. As a result, the actual impact of any given level of networking is lessened overall. Having to deal with several important sources of funding means that managers likely have to handle higher levels of goal conflict – a circumstance that would also complicate the task. Whereas some literature implies that operating in a networked world is something that adept managers should be able to master (for example, Mandell 2001), these findings raise the question of whether networks of a certain complexity, and perhaps a degree of goal conflict, strain or surpass even active networkers' abilities to perform their managerial role effectively. The answer to this question carries implications not only for those interested in networks and the performance of public programs, but also for those who care about intergovernmental programs and their management.

This sort of logic, combined with the findings on state aid, might lead to the expectation that personnel stability should matter more in the high-funding-diversity school districts. These are the ones in more complex and perhaps conflictual intergovernmental networks, at least in a fiscal sense. If the earlier discussion can be applied here, the more complex settings should also be ones in which the stability of personnel can contribute more to performance. The results provide some support for this idea. Here management stability seems clearly more important in the high-diversity settings; seven sets of equations point in this direction, only one (for the state exam pass rate for black students) in the opposite direction.[14] In several of the cases, the differences in slopes for management stability were considerable between the two parts of the sample. Again, this finding makes sense, in that experienced top managers are more likely to be effective in navigating the complex and conflictual world of intergovernmental funding to produce effective performance. The impacts of teacher stability on performance do not vary consistently between high- and low-diversity settings. For five of the ten measures, teacher stability matters more when funding is spread among several sources. For four measures, it matters more when funding is concentrated as to source.[15] Since teachers themselves are virtually never involved in negotiating intergovernmental aid or dealing with the complexity of a school district's intergovernmentally networked surroundings, the mixed results here are not very surprising.

If we treat funding diversity, then, as a measure of network complexity, the findings overall are rather straightforward. More concentrated funding streams mean that top managerial networking and quality are more important. Managerial stability becomes consistently more important with diverse funding sources. Managers matter for performance in intergovernmentally networked settings, but they appear to have larger impacts when the networks are not too complex and conflictual, so that they are presumably able to concentrate their external efforts where it will do some good. Where the setting is more complex, managerial longevity helps more.

Conclusions

Among the most important kinds of networked contexts is the set of situations in which the intertwining of interdependent actors is a product of conscious design rather than evolution or chance. The most explicit and longstanding kind of designed interdependence is the intergovernmental governance system. In some contexts, such as the emerging forms of the European Union, such multilevel governance is a fairly recent and immensely important product of expanding networked action. In other contexts, such as a range of intergovernmental programs in federal systems such as that in the United States, intergovernmental patterns are many, variegated, constitutionally legitimated, and of longstanding operation. All such settings deserve systematic analytical attention, and the burgeoning interest in networks portends increasing focus on intergovernmental governance and management.

This trend is propitious, not only because the topic is important and will likely grow in salience, but also because the subject of intergovernmental management, while critically important, remains in need of theoretical approaches. Developments on the subject of networks may be able to help in this regard. Our effort to explore this notion has been constructed from a general theory of networks and public management developed without particular attention to intergovernmental program management but with potential applicability there.

We have applied a simplified version of our model to an enduring and distinctively American set of cases, school system management, that nevertheless should be instructive regarding the role and importance of public management in intergovernmentally networked settings. The model provides help in unpacking an exceedingly complex set of relationships. It, and the findings of this chapter, can offer both hypotheses and guidance for further research on intergovernmental management in networked settings.

The evidence is clear that managerial networking, managerial quality, and selected stabilizing features (most systematically, personnel stability) contribute positively to program performance, at least for many measures associated with education in Texas. The evidence is also overwhelming that nonlinear interactions between structure, management, and environmental forces are commonplace in the world of networked public programs.

Further, discussions of networks and networking can benefit from more conceptual clarity. In particular, the networking behavior of managers (and others) is not the same thing as the structural interdependence that often binds elements of networks together. Our model helps to elucidate this distinction by labeling the behavioral aspect as a component of management – M_2 – and the structural part as one aspect of the environmental vector – X_i. We have measured these separately; in fact, we have tried to tap the latter in two ways regarding the intergovernmental fiscal interdependence of school districts and sought to explore how these are related. While managers may do a lot of networking in either high- or low-dependence settings, their efforts pay off more when the structural environment reflects more reliance on external resources. When managers face dependences from several directions, their networking efforts are less effective than when they can concentrate their efforts on limited sources. Behavioral networking helps, but it helps more in certain kinds of networks; and the intergovernmental structure is part of the explanation.

Rather than treating stability as an enemy of networks and networking, and the converse, this chapter shows that, in intergovernmental settings, some kinds of stability may actually be a help or precondition to more effective networked action. When school districts operate in more fiscally interdependent and complex settings, managerial stability and personnel stability seem to provide greater contributions to more effective performance. Stability as a platform for risk taking, entrepreneurial action in networks: this idea deserves further careful exploration, especially as governance systems expand and multilevel intergovernmental arrays are increasingly developed. How to deliver performance in such settings becomes a critical issue, and the findings here suggest that certain subtleties may be part of the answer.

The stability and networks relationship in this chapter might also be linked to our earlier findings on managerial capacity. In that case, another form of stability, a large managerial cadre, facilitated the organization's ability to perform in the face of a crisis. Crises and networks are forms of uncertainty; stability and management capacity are both forms of organizational presence, perhaps even of bureaucracy. Organizations that run counter to less certain environments appear to be better performers in both cases. Because these findings are generally contrary to current ideologies of management consulting, they hold important lessons for public managers and the design of governance institutions alike.

Our findings about managerial quality also deserve mention and are related to this theme. Quality matters, but not in the same way and to the same extent in all settings. Finding and retaining first-rate managers clearly pays off in performance; the analyses reported here indicate support for this point. In the more interdependent and more complicatedly networked intergovernmental contexts, however, the impact of good managers, ceteris paribus, is somewhat less. A number of implications might flow from this finding, especially if further support is found in other settings and other policy fields.

Rather than tease these out in detail here, however, we end the chapter by emphasizing some of the tasks yet to accomplish. The general model of public management continues to show promise, and the role of management, directly (in terms of networking and quality) and indirectly (in the recruitment and retention patterns of personnel), is clearly a crucial feature of successful performance for public education in Texas. The complex set of managerial influences deserves analysis in other places, other policy sectors, and other countries. Additional dimensions of intergovernmental structure, including those beyond the fiscal, are worth attention as well. Other stabilizing forces should also be explored. So, while the results here are complex and promising, they point toward yet more puzzles and should encourage still more research.

NOTES

1. Influences emanating from the environment of a public organization are properly treated as part of the "X" term when one is analyzing management and performance at the organizational level of analysis. If one were examining the system at the network level of analysis, network structural arrangements would be considered part of the vector of stabilizing features, S_n, of the larger array (see the coverage of modeling at the network level in Chapter 2).
2. The analyses in this chapter follow the presentation by O'Toole and Meier (2004c).
3. We cite information here from earlier years, since the data we analyze in this chapter pertain to an earlier five-year period, but the general points made about the fiscal structure of the system and variation nationwide continue to hold.

4. The total revenue for public school systems in United States for 1998/9 was more than $200 billion, of which approximately $24 billion derived from the national government. The vast majority of the nationwide elementary and secondary education dollars are raised directly by local districts, primarily from their own taxes, with some coming from other local governments and some from charges imposed by the districts. See CSG 2002.

5. We use state funds rather than state and federal funds because, for most districts, the percentage of federal funds is relatively small. For a small number of districts with major federal facilities, such as military bases, federal aid is the largest source of funds. These "federal impact" districts are fundamentally different from districts that depend on state sources, in that federal funds essentially substitute for local monies. Including federal funds in the analysis results in generally similar results to those reported here, but the federal impact districts tend to muddy the findings. The diversity measure also picks up the federal impact districts.

6. Management quality is also uncorrelated with both measures of personnel stability (-0.02 for each), as is managerial networking (0.04 correlation with teacher stability, -0.08 with management stability).

7. The relationship between the percentage of students taking the tests and the test scores in Texas is actually positive but explains less than 2 percent of the variance.

8. Of the twenty-eight non-significant relationships, nineteen are in the predicted direction.

9. For one performance measure, TAAS pass rates for low-income students, neither coefficient was statistically significant.

10. Even if it were, the slope is substantially smaller.

11. Their focus is on another aspect of stability: constancy of the key network organizational members – in contracted relations for service provision – over a several-year period.

12. Given the findings analyzed here, this may be the case not only for M_1, the internal management of operations that has been omitted altogether in the simplified model, but also for overall managerial quality.

13. For both networking and quality, the dropouts performance equation contained anomalous results. Given the quality of the data, therefore, the pattern can be considered even stronger than the summary numbers suggest.

14. The equations for the two low-end performance measures all show insignificant results for managerial stability.

15. For the dropout rate, the teacher coefficient was insignificant for both halves of the sample.

8 Public management and performance: what we know, and what we need to know

This book has presented a perspective, a model, and a large set of empirical findings. The results speak to a broad agenda occupying many scholars and practitioners: understanding how public managers shape agency and program performance. In this chapter we draw the volume to a close by undertaking two tasks. First, we review and tie together what we have learned about public management and performance. We then sketch a new agenda for some of what, we believe, remains to be explored.

What does the evidence show?

This research program has developed many findings about whether, how, and how much public management influences the performance of public organizations. Most findings explain what is going on in school districts within one state; but, we argue strongly, this "limitation" should not diminish the record. Although this work should be replicated in other empirical settings – and although we have initiated that ourselves, as have others discussed in earlier chapters – the patterns analyzed here should not be marginalized. First, the sample included in most of our empirical studies consists of more than 1 percent of all governments in the United States. Second, no larger sample of public organizations has ever been analyzed for determinants of performance. Third, the analyses develop and report on numerous types of managerial influence. While the findings sometimes show that managers shape performance in ways that some might find to be expected, the results do not merely theorize or speculate about such channels of influence; they *demonstrate* the influence with systematic evidence. This sort of contribution is unusual. The approach here, therefore, is what can be considered to constitute evidence-based public management. Fourth, the characteristics of these organizations suggest that many of the results here are likely generalizable to other public organizations that are highly professionalized and operate via a relatively decentralized structure, especially when such organizations function as street-level bureaucracies (Lipsky 1980). Fifth, substantial practical limitations currently restrict the options for large-N empirical studies seeking to explain performance: the relative lack of valid and reliable performance measures; the limited sets of such measures available in time series; the typical lack of a common performance metric across the cases (the "apples and oranges" problem); the restricted number of data sets that contain multiple performance measures, despite the fact that public organizations are virtually never asked to do one and only one thing; and the difficulties plaguing such available, putative performance measures as the federal government's Program Assessment Rating Tool. Consequently, we certainly cannot say that the findings developed here hold for all public organizations; but they are built on a better-developed and sounder empirical base than has been the case for other research programs in the field.

The model we have developed from the case study literature reduces the innumerable complications and subtleties of the practical world to a few clusters of variables: management; stabilizing features in and of public organizations; external forces that work as opportunities or constraints on programs; and, of course, performance itself. This simplified model is not without its complexities. It considers the performance of public organizations, essentially, as inertial – and yet as subject to influences, even in the short term, including by management. It treats management as a multifunctional enterprise and indicates that different managerial functions have different – and nonlinear – impacts on performance. It can be simplified further by bundling managerial functions into externally oriented and internally focused management. Moreover, as shown repeatedly throughout this book, it offers opportunities to test parts of the model through further simplifications, when these can be justified by the research focus of interest and the features of the empirical setting.

Managers, the model proposes, work in the organization's environment to draw in resources and take advantage of opportunities for the agency and its mandated programs – while also protecting the core organizational tasks from disruption triggered by outside jolts or shocks. Managers also, the model asserts, perform multiple tasks to encourage and support the internal production of the organization. While the model does not explicitly emphasize this point, it also implies that these managerial functions include both a quantity element (how much effort and energy do managers invest in various functions?) and a quality element (how good are the managers at doing what they do in seeking to shape performance?). Public organizations also reap performance advantages from stability, the model further claims, even though today's popular rhetoric extols change and reinvention. The model admits that change can boost performance, but it emphasizes the underheralded virtues of stability. Finally, the model is also framed explicitly in an open-systems fashion so that the world external to the public organization offers both prospects for improvement and threats to the delivery of policy results.

The model therefore incorporates a number of assertions and assumptions, some of which seem almost obvious, others of which are certainly somewhat speculative. The important question is not how the model is built, but what the evidence actually shows. In answer to this question, we can say: "Many things." In most respects the model holds up surprisingly well to systematic empirical investigation. On a set of issues the jury is still out. Finally, on a few points, the model may need to be revised, at least for certain sorts of practical settings.

In summarizing here what we know about public management and performance from our empirical studies, we begin with the second, or environmental, term of the model, and focus especially on managerial networking. Do public managers in fact devote substantial effort to interact with a variety of external actors – do they network? The answer is clearly "Yes," at least for top managers, and pretty clearly (on the basis of our analysis of data from English local authorities and police departments) for other managers at subordinate levels. We also know that the variation in the extent of networking by managers – even those in the same positions in the same sorts of organizations – is considerable. In work not included in this book, we have explored whether networking behavior by top managers can be explained by features of the organization and the environment. Virtually none of the networking behavior is related to these features of the context; and, as Chapter 3 shows, we have strong evidence that managers' networking patterns are rather stable over time and related to the individual manager and his or her characteristics.

Can we be more specific about how the managerial networking boosts performance? Although exploring relationships in hundreds of organizations across a number of years means not being able to trace the precise processes through which managers' networking efforts assist production, we expect that the interactions serve multiple functions. Managers working in their networked environment can draw useful information into their organizations (for example, with regard to programs, policies and innovations worth considering), can negotiate and receive technical assistance, can tap the efforts and production potential of other organizations in patterns of coproduction, and can strengthen the organization's political position with other actors and institutions. They can also help to fend off threats and shocks from outside.

As Chapter 3 highlighted, we know that, in this set of public organizations, networking adds to performance not in a simple linear fashion but by interacting with selective resources (opportunities) in the environment, thus leveraging and strengthening the impact of these resources on the outcomes of interest. In other words, the nonlinear, interactive relationship between networking and environmental forces (the "X" term of our model) is supported by the evidence. In a paradoxical finding, we discovered that those organizations performing especially well are less inertial than those seemingly more trapped in a mediocre production process.

We also know that it is possible to create a good measure of managerial networking across many organizations without expending huge amounts of time and expense in sketching the full networks in which managers may be situated. Considering such networking as a general behavior and one that is practically important makes sense: more networking by top managers means better organizational performance. As one might expect, nevertheless, one can overdo it. We have shown that the marginal contributions of managerial networking by top managers decline at higher levels of networking – although incorporating a consideration of managerial quality (an aspect to be reviewed shortly) eliminates the diminishing marginal returns.

Although managerial networking improves performance, it does not do so in an undifferentiated fashion. Because the externally oriented actions of managers take place in a political environment, the external interactions influence organizational performance to improve outcomes for the more advantaged and powerful stakeholders in that environment. Performance is improved on the most salient performance measure and those that are most important to advantaged clientele, while there is little or no effect for outcomes that matter most to the less advantaged. Managerial networking has real payoffs, but not inevitably and not for everyone.

Although networking by top managers has been carefully investigated in this book, we have not explored the impact of networking at other levels in the organization. We know from the English local government data that substantial networking takes place at different echelons in these governmental organizations. We have not estimated any performance impacts of networking at different levels within an organization, however.

Managerial networking is a set of behaviors. Public organizations and their programs often also are situated in networks – patterns of interdependence across organizations that have structural properties. We began to explore how such networks, or network properties, might help to shape program outcomes, in Chapter 7. That initial foray into the topic demonstrated that structural features of intergovernmental networks and networking behavior by top managers both influence educational outcomes. The structural and behavioral elements also interact with each other, but much remains to be learned here.

The specific investigations of managerial networking tap the amount of networking and then explore whether it makes a difference to performance. In recognition of the obvious fact that management entails a quality dimension as well as a quantity one, we also developed a measure of managerial quality to assess the relationship of managerial quality to performance. We have validated such a measure, based on the portion of top managers' salaries that is not explained by conventional determinants of salary. We have argued that this measure is correlated with local school boards' assessment of the quality exhibited by top management in their districts and have shown that the measure is positively related to many indicators of performance. Chapter 4 was devoted to this work. Although we have not developed this line of research further to additional levels of management, other recent work shows that a similar measure of middle management quality, also based on salary data, can be developed and is, separately, related to performance (Johansen 2008). A salary residual measure cannot be used in tapping managerial quality in all public organizations, of course, in particular because constrained salary ranges are often stipulated as a part of civil service systems. Attention should therefore be devoted to alternative approaches – including some possibilities based on surveys of decision makers in public organizations and/or of those responsible for holding such organizations accountable (for an interesting survey-based approach developed for and implemented in business organizations, see Bloom and van Reenen 2007).

With regard to the environmental term of the model, we have also investigated externally generated shocks and how public organizations buffer themselves from their sometimes turbulent environment. We examined two types of jolts or shocks: unexpected and sizable budget cuts and the displacement of thousands of students due to two hurricanes – natural disasters that were consequential for public education and many other functions as well. We have also been exploring environmental jolts of another sort in a different empirical setting: unexpectedly large influxes of eastern European immigrants into England, and the consequent strains on the systems there for delivering public services (see, for instance, Andrews *et al.* 2009, 2010b).

All these analyses, including the one focusing on English local government, show similar patterns with respect to performance. Negative shocks, whether budgetary or otherwise, impede performance; when the shock penetrates the organization, though, managers are able to operate internally to reduce the performance-related hit. Chapter 5 provided extensive evidence in this regard, particularly concerning subtle adjustments in budgetary and staffing patterns that focus the organization's attention on its core business. (We noted there, and repeat here, that such efforts over the short term could carry negative consequences for other performance objectives, especially if such efforts are repeatedly called upon to mitigate shocks. We observed the irony that, to the extent that managers are successful in such efforts, they may weaken the political argument and coalition for budgetary assistance going forward.) These sorts of moves mitigate the performance-related effects of shocks and are an aspect of the internal management of the organization. Internal management comprises a host of possible functions. In this volume we have explored a number of these, but substantial additional work will be required to demonstrate fully the manifold ways internal management can shape outcomes.

Although managers can work to protect the core production processes from unwanted disruption, they cannot always *eliminate* the negative performance impacts of shocks from the external world. In such cases, our studies of three kinds of shocks – unexpected budget cuts, the unexpected arrival of needy hurricane refugees who also need to be educated, and the arrival in England of immigrants from eastern Europe in much greater than anticipated numbers – show an identical, and important, finding: management capacity, measured as the relative size of the central office staff, can mitigate the negative performance impact of such jolts to the system.

Why does management capacity help? Our earlier discussion in Chapter 6 offered a number of clues, but we cannot be completely sure without additional research. The strongest arguments on behalf of more capacity seem to focus on the ability to analyze nonroutine situations, such as jolts from the environment, and to deploy human resources to address the most pressing or fundamental challenges presented by those circumstances. We have also been able to determine, as the evidence in the same chapter shows, that more capacity does more than "merely" wipe out the untoward impacts of shocks. It also enhances the performance-related value of networking by managers themselves. Here too we see the value of capacity primarily in helping managers sort through the multiple and sometimes complex "games" in which they must or might engage externally. Thus analytical ability and the possible delivery of results and resources valued by external parties enhance the simple value of networking in the environment.

Managerial capacity offers much of value to public organizations, but the issue is two-pronged. It may be good to keep on hand substantial managerial capacity, in case lightning (or hurricanes, or budget disaster, or huge influxes of immigrants) strikes. The opportunity costs must also be considered, however. A practical, and complicated, question is how to assess the relative risks of being overwhelmed by the need for additional management help versus the real financial (and perhaps other) costs of carrying additional trained managerial professionals to deal with unexpected contingencies. Different organizations, situated in different contexts, should assess the relative risks differently. A practical issue, therefore, is how prone a public organization is to disruptions or unpleasant shocks that are substantially out of the ordinary. If the scenario is a rare one, perhaps it makes sense simply to ride it out when it occurs. If, on the other hand, shocks are likely to occur with a fair amount of frequency, building in the advantages of managerial capacity (and thus slack) might make sense. Our advice to public managers is direct, even if nuanced: make a determination about the amount of managerial capacity to develop and maintain on the basis of the expectations and needs facing your own public organization.

We have been discussing shocks and managerial capacity here as if it were inevitable that, once turbulence buffets the organizational system, it penetrates and forces managerial (and other) responses – otherwise disruption happens. We have also seen, however, that the buffering of shocks from the environment can keep disruption away from the internal workings of public organizations. We have treated buffering, a venerable concept in organization theory, in terms of the denominator of the environmental term of our model (S_eM_4) – a combination of stability-inducing features along with the protective efforts of managers who interact with forces in the environment to keep them out of the organization even before they penetrate the system of production. Unfortunately, our research agenda has not yet progressed to the point at which we have been able to measure – separately – the stabilizing organizational elements and the protective moves of managers. The combined buffering term was the subject of some work reported in Chapter 6, however. Clearly, buffering helps performance. What is less clear is whether the relationship is nonlinear with respect to the environmental shock itself. In our initial efforts, we concluded that the interactive effect we hypothesized does not add to the explanatory power of the model, but a more definitive conclusion awaits more extensive testing.

In short, therefore, we have explored rather extensively – even if not definitively – the second term of our model. We have shown that an overall measure of managerial quality also generates positive outcomes. What of the first term – the portion of the model focused on internal management and its purported relationship to performance? This book contains some findings in this respect as well. Indeed, in this section we have already mentioned one such finding: that managers can adjust budgets and staffing patterns to reduce or remove disruptions emanating from outside the organizations.

The book has offered additional evidence as well, evidence centering on human resources and their effective management. Stability in staffing patterns – of top managers and especially of front-line professionals in school districts – contributes positively to educational outcomes. This set of patterns can be interpreted as partial validation of the stability-related, or "S," term of our model. Personnel stability is also a function of HR management, however, and is therefore a partial manifestation of the beneficial contribution of internal management. As additional research ensues, it would be useful to try to estimate the impact of other elements of the stabilizing vector. In the case of school districts, curricular stability and stability in procedures could be of particular interest.

More generally, an important line of work that has yet to be explored has to do with the *structural* stability of administrative systems. The Texas school districts data set offers many advantages, as we have explained, but it also has its limits. One of these is the link between structure and performance. School districts differ in many ways, but they are structurally rather similar; they also tend toward structural stability over time. Ideally, therefore, future empirical work in settings offering both cross-sectional structural variation and some structural reorganizations over time can explore this important aspect of the "S" vector.

The management of organizations' human capital also contributes to performance, as still more evidence presented in Chapter 5 demonstrates – thus validating a proposition at the heart of the specialty of public HR management and bringing to the fore the practical importance of governments addressing what has been called the human capital "crisis" on the horizon. As we indicated at the outset of this volume, internal management encompasses a huge number of options and functions, often summarized by

Table 8.1 Intercorrelations of management measures

"M" measures	Quality	Mnetworking	Mstability	Tstability	Buffering[1]	Capacity
Mnetworking	−0.01	x	x	x	x	x
Mstability	−0.03	−0.07	x	x	x	x
Tstabililty	−0.02	0.05	0.00	x	x	x
Buffering	0.05	−0.05	−0.05	−0.05	x	x
Capacity	0.10	−0.04	−0.04	−0.12	0.27	x
Human resources M	0.07	−0.05	0.10	0.12	−0.04	−0.002

Notes: [1] Technically, this term measures M_4S_e, the denominator of the second term in the model. It includes a management component, and so we include it here.

the venerable term POSDCORB but sometimes extending beyond even this set of activities. Our work has examined only a modest fraction of these. Thus another part of the research agenda is to expand empirical analyses to estimate the performance-relevant impacts of other internal management efforts.

Overall, we have shown numerous measurable and practically important influences of public management on policy outcomes. Nevertheless, we should avoid the temptation to embrace managerialism – the assumption that better management is a cure-all for a wide range of economic and social problems (see Pollitt 1990: 1). Numerous other influences need to be taken into account, and, indeed, we have already written another book about the interaction between managers and the broader political system (Meier and O'Toole 2006). Managers are not superheroes, even if their intention and efforts are often noble and heroic; but neither should we underestimate the effect that management can have. Even taking into account only those performance results that we have thus far been able to link to one or other aspect of management, and even omitting the obviously relevant performance impacts that middle management is almost certain to have, we estimate roughly that we can attribute approximately 20 percent of the overall variance in performance across organizations to the effects of top management (see Meier and O'Toole 2009b). This is hardly a trivial quantity.

Equally interesting is the *pattern* of managerial influence across the several different aspects of management. Table 8.1 shows the correlation matrix between the six different management measures. Of the twenty-one intercorrelations, all but one are at 0.12 or lower; and the one exception is also exceedingly modest (0.27 between buffering and management capacity). For practical purposes almost all the measures are virtually uncorrelated.

Table 8.2 Practical lessons for managers

(1) Managerial networking can lead to performance gains either through the acquisition of technical knowledge or the development of political/public support.

(2) Managerial networking can interact with some organizational resources to increase their impact several-fold. Given this relationship, managers need to exercise choice with regard to how to pursue environmental opportunities.

(3) Managerial networking is subject to diminishing marginal returns; the best managers limit their networking activities before reaching this point.

(4) Managerial networking has distributive consequences. Network demands are more likely to come from well-established and well-endowed network nodes.

(5) The impact of managerial networking depends on the structural context. Managerial networking is more valuable in structural networks.

(6) Management needs to build excess managerial capacity to deal with shocks and other unexpected environment problems.

(7) Management capacity enhances the impact of managerial networking.

(8) Managers need to recognize that building managerial capacity results in tradeoffs. In particular, investments in managerial capacity can limit current levels of production.

(9) Loosely coupled organizations generally perform better; this is especially the case with regard to disadvantaged clientele.

(10) The stability of front-line workers leads to higher productivity. This relationship is stronger for programs that affect disadvantaged clientele.

(11) Managerial stability is positively related to performance.

(12) The development of human capital is the management activity with potentially the largest payoff for performance.

(13) Management actions are generally independent of each other, so that improvements in one area are not necessarily related to management abilities in other areas.

This pattern is interesting, for at least two reasons. First, it suggests that the contributions that various management functions make to performance can be treated basically as additive. Second, the set of (non)relationships shows that "good management" comes in many flavors – or, more precisely, that management is clearly a multifunctional enterprise. Managers who excel at one aspect are no more (or less) likely to do well at another. These results are intriguing and call for more sustained analysis both within and among these and other managerial functions.

Although our purpose has been to contribute to the scholarly literature on public management rather than provide advice to practicing public managers, we are aware that our work has significant implications for how organizations should be managed. Under the guise of evidence-based public management, we have discussed this issue in some detail (see Meier and O'Toole 2009b). Table 8.2 provides a summary of findings that we think have practical application to the real world of public management. These should be considered no more than tentative, because we have not worked with public organizations to apply these lessons systematically and measure the results. At the same time, much of the list accords with what are considered to be good management practices in the literature (see Rainey 2009).

For all that we have learned, nonetheless, there is a great deal that remains to be done. As we bring the present study to a conclusion, therefore, it is appropriate to indicate some of what still lies before the research community.

What remains to be explored?

Even as we have summarized the research findings in this book, we have indicated additional avenues to be explored. In particular, we note that this research agenda needs to move to venues beyond school districts in Texas; should encompass managerial influences below as well as including the top echelon of public organizations; would, ideally, explore the multiple influences of management in settings more thoroughly networked than public education; could explore additional measures of managerial quality that could be applied in more conventional civil service systems; might reach to include additional aspects of internal management; should address other terms of the model that have not been systematically analyzed thus far; and would focus as well on the functional form of several of the relationships hypothesized in that model to clarify and develop a better understanding of the causal patterns.

All these items on the agenda were mentioned earlier, but a few additional comments about some of them can be helpful here. With regard to the heavy use of the Texas school districts data set, we explained earlier its unique value and its enhanced utility over time as additional validated measures have been developed. We should note that we have been exploring the management-and-performance agenda in other venues as well. Thus far, we have developed findings from English local governments, as alluded to in this book, and in state unemployment insurance programs. We have initiated collaborations with public management researchers in two other European countries to explore the impact of management on performance in public education in these settings as well. The findings there should help to test further the relationships we have found in Texas school districts and also broaden the research agenda to include additional matters. This new work, for example, is designed to tap managerial influences at more than one level, and thus below the top echelon. This sort of cross-national work also can link public management studies to their broader governance structures. The United States situates management in the midst of pluralist governance arrangements, but some of the relationships might operate differently in, for instance, more corporatist settings. Some of the emergent work, therefore, offers the potential to explore such themes of governance, which have been considered important but essentially unverified in recent work in the field. In addition to these ongoing projects, we are initiating work on the management of hospitals and nursing homes. Both data sets include public, private, and nonprofit organizations.

We have also expanded the Texas schools data set by inviting other scholars to nominate survey items for inclusion in the superintendent surveys. Several such questions on performance management, social capital, trust, and diversity were included in the 2009 survey. We are also at the early stages of examining data on charter schools. We have collected data on these over time and are now working with a colleague to examine public management in these organizations, which effectively operate as nonprofit organizations subject to some state regulation and funding. The analyses there may speak to the themes developed in the research literature on nonprofit organizations.

What is likely to be more challenging by far is any effort to estimate the full range of managerial influences in more thoroughly networked settings. As explained in Chapter 2, we expect public management in networks to be perhaps even more consequential than in more traditional settings (O'Toole 2000b), but practical impediments make it especially difficult to conduct large-N empirical explorations of the question. Modeling managerial impacts in networks requires adding more management functions and vectors of influence, managers themselves may have strategic reasons to disguise their own efforts to shape results in such settings, multiple managers in very different organizations may simultaneously be attempting to move performance along (albeit not necessarily in the same direction), and the structural dimensions of the program setting are less transparent and may need to be mapped with significantly more labor-intensive research efforts. This agenda item remains important, but progress is likely to be slow.

We are more optimistic about the agenda with regard to internal management and performance. Thus far we have triangulated around the internal management function but not specified it as completely as would be ideal. A number of additional managerial efforts that are focused internally can be examined in principle so long as the data are gathered systematically from managers or other sources. Certain additional managerial functions have already been the focus of research effort on our part. Along with colleagues, we have explored whether the content of managers' (and organizations') strategy is related to performance in the ways hypothesized by some generic management theorists (see Meier *et al.* 2007 and Andrews *et al.* 2010a). Strategy can be considered an aspect of management that entails both internal and external attention. Other management efforts that are directed primarily at internal coordination, planning, resource allocation, communication, and so forth are all – in principle – amenable to empirical analysis. The research agenda going forward needs to include such studies if we are to reach a fuller understanding of the management–performance relationship. Some of the points just mentioned, along with a set of additional ones, can be unpacked more fully in this coverage of the research agenda that remains to be addressed.

Governance structures

The broader set of institutional arrangements for public managerial efforts needs to be explored in any thoroughgoing examination (see, for instance, Lynn, Heinrich, and Hill 2001). In this volume we have analyzed a range of managerial influences, but we have done so while largely ignoring the system's larger governance structure. For the most part we have examined independent agencies within a decentralized governance system in a fragmented political system. All these characteristics of governance systems vary both within nations and between them. Similarly, the political context also needs to be taken into account, as does the larger network in which many public organizations conduct their efforts. Further, multiple levels in governance arrangements can also shape policy results, and the interplay among these is clearly worth systematic investigation (for one such effort, see Meier, O'Toole, and Nicholson-Crotty 2004). Combining all such elements in a complex governance structure and exploring their interactive effects across many cases poses a formidable challenge – and especially so if the variation in governance structures cross-nationally in quite different systems is taken seriously. Analyzing such patterns for their performance-related effects is necessary for a full understanding of the role management plays in implementing public programs.

Politics and management

The study of governance structures brings to the forefront the relationship between politics and public managerial systems – an understudied topic. Public programs are governed by a mix of career administrators and political actors. Several aspects of these hybrid governance systems should be of particular interest.

First, how public organizations and their managers interact with political actors and institutions deserves much more careful attention. Most of the literature on this subject is qualitative and of a case study nature. A more quantitative literature focuses only on simple principal–agent models. These literatures are interesting and provocative but necessarily limited in what they can offer. Large-N studies of this topic that recognize the complexity of the political–administrative interface are clearly in order. Second, and in a related vein, the relative importance of political and administrative systems for performance needs much more attention. In work that has not been covered in this book, we have sought to determine what happens when political bodies fail to represent the broader public (Meier and O'Toole 2004b). In the empirical settings we have examined, managerial influence expands when political institutions do an inadequate job at their political task. We believe that this pattern is likely to be a more general one, but the research on it has only just begun.

Third, how public organizations and their managers marshal public support is also important and deserving of similar careful, quantitative examination. Finally, it may be time for public management researchers to think big – even imperialistically. Administrative agencies are not the only institutions in a political system that require management. The judiciary, legislatures, and other relevant political bodies also present appropriate venues for the systematic study of public management. These bodies produce outputs and outcomes, and they are not anarchies. There is no good reason to restrict the systematic study of public management and performance to bureaucratic bodies alone (Lynn 1996). One of us has already proposed that public management as a research field should expand in hegemonic fashion to cover the institutions traditionally included in the embrace of political science (Meier 2007; see also Vaughn and Villalobos 2009).

Social capital

A topic that can be mentioned in conjunction with more detailed coverage of governance structures is that of social capital. This is not the place for anything more than a cursory mention of this subject, but it should be clear from work done on nonprofit organizations, as well as some of the contributions in political science, that social capital can offer a number of advantages, including the enhancement of what government organizations themselves can accomplish (Putnam 1993, 2000). The research literature of public management has paid little attention thus far to how social capital helps to shape program outcomes, however.

Specific kinds of research questions present themselves. One has to do with whether and how the general level of community organization might leverage enhanced public program performance – for instance, can social capital help to blunt the negative performance consequences that governments might otherwise experience when public organizations are faced with the kinds of environmental shocks we have examined in this book? We have begun to explore this question, and plan to address it more fully in the future (Andrews *et al.* 2009). Another is whether managers of public organizations can place themselves appropriately in their networked environment so as to take advantage of key external parties and organizations to enhance public program performance. The theory of structural holes offers potential as a source of testable propositions worthy of careful empirical testing in this regard (see, for instance, Burt 1992, 1997). Here too we have begun some systematic analysis (Andrews *et al.* forthcoming (a)), but the field as a whole should be encouraged to explore such questions in considerably more depth.

Yet another potentially important topic, related to the role of social capital in public management, is how trust – sometimes considered an important aspect of social capital more generally – operates in social systems to facilitate exchanges between coproducing actors, enhances community support for the production of public services, reduces actors' discount rates into the future to achieve benefits for which the main cost must be borne in the short term, improves flows of accurate information, and reduces coordination costs among interdependent organizations and individuals (see Edelenbos and Klijn 2007). Additional work along these lines, clearly related to the theme of social capital, should also be revealing.

The literature on social capital distinguishes between bonding and bridging social capital. Bonding social capital occurs in homogeneous groups and might have negative consequences for effective governance, since it may be correlated with hostility across groups in society. Bridging social capital, in contrast, consists of those bonds across groups that tie individuals to more diverse individuals in other groups. Bridging social capital is perceived to make positive contributions to society and governance. Unexplored in the management literature is what public management does to build both bridging and bonding social capital. Any public program that relies on citizen production also seeks to build social capital in the community. The role that public management plays in fostering social capital, particularly bridging social capital, could well be one of management's more important contributions to democracy.

M_3 exploiting the environment

Our research program has made progress in examining several of the relationships hypothesized in our model. We have not, however, made progress in examining managers' explicit efforts to tap or exploit opportunities or resources in the environment. This managerial function is labeled M_3 in our model. We have hypothesized that such managerial exploitation is likely to enhance outcomes and is likely to interact with at least some of the environmental (or "X") forces rather than merely add in a linear fashion to performance. At this point, however, we have not developed a defensible measure of managerial exploitation itself (apart from its inclusion in the broader networking measure) and are unable to document how such efforts actually operate to shape performance. This topic too therefore remains on the agenda and should receive attention in the future.[1]

Performance, writ more broadly

One theme emphasized in this book has been that public organizations are typically charged with multiple goals and, therefore, should be assessed via multiple performance measures. We have done so in many of the analyses presented in earlier chapters, and we have seen that the patterns revealed across a full array of performance measures can be quite telling. This cannot be the end of the story, though. In all the measures used in this study, performance is interpreted implicitly as quantity of outputs or outcomes over some designated time period, but additional ways of conceptualizing performance should be considered as well.

As Boyne has pointed out (2003), performance can be considered along a number of additional dimensions. Two of the most important are efficiency (the ratio of outputs or outcomes to financial inputs) and equity (the "fairness of the distribution of service costs and benefits between different groups" (Boyne 2003: 368)). In this book we have ignored the subject of efficiency, treating financial inputs as control variables as we have sought to estimate managerial effects on service outputs and outcomes.[2] Furthermore, while we have explored an aspect of equity in our consideration of whether networking by top managers produces benefits skewed toward the most advantaged clientele, we have not gone into this theme in depth. For instance, we have ignored the distribution of service costs across social groups. Efficiency and equity have been persistently important themes in the practical world of public management and have been recognized by researchers as central as well. Still, as Boyne documents, their empirical examination in larger-N studies of performance has been rare. It is time for the studies of performance and public management to begin to address these additional subjects as well. A range of thus far untapped dependent variables can be the focus of research attention.

Even Boyne's range of indicators might be perceived as too narrow from one perspective. Many feel that education should not be narrowly defined in terms of test scores, but should also include broader elements of producing effective democratic citizens (Smith 2003). Similar performance goals can be envisioned for all government agencies, as they provide fora for citizen development (Cook 1996).

This study has relied on performance indicators established by external political actors. It differs from some analyses on this dimension by avoiding the use of managers' own perceptions of how well the organization is doing (a relatively common practice in the public management literature). Although we find the relationship between internal perceptual measures of performance and external objective measures of performance interesting and plan to investigate this link further (see Meier and O'Toole 2010), the real world of governance eschews self-assessments of performance and therefore operates consistently with the emphasis in this book.

Another M?

In its formalization of the role of internal management in shaping performance, our model emphasizes the point that public management can reinforce, prop up, or stabilize the ongoing production process of organizations. We have observed in this book that there are many ways of doing so, and our empirical treatment of this function has investigated a few of these. The model makes no mention of another potential source of managerial influences on performance, however: efforts by management to *disrupt* internal routines and production processes in the interest not of reinforcing current efforts but changing and improving them.

We have downplayed this potential aspect of management in our studies, in part because we have been skeptical of the frequent claims that innovation and entrepreneurial public management are the sole routes to high perform-ance. Some well-established themes in the research literature as well as in practice, however, strongly emphasize organizational change and develop-ment. Managerial efforts to alter rather than reinforce the inertial produc-tion systems of public organizations are certainly worthy of systematic study. Indeed, we have noted in this volume that the more highly performing portions of our sample of school districts are also less autoregressive than those doing less well. Therefore, another item on the research agenda, going forward, is to investigate managerial efforts at organizational change and the reform of extant processes to explore performance-related effects. It might be the case, for instance, that the results of such managerial efforts are negative in the short term but sometimes positive over the longer haul.

Extending to other sectors

Our model was developed from the literature on public management, which is based largely on case studies, and has been used to explore relationships in public organizations. Nothing in the model is restricted only to traditional government-owned organizations, however. We have already mentioned the potential applicability to nonprofit organizations. In addition, the same might be said with regard to private, for-profit organizations.

Here matters are not quite so simple, because "publicness" and "private-ness" can be considered on more than one dimension, not simply ownership (see Perry and Rainey 1988). In particular, the source of funding and the form of social control also constitute criteria for distinguishing the sectors. The public–private distinction might also be considered in terms of multiple categories or via a continuum rather than a dichotomy. Bozeman (1987), for example, has even argued that "all organizations are public" – at least in some respects.

The research literature has not sorted out the question of whether pub-licness, in whatever form, renders the managerial functions distinctive with respect to determinants of organizational performance. To the extent that management can be considered a generic function, an approach typically taken by business management researchers, a model and set of findings valid for public organizations should presumably be generalizable to organizations more broadly. Accordingly, one approach would be to test the various hypotheses implicit in the model in empirical work on, for instance, private and for-profit organizations. If the patterns and results are similar, such findings would strengthen the argument for generic management. If they are different in consistent ways, such findings would inductively build the argument for distinctive theoretical spheres – or, at least, for treating publicness as a theoretically important variable.

Another approach, however, would be to use the currently available research literature on public and private organizations to inform a consideration of how a general model – for instance, the one we have put forward in this book – might be affected by sector with regard to how performance is shaped. So, for example, should we expect a given quantity of the internal management function (M_1) to have a larger or smaller effect on performance in more public or more private organizations? The current set of research findings on publicness can be used to develop a set of testable hypotheses. We have made an initial theoretical effort along these lines (see Meier and O'Toole forthcoming (b)), although the argument has not been included in this volume. The validity of such a logic, of course, awaits empirical testing.

Better measures, more data

As is clear from this book, it is possible to develop valid and reliable measures of aspects of public management and test their performance effects with data on hundreds of organizations. As discussion in the current chapter makes clear, these can be improved in a number of respects. As public management goes forward, it is important to build additional data sets that share many of the strengths of the Texas school districts data set and perhaps add still others – structural variation, for instance, and network characteristics. To those who would criticize the school districts data set for some of its limitations, we would say, simply, that the answer is to improve on what is now available; to organize and collect more data on more public organizations; to do it in more policy fields; to build a longer time series; to do so with an array of performance measures; and, above all, to gather excellent data on management. This last kind of item – the behavior, efforts, and skill of public managers – is the type typically neglected. Even with the current popularity of the so-called performance movement, governments as well as researchers have little solid information about what managers do and how well they operate as they tackle their responsibilities. While calling for better measures and better data is almost a cliché, the fact is that we will not make much more progress in understanding the relationship between public management and performance without significant developments on both fronts.

There is much more work to be done, therefore, if we are to implement fully the sort of research agenda that can demonstrate the entire range of managerial impacts on the outputs and outcomes of public organizations. It will take time, and many researchers, and undoubtedly some false starts. At this point in the research program, we have begun the task, and a number of other researchers have joined the effort, often by expanding the range of questions that can be addressed with the data at hand and sometimes by identifying new and promising sources – whether it be the influence of diversity and representation on performance (Pitts 2005), organizational leadership and its effects (Fernández 2005), gender and performance (Johansen 2007), mayoral influences on results in Colombia (Avellañeda 2009b), or managerial effects in state governments (Donahue *et al.* 2004), to mention but a sample of the recent work. The questions are large and important, the need for answers pressing, and the results thus far promising. We welcome many more to join the challenge.

NOTES

1. What we have explored is managerial strategy, particularly the notion of prospecting, which could be very similar to efforts to exploit the environment (see Meier et al. 2007). Prospecting does not appear to have much impact in our analyses, thus suggesting that the effort to exploit environmental opportunities is something different from a prospecting strategy.
2. In some cases efficiency is clearly a secondary goal. The school districts in our study seek to maximize outputs relative to the resources they are allocated. In this process they might go beyond the most efficient point of production and get diminishing returns. Because districts are evaluated on their test scores, not on whether they attained the scores in the most efficient manner, they have an incentive to spend all their resources in order to attain the maximum performance possible.

Glossary

Above criterion is a US college board score of more than 1,110 on the SAT or its ACT equivalent. This is, essentially, equal to a score that would rank a student in the top 20 percent nationally. The Texas Education Agency defines this score as one designating college-ready students.

ACT is a college aptitude examination, formerly known as the American College Test, that high school students take. The exam is used primarily by Midwestern colleges and universities.

All-pass rate is the percentage of students in a district who have passed all portions of the TAAS or the TAKS exam for that year.

Anglo pass rate is the percentage of Anglo students (white non-Latinos) in a district who have passed all portions of the TAAS or TAKS for that year.

Attendance is a performance indicator that is the percentage of all students in a district who attend classes on average – i.e. the average of the average daily attendance percentages.

Autoregressive systems are inertial systems. In an autoregressive system, current outputs can be expected to be strongly influenced by past outputs. Formal organizations are typically designed to be autoregressive. See also *Outputs*.

Black pass rate is the percentage of black students in a district who have passed all portions of the TAAS or TAKS exam for that year.

Buffering (SM$_4$) is a measure of how loosely coupled the organization is, consistent with the theoretical notion that a loosely coupled organization is more able to take a shock to the system and dissipate it rapidly. This measure is based on the correlation of the organization's outputs from 1988 to 1994 (a time period before the current study). That correlation subtracted from 1.0 is the measure of buffering used.

Bureaucracy is a type of formal organization with certain distinctive features, including a hierarchy of superior–subordinate relations, the appointment of experts on the basis of merit criteria, fixed and limited jurisdictions, decision making on the basis of rules, and reliance on written records.

Capacity; see *Managerial capacity*.

College boards are aptitude exams that are given to high school students to measure their readiness for college. See *ACT, SAT*.

College-ready; see *Above criterion*.

Dropouts are students who leave school without completing their degree program. The state of Texas has two dropout measures: the four-year dropout measure and the six-year dropout measure. The difference is in whether the base measure is calculated over the last four years of school or the last six. Dropouts are only rarely used as performance indicators in this book, because they are conceded to contain substantial measurement error.

Governance, in today's parlance, refers to the full set of formal institutions and informal ones, along with the associated patterns of action that produce policy results. A governance system for a particular policy or program may involve an organization such as a public agency or a large and complex network of organizations and actors. Governance systems may include public, for-profit, and nonprofit units.

Human resources management; see *Internal management*.

Independent school district is a US governance structure for school districts. These are essentially special-purpose units that are created for the express purpose of operating public schools. School districts generally do not have boundaries that are coterminous with other jurisdictions – even those that share the same name. The "independent" portion of the title means that the school district has an independently elected governing board and has the authority to levy taxes for the support of public education. Except for a single municipal school district, all districts in Texas are governed as independent school districts.

Internal management (M_1) is management's efforts to manage inside the organization. We measure internal management with five items: the superintendent's assessment of the quality of the principals' management skills, experienced teachers, professional development (on a scale of 5 = excellent to 1 = inadequate), and whether the superintendent agreed or disagreed on a four-point scale with two other items: "With the people I have in this organization, we can make virtually any program work" and "I am quite likely to recommend a subordinate for a superintendent position in another district." The measure is a factor analysis of these items, resulting in a single factor.

Latino pass rate is the percentage of Latino students in a district who have passed all portions of the TAAS or TAKS exam for that year.

Low-income pass rate is the percentage of low-income students in a district who have passed all portions of the TAAS or TAKS for that year.

Low-income student is a student who is eligible for free or reduced price school lunches. The exact criteria are based on federal poverty levels for a given size of household.

M_1; see *Internal management*.

M_2; see *Managerial networking*.

Managerial capacity is the percentage of all employees who are located in central office administration.

Managerial networking (M_2) is a measure of how frequently top managers interact with key actors in the environment. Superintendents are asked how frequently they interact with a set of individuals on a scale of daily (6) to never (1). The actual score is a factor analysis of the set of external actors. The initial measure included local business leaders, state legislators, other superintendents, the Texas Education Agency, and school board members. Later measures omitted contact with the school board and treated that as a separate measure (often termed "managing upward"). The factor analysis consistently generates only a single significant factor, with all indicators loading positively on that factor. An increase in the number of external actors appears to have little impact on the measurement of this factor. *Managerial networking* is also the measure of managing outward.

Managerial quality is a measure that is based on a regression equation predicting the salary of the school superintendent. Essentially, the strategy (see Chapter 4) takes all the factors that should predict a superintendent's salary (district size, past performance, age, etc.) and uses these as independent variables in a regression. The residual from this equation – that is, the part that cannot be explained by known factors – is taken as a judgment by the school board as to the quality of the manager.

Managerial stability (S_m) is the number of years the superintendent has been employed by the district in any capacity.

Managing downward is a measure of how frequently the superintendent interacts with school principals, on a scale of daily (6) to never (1).

Managing outward; see *Managerial networking*.

Managing upward is a measure of how frequently the superintendent interacts with members of the school board, on a scale of daily (6) to never (1).

Networking; see *Managerial networking*.

Networks are structures of interdependence involving multiple organizations or parts thereof, in which one unit is not merely the formal subordinate of the others in some larger hierarchical arrangement.

Outcomes of an organization or program refer to the eventual impact of policy actions, along with the results of other causal variables, on the ultimate issue or concern prompting the initial policy intervention. See also *Outputs*.

Outputs of an organization or program are the immediate consequences of policy and management efforts, such as bridges built, cases processed, environmental permits issued. See also *Outcomes*.

Percentage tested is the percentage of students who take either the ACT or the SAT. This measure is a rough indicator of students going on to college, since a student who takes neither exam is unlikely to attend college.

Performance of an organization or public program is the achievement of such organizations and programs in terms of the outputs and outcomes that they produce. There can be numerous measures of performance, and the concept can be considered to have a number of dimensions, including efficiency, effectiveness, equity, and public satisfaction.

Personnel stability (S_p) is a measure of the stability of teaching personnel. It is the percentage of the teachers last year who were employed by the district at the start of the current year. This calculation avoids imputing turnover to districts that are rapidly growing.

Principal is the title given to the individual who oversees a school within a school district. Principals can be thought of as middle managers who oversee the production personnel (the teachers) of the districts.

Public management is the coordination of people and resources toward the accomplishment of collective purpose; public management also involves tapping the interdependent organizational environment in support of such purpose and to protect the organization's efforts from potential disturbances.

S_m; see *Managerial stability.*

SM_4; see *Buffering.*

S_p; see *Personnel stability.*

SAT is a college aptitude examination, formerly known as the Scholastic Aptitude Test, that is used by most colleges and universities for admissions decisions. The test ranges from 200 to 800 for three tests – math, verbal, and analytical. The school districts generally report the sum of math and verbal scores.

School boards are the governing body of US school districts. In Texas, school boards are elected via a nonpartisan ballot. The board has the authority to set general education policy, to levy taxes, and to hire a superintendent to operate the school.

Stability; see *Managerial stability, Personnel stability.*

Superintendent is the chief operating officer of the school district. The superintendent is appointed by the school board, generally for a fixed-term contract.

TAAS is the Texas Assessment of Academic Skills, a standardized test administered to Texas students until 2003. The test was administered to different grades of students in different years (with a general expansion of the number of grades). There were also specialized tests given to assess knowledge gained from specific courses – e.g. an end of algebra exam. This evolved into a high-stakes test that students had to pass in order to receive a regular diploma from the state of Texas. The data used are the percentage of students passing all TAAS exams that they took. See *TAKS.*

TAKS is the Texas Assessment of Knowledge and Skills, a standardized test used in Texas from 2003 onward. It replaced the TAAS, and, although it is more difficult than the TAKS, the scores under it are highly correlated. See *TAAS.*

Texas Education Agency is a state agency in Texas that oversees the state's school districts. The TEA is also the agency that collects a wide range of performance data on Texas schools and school districts. The agency has regulatory authority and is the pass-through agency for funds allocated to the school district from the states.

References

Agranoff, Robert. 1986. *Intergovernmental Management: Human Services Problem-Solving in Six Metropolitan Areas.* Albany, NY: SUNY Press.

2007. *Managing within Networks: Adding Value to Public Organizations.* Washington, DC: Georgetown University Press.

Agranoff, Robert, and Michael McGuire. 2003. *Collaborative Public Management: New Strategies for Local Governments.* Washington, DC: Georgetown University Press.

Allison, Graham. 1971. *Essence of Decision: Explaining the Cuban Missile Crisis.* Boston: Little, Brown.

Altshuler, Alan A., and Robert D. Behn (eds.). 1997. *Innovation in American Government: Challenges, Opportunities, and Dilemmas.* Washington, DC: Brookings Institution Press.

Andersen, Simon Calmar, and Peter B. Mortensen. 2010. "Policy stability and organizational performance: is there a relationship?" *Journal of Public Administration Research and Theory* **20**, 1: 1–20.

Andrews, Rhys, George A. Boyne, Jennifer Law, and Richard M. Walker. 2005. "External constraints and public sector performance: the case of Comprehensive Performance Assessment in English local government." *Public Administration* **83**, 4: 639–56.

Andrews, Rhys, George A. Boyne, Kenneth J. Meier, Laurence J. O'Toole, Jr., and Richard M. Walker. 2009. "Immigration, local government capacity and public service performance: evidence from England." Working paper. Cardiff University.

2010a. "Alignment and results: testing the interaction effects of strategy, structure, and environment from Miles and Snow." *Administration and Society* **42**, 2: 160–92.

2010b. "The micro-politics of European immigration: local government capacity and public service performance in England." Working paper. Cardiff University.

2010c. "Wakeup call: strategic management, network alarms and performance." *Public Administration Review* **70**, 5: 731–41.

Forthcoming (a). "Environmental and organizational determinants of external networking." *American Review of Public Administration.*

Forthcoming (b). "Vertical strategic alignment and public service performance." *Public Administration.*

Andrews, Rhys, George A. Boyne, and Richard M. Walker. 2006. "Strategy content and organizational performance: an empirical analysis." *Public Administration Review* **66**, 1: 52–63.

Appleby, Paul H. 1949. *Policy and Administration.* University, AL: University of Alabama Press.

Argyris, Chris. 1957. *Personality and Organization: The Conflict between System and Individual.* New York: Harper.

Avellañeda, Claudia N. 2009a. "Mayoral quality and local government finance." *Public Administration Review* **69**, 3: 469–86.

2009b. "Municipal performance: does mayoral quality matter?" *Public Administration Research and Theory* **19**, 2: 285–312.

Ban, Carolyn. 1995. *How Do Public Managers Manage? Bureaucratic Constraints, Organizational Culture, and the Potential for Reform.* San Francisco: Jossey-Bass.

Ban, Carolyn, and Norma N. Riccucci (eds.). 2002. *Public Personnel Management: Current Concerns, Future Challenges*, 3rd edn. New York: Longman.

Bardach, Eugene. 1998. *Getting Agencies to Work Together: The Practice and Theory of Managerial Craftsmanship.* Washington, DC: Brookings Institution Press.

Barnard, Chester I. 1938. *The Functions of the Executive.* Cambridge, MA: Harvard University Press.

Bartle, John R. 1996. "Coping with cutbacks: city response to aid cuts in New York state." *State and Local Government Review* **28**, 1: 38–48.

Barzelay, Michael. 2001. *The New Public Management: Improving Research and Policy Dialogue.* Berkeley: University of California Press.

Barzelay, Michael, and Babak J. Armajani. 1992. *Breaking through Bureaucracy: A New Vision for Managing in Government.* Berkeley: University of California Press.

Beam, David R., Timothy J. Conlan, and David B. Walker. 1983. "Federalism: the challenge of conflicting theories and contemporary practice." In Ada W. Finifter (ed.). *Political Science: The State of the Discipline*: 247–82. Washington, DC: American Political Science Association.

Beam, George. 2001. *Quality Public Management: What It Is and How It Can Be Improved and Adapted.* Chicago: Burnham.

Behn, Robert D. 1991. *Leadership Counts: Lessons for Public Managers.* Cambridge, MA: Harvard University Press.

2001. *Rethinking Democratic Accountability.* Washington, DC: Brookings Institution Press.

Bennis, Warren. 1993. *An Invented Life: Reflections on Leadership and Change.* Reading, MA: Addison-Wesley.

Bertelli, Anthony M., and Laurence E. Lynn, Jr. 2006. *Madison's Managers: Public Administration and the Constitution.* Baltimore: Johns Hopkins University Press.

Bilmes, Linda, and Jeffrey Neal. 2003. "The people factor: human resources reform in government." In John Donahue and Joseph Nye (eds.). *For the People: Can We Fix Public Service?*: 113–33. Washington, DC: Brookings Institution Press.

Bingham, Lisa Blomgren, and Rosemary O'Leary. 2008. *Big Ideas in Collaborative Public Management.* Armonk, NY: M. E. Sharpe.

Bloom, Nicholas, and John van Reenen. 2007. "Measuring and explaining management practices across firms and countries." *Quarterly Journal of Economics* **122**, 4: 1351–408.

Bogason, Peter, and Theo A. J. Toonen (eds.). 1998. "Comparing networks." Symposium in *Public Administration* **76**, 2: 205–407.

Bohte, John. 2004. "Examining the impact of charter schools on performance in traditional public schools." *Policy Studies Journal* **32**, 4: 501–20.

Bohte, John, and Kenneth J. Meier. 2000. "Goal displacement: assessing the motivation for organizational cheating." *Public Administration Review* **60**, 2: 173–82.

Bollen, Kenneth. 1989. *Structural Equations with Latent Variables.* New York: Wiley.

Bowles, Samuel, and Herbert Gintis. 1976. *Schooling in Capitalist America: Educational Reform and the Contradictions of Economic Life.* New York: Routledge & Kegan Paul.

Boyd, Donald, Hamilton Lankford, Susanna Loeb, and James H. Wyckoff. 2003. "Analyzing the determinants of the matching of public school teachers to jobs: estimating compensating differentials in imperfect labor markets." Working Paper no. 9878. Cambridge, MA: National Bureau of Economic Research [NBER] (available at http://ssrn.com/abstract=430592).

Boyne, George A. 2003. "Sources of public service improvement: a critical review and research agenda." *Journal of Public Administration Research and Theory* **13**, 3: 367–94.

Boyne, George A., and Alex A. Chen. 2007. "Performance targets and public service improvement." *Journal of Public Administration Research and Theory* **17**, 3: 455–77.

Boyne, George A., Kenneth J. Meier, Laurence J. O'Toole, Jr., and Richard M. Walker (eds.). 2006. *Public Service Performance: Perspectives on Measurement and Management.* Cambridge University Press.

Boyne, George A., and Richard M.Walker. 2006. "Strategy content and public service organizations." *Journal of Public Administration Research and Theory* **14**, 2: 231–52.

Bozeman, Barry. 1987. *All Organizations Are Public: Bridging Public and Private Organizational Theories.* San Francisco: Jossey-Bass.

Brambor, Thomas, William Roberts Clark, and Matt Golder. 2006. "Understanding interaction models: improving empirical analyses." *Political Analysis* **14**, 1: 63–82.

Bressers, Hans, Laurence J. O'Toole, Jr., and Jeremy Richardson (eds.). 1995. *Networks for Water Policy: A Comparative Perspective.* London: Frank Cass.

Bretschneider, Stuart, Frederick J. Marc-Aurele, and Jiannan Wu. 2005. "'Best practices' research: a methodological guide for the perplexed." *Journal of Public Administration Research and Theory* **15**, 2: 307–23.

Breul, Jonathan D., and Nicole W. Gardner (eds.). 2004. *Human Capital 2004.* New York: Rowman & Littlefield.

Brewer, Gene A. 2005. "In the eye of the storm: frontline supervisors and federal agency performance." *Journal of Public Administration Research and Theory* **15**, 4: 505–27.

    2006. "All measures of performance are subjective: more evidence on US federal agencies." In George A. Boyne, Kenneth J. Meier, Laurence J. O'Toole, Jr., and Richard M. Walker (eds.). *Public Services Performance: Perspectives on Measurement and Management*: 35–54. Cambridge University Press.

Brewer, Gene A., and Sally C. Selden. 2000. "Why elephants gallop: assessing and predicting organizational performance in federal agencies." *Journal of Public Administrative Research and Theory* **10**, 4: 685–711.

Burt, Ronald S. 1992. *Structural Holes: The Social Structure of Competition.* Cambridge, MA: Harvard University Press.

    1997. "The contingent value of social capital." *Administrative Science Quarterly,* **42**, 2: 339–65.

Burtless, Gary (ed.). 1996. *Does Money Matter? The Effect of School Resources on Student Achievement and Adult Success.* Washington, DC: Brookings Institution Press.

Carmines, Edward, and R. Zeller. 1979. *Reliability and Validity Assessment.* Newbury Park, CA: Sage.

Christensen, Robert K., and Beth Gazley. 2008. "Capacity and public administration: analysis of meaning and measurement." *Public Administration and Development* **28**, 4: 265–79.

Chubb, John, and Terry M. Moe. 1990. *Politics, Markets and America's Schools.* Washington, DC: Brookings Institution Press.

Chun, Young Han, and Hal G. Rainey. 2005. "Goal ambiguity and organizational performance in US federal agencies." *Journal of Public Administration Research and Theory* **15**, 4: 529–57.

2006. "Consequences of goal ambiguity for public organizations." In George A. Boyne, Kenneth J. Meier, Laurence J. O'Toole, Jr., and Richard M. Walker (eds.). *Public Services Performance: Perspectives on Measurement and Management*: 92–112. Cambridge University Press.

Coggburn, Jerrell D., and Saundra K. Schneider. 2003. "The quality of management and government performance: an empirical analysis of the American states." *Public Administration Review* **63**, 2: 206–13.

Cohen, David B., Justin S. Vaughn, and José D. Villalobos. 2010. "Subjective performance indicators and White House management." Paper presented at the sixty-eighth annual national conference of the Midwest Political Science Association. Chicago, April 23.

Cohen, Steven, and William Eimicke. 1995. *The New Effective Public Manager: Achieving Success in a Changing Government.* San Francisco: Jossey-Bass.

Conan Doyle, Arthur. 1894. *The Memoirs of Sherlock Holmes.* London: George Newnes.

Cook, Brian J. 1996. *Bureaucracy and Self-Government: Reconsidering the Role of Public Administration in American Politics.* Baltimore: Johns Hopkins University Press.

Council of State Governments. 2002. *The Book of the States 2002.* Lexington, KY: CSG.

Cyert, Richard M., and James G. March. 1963. *A Behavioral Theory of the Firm.* Englewood Cliffs, NJ: Prentice-Hall.

Dalton, Dan R., William D. Todor, Michael J. Spendolini, Gordon J. Fielding, and Lyman W. Porter. 1980. "Organizational structure and performance: a critical review." *Academy of Management Review* **5**, 1: 49–64.

Dee, Thomas, and Martin West. 2008. "The non-cognitive returns to class size." Working Paper no. 13994. Cambridge, MA: NBER (available at www.nber.org/papers/w13994).

Derthick, Martha. 1970. *The Influence of Federal Grants: Public Assistance in Massachusetts.* Cambridge, MA: Harvard University Press.

Doig, Jameson W., and Erwin C. Hargrove. 1987. *Leadership and Innovation: A Biographical Perspective on Entrepreneurs in Government.* Baltimore: Johns Hopkins University Press.

1990. *Leadership and Innovation: A Biographical Perspective on Entrepreneurs in Government*, abridged edn. Baltimore: Johns Hopkins University Press.

Donahue, Amy K., Willow S. Jacobson, Mark D. Robbins, Ellen V. Rubin, and Sally C. Selden. 2004. "Management and performance outcomes in state government." In Patricia W. Ingraham and Laurence E. Lynn, Jr. (eds.). *The Art of Governance: Analyzing Management and Administration*: 123–51. Washington, DC: Georgetown University Press.

Donahue, Amy K., Sally C. Selden, and Patricia W. Ingraham. 2000. "Measuring government management capacity: a comparative analysis of city human resources management systems." *Journal of Public Administration Research and Theory* **10**, 2: 381–411.

Drucker, Peter. 1967. *The Effective Executive.* New York: Harper & Row.

Dull, Matthew. 2006. "Why PART? The institutional politics of presidential budget reform." *Journal of Public Administration Research and Theory* **16**, 2: 187–215.

Dunn, Delmer D. 1997. *Politics and Administration at the Top: Lessons from Down Under.* University of Pittsburgh Press.

Edelenbos, Jurian, and Erik-Hans Klijn. 2007. "Trust in complex decision-making networks: a theoretical and empirical exploration." *Administration and Society* **39**, 1: 25–50.

Ehrenberg, Ronald G., Richard P. Chaykowski, and Randy A. Ehrenberg. 1988a. "Determinants of the compensation and mobility of school superintendents." *Industrial and Labor Relations Review* **41**, 3: 386–401.

1988b. "Are school superintendents rewarded for performance?" In D. H. Monk (ed.). *Micro-Level School Finance: Issues and Implications for Policy*: 337–64. Cambridge, MA: Ballinger.

Ellingsen, Tore, and Magnus Johannesson. 2007. "Paying respect." *Journal of Economic Perspectives* **21**, 4: 135–49.

Elmore, Richard F. 1997. "The paradox of innovation in education: cycles of reform and the resilience of teaching." In Alan A. Altshuler and Robert D. Behn (eds.). *Innovation in American Government: Challenges, Opportunities, and Dilemmas*: 246–73. Washington, DC: Brookings Institution Press.

Enticott, Gareth, George A. Boyne, and Richard M. Walker. 2009. "The use of multiple informants in administration research: data aggregation using organizational echelons." *Journal of Public Administration Research and Theory* **19**, 2: 229–53.

Fennell, Mary L., and Jeffrey A. Alexander. 1987. "Organizational boundary spanning in institutionalized environments." *Academy of Management Journal* **30**, 3: 456–76.

Ferlie, Ewan, Lynn Ashburner, Louise Fitzgerald, and Andrew Pettigrew. 1996. *The New Public Management in Action*. Oxford University Press.

Ferlie, Ewan, Laurence E. Lynn, Jr., and Christopher Pollitt (eds.). 2005. *The Oxford Handbook of Public Management*. Oxford University Press.

Fernández, Sergio. 2005. "Developing and testing an integrative framework of public sector leadership: evidence from the public education arena." *Journal of Public Administration Research and Theory* **15**, 2: 197–217.

Forbes, Melissa, and Laurence E. Lynn, Jr. 2005. "How does public management affect government performance? Findings from international research." *Journal of Public Administration Research and Theory* **15**, 4: 559–84.

Frederickson, H. George. 1999. "The repositioning of American public administration." *PS: Political Science and Politics* **32**, 4: 701–11.

Freeman, J. Leiper. 1965. *The Political Process: Executive Bureau–Legislative Committee Relations*. New York: Random House.

Gage, Robert W., and Myrna P. Mandell (eds.). 1990. *Strategies for Managing Intergovernmental Policies and Networks*. New York: Praeger.

Galbraith, Jay R. 1973. *Designing Complex Organizations*. Reading, MA: Addison-Wesley.

General Accounting Office. 1999. *Managing for Results: Opportunities for Continued Improvements in Agencies' Performance Plans*. Washington, DC: Government Printing Office.

Gerth, H. H., and C. Wright Mills (eds.). 1958. *From Max Weber: Essays in Sociology*. Oxford University Press.

Gilmour, John D., and David E. Lewis. 2006. "Assessing performance budgeting at OMB." *Journal of Public Administration Research and Theory* **16**, 2: 169–86.

Goerdel, Holly T. 2006. "Taking initiative: proactive management and organizational performance in networked environments." *Journal of Public Administration Research and Theory* **16**, 3: 351–67.

Golembiewski, Robert T. 1962. *The Small Group: An Analysis of Research Concepts and Operations*. University of Chicago Press.

1990. "Differences in burnout, by sector: public vs. business estimates using phases." *International Journal of Public Administration* **13**, 4: 545–59.

Goodsell, Charles. 1993. "Reinventing government or rediscovering it?" *Public Administration Review* **53**, 1: 85–6.

Gore, Al. 1993. *From Red Tape to Results: Creating a Government that Works Better and Costs Less*. Washington, DC: Government Printing Office.

Graue, Elizabeth, Kelly Hatch, Kalpana Rao, and Denise Oen. 2007. "The wisdom of class size reduction." *American Educational Research Journal* **44**, 3: 670–700.

Gulick, Luther. 1937. "Notes on the theory of organization." In Luther Gulick and Lyndall Urwick (eds.). *Papers on the Science of Administration*: 3–35. New York: Institute of Public Administration.

Guyatt, G., J. Cairns, D. Churchill, *et al.* 1992. "Evidence-based medicine: a new approach to teaching the practice of medicine." *Journal of the American Medical Association* **268**, 17: 2420–5.

Hall, Thad E., and Laurence J. O'Toole, Jr. 2000. "Structures for policy implementation: an analysis of national legislation, 1965–1966 and 1993–1994." *Administration and Society* **31**, 6: 667–86.

2004. "Shaping formal networks through the regulatory process." *Administration and Society* **36**, 2: 186–207.

Hamilton, James D. 1994. *Time Series Analysis*. Princeton University Press.

Hanushek, Eric. 1996. "School resources and student performance." In Gary Burtless (ed.). *Does Money Matter? The Effect of School Resources on Student Achievement and Adult Success*: 43–73. Washington, DC: Brookings Institution Press.

Hanushek, Erik A., John F. Kain, Steven G. Rivkin. 1998. "Teachers, schools, and academic achievement." Working Paper no. 6691. Cambridge, MA: NBER (available at http://ssrn.com/abstract=122569).

Hargrove, Erwin C., and J. C. Glidewell (eds.). 1990. *Impossible Jobs in Public Management*. Lawrence, KS: University of Kansas Press.

Hawes, Daniel P. 2006. "Haven't we been here before? Political institutions, public management, and bureaucratic performance." Paper presented at the conference "Empirical studies of organizations and public management." College Station, TX, May 6.

Heclo, Hugh. 1977. *A Government of Strangers: Executive Politics in Washington*. Washington, DC: Brookings Institution Press.

Hedges, Larry V., and Rob Greenwald. 1996. "Have times changed? The relation between school resources and student performance." In Gary Burtless (ed.). *Does Money Matter? The Effect of School Resources on Student Achievement and Adult Success*: 74–92. Washington, DC: Brookings Institution Press.

Heinrich, Carolyn J. 2007. "Evidence-based policy and performance management." *American Review of Public Administration* **37**, 3: 255–77.

Hennessey, J. Thomas. 1998. "'Reinventing' government: does leadership make the difference?" *Public Administration Review* **58**, 5: 522–32.

Hess, Frederick M. 1999. *Spinning Wheels: The Politics of Urban School Reform*. Washington, DC: Brookings Institution Press.

Hicklin, Alisa K. 2006. "The quest for diversity: increasing minority student representation at American public universities." Unpublished Ph.D. dissertation. Department of Political Science, Texas A&M University, College Station.

Hicklin, Alisa, Laurence J. O'Toole, Jr., and Kenneth J. Meier. 2008. "Serpents in the sand: managerial networking and nonlinear influences on organizational performance." *Journal of Public Administration Research and Theory* **18**, 2: 253–73.

Hicklin, Alisa K., Laurence J. O'Toole, Jr., Kenneth J. Meier, and Scott E. Robinson. 2009. "Calming the storms: collaborative public management, Hurricanes Katrina and Rita, and disaster response." In Rosemary O'Leary and Lisa Bingham (eds.). *The Collaborative Manager: New Ideas for the Twenty-First Century*: 95–114. Washington, DC: Georgetown University Press.

Hill, Carolyn J., and Laurence E. Lynn, Jr. 2005. "Is hierarchical governance in decline? Evidence from empirical research." *Journal of Public Administration Research and Theory* **15**, 2: 173–95.

Hill, Gregory C. 2009. "The effect of frequent managerial turnover on organizational performance." *Social Science Journal* **46**, 3: 557–70.

Holzer, Marc, and Kathe Callahan. 1998. *Government at Work: Best Practices and Model Programs*. Thousand Oaks, CA: Sage.

Hood, Christopher. 1991. "A public management for all seasons." *Public Administration* **69**, 1: 3–19.

Hufen, Hans, and Arthur Ringeling (eds.). 1990. *Beleidsnetwerken: Overheids-, semi-overheids-, en particuliere organisaties in wisselwerking*. The Hague: VUGA.

Huxham, Colin. 2000. "The challenge of collaborative governance." *Public Management Review* **2**, 3: 337–52.

Ingraham, Patricia W. 1993. "Of pigs in pokes and policy diffusion: another look at pay for performance." *Public Administration Review* **23**, 4: 348–56.

(ed.). 2007. *In Pursuit of Performance: Management Systems in State and Local Government*. Baltimore: Johns Hopkins University Press.

Ingraham, Patricia W., Philip G. Joyce, and Amy Kneedler Donahue. 2003. *Government Performance: Why Management Matters*. Baltimore: Johns Hopkins University Press.

Ingraham, Patricia W., and Laurence E. Lynn, Jr. 2004. *The Art of Governance: Analyzing Management and Administration*. Washington, DC: Georgetown University Press.

Ingraham, Patricia W., Sally C. Selden, and Donald Moynihan. 2000. "People and performance: challenges for the future of the public service: the report from the Wye River conference." *Public Administration Review* **60**, 1: 54–60.

Jacobs, Ronald L., and Christopher Washington. 2003. "Employee development and organizational performance: a review of literature and directions for future research." *Human Resource Development International* **6**, 3: 343–54.

Jacobson, Willow S., Christine Kelleher Palus, and Cynthia J. Bowling. 2010. "A woman's touch? Gendered management and performance in state administration." *Journal of Public Administration Research and Theory* **20**, 2: 477–504.

Jencks, Christopher, and Meredith Phillips (eds.). 1998. *The Black–White Test Score Gap*. Washington, DC: Brookings Institution Press.

Johansen, Morgen S. 2007. "The effect of female strategic managers on organizational performance." *Public Organization Review* **7**, 3: 269–79.

2008. "Measuring middle manager quality and its effect on organizational performance." Paper presented at the third conference on "Empirical studies of organizations and public management." College Station, TX, May 2.

Jones, Bryan D. 1985. *Governing Buildings and Building Government: A New Perspective on the Old Party.* University: University of Alabama Press.

Katz, Daniel, and Robert L. Kahn. 1978. *The Social Psychology of Organizations*, 2nd edn. New York: Wiley.

Kaufman, Herbert. 1960. *The Forest Ranger: A Study in Administrative Behavior.* Baltimore: Johns Hopkins University Press.

1991. *Time, Chance, and Organizations: Natural Selection in a Perilous Environment*, 2nd edn. Chatham, NJ: Chatham House.

Keiser, Lael R., Vicky M. Wilkins, Kenneth J. Meier, and Catherine Holland. 2002. "Lipstick or logarithms: gender, identity, institutions and representative bureaucracy." *American Political Science Review* **96**, 3: 553–64.

Kellough, J. Edward. 2006. "Employee performance appraisal in the public sector: uses and limitations." In Norma M. Riccucci (ed.). *Public Personnel Management: Current Concerns, Future Challenges*, 4th edn.: 177–89. New York: Longman.

Kellough, J. Edward, and Lloyd G. Nigro. 2006. "Personnel policy and public management: the critical link." In J. Edward Kellough and Lloyd G. Nigro (eds.). *Civil Service Reform in the States: Personnel Policy and Politics at the Subnational Level*: 1–10. Albany, NY: SUNY Press.

Kellough, J. Edward, and Will Osuna. 1995. "Cross-agency comparisons of quit rates in the federal service: another look at the evidence." *Review of Public Personnel Administration* **15**, 4: 58–68.

Kelman, Steven. 2008. "Public administration and organization studies." In James P. Walsh and Arthur P. Brief (eds.). *The Academy of Management Annals*, vol. I: 225–67. New York: Lawrence Erlbaum Associates.

Kickert, Walter J. M., Erik-Hans Klijn, and Joop F. M. Koppenjan (eds.). 1997. *Managing Complex Networks: Strategies for the Public Sector.* London: Sage.

Kim, Sangmook. 2005. "Individual-level factors and organizational performance in government organizations." *Journal of Public Administration Research and Theory* **15**, 2: 245–61.

Klijn, Erik-Hans. 1996. *Regels en sturing in netwerken: De invloed van netwerkregels op de herstructurering van naoorlogsewijken.* Delft: Eburon.

Koch, Marianne J., and Rita G. McGrath. 1996. "Improving labor productivity: human resource management policies do matter." *Strategic Management Journal* **17**, 5: 335–54.

Kooiman, Jan. 2003. *Governing as Governance.* London: Sage.

Kozol, Jonathan. 1991. *Savage Inequalities: Children in America's Schools.* New York: Crown Publishers.

Krause, George A., and James W. Douglas. 2005. "Institutional design versus reputational effects on bureaucratic performance: evidence from US government macroeconomic and fiscal projections." *Journal of Public Administration Research and Theory* **15**, 2: 281–306.

Krueathep, Weerasak, Norma M. Riccucci, and Charas Suwanmala. 2010. "Why do agencies work together? The determinants of network formation at the subnational level of government in Thailand." *Journal of Public Administration Research and Theory* **20**, 1: 157–85.

Laczko-Kerr, Ildiko, and David C. Berliner. 2002. "The effectiveness of 'Teach for America' and other under-certified teachers on student academic achievement: a case of harmful public policy." *Education Policy Analysis Archives* **10**, 37, http://epaa.asu.edu/epaa/v10n37.

Lankford, Hamilton, Susanna Loeb, and James Wyckoff. 2002. "Teacher sorting and the plight of urban schools: a descriptive analysis." *Educational Evaluation and Policy Analysis* **24**, 1: 37–62.

Lawrence, Paul R., and Jay W. Lorsch. 1967. *Organization and Environment: Managing Differentiation and Integration.* Cambridge, MA: Harvard University Press.

Lazear, Edward P., and Kathryn L. Shaw. 2007. "Personnel economics: the economist's view of human resources." *Journal of Economic Perspectives* **21**, 4: 91–114.

Levine, Charles H. 1978. "Organizational decline and cutback management." *Public Administration Review* **38**, 4: 316–25.

  (ed). 1980. *Managing Fiscal Crisis: The Crisis in the Public Sector.* Chatham, NJ: Chatham House.

Li, Ling X. 2000. "An analysis of sources of competitiveness and performance of Chinese manufacturers." *International Journal of Operations and Production Management* **28**, 3: 375–92.

Light, Paul C. 1997. *The Tides of Reform: Making Government Work, 1945–1995.* New Haven, CT: Yale University Press.

  1998. *Sustaining Innovation: Creating Nonprofit and Government Organizations that Innovate Naturally.* San Francisco: Jossey-Bass.

  1999. *The True Size of Government.* Washington, DC: Brookings Institution Press.

  2008. "A government ill executed: the depletion of the federal service." *Public Administration Review* **68**, 3: 413–19.

Lineberry, Robert. 1977. *Equality and Urban Policy: The Distribution of Municipal Public Services.* Beverley Hills, CA: Sage.

Lipsky, Michael. 1980. *Street-Level Bureaucracy: Dilemmas of the Individual in Public Services.* New York: Russell Sage Foundation.

Lundin, Martin. 2007. "Explaining cooperation: how resource interdependence, goal congruence, and trust affect joint actions in policy implementation." *Journal of Public Administration Research and Theory* **17**, 4: 651–72.

Lynn, Laurence E., Jr. 1984. "The Reagan administration and the renitent bureaucracy." In Lester M. Salamon (ed.). *The Reagan Presidency and the Governing of America*: 339–70. Washington, DC: Urban Institute.

  1996. *Public Management as Art, Science, and Profession.* Chatham, NJ: Chatham House.

  2001. "The myth of the bureaucratic paradigm: what traditional public administration really stood for." *Public Administration Review* **61**, 2: 144–60.

  2006. *Public Management: Old and New.* New York: Routledge.

Lynn, Laurence E., Jr., Carolyn J. Heinrich, and Carolyn J. Hill. 2000. "Studying governance and public management: Why? How?" In Carolyn J. Heinrich and Laurence E. Lynn, Jr. (eds.). *Governance and Performance: New Perspectives*: 1–33. Washington, DC: Georgetown University Press.

  2001. *Improving Governance: A New Logic for Empirical Research.* Washington, DC: Georgetown University Press.

Lynn, Monty L. 2005. "Organizational buffering: managing boundaries and cores." *Organizational Studies* **26**, 1: 37–61.

McGregor, Douglas. 1960. *The Human Side of Enterprise*. New York: McGraw-Hill.

    2006. *The Human Side of Enterprise*, annotated edn., updated and with commentary by J. Cutcher-Gershenfeld. New York: McGraw-Hill.

McGuire, Michael. 2006. "Collaborative public management: assessing what we know and how we know it." *Public Administration Review* **66**, 6 (Supplement): 33–43.

Malysa, Lani Lee. 1996. "A comparative assessment of state planning and management capacity: tidal wetlands protection in Virginia and Maryland." *State and Local Government Review* **28**, 3: 205–18.

Mandell, Myrna P. (ed.). 2001. *Getting Results through Collaboration: Networks and Network Structures for Public Policy and Management*. Westport, CT: Quorum Books.

Martin, Stephen, and Peter C. Smith. 2005. "Multiple public service indicators: towards an integrated statistical approach." *Journal of Public Administration Research and Theory* **15**, 4: 599–613.

Meier, Kenneth J. 2007. "The public administration of politics, or what political science could learn from public administration." *PS: Political Science and Politics* **40**, 1: 3–9.

Meier, Kenneth J., Carl Doerfler, Daniel Hawes, Alisa K. Hicklin, and Rene R. Rocha. 2006. "The role of management and representation in improving performance of disadvantaged students: an application of Bum Phillips's 'Don Shula rule.'" *Review of Policy Research* **23**, 5: 1095–110.

Meier, Kenneth J., Warren Eller, and Michael Pennington. 2005. "Race, sex, and Clarence Thomas: representation change in the EEOC." *Public Administration Review* **65**, 2: 171–9.

Meier, Kenneth J., and Jeff Gill. 2000. *What Works: A New Approach to Program and Policy Analysis*. Boulder, CO: Westview Press.

Meier, Kenneth J., and Alisa K. Hicklin. 2008. "Employee turnover and organizational performance: testing a hypothesis from classical public administration." *Journal of Public Administration Research and Theory* **18**, 4: 573–90.

Meier, Kenneth J., and Jill Nicholson-Crotty. 2006. "Gender, representative bureaucracy, and law enforcement: the case of sexual assault." *Public Administration Review* **66**, 6: 850–60.

Meier, Kenneth J., and Laurence J. O'Toole, Jr. 2001. "Managerial strategies and behavior in networks: a model with evidence from US public education." *Journal of Public Administration Research and Theory* **11**, 3: 271–95.

    2002. "Public management and organizational performance: the impact of managerial quality." *Journal of Policy Analysis and Management* **21**, 4: 629–43.

    2003. "Public management and educational performance: the impact of managerial networking." *Public Administration Review* **63**, 6: 675–85.

    2004a. "Conceptual issues in modeling and measuring management and its impacts on performance." In Patricia W. Ingraham and Laurence E. Lynn (eds.). *The Art of Governance: Analyzing Management and Administration*: 195–223. Washington, DC: Georgetown University Press.

    2004b. "Unsung impossible jobs: the politics of public management." Unpublished paper.

    2005. "Managerial networking: issues of measurement and research design." *Administration and Society* **37**, 5: 523–41.

2006. *Bureaucracy in a Democratic State: A Governance Perspective.* Baltimore: Johns Hopkins University Press.

2008. "Management theory and Occam's razor: how public organizations buffer the environment." *Administration and Society* **39**, 8: 931–58.

2009a. "The dog that didn't bark: how public managers handle environmental shocks." *Public Administration* **87**, 3: 485–502.

2009b. "The proverbs of new public management: lessons from an evidence-based research agenda." *American Review of Public Administration* **39**, 1: 4–22.

2010. "I think (I am doing well), therefore I am: assessing the validity of administrators' self-assessments of performance." Paper presented at the sixty-eighth annual national conference of the Midwest Political Science Association. Chicago, April 24.

Forthcoming (a). "Beware of managers not bearing gifts: how management capacity augments the impact of managerial networking." *Public Administration.*

Forthcoming (b). "Comparing public and private management: theoretical expectations." *Journal of Public Administration Research and Theory.*

Meier, Kenneth J., Laurence J. O'Toole, Jr., George A. Boyne, and Richard M. Walker. 2007. "Strategic management and the performance of public organizations: testing venerable ideas against recent theories." *Journal of Public Administration Research and Theory* **17**, 3: 357–77.

Meier, Kenneth J., Laurence J. O'Toole, Jr., and Alisa K. Hicklin. 2009. "Comparing the impact of public and private sector management: a preliminary analysis using colleges and universities." Paper presented at the annual meeting of the American Political Science Association. Toronto, September 3.

2010. "I've seen fire and I've seen rain: public management and performance after a natural disaster." *Administration and Society* **41**, 8: 979–1003.

Meier, Kenneth J., Laurence J. O'Toole, Jr., and Yi Lu. 2006. "All that glitters is not gold: disaggregating networks and the impact on performance." In George Boyne, Kenneth Meier, Laurence J. O'Toole, Jr., and Richard Walker (eds.). *Public Service Performance: Perspectives on Measurement and Management*: 152–70. Cambridge University Press.

Meier, Kenneth J., Laurence J. O'Toole, Jr., and Sean Nicholson-Crotty. 2004. "Multilevel governance and organizational performance: investigating the political-bureaucratic labyrinth." *Journal of Policy Analysis and Management* **23**, 1: 31–47.

Meier, Kenneth J., and Joseph Stewart. 1991. *The Politics of Hispanic Education: Un Paso Pa'lante y dos Pa'tras.* Albany, NY: SUNY Press.

Meyer, John W., and Brian Rowan. 1977. "Institutionalized organizations: formal structure as myth and ceremony." *American Journal of Sociology* **83**, 2: 340–63.

Miles, Raymond E., and Charles C. Snow. 1978. *Organizational Strategy, Structure, and Process.* New York: McGraw-Hill.

Milward, H. Brinton, and Keith G. Provan. 2000. "Governing the hollow state." *Journal of Public Administration Research and Theory* **20**, 2: 359–79.

Miner, Anne S., Terry L. Amburgey, and Timothy M. Stearns. 1990. "Interorganizational linkages and population dynamics: buffering and transformational shields." *Administrative Science Quarterly* **35**, 4: 689–713.

Mintzberg, Henry. 1973. *The Nature of Managerial Work.* New York: Harper & Row.

Mladenka, Kenneth R. 1980. "The urban bureaucracy and the Chicago political machine: who gets what and the limits to political control." *American Political Science Review* **74**, 4: 991–8.

Moe, Ronald C. 1994. "The 'Reinventing government' exercise: misinterpreting the problem, misjudging the consequences." *Public Administration Review* **54**, 2: 111–22.

Molnar, Alex, Philip Smith, John Zahorik, Amanda Planer, and Anke Halbach. 1999. "Evaluating the SAGE program: a pilot program in targeted pupil–teacher reduction in Wisconsin." *Educational Evaluation and Policy Analysis* **21**, 2: 165–77.

Moore, Mark H. 1995. *Creating Public Value: Strategic Management in Government.* Cambridge, MA: Harvard University Press.

Moynihan, Donald. 2006. "What do we talk about when we talk about performance? Dialogue theory and performance budgeting." *Journal of Public Administration Research and Theory* **16**, 2: 151–68.

2008. *The Dynamics of Performance Management: Constructing Information and Reform.* Washington, DC: Georgetown University Press.

Murphy, Kevin R., and Jeanette Cleveland. 1995. *Understanding Performance Appraisal: Social, Organizational, and Goal-Based Perspectives.* Thousand Oaks, CA: Sage.

National Commission on Excellence in Education. 1983. *A Nation at Risk: The Imperative for Education Reform.* Washington, DC: Government Printing Office.

Nicholson-Crotty, Sean, and Laurence J. O'Toole, Jr. 2004. "Public management and organizational performance: the case of law enforcement agencies." *Journal of Public Administration Research and Theory* **14**, 1: 1–18.

Nigro, Lloyd, Felix Nigro, and J. Edward Kellough. 2007. *The New Public Personnel Administration,* 6th edn. Belmont, CA: Thomson Wadsworth.

O'Leary, Rosemary, and Lisa Blomgren Bingham (eds.). 2009. *The Collaborative Public Manager: New Ideas for the Twenty-First Century.* Washington, DC: Georgetown University Press.

O'Toole, Laurence J., Jr. 1990. "Theoretical developments in public administration: implications for the study of federalism." *Governance* **3**, 4: 394–415.

1996. "Rational choice and the public management of interorganizational networks." In Donald F. Kettl and H. Brinton Milward (eds.). *The State of Public Management*: 241–63. Baltimore: Johns Hopkins University Press.

1997. "Treating networks seriously: practical and research-based agendas in public administration." *Public Administration Review* **57**, 1: 45–52.

1998. *Institutions, Policy, and Outputs for Acidification: The Case of Hungary.* Aldershot: Ashgate.

(ed.). 2000a. *American Intergovernmental Relations: Foundations, Perspectives, and Issues,* 3rd edn. Washington, DC: CQ Press.

2000b. "Different public managements? Implications of structural context in hierarchies and networks." In Jeffrey Brudney, Laurence J. O'Toole, and Hal G. Rainey (eds.). *Advancing Public Management: New Developments in Theory, Methods, and Practice*: 19–32. Washington, DC: Georgetown University Press.

O'Toole, Laurence J., Jr., and Kenneth J. Meier. 1999. "Modeling the impact of public management: implications of structural context." *Journal of Public Administration Research and Theory* **9**, 4: 505–26.

2003a. "Bureaucracy and uncertainty." In Barry C. Burden (ed.). *Uncertainty in American Politics*: 98–117. Cambridge University Press.

2003b. "Plus ça change: public management, personnel stability, and organizational performance." *Journal of Public Administration Research and Theory* **13**, 1: 43–64.

2004a. "Desperately seeking Selznick: cooptation and the dark side of public management in networks." *Public Administration Review* **64**, 6: 681–93.

2004b. "Parkinson's law and the new public management? Contracting determinants and service quality consequences in public education." *Public Administration Review* **64**, 3: 342–52.

2004c. "Public management in intergovernmental networks: matching structural networks with managerial networking." *Journal of Public Administration Research and Theory* **14**, 4: 469–94.

2006. "Networking in the penumbra: public management, cooptative links, and distributional consequences." *International Public Management Journal* **9**, 3: 271–94.

2007. "Public management and the administrative conservator: empirical support for Larry Terry's prescriptions." *Administrative Theory and Praxis* **29**, 1: 148–56.

2009. "The human side of public organizations: contributions to organizational performance." *American Review of Public Administration* **39**, 5: 499–518.

2010. "In defense of bureaucracy: public managerial capacity, slack, and the dampening of environmental shocks." *Public Management Review* **12**, 3: 341–61.

O'Toole, Laurence J., Jr., Kenneth J. Meier, and Sean Nicholson-Crotty. 2005. "Managing upward, downward, and outward: networks, hierarchical relationships and performance." *Public Management Review* **7**, 1: 45–68.

O'Toole, Laurence J., Jr., and Robert S. Montjoy. 1984. "Interorganizational policy implementation: a theoretical perspective." *Public Administration Review* **44**, 6: 491–503.

OECD. 1995. *Decision-Making in 14 OECD Education Systems*. Paris: OECD.

Osborne, David, and Ted Gaebler. 1992. *Reinventing Government: How the Entrepreneurial Spirit Is Transforming the Public Sector from Schoolhouse to Statehouse, City Hall to the Pentagon*. Reading, MA: Addison-Wesley.

Osborne, David, and Peter Plastrik. 1997. *Banishing Bureaucracy: The Five Strategies for Reinventing Government*. Reading, MA: Addison-Wesley.

Palmer, Harvey D., and Guy D. Whitten. 1999. "The electoral impact of unexpected inflation and economic growth." *British Journal of Political Science* **29**, 4: 623–39.

Pammer, William J. 1990. *Managing Fiscal Strain in Major American Cities: Understanding Retrenchment in the Public Sector*. Westport, CT: Greenwood Press.

Perrow, Charles. 1986. *Complex Organizations: A Critical Essay*, 3rd edn. New York: Random House.

Perry, James L., and Hal G. Rainey. 1988. "The public–private distinction in organization theory: a critique and research strategy." *Academy of Management Review* **13**, 2: 182–201.

Peters, B. Guy, and Donald J. Savoie (eds.). 2000. *Governance in the Twenty-First Century: Revitalizing the Public Service*. Montreal: McGill-Queen's University Press.

Peterson, John, and Laurence J. O'Toole, Jr. 2001. "Federal governance in the United States and the European Union: a policy network perspective." In Kalypso Nicolaidis and Robert Howse (eds.). *The Federal Vision: Legitimacy and Levels of Governance in the United States and the European Union*: 300–34. Oxford University Press.

Petrovsky, Nicolai. 2006. "Public management theory and federal programs: a test using PART scores." Paper presented at the conference "Empirical studies of organizations and public management." College Station, TX, May 5.

Pfeffer, James. 2007. "Human resources from an organizational behavior perspective: some paradoxes." *Journal of Economic Perspectives* **21**, 4: 115–34.

Pfeffer, Jeffrey, and Gerald R. Salancik. 1978. *The External Control of Organizations: A Resource Dependence Perspective.* New York: Harper & Row.

Pindyck, Robert S., and Daniel L. Rubinfeld. 1991. *Econometric Models and Economic Forecasts.* New York: McGraw-Hill.

Pitts, David W. 2005. "Diversity, representation, and performance: evidence about race and ethnicity in public organizations." *Journal of Public Administration Research and Theory* **15**, 4: 615–31.

2009. "Diversity management, job satisfaction, and performance: evidence from US federal agencies." *Public Administration Review* **69**, 2: 328–38.

Pollitt, Christopher. 1990. *Managerialism and the Public Services: The Anglo-American Experience.* Oxford: Blackwell.

Pollitt, Christopher, and Geert Bouckaert. 2000. *Public Management Reform: A Comparative Analysis.* Oxford University Press.

Powell, Walter W., and Paul J. DiMaggio (eds.). 1991. *The New Institutionalism in Organizational Analysis.* University of Chicago Press.

Pressman, Jeffrey. 1975. *Federal Programs and City Politics: The Dynamics of the Aid Process in Oakland.* Berkeley: University of California Press.

Pressman, Jeffrey, and Aaron Wildavsky. 1984. *Implementation: How Great Expectations in Washington Are Dashed in Oakland; Or, Why It's Amazing that Federal Programs Work at all, This Being a Saga of the Economic Development Administration as Told by Two Sympathetic Observers Who Seek to Build Morals on a Foundation of Ruined Hopes,* 3rd edn. Berkeley: University of California Press.

Provan, Keith G., and H. Brinton Milward. 1991. "Institutional-level norms and organizational involvement in a service-implementation network." *Journal of Public Administration Research and Theory* **1**, 4: 391–417.

1995. "A preliminary theory of interorganizational network effectiveness: a comparative study of four community mental health systems." *Administrative Science Quarterly* **40**, 1: 1–33.

Putnam, Robert. 1993. *Making Democracy Work: Civic Traditions in Modern Italy.* Princeton University Press.

2000. *Bowling Alone: The Collapse and Revival of American Community.* New York: Simon & Schuster.

Radin, Beryl A. 2006. *Challenging the Performance Movement: Accountability, Complexity, and Democratic Values.* Washington, DC: Georgetown University Press.

Raffel, Jeffrey A. 2007. "Why has public administration ignored public education, and does it matter?" *Public Administration Review* **67**, 1: 135–51.

Rainey, Hal G. 2003. *Understanding and Managing Public Organizations,* 3rd edn. San Francisco: Jossey-Bass.

2009. *Understanding and Managing Public Organizations,* 4th edn. San Francisco: Jossey-Bass.

Rainey, Hal G., and Paula Steinbauer. 1999. "Galloping elephants: developing elements of a theory of government organizations." *Journal of Public Administration Research and Theory* **9**, 1: 1–32.

Rattsø, Jørn. 1999. "Aggregate local public sector investment and shocks: Norway 1946–1990." *Applied Economics* **31**, 4: 577–84.

Rethemeyer, R. Karl, and Deneen M. Hatmaker. 2008. "Network management reconsidered: an inquiry into management of network structures in public sector service provision." *Journal of Public Administration Research and Theory* **18**, 4: 617–46.

Rhodes, R. A. W. 1997. *Understanding Governance: Policy Networks, Governance, Reflexivity and Accountability.* Maidenhead: Open University Press.

Riccucci, Norma M. 1995. *Unsung Heroes: Federal Executives Making a Difference.* Washington, DC: Georgetown University Press.

   2005. *How Management Matters: Street-Level Bureaucrats and Welfare Reform.* Washington, DC: Georgetown University Press.

Rittel, Horst, and Melvin Webber. 1973. "Dilemmas in a general theory of planning." *Policy Sciences* **4**, 2: 155–69.

Rivkin, Steven, G., Erik A. Hanushek, and John F. Kain. 2005. "Teachers, schools, and academic achievement." *Econometrica* **73**, 2: 417–58.

Robinson, Scott, Kenneth J. Meier, Floun'say Caver, and Laurence J. O'Toole, Jr. 2007. "Explaining policy punctuations: bureaucratic centralization, organizational size, and the punctuated equilibrium theory of public agency budgets." *American Journal of Political Science* **51**, 1: 140–50.

Roch, Christine H., and David W. Pitts. 2010. "Differing effects of representative bureaucracy in charter schools and traditional public schools." Unpublished paper. Department of Public Management and Policy, Georgia State University, Atlanta.

Roch, Christine H., David W. Pitts, and Ignacio Navarro. 2010. "Representative bureaucracy and policy tools: ethnicity, student discipline and representation in public schools." *Administration and Society* **42**, 1: 38–65.

Rose, Richard. 1993. *Lesson-Drawing in Public Policy: A Guide to Learning across Time and Space.* Chatham, NJ: Chatham House.

Rubin, Irene S. 2005. *The Politics of Public Budgeting: Getting and Spending, Borrowing and Balancing*, 5th edn. Washington, DC: CQ Press.

Salisbury, Robert. H. 1984. "Interest representation: the domination of institutions." *American Political Science Review* **78**, 1: 64–76.

Sandfort, Jodi R. 1999. "The structural impediments to human service collaboration: the case of welfare reform." *Social Service Review* **73**, 3: 314–39.

Sargent, Stephen. 2009. "The impact of internal management on organizational performance." Unpublished Ph.D. dissertation. Deptartment of Political Science, Texas A&M University, College Station.

Schalk, Jelmer, René Torenvlied, and Jim Allen. 2010. "Network embeddedness and public agency performance: the strength of strong ties in Dutch higher education." *Journal of Public Administration Research and Theory* **20**, 3: 629–53.

Scharpf, Fritz W. (ed.). 1993. *Games in Hierarchies and Networks: Analytical and Empirical Approaches to the Study of Governance Institutions.* Frankfurt: Campus.

1997. *Games Real Actors Play: Actor-Centered Institutionalism in Policy Research.* Boulder, CO: Westview Press.

Schattschneider, E. E. 1960. *The Semi-Sovereign People: A Realist's View of Democracy in America.* New York: Holt, Rinehart and Winston.

Scholzman, Kay Lehman. 1984. "What accent the heavenly chorus? Political equality and the American pressure system." *Journal of Politics* **46**, 4: 1006–32.

Seidman, Harold. 1998. *Politics, Position, and Power: The Dynamics of Federal Organization,* 5th edn. New York: Oxford University Press.

Selden, Sally C. 1997. *The Promise of Representative Bureaucracy: Diversity and Responsiveness in a Government Agency.* New York: M. E. Sharpe.

Selden, Sally C., and Willow Jacobson. 2007. "Government's largest investment: human resource management in states, counties, and cities." In Patricia W. Ingraham (ed.). *In Pursuit of Performance: Management Systems in State and Local Government;* 82–116. Baltimore. Johns Hopkins University Press.

Selznick, Philip. 1949. *TVA and the Grass Roots: A Study in the Sociology of Formal Organization.* Berkeley: University of California Press.

Shafritz, Jay M., David H. Rosenbloom, Norma M. Riccucci, Katherine C. Naff, and Al C. Hyde. 2001. *Personnel Management in Government: Politics and Process,* 5th edn. New York: Marcel Dekker.

Simon, Herbert A. 1946. "The proverbs of administration." *Public Administration Review* **6**, 1: 53–67.

1997. *Administrative Behavior: A Study of Decision-Making Processes in Administrative Organizations,* 4th edn. New York: Free Press.

Smith, Kevin B. 2003. *The Ideology of Education: The Commonwealth, the Market and America's Schools.* Albany, NY: SUNY Press.

Sorenson, Olav. 2003. "Interdependence and adaptability: organizational learning and the long-term effect of integration." *Management Science* **49**, 4: 446–63.

Spicer, Michael W., and Larry D. Terry. 1993. "Legitimacy, history and logic: public administration and the constitution." *Public Administration Review* **53**, 3: 239–45.

Stoker, Gerry (ed.). 1999. *The New Management of British Local Governance.* Basingstoke: Macmillan.

Stoker, Robert. 1992. *Reluctant Partners: Implementing Federal Policy.* University of Pittsburgh Press.

Terry, Larry D. 2002. *Leadership of Public Bureaucracies: The Administrator as Conservator,* 2nd edn. Armonk, NY: M. E. Sharpe.

Thompson, Fred, and Lawrence R. Jones. 1994. *Reinventing the Pentagon: How the New Public Management Can Bring Institutional Renewal.* San Francisco: Jossey-Bass.

Thompson, James D. 1967. *Organizations in Action: Social Science Bases of Administrative Theory.* New York: McGraw-Hill.

Todd, Petra E., and Kenneth I. Wolpin. 2003. "On the specification and estimation of the production function for cognitive achievement." *Economic Journal* **113**, 1: F3–F33.

Tyack, David. 1974. *The One Best System: A History of American Urban Education.* Cambridge, MA: Harvard University Press.

US Census Bureau. 2008. *2007 Census of Governments.* Washington, DC: Government Printing Office.

Vaughn, Justin, and José Villalobos. 2009. "The managing of the presidency: applying theory-driven empirical models to the study of White House bureaucratic performance." *Political Research Quarterly* **62**, 1: 158–63.

Verba, Sidney, and Norman Nie. 1972. *Participation in America: Political Democracy and Social Equality.* New York: Harper & Row.

Wagner, Kevin, and Jeff Gill. 2005. "Bayesian inference in public administration research." *International Journal of Public Administration* **28**, 1: 5–35.

Walker, David M. 2001. *Human Capital: Taking Steps to Meet Current and Emerging Human Capital Challenges.* Washington, DC: General Accounting Office.

Walker, Richard M., and George A. Boyne. 2006. "Public management reform and organizational performance: an empirical assessment of the UK Labour government's public service improvement strategy." *Journal of Policy Analysis and Management* **25**, 2: 371–93.

Walker, Richard M., Laurence J. O'Toole, Jr., and Kenneth J. Meier. 2007. "It's where you are that matters: an empirical analysis of the networking behaviour of English local government officers." *Public Administration* **85**, 3: 739–56.

Wamsley, Gary L., Robert N. Bacher, Charles T. Goodsell, Philip S. Kronenberg, John A. Rohr, Camilla M. Stivers, Orion F. White, and James F. Wolf. 1990. *Refounding Public Administration.* Newbury Park, CA: Sage.

Wenger, Jeffrey B, Laurence J. O'Toole, Jr., and Kenneth J. Meier. 2008. "Trading speed for accuracy? Managing goal conflict and accommodation in the US Unemployment Insurance Program." *Policy Studies Journal* **36**, 2: 175–98.

Wenglinsky, Harold. 1997. *How Educational Expenditures Improve Student Performance and How They Don't.* Princeton, NJ: Educational Testing Service.

Wilkins, Vicky M., and Lael R. Keiser. 2006. "Linking passive and active representation by gender: the case of child support agencies." *Journal of Public Administration Research and Theory* **16**, 1: 87–102.

Wilson, James Q. 1989. *Bureaucracy: What Government Agencies Do and Why They Do It.* New York: Basic Books.

Wilson, Woodrow. 1887. "The study of administration." *Political Science Quarterly* **2**, 2: 197–222.

Wirt, Frederick, and Michael Kirst. 2005. *The Political Dynamics of American Education.* Berkeley, CA: McCutchan Publishing.

Wolf, Patrick J. 1993. "A case survey of bureaucratic effectiveness in US Cabinet agencies: preliminary results." *Journal of Public Administration Research and Theory* **3**, 2: 161–81.

Wong, Kenneth K. 1999. *Funding Public Schools: Politics and Policies.* Lawrence: University Press of Kansas.

Wood, Stephen. 1999. "Human resource management and performance." *International Journal of Management Reviews* **1**, 4: 367–414.

Woodward, Joan. 1965. *Industrial Organization: Theory and Practice.* Oxford University Press.

Wright, Deil S. 1988. *Understanding Intergovernmental Relations*, 3rd edn. Pacific Grove, CA: Brooks/Cole.

1990. "Federalism, intergovernmental relations, and intergovernmental management: historical reflections and conceptual comparisons." *Public Administration Review* **50**, 2: 168–78.

Wrinkle, Robert D., Joseph Stewart, and Jerry L. Polinard. 1999. "Public school quality, private schools and race." *American Journal of Political Science* **43**, 4: 1248–53.

Wulf, Henry S. 2002. "Trends in state government finances." In Council of State Governments. *The Book of the States 2002*: 269–74. Lexington, KY: CSG.

Yukl, Gary. 2006. *Leadership in Organizations*, 6th edn. Upper Saddle River, NJ: Prentice Hall.

Zeigler, L. Harmon, and G. Wayne Peak. 1972. *Interest Groups in American Society*. Englewood Cliffs, NJ: Prentice-Hall.

Index

Note: page numbers in *italic* indicate Glossary items.

above criterion *287*
ACT scores 48, *287*
administrative function
  conservatorship role 134
  role in managerial networking 115, 117–18,
    121–3
  stability 133–4, 135–8
all-pass rate *287*
Anglo pass rate *287*
Appleby, Paul 2
attendance rates 49, *287*
autoregressive models 75–81
  autoregressive function 68, 69, 70
  impact of networking on future
    performance 75–7
  nonlinear future impacts of networking
    77–81
autoregressive systems *287*
  modeling 28–30
  public organizations as xii

black pass rate *287*
budget shocks, summary of findings 271–4
  see also decision-making study; managerial
    capacity and budget shocks
buffering (SM$_4$) *287*
  effects of managerial slack 185–6
  impacts on performance 234–5
  impediments to performance 68–75
  modeling 31–2
  summary of findings 273–4
buffering and managerial capacity 185–6, 194–7,
    202–6, 207, 218–35
  approach to measuring buffering 221–6
  blockade-type buffers 219
  buffering mechanisms 219
  dampener-type buffers 219
  data 226–7
  definition of buffering 218–19
  definition of buffers 218–19

distributional consequences of buffering 233
  English local government example 234
  environmental factors (X) 227
  findings 227–32
  forms of adaptive response 219
  implications for performance 232–3
  management variables (M) 227
  managerial buffering elements 218–19, 221, 222
  measurement 226–7
  modeling a measure of buffering 219–21,
    222–6
  Occam's razor principle 226, 232, 233
  outcome measures (O) 226–7
  selective filters 219
  structural buffering elements 218–19, 221–2
  types of buffering functions 219
bureaucracy 132–3, 134, 182, 183, 194–7, *287*
burnout-generated turnover 136, 137
Bush, George W. 11–12, 124–5

capacity *see* managerial capacity
change *see* organizational change
collaboration through networks 57
  see also managerial networking
college boards *287*
college-bound student performance
  measures 48
college-ready student *288*
common-source bias 13
Comprehensive Performance Assessment
  (Audit Commission) 13–14
Conan Doyle, Arthur 162–3, 182
conserving activities 102, 134
Core Service Performance (Audit Commission)
  13–14

dark side hypothesis, managerial networking
  82–3, 83–6, 86–93
data sets xiii
  developing additional data sets 285–6

data sets (cont.)
    exploration of other data sets 277–8
    extending to other sectors 284–5
    variety of data used 45–6
    see also Texas school district data set
decision-making study 161–74
    budgetary shock context 161–3
    controls 164
    dependent variables 164
    environmental shocks 161–2
    findings 164–72
    implications 172–4
    long-term costs 173–4
    maintaining performance during budget
        cuts 162–3, 172–4
    measuring budget shocks 163–4
    mitigating negative budgetary shocks
        162–3, 172–4
    short-term costs 173
distributional consequences
    of buffering 233
    of networking 82–3, 83–6, 86–93, 270
dropout rates 49, *288*

economic equity measure 48
effectiveness of public management 2, 7–8, 14
efficiency and performance 2
English local government example, managerial
    capacity 234
entrepreneurial management 102, 133–4
environment
    exploiting opportunities in (M_3) xiii,
        68–75, 282
    organizational relationships with xiii
    threats from xiii
environmental factors (X) 227
environmental shocks 161–2
    modeling 30–1
    nature of response to 68–75
    summary of findings 271–4
    term (X') 186–7
    see also decision-making study; managerial
        capacity and budget shocks; managerial
        capacity and natural disasters
environmental typology 40–1
    pooled environments 40, 41
    reciprocal environments 40, 41
    sequentially structured environments 40, 41
equity and performance 2
European Union 263
evidence-based approach to public
    management 4–5

Ford Foundation 133

governance *288*
    future research 279
    model 15, 37
    patterns 3
government, policy implementation
    challenges 1–4
Government Performance and Results Act
    (1973) 11
Government Performance Project (GPP) 12,
    103, 152

hierarchy 24–5
human resources management 274
    contribution to performance 152–3, 159–61
    findings 156–9
    human capital as a long-term asset 160
    implications 159–61
    link with performance 150
    measures 153–5
    modeling the impact of 151–2
    need for investment in people 160
    sample 153–5
    theorizing about the content of M_1 152–3
Hurricane Katrina 197–8
Hurricane Rita 198

independent school district *288*
individual performance appraisal 104
inequality, consequences of networking 82–3,
    83–6, 86–93, 270
inertial systems
    modeling 28–30
    public organizations as xii
    see also autoregressive models; autoregressive
        systems
innovation in public management 133–4
institutional design and reputation 6
intergovernmental aid 243
intergovernmental networks 240–6
    behavioral aspect of networking 245–6
    intergovernmental aid 243
    intergovernmental landscape 241–2
    intergovernmental management 241–2
    intergovernmental ties as networked
        relations 242–3
    network terminology 245–6
    networked environment of public education
        243–5
    structural networks 240–1, 245–6
intergovernmental networks and public
    management 247–65
    behavioral aspect of networking 249–50, 264
    conclusions 263–5
    control variables (X'_t) 247, 251

findings 251–63
influences on performance 263–5
intergovernmental context 250–1
management measures (M_2) 249–50, 264
managerial networking 249
managerial quality 249
managerial stability 250
measures 249
modeling 247–9
outcome measures (O) 251
performance measures (O) 251
stability measures (S) 250
structural dimension (X_i) 247, 250–1, 264
teacher stability 250
units of analysis 249
internal management (M_1) *288*
    functions 131–2
    theorizing about the content of M_1 152–3
internal management and performance 131
    human resources management 150
    making quality decisions 161–74
    organizational stability 132–50
    range of functions and challenges 131–2
    review of studies in other settings 174–8
    summary of findings 272, 274–5

Kennedy School of Government 133

Latino pass rate *288*
leadership 101–2, 103–4
leadership stability 136
local governments, policy implementation 1–2
low-income pass rate *288*
low-income student *288*

M terms, quality component 100
M_1 *see* internal management
M_2 *see* managerial networking
M_3 *see* environment
management quality hypothesis 100–1
managerial capacity *288*
    as managerial potential 183–6
    in non-crisis times 207–18
    summary of findings 272–3
managerial capacity and budget shocks 183–97
    amount of protection to build in 195–6
    approach to measuring managerial capacity 185–6
    buffering effect of managerial capacity 194–7
    buffering effect of managerial slack 185–6
    capacity as managerial potential 183–6
    control variables 189
    costs of surplus capacity 195–6
    environmental shock term (X') 186–7

findings 189–94
identifying slack in managerial resources 185–6
implications 194–7
location of slack in the system 196
managerial capacity measurement 188
managerial reserve available 183–6
measures 187–9
measuring shocks 187–8
methods 189
organization theory approach 183
performance indicators 188–9
performance priorities 195–6
positive aspects of bureaucracy 194–7
potential to mitigate budgetary shocks 183–6
protection and defense functions 183–6
reduced model 186–7
sample 187–9
views on bureaucracy 183
managerial capacity and buffering 185–6, 194–7, 202–6, 207, 218–35
    approach to measuring buffering 221–6
    blockade-type buffers 219
    buffering mechanisms 219
    dampener-type buffers 219
    data 226–7
    definition of buffering 218–19
    definition of buffers 218–19
    distributional consequences of buffering 233
    English local government example 234
    environmental factors (X) 227
    findings 227–32
    forms of adaptive response 219
    impacts on performance 234–5
    implications for performance 232–3
    management variables (M) 227
    managerial buffering elements 218–19, 221, 222
    measurement 226–7
    modeling a measure of buffering 219–21, 222–6
    Occam's razor principle 226, 232, 233
    outcome measures (O) 226–7
    selective filters 219
    structural buffering elements 218–19, 221–2
    types of buffering functions 219
managerial capacity and managerial networking 207–18
    control variables 211
    data and measurement 210–11
    findings 212–17
    impacts on performance 217–18
    implications 217–18
    links between 207–9
    management variables (M) 211
    managerial capacity (M_c) 211
    managerial networking (M_2) 211

managerial capacity and managerial networking
    (cont.)
  managerial quality (M_q) 211
  managerial stability 211
  managing upward 211
  modeling the impact of managerial capacity
      209–10
  networking strategy and resources 207–9
  outcome measures (O) 211
  personnel stability variables 211
  potential impacts on performance 207–9
  role of managerial capacity in networking 207–9
  workforce stability 211
managerial capacity and natural disasters 197–207
  autoregressive model 201–2
  buffering effects 202, 6, 207
  control variables 201–2
  data 199–202
  environmental shock term (X') 199–200
  findings 202–6
  Hurricanes Katrina and Rita 197–8
  implications 207
  measuring the environmental shock (X')
      199–200
  nonlinear effects 202–6, 207
  outcome measures (O) 200–1
managerial functions, modeling 26–7, 278–9
managerial influence
  extent of 275
  modeling 32–6
  patterns of 275–6
managerial networking (M_2) 55–96, 288
  autoregressive models 75–81
  buffering impediments to performance 68–75
  building support for programs 56
  collaboration 57
  comparing different public organizations 64–6
  dark side hypothesis 82–3, 83–6, 86–93
  diminishing returns 115, 116–21
  distributional consequences 82–3, 83–6,
      86–93, 270
  exploitation of environmental opportunities
      68–75
  fending off threats 56
  functionalist perspective 83–6, 86–93
  government requirement for 56–7
  impact on future performance 75–7
  impact on organizational performance 66–75
  implications 81–2
  influence of managerial quality 120–1
  interactions with external parties 59–66
  managerial balancing act 116–21
  measuring extent and frequency 59–66
  measuring impact of M_2 68–75

measuring impact on performance 68–75
  measuring M_2 61–4
  mechanisms of performance enhancement 81–2
  nature of response environmental shocks 68–75
  nature of the link with performance 114–15,
      116–21
  network-related activities 8, 9
  nonlinear impacts on future performance 77–81
  nonlinear impacts on performance 68–75,
      114–15, 116–21
  opportunity costs 115, 116
  organization theory context 93
  organizational influences on 121–3
  political issues 82–3, 83–6, 86–93
  politics of program management 85–6, 86, 93
  potential for diminishing returns 115, 116–21
  public–private partnerships 57
  quality (skill) aspect 100, 117
  quantity (effort) aspect 117
  role of administrative support staff 115,
      117–18, 121–3
  strategic choices by managers 66–8, 75
  studies of performance effects 93–6
  summary of findings 269–71
  tendency toward inequality 82–3, 83–6, 86–93
  tradeoffs 115, 116
  use of resources and time 116–21
  voluntary linkages 57
managerial networking and managerial
      capacity 207–18
  control variables 211
  data and measurement 210–11
  findings 212–17
  impacts on performance 217–18
  implications 217–18
  links between 207–9
  management variables (M) 211
  managerial capacity (M_c) 211
  managerial networking (M_2) 211
  managerial quality (M_q) 211
  managerial stability 211
  managing upward 211
  modeling the impact of managerial capacity
      209–10
  networking strategy and resources 207–9
  outcome measures (O) 211
  personnel stability variables 211
  potential impacts on performance 207–9
  role of managerial capacity in networking 207–9
  workforce stability 211
managerial networking and managerial quality
      see managerial quality and managerial
      networking
managerial quality 289

managerial quality and managerial networking
    114–23
  managerial balancing act 116–21
  nature of the link with performance 114–15,
    116–21
  nonlinear relationships 114–15, 116–21
  opportunity costs 115, 116
  organizational differences 121–3
  potential for diminishing returns 115, 116–21
  quality (skill) aspect of networking 117
  quantity (effort) aspect of networking 117
  role of administrative support staff 115,
    117–18, 121–3
  tradeoffs 115, 116
  use of resources and time 116–21
managerial quality and performance 100–28
  approach to measurement 104, 105–6
  causal paths 107
  characterizing managerial quality 101–4
  entrepreneurial management 102
  individual performance appraisal 104
  leadership 101–2, 103–4
  management quality concept 101–4
  management quality hypothesis 100–1
  managerial quality studies 123–5
  measurement challenge 102
  measuring managerial quality 107–10
  measuring superintendent quality 105–6
  modeling performance 110–14
  pay for performance systems 104
  performance appraisal 104
  protective and conserving activities 102
  quality component of the M terms 100
  quality management perspective 102
  review of related studies 103–4
  risk-taking activities 102
  salary-based measures 104, 105–6
  salary model 107–10
  summary of research findings 125–8, 271
managerial stability (S_m) 289
managerialism xii, 4, 5, 275
managing downward 289
managing outward see managerial networking
managing upward 211, 289
Merit Principles Survey 12–13
mission stability 24, 135
model of public management and performance 23,
    28–38, 38–42
  aims of the approach 15
  alternative approach 15
  approach to modeling 36–8
  autoregressive (inertial) systems 28–30
  buffering 31–2
  data sets used for testing xiii

elements of a model 23–8
environmental shocks 30–1
governance model 15
hierarchy 24–5
inductive approach 16
inertial (autoregressive) systems 28–30
influence of multiple managers 27–8
limitations of the approach 17–18
managerial functions (M) 26–7
managerial influences 32–6
network-level modeling 38–42
networks 16–17, 25–6
operation at multiple levels 27–8
parsimonious and formal approach 14–18
role of internal management 16
shocks 30–1
stabilizing forces 24, 35–6
strengths of the approach 17
testing hypotheses 36, 38
theoretical influences 15–16
underlying principles xiii
modeling
  managerial functions 26–7, 278–9
  managerial influence 32–6
modeling performance 110–14
  control variables 110
  findings 111–14
  performance measures 110–11
multiorganizational action 3

National Performance Review 133
natural disasters see managerial capacity and
    natural disasters
network-level modeling 38–42
  pooled environments 40, 41
  reciprocal environments 40, 41
  sequentially structured environments 40, 41
  typology of environments 40–1
networking
  as behavior 245–6
  uses of the term 245–6
  see also managerial networking
networks 25–6, 289
  advantages of 56–7
  approach to investigation 57–9
  characteristics of 55
  coordination challenges 25–6
  dealing with "wicked problems" 56
  fluidity of 25–6
  inducements to use 56–7
  managerial challenges 56
  means of avoiding difficult issues 84
  nodes 25
  policy-related problem solving 56

networks (cont.)
    political pressure within 85–6, 86–93
    shifts in policy emphasis 84–5
    stability in 25
    structural and behavioral elements 271
    structural meaning 240–1, 245–6
    uses of the term 245–6
    see also intergovernmental networks
new public management xii, 5, 7, 102, 134,
        177, 194, 197
nonlinear relationships between variables
        xiii, 182–235
    buffering 218–35
    future impacts of networking 77–81
    managerial capacity and budget shocks 183–97
    managerial capacity and managerial
        networking 207–18
    managerial capacity and natural disasters
        197–207
    managerial capacity and performance 234–5
    managerial capacity in non-crisis times 207–18
    managerial networking and managerial
        capacity 207–18
    managerial networking and managerial quality
        114–15, 116–21
    managerial networking and performance 68–75
    managerial quality and managerial networking
        114–15, 116–21
    public management and performance 9
    stability in public management 145–8
    summary of findings 270
nonlinearity and buffering 218–35
    approach to measuring buffering 221–6
    blockade-type buffers 219
    buffering mechanisms 219
    dampener-type buffers 219
    data 226–7
    definition of buffering 218–19
    definition of buffers 218–19
    distributional consequences of buffering 233
    environmental factors (X) 227
    findings 227–32
    forms of adaptive response 219
    impacts on performance 234–5
    implications for performance 232–3
    management variables (M) 227
    managerial buffering elements 218–19, 221, 222
    managerial capacity in English local
        government 234
    measurement 226–7
    modeling a measure of buffering 219–21, 222–6
    Occam's razor principle 226, 232, 233
    outcome measures (O) 226–7
    selective filters 219

structural buffering elements 218–19, 221–2
    types of buffering functions 219

Occam's razor principle 226, 232, 233
opportunity costs, managerial networking
        115, 116
organization theory 182, 183
    context for networking 93
organizational change 133–4
    managerial efforts to bring about 283–4
organizational goal ambiguity 6
organizing through structures and procedures xiii
outcomes of an organization or program 289
outputs of an organization or program 289

PART (Program Assessment Rating Tool) 6, 12,
        124–5, 268
pay for performance systems 6, 104
percentage tested 289
performance 289
    and effectiveness 2
    and efficiency 2
    and equity 2
    and governance patterns 3
    and organizations 3
    and public management 3–4
    and public satisfaction 2
    broader measures of 282–3
    definitions 2
    link with public management 2
    nonlinear relationship with management 9
    research findings 6–7, 9–10
performance appraisal 104
performance measurement 10–14
    challenges 10–11
    developing better measures 285–6
    link to management effectiveness 14
    measurement process examples 11–14
    Texas school district data set 46–9
performance targets 6
personnel stability (S_p) 24, 135–6, 274, 290
personnel stability analysis 136–8
    burnout-generated turnover 136, 137
    conclusions about stability 149–50
    consequences of personnel instability 136–8
    findings 140–5
    influence on performance 140–5
    interaction between variables 145–8
    leadership stability 136
    measures of personnel stability 140
    measures used 140
    modeling personnel stability (S_p) 138–40
    modeling the impact of stability (S) 138–40
    nonlinear relationships 145–8

policy implementation
  avoiding difficult issues 84
  challenges faced by governments 1–4
  definitions of performance 2
  multiorganizational action 3
  networks of organizations 3
  patterns of governance 3
  performance 2
  role of public management 2
  role of subnational governments 1–2
  scale and scope of public organizations 3
  shifts in policy emphasis 84–5
policy-related problem solving, use of networks 56
political issues 270
  in networking 82–3, 83–6, 86–93
  future research 279–80
political pressure within networks 85–6, 86–93
political science perspective 4–5
politics of program management 85–6, 86–93
population ecology perspective xii, 4–5
principal (of a school) 290
procedural stability 24, 135
production function variables 49–51
production stability 24, 135
program management, political issues
    85–6, 86–93
protective activities, management function 102
public education, networked environment 243–5
public management 290
  as impediment to service delivery xii
  definition 2
  managerialist view xii
  new public management view xii
  population ecology view xii
  range of theoretical approaches xi–xii
  role in policy implementation 2
  views on effectiveness xi–xii
public management and performance 2, 3–4
  evidence-based perspective 4–5
  managerialist perspective 4, 5
  multiple influences 5
  new public management perspective 5
  political science perspective 4–5
  population ecology perspective 4–5
  research findings 6–7, 9–10
public management principles xii–xiii
  autoregressive (inertial) systems xii
  dealing with threats in the environment xiii
  exploiting opportunities in the environment xiii
  managing within the organization xiii
  mathematical model xiii
  nonlinear relationships between variables xiii
  organizing through structures and procedures xiii
  relationships with the environment xiii

public management research, findings
  approach to analysis 267–8
  budget shocks 271–4
  buffering of shocks 273–4
  distributional consequences of networking 270
  environmental shocks 271–4
  extent of managerial influence 275
  features of the model 268–9
  generalization from findings 267–8
  human resources management 274
  internal management 272, 274–5
  managerial capacity 272–3
  managerial networking 269–71
  managerial quality 271
  nature of the data set 267–8
  nonlinear interactions 270
  patterns of managerial influence 275–6
  personnel stability 274
  political issues 270
  practical applications 276–7
  relevance of the findings 267–8
  stabilizing forces 274
  structural and behavioral elements
    of networks 271
  structural stability 274
  what the evidence shows 267–77
public management research, future agenda
  additional data sets 285–6
  broader assessment of performance 282–3
  developing better measures 285–6
  expansion of the Texas schools data set 278
  exploiting the environment (M_3) 282
  exploration of other data sets 277–8
  extending to other sectors 284–5
  governance structures 279
  managerial efforts to bring about
    change 283–4
  modeling the full range of managerial
    functions 278–9
  politics and management 279–80
  social capital 280–2
  what remains to be explored 277–86
public management studies, review
  competing theories 10
  difficulty of assessing performance 10–14
  distinctiveness of public management 7
  effectiveness of public management 7–8
  importance of public management 7–8
  interactive effects 9
  key themes and findings 7–9
  lack of consensus about performance 9–10
  managers catalyze action 9
  multifaceted nature of management 8–9, 9–10
  network-related activities 8, 9

public management studies, review (cont.)
    nonlinear relationship with performance 9
    public sector performance 6–7, 9–10
    range of approaches 5–7
public organizations
    multiorganizational action 3
    networks of organizations 3
    scale and scope of 3
public–private partnerships 57
public satisfaction, and performance 2

quality management perspective 102
quality of public management *see* managerial
    quality

racial equity measure 48
representative bureaucracy 176
research *see* public management research
resources, measures of 50
risk taking by managers 102

S *see* stability
salary-based measures of quality 104, 105–6
salary model 107–10
SAT scores 48, *290*
school boards *290*
Selznick, Philip 85, 89, 92
shocks *see* environmental shocks
S_m *see* managerial stability
SM_4 *see* buffering
social capital 280–2
S_p *see* personnel stability
stability (S) in public management 132–50
    administrative conservatorship 134
    administrative stability 133–4, 135–8
    bureaucracy *1*, 132–3, 134, 182, 183, 194–7
    burnout-generated turnover 136, 137
    changing views on 132–3
    conclusions about stability 149–50
    consequences of personnel instability 136–8
    criticism of 133–4
    drive for innovation 133–4
    emphasis on organizational change 133–4
    entrepreneurial management 133–4
    influence on performance 140–5
    interaction between variables 145–8
    leadership stability 136
    measures of personnel stability 140
    mission stability 135
    modeling personnel stability (S_p) 138–40
    modeling the impact of stability (S) 138–40
    nonlinear relationships 145–8
    personnel stability 135–6
    personnel stability analysis 136–8

procedural stability 135
production stability 135
    relationship to performance 132–3
    stabilizing forces 24, 25, 35–6, 274
    structural stability 24, 25, 135, 274
    support for 134
    technology stability 135
    unpopularity of , 133–4
    see also managerial stability; personnel stability
stabilizing forces 24, 25, 274
    modeling 35–6
strategic choices, managerial networking 66–8, 75
structural and behavioral elements of
    networks 271
structural fluidity 25–6
structural networks 240–1, 245–6, 247, 250–1, 264
structural stability 24, 25, 135, 274
subnational governments, policy implementation
    challenges 1–2
substantively weighted analytical technique
    (SWAT) 77–8
superintendent *290*
    quality measurement 105–6

TAAS (Texas Assessment of Academic Skills)
    scores 46–9, *290*
TAKS (Texas Assessment of Knowledge and Skills)
    scores 46–9, *290*
tapping performance 10–14
    link to management effectiveness 14
    measurement process examples 11–14
    performance measurement challenges 10–11
task difficulty, measures of 50
technology stability 24, 135
Texas Education Agency (TEA) *290*
Texas school district data set xiii, 42–52, 267–8
    ACT scores 48, *287*
    attendance rates 49, *287*
    college-bound student performance
        measures 48
    dropout rates 49, *288*
    economic equity measure 48
    future expansion 278
    measures of resources 50
    measures of task difficulty 50
    performance measures 46–9
    presentation of findings 51
    production function variables 49–51
    racial equity measure 48
    research value of the data set 44–6
    SAT scores 48, *290*
    structure of the Texas districts 44
    TAAS/TAKS exam scores 46–9, *290*
    Texas context 43

United Kingdom
   Audit Commission performance measures 13–14
   English local government example 234
United States
   General Accounting Office 11
   Government Accountability Office 11
   Government Performance and Results Act
      (1973) 11

Merit Systems Protection Board 12–13
Office of Management and Budget 11–12
The President's Management Agenda (2002)
   11–12

"wicked problems," use of networks 56

X *see* environmental factors